Addressing Tipping Points for a Precarious Fı

Addressing Tipping Points for a Precarious Future

Edited by

Tim O'Riordan and Tim Lenton

Published for THE BRITISH ACADEMY
by OXFORD UNIVERSITY PRESS

Oxford University Press, Great Clarendon Street, Oxford OX2 6DP

First edition published in 2013

British Library Cataloguing in Publication Data
Data available

Library of Congress Cataloging in Publication Data
Data available

Typeset by Keystroke, Station Road, Codsall, Wolverhampton
Printed in Great Britain by
T.J. International, Padstow, Cornwall

ISBN 978-0-19-726553-6

For our next generation
who will live through what we create for them
James, Zoë, Joseph, Esther, Edward and Sammy

Contents

Figures and tables

Figures

Tables

Foreword

SIR CRISPIN TICKELL

'Tipping points' mean different things to different people. Most of them with their implications are well explored in this book. For me a tipping point is when an accumulation of small or even big changes suddenly causes a critical change. Usually we cannot identify a tipping point until we have passed it.

One of the best demonstrations of tipping points is in the behaviour of ecosystems. Within the infinite complexity of living systems in which different organisms depend on each other, one break in the chain or tipping point can bring rapid change to the others linked within it. For some this means disaster; for others it means rapid, perhaps favourable, change within a new chain. This is part of the phenomenon of life.

We can see this in the history of the human animal. Tribes, cities, and societies can rapidly crash or flourish. As ever, the tipping point could not have been foreseen. Usually it was a combination of unusual circumstances. Changes in patterns of rainfall came together with social and economic difficulties to bring about the collapse of classic Maya society. The Black Death coincided with the beginnings of the Little Ice Age to transform mediaeval society. A new merchant elite was able to tip over the monarchies of King Charles I and later King James II, and thereby create the circumstances of the industrial revolution in the following century.

We are certainly in turbulent times today. Our current epoch has been labelled 'the Anthropocene' by many geologists: it marks the period since the industrial revolution in which the human species has vastly increased its numbers; exploited the natural, often irreplaceable resources of the Earth; upset longstanding ecosystems, thereby destroying countless other species; and changed the chemistry of the land, sea, and air of the Earth in ways we have yet to understand. For example, we can observe the current destabilization of climate with prospects for global warming, but can only guess at the consequences for future distribution of water and new means for producing the energy which drives our society. Whereas in the past the rise and fall of civilizations was something regional and distinct, we are now more interconnected than ever before, and as the present economic crisis demonstrates, what happens in one place immediately affects what happens in others.

So what, if anything, can we do about all this? Can we discern future tipping points? Which ways could they tip us? It is fair to say that the conventional wisdom, which has led us to where we are, is under increasing challenge. Some politicians may still call for more respect for market forces, and argue about the effects of inflation or deflation, the supply of money, and the need for growth, however defined. But others are painfully aware of the wider issues: concern for the environment in all its aspects, our unhealthy dependence on certain technologies, including being locked into old ones, and human prospects in general. Are we measuring the right things in the right way, in particular our wealth, health, and happiness? Are our brains changing so that we see things in pictures rather than think in words? Can we still see the wood for the trees? Does globalization of society imply loss of local identity, or – worse – a return to nationalisms and local rivalries, with lethal struggles over resources?

No one knows the answers. But it is clearer than ever that we need to work globally, and above all identify the common interest in tackling the problems of the Anthropocene. This may require an assembly of regional interests, so-called 'pluralities', within a global framework, which reflect the current changes in the balance of power. Change usually comes about for three main reasons: leadership from those who effectively run our society; pressure from ordinary people through the means at their disposal; and occasionally from what I call 'benign catastrophes', when something goes visibly and attributably wrong and thereby illustrates the need for action. These will be the vital tipping points.

Above all we need to think differently. Only then will we be able to act differently.

Preface

This book originates from a 2011 conference generously funded by the British Academy and the Global Environmental Change Committee of the Royal Society.

The aims of the conference were to address and answer three questions:

1. Are we designing our governing institutions for sufficiently flexible, yet equitable, adaptation and resilience in the face of possibly unknowable, but potentially catastrophic, events or combinations of events in both Earth systems and social systems?
2. Are we creating, year by year, a set of governing arrangements that are brittle, fragmented, and increasingly vulnerable, in the face of potentially convulsive change?
3. Is it possible, creatively and purposefully, to shape our governing ways, our cultural mores, our economic approaches, and our commitments to long-term social justice, to prepare society for transformational tipping points in a benign and caring manner in sufficient time?

The conference was preceded by a scene-setting workshop held in the British Academy in January 2011. This greatly clarified the issues, and enabled the participants to feel a common purpose. It encouraged authors to draft their initial contributions, and to sense the connections between their arguments. It set the scene for the complete agenda for the subsequent April conference held in the Kavli Centre and managed by the Royal Society.

The great value of the Kavli conference was to bring together a wide range of scientists, social scientists, and humanities specialists to combine their experiences and expertise for understanding the many interpretations of tipping points. These facets included:

*   the physical and dynamical properties of Earth system processes;
*   the scientific understanding of the early warnings of reduced resilience;
*   the social sciences of economics and governing which suggest how the messy management of human affairs may reach brittle stress points;

- the liberating interaction of the two sets of stress-related physical and social processes through the media of the arts and narrative;
- the moral, spiritual and cultural dimensions of the scope for coping with abrupt change.

One of the very rich aspects of the conference was the ways in which the creative minds of the historian, theologian, and novelist can deal with uncertain but possibly sudden shifts in these systems – the generation of convulsive combinations of developments. This is the skill of those who can craft deep metaphors and the 'storyline' – lessons from what has happened before, and about the strength of moral positioning over how to adapt fairly and securely.

The conference also received ideas and commentary from the worlds of business, of media and communication, of diplomacy, and of governing in the broadest sense. These perspectives added greatly to the richness of the discussions and of the nuances of analysing both the contours of tipping points and the answers to the questions of whether we are creating inappropriate governance arrangements. Indeed, it is very likely we are not prepared culturally or politically for adaptation to combinations of tipping points, which could indeed be generated within a few decades. We seem to be creating conditions of maladaptation and dangerous 'lock-in'. One outcome is that, unless the most successful experiences of adaptive learning spontaneously and imaginatively arising from many parts of the planet are fully reported and understood, humanity may not be able to adapt with sufficient social justice to enable future societies to cope fairly and tolerably with disruptive change.

This book is primarily designed to place tipping points in their scientific, economic, governmental, creative, and spiritual contexts. Its contributions cover the various interpretations and metaphors of tipping points, the scope for anticipating their onset, and the capacity both for resilience in the face of their impending arrival and for better ways of communicating and preparing societies, economies, and governments for accommodating to them and hence to turn them into responses which buffer and better human well-being. Above all, the possibility of preparing society and its governing institutions for creative and benign 'tips' provides a unifying theme for the book.

The big lessons from the conference are these: that we can assess tipping points and critical thresholds on many dimensions; that we can begin to see the early warnings of their appearance; and that we do have time still to attend to the conditions which answer Question 3. But at best, we only have this decade to begin in earnest this comprehensive adjustment. This volume is therefore very timely. The widespread dismay over the prevarication and seeming inability of world heads of state (many of whom did not even attend) to address the plight of all peoples on this disrupted planet at the UN Conference on Sustainable Development ('Rio+20', held in Rio de Janeiro in June 2012) is leading many to the dangerous conclusion that political leadership is unavailable. The 'wicked problems' of climate disruption and unsustainable use of ecosystems simply defeat conventional politics, whether of the democratic or autocratic worlds, dependent as both are on evidently unsustainable patterns of growth and exploitation of resources. Despite some recognition for a transition to a so-called 'green' economy, though not a sustainable one, there is every sign that the very characteristics of markets, politics, and inequalities which have led to the current global recession and social malaise are being blindly pursued, apparently because there is neither vision nor the willingness to change course. At an Oxford University conference in July 2012 on resource security and sustainability, David Miliband MP, a former Secretary of State for the Environment, Food and Rural Affairs in the UK, argued that we must hold fast to faith in democracy as the best available political model for achieving the transition to sustainability. But he was also driven to admit that among the policymaking elites of the West there was still far too little will-power, passion, or conviction behind sustainable development. Too many politicians, he concluded, in their hearts and heads do not yet accept the diagnosis of unsustainability and the approach of tipping points, still less wish to act on it.

The book is divided into eight Parts, which consist of 'chapters' and 'commentaries', numbered sequentially. The fourteen main chapters were all presented at one or other of the conference sessions, where they were discussed in detail. The other contributions are designed as short commentaries. For the most part these were commissioned from people who were not at the conference sessions. The text is edited to create cohesion between the contributions so that the various nuances of science, social science, and humanity perspectives are enabled to merge. The intended readership is informed policymakers, policy analysts, researchers, and those in the general public who seek to understand what possible future outcomes they and their offspring may face before this current century passes its halfway stage. The text is also shaped to offer a combination of distress at what may happen if the warnings are not heeded, and hope that there is time to change course, admittedly in an increasingly difficult manner if conscious delay is continued, and that the ultimate prize is worth sacrificing and fighting for. Humanity has triumphed over adversity, though not always have earlier civilizations succeeded. What is special now is that the whole of humanity faces the same awkward dilemmas, not just the overambitious few. Having edited this book we are not confident that there is a happy outcome, as the disruptive journey has not yet been sufficiently altered to offer confidence that real learning is taking place. Readers are encouraged to make up their own minds when reading the pages that follow.

Tim O'Riordan and Tim Lenton
September 2012

Acknowledgements

We are especially grateful to the British Academy and to the Royal Society Global Environmental Change Committee for having the faith in the whole enterprise. We have been supported throughout by Fellows of both learned Academies as well as by their very competent administrators.

About the cover art: still image from "Critical Transitions" by Tone Bjordam

Norwegian artist Tone Kristin Bjordam works with video, animation films, photography, painting, drawing and installation. Bjordam has for many years been working on projects visualizing the movement and progression of liquid color in fluids and unfolding organic forms in motion. She stages controlled, yet playful experiments and creates imaginary landscapes.

The art video "Critical Transitions" was made in 2012, inspired by discussions with scientist Marten Scheffer who studies the nature of change in complex systems.

Climate, forests, coral reefs, financial markets and even our minds occasionally reach a tipping point where they go through a radical transformation. Foreseeing such critical transitions or even noticing that they are unfolding is challenging as they are embedded in the omnipresent permanent flow of change.

Dazzled by myriads of such minimal motions, how can we see that they sometimes erupt into transforming change? Emerged in chaotic and turbulent transformation how can we see where we are going? Science seeks universal early warning signals for critical transitions, but often we may only realize the world is not the same anymore in the hindsight.

For more information about this project: www.tonebjordam.com

Contributors

Tim O'Riordan is Emeritus Professor of Environmental Sciences at the University of East Anglia, Norwich. He is a Deputy Lieutenant of the County of Norfolk, a Fellow of the British Academy, and received an OBE in 2010. Email: t.oriordan@uea.ac.uk

Tim Lenton is Professor of Climate Change and Earth System Science at the University of Exeter. He holds a Royal Society Wolfson Research Merit Award and is a Fellow of the Geological Society, the Linnean Society, and the Society of Biology. Email: t.m.lenton@exeter.ac.uk

Sir Crispin Tickell GCMG KCVO, a former British Permanent Representative to the United Nations, is a member of the Advisory Council of the Martin School at Oxford University. He is the author of many papers and books on environmental and international issues. Email: ct@crispin tickell.net

David Atkinson retired as Bishop of Thetford in 2009. After doctoral work in organic chemistry, he was ordained in the Church of England, then a Fellow of Corpus Christi College Oxford, Canon of Southwark Cathedral, and Archdeacon of Lewisham. He serves on the Board of Operation Noah. Email: davidatkinson43@virginmedia.com

Mike Barry is Head of Sustainable Business at Marks and Spencer, helping drive forward their sustainability plan, Plan A. He believes that business is reaching a tipping point, where 'less bad' is no longer good enough. The real, practical challenges of responding to resource competition, extreme weather, new social expectations, greater transparency and new economic models based around the sharing/circular economy mean that business has to strike out and build a new, better approach, one that delivers social, environmental and economic benefit in equal measure.

Emily Boyd is Reader in Geography, University of Reading.

Paul Brown is co-editor of the Climate News Network, an internet service providing daily news of the science and politics of climate change for journalists. He is a former environment correspondent of the *Guardian* and Fellow of Wolfson College Cambridge. Email: paulbrown5@mac.com

Ian Christie is a Fellow of the Centre for Environmental Strategy, University of Surrey, Guildford. He has worked for many years on sustainable development and environmental issues in central and local government, business consultancy, and think tanks in the UK.

Charles Clarke is a former Cabinet Minister. After 25 years in active politics, he became a Visiting Professor in Politics at the University of East Anglia, where he organised the 'Too Difficult Box' series of lectures (see www.charlesclarke.org).

Keith Clarke is a qualified architect with nearly 50 years' experience in city planning and the design and construction of buildings and major infrastructure throughout the world. Until recently he was the CEO of the largest consulting engineering consultancy in the UK, WS Atkins, a FTSE 250 company.

Andrew Dobson is Professor of Politics at Keele University. Email: a.n.h.dobson@keele.ac.uk

Paul Ekins is Professor of Resources and Environmental Policy and Director of the UCL Institute for Sustainable Resources at University College London. He received a UNEP Global 500 Award for 'outstanding environmental achievement' in 1994 and was a member of the Royal Commission on Environmental Pollution, 2002–2008.

John Elkington is co-founder and Executive Chairman of Volans (2008), and co-founder of Environmental Data Services (ENDS) (1978) and SustainAbility (1987). He is author or co-author of eighteen books, most recently *The Zeronauts: Breaking the Sustainability Barrier* (Oxford: Earthscan/Taylor & Francis, 2012).

Giles Foden is a novelist (*The Last King of Scotland, Turbulence*) and Professor of Creative Writing at UEA. He was rapporteur to workshops of the European Commission's Global Systems Dynamics and Policies co-ordination action (2008–2010).

Laurence Freeman is Director of Meditatio.

Toby Gardner is a research fellow in the Zoology Department of the University of Cambridge, as well as a visiting researcher at the Goeldi Museum and the International Institute for Sustainability in Rio de Janeiro, Brazil. At the time of writing Dr Gardner co-leads the Sustainable Amazon Network (www.redeamazoniasustentavel.org), a multi-disciplinary research initiative aimed at understanding challenges and opportunities facing land-use sustainability in the Brazilian Amazon.

Patricia Howard is Research Professor in the Department of Social Sciences at Wageningen University in the Netherlands, and Honorary Professor in the School of Anthropology and Conservation at the University of Kent in the UK, working on the relations between biodiversity and human well-being. She leads the Ecosystem Services and Poverty Alleviation (ESPA) Project 'Human Adaptation to Biodiversity Change'.

John Ingram is 'Food Security Leader' for the Natural Environment Research Council, and is based in the Environmental Change Institute, University of Oxford. His main interest is the interaction between food systems and environment.

Tim Lang is Professor of Food Policy at City University London's Centre for Food Policy. The Centre studies food systems through the lens of public health, environment, citizenship, and social justice, exploring whether and how policy reflects these concerns. Email: t.lang@city.ac.uk

Thomas Lingard is Global Advocacy Director at Unilever. He also serves on the World Economic Forum's Global Agenda Council on Governance for Sustainability, the Oxfam Association, and the International Advisory Committee of the STEPS Centre at the University of Sussex. He was previously Deputy Director of the policy think tank Green Alliance.

Amanda Long is Executive Officer, Marketing, Membership and Media at the East of England Co-Operative.

Sara Parkin is Founder Director of Forum for the Future, Board member of the European Training Foundation, and former Co-secretary of the European Greens. She was awarded an OBE for services to education and sustainability in 2001. Her latest book is *The Positive Deviant: Sustainability Leadership in a Perverse World*. Email: saraparkinoffice@forumforthe future.org

Joe Ravetz is Co-Director of the Centre for Urban & Regional Ecology at Manchester, and leads on sustainable cities and regions. A former architect/planner, he is also a graphic facilitator, foresight trainer and policy adviser. His books include *City-Region 2020* and the forthcoming *Urban 3.0: Synergistic Pathways for a One Planet Century.*

Jonathan Sinclair-Wilson was for 20 years Managing Director of Earthscan, the leading English-language publisher on sustainable development.

Joe Smith is Senior Lecturer in Environment at the Open University, and works on environmental policy and communications. He has worked extensively with the BBC since the mid-1990s and is also Director of the historic clock-making company Smith of Derby Ltd. Email: joe.smith@open.ac.uk

Matthew Taylor became Chief Executive of the RSA in November 2006. Prior to this appointment, he was Chief Adviser on Political Strategy to the Prime Minister, and Director of the Institute for Public Policy Research between 1999 and 2003.

Camilla Toulmin is Director of IIED, the International Institute of Environment and Development. An economist by training, she has worked mainly in Africa on agriculture, land, climate and livelihoods, mixing research, policy analysis and advocacy. She is Board chair of ICARDA, Trustee of the Franco-British Council, and sits on the Advisory Boards of the Grantham Institute London, and IDDRI Paris.

PART 1
TIPPING POINTS AND CRITICAL THRESHOLDS

1.1
Metaphors and systemic change

TIM O'RIORDAN, TIM LENTON, AND IAN CHRISTIE

Setting the scene

This chapter has its origins in an introduction to a seminar jointly convened through the funding kindness of the British Academy and the Royal Society. Its purpose was to explore the various meanings and possible consequences of 'tipping points' over the coming decades. The seminar took place in the spring of 2011 at the Kavli Centre run by the Royal Society. It comprised ten speakers and twenty-five commentators. Participants represented a wide range of backgrounds, covering Earth system science, natural resource policies, economics, politics, media and communications, international relations, business, literature, and religion. What was fascinating was their enthusiasm for the creative fusion of highly diverse contributions and ideas. Participants embraced the wide range of meanings associated with 'tipping points' and grasped the significance of the concept for the disturbing age in which we find ourselves.

This introductory chapter surveys various ways of approaching and interpreting tipping points, and explains the contexts in which the contributions that follow fit into this framework. Thus, it seeks to provide a perspective for the whole book.

We took as our starting point the idea that tipping points are perhaps best understood as metaphors to help deal with uncertainty and complexity, wholeness, and the unpredictability of the future. Tipping points are processes of discontinuous, and at times disruptive, change. Generically they are *critical thresholds*, which offer various timescales of onset and impact. These thresholds may manifest themselves across the whole globe, or regionally, or locally. They can come in the form of planetary processes, of ecosystem adjustments, of military, terrorist, or convulsive political action, or of profound shifts in economic performance, cultural outlooks and social behaviour. Indeed, tipping points can arise out of combinations of physical and social systems and the strains and stresses affecting them, all working in complex loops of influence and impact. What concerns us here, and in our concluding chapter (8.1), is that tipping points may sit at the cusp of being transformational for the worsening or bettering of human existence. 'Tipping points' in this book actually refer to a series of transitions and transformations, some predictable and some unforeseeable.

Three ways in which tipping points can be characterized relate to:

- The science of global physical systems, their measurement and predictability, singly or in combination, as addressed by Tim Lenton in Part 2;
- The social science of governance through means of anticipating and adapting to possible shifts in such system states, approached in Parts 4, 6, and 7;
- The creative processes of constructing ways forward for society, which contribute to betterment and accommodation, by procedures which are socially fair, build resilience through adaptation, and reinforce the fundamental integrity of the ecosystem life-support processes, explored in Parts 5, 6, 7, and 8.

Lying behind this framing of tipping points are four sets of propositions. The first is that we could be entering a time in which *unintended worsening* of policy makes for a drastic worsening of environmental problems and socio-economic conditions. By our particular ways of governing ourselves, we may be creating conditions of economy, of decision bias, of social conditioning, and of ethics which actually reinforce (lock in) the likelihood of tipping points in both physical and social realms.

Second, we could be creating conditions of *induced vulnerabilities* – the generation of further risks – through tendencies already apparent in policy, production and consumption. The ways in which we seek to adapt, because of this inbuilt tendency to create greater tensions (dependency, powerlessness, incapacity to adapt), can also lead to more intense and unanticipated combinations of both social and physical/ecological stresses.

Third, the uncertainties surrounding the idea of tipping points and their manifestations raise the problem of *incoherence* in communication and response. We have yet to consider suitable means for explaining the various narratives, or ways of visualizing and instilling meaning to tipping points in all of their manifestations, which could lead to constructive adaptation and collective mitigation (as examined in Part 7).

Our final proposition is that tipping points must be conceived not only as risks and threats, but also as potential moments of *restorative redirection*. It is still possible for a series of positive transformational tipping points to be combined. These would prepare society for forms of governing, of designing economies, and of creating the social conditions for combined preventative action that can stave off the 'malign' tipping points, in favour of robust, resilient and adaptive values and governing procedures. This would be the creative and 'super-adjusting' tipping point, of which, at present, we see only glimpses – in social movements of ecological localism, and in many parts of developing economies where continuous resilience and adaptation are essential.

Achieving restorative redirection presents an immense challenge, but it is an experience which the planet has been through several times before, admittedly without conscious steering (Duarte Santos 2011; Lenton and Watson 2011). This particular transition will be hugely different. It will involve both profound shifts in social outlooks and associated adjustments. It will also require collectively agreed recognition and capacity to restore and nurture life-support processes, often under conditions of unfriendly and unbending economic incentives, and inbuilt vulnerabilities. Hence the shift towards so-called 'benign' tipping points, as 'malign' tipping points continue to engulf us, will neither be easy, nor in the absence of ingenuity and extremely determined and creative leadership, democratically popular. We only see tough times ahead.

Tipping points as metaphors

Metaphors can elicit new concepts by 'throwing together' pre-existing lines of thought into fresh perspectives, as Giles Foden argues in Chapter 3.1. Metaphors are conveyors of meaning and storytelling. Metaphors enable imagery and ideas to fuse and to recombine, to unify through experimental exploration. Shifts in manners of thinking and of meanings of values are easier to explore through metaphor. They allow continuous rediscovery from any starting point, especially where there are many possible endings. Metaphors stimulate the imagination, and loosen the mental bounds that restrict our perception of actual and potential realities. But metaphors can also confuse, because meanings are not always aligned to appreciate their novelty. Metaphors may be contested and unruly, trampling on established patterns of thought and analysis. As a consequence, the science of tipping points (Part 2) and the politics (Part 6) are beset with conflicting interpretations as metaphorical pathways collide.

Metaphors may be created on the basis of past evidence, interactive models, creative interpretations of futures, simplifications of complexity, exploration of intriguing mathematical formulations, storytelling, and popular, misguided and sloppy usage. All these devices are means for characterizing, and giving shape to, uncertainty, interdependence, turbulence, and crises, and for unleashing the creative power of imagining. Metaphors are employed to assist in the ordering of chaos, for carving out meaningful narratives and stories from apparently seamless continuity, for creating understanding through patterns of skilful construction, and for firming up the shifting sands of unpredictability in order to obtain plausible assurance about what could happen next.

Three classes of tipping point and related metaphors attracted the attention of the seminar participants.

1. Threshold conditions, chaotic transformations, bifurcations, and revolutions

These are qualities found in mathematics; risk theory; catastrophe theory; abrupt change dynamics; the coupling of systems to sudden phase changes in local environments, macro-scale Earth systems, and in geopolitical outlooks. Such transformations take place in a variety of circumstances: from stress points found in pathways of order and reason; to sudden shifts of political arrangements; to new patterns of power; to innovative processes of measurement and making choices. They are characterized by intervening periods of adjustment, which eventually reach a stage where inbuilt procedures for accommodation, or protecting existing institutions of decision taking, can no longer rely on 'more of the same'. Things simply have to shift.

Physicists, mathematicians, ecologists, epidemiologists and sociologists, in their various ways, have identified 'bifurcations'. These are points where a small additional 'forcing' or 'nudge' takes a complex system abruptly into a qualitatively different state or into the orbit of another system or set of properties in the environment, known as an 'attractor'. The interesting quality here is their apparent unpredictability, even though after a 'change event', it may be possible to spot the clues of onset. In the arena of political transformation, for example, the fall of communism in the early 1990s, and the 'Arab Spring' of 2011 have been analysed for their precursors in the internal social and political dynamics of restless and networked societies, and oppressive regimes. Tipping points are rarely wholly unpredictable. There is currently much excitement about the prospects for early warning of such 'critical transitions' in a range of complex systems (Scheffer 2009), and perhaps even on the basis of identification of large-scale recurrent patterns in social evolution and upheavals (Turchin and Nefedov 2009; Turchin 2011).

2. Prediction, adaptation, resilience, accommodation, path dependency, and tenacity in holding on to the familiar

These are all variants of responses to confronting or actually experiencing such threshold conditions. Doing nothing is not considered a viable or sensible option, but any sudden shifts of policy or behaviour carry all manner of risks and potential casualties, and any new rules of decision taking are usually unfamiliar and weakly formulated. Changing tardily patterns of power, clinging on to conceptions of morality and fairness, and relying on the process of 'muddling through', all play their part. So too does the tendency to cling to existing commitments of political dependence, or the failure to adapt because too much sunk investment is at stake.

One cause of the collapse of earlier civilizations might have been the unwieldy scale of large urban complexes, and the associated stubborn adherence to living with the 'sunk costs' of existing, costly, and inflexible infrastructural investments (Scheffer 2009). But 'sunk costs' also apply to political power structures, worldviews, and frighteningly interdependent economic institutions. This applies today in cases such as the banks, particularly in the Eurozone countries. A related but uniquely frustrating phenomenon of 'systems that fail to tip' can be found in political and economic crises where nearly everyone agrees that something has to give (see Sara Parkin (6.3)). Tim Lang and John Ingram (4.1) offer an equivalent perspective on the increasing elusiveness of food security.

The very nature of nascent tipping points makes it difficult to shift attitudes, values and behaviour. Tipping points are visible clearly, if at all, only in the historical record, and thus lack compelling force in the present. The overwhelming temptation and pressures are to wait and see, to hope that something turns up to eliminate the projected risk, and to enable business as usual to persist, or to assume that we can always fall back on adaptation.

Note, however, that even adaptation does not always result in positive coping. Ill-designed adaptation can reinforce vulnerability and the brittleness of power and authority, unsuited to emerging threshold conditions, where established mechanisms for adaptation and adjustment can no longer hold. Emily Boyd (7.2) points out that weak adaptation, even in the face of crisis, may arise from the mixing of informal social preferences and cultural norms with formal and less flexible political and economic institutions, further muddled by clumsy media and communications misunderstandings. Adaptive governance, she notes, 'consists of four fundamentals: explicit understanding of the system; monitoring; flexibility in management and administration through networks; and preparation for "surprise"'.

3. Social construction, opportunism, media formulation, marketing, and organising bias

Tipping points are now invoked in all manner of publications, of communications, of language and knowledge, almost whenever the notion of threat, of crisis, of fear, of helplessness, and of a call for dramatic transformational approaches to the messy governing of economies and societies, is called upon. Here the notion of tipping points loses its shape, tends to be overused and blurred, and hence can become unhelpful as a narrative for coping. This is precisely the danger of metaphor which Giles Foden counsels against in Chapter 3.1. The tendency for universality, for sloppy comparison, and for meaningless preparation, may yet prove the nemesis of the tipping point metaphor. Metaphors can guide, but they can also muddle. This aspect is explored by Tim Lang and John Ingram (4.1), and by Patricia Howard (4.2) in her various ecological, cultural and linguistic interpretations of biodiversity. Tipping points, like the highly necessary but deeply contested concept of sustainability, are already in danger of being over-defined, chaotically misinterpreted, and chronically abused by overreliance on ubiquitousness.

A sense of foreboding

Lying beneath these formulations of tipping points is a sense of foreboding. We appear to be entering a stage in world affairs where rapid change, spurred by instant communication and an overwhelming desire to dramatize events to gain competitive media attention, appears convulsive, cataclysmic, and beyond any sense of benign rational management. It is so tempting to ignore warnings, to cling on to the familiar, to hold on to sunk investments, and to seek pathways which are already damaged by protective power and false promises. This is particularly so in the many cases where the timing of possibly tragic outcomes is not provable, and is subject to very wide variations in estimates. Denial, delay, and dissonance capture the desperation of hanging on.

The emerging worlds of interconnected systems dynamics, and the sweet fruits of interdisciplinarity, tempt thinkers to try and understand our predicament by modelling it. Modelling with huge banks of data is now possible on scales almost unimagined a decade ago. There seems to be no limit to the scope for amassing meaningful patterns from seemingly chaotic cascades of information, apart from the imagination needed to create and make sense of these patterns. And the more the requirement to organize and give meaning, the more there needs to be fusion of both a narrative for creative exploration and a model for analytical ordering and forecasting. Yet the very capacity of modelling nowadays draws our attention to the significant voids in data arrays. For example, ocean acidification may or may not be catastrophic, not just hazardous, for calcareous marine life: we do not yet have the necessary instrumentation or the time series trends to be sure.

Such modelling is now so sophisticated that it can encompass both physical and social systems, and can combine the talents of academia, business and government. So the scope for extraordinary integration between disciplines, and means of shaping innovative decisions, is becoming very exciting. Here the mathematics and the narrative can be combined creatively. Tipping points could be expressions of wholly new forms of reasoning and imagining, of cross-cultural communication, and of preparing for fundamentally fresh ways to discover the 'complete human condition' in an age of real threat to the betterment of all life on this beleaguered planet. Novel forms of communication, such as those advancing on social networks, offer ways to translate the metaphors of thresholds and scenarios. Joe Smith (7.1) and Paul Brown (7.3) show that there are fundamental difficulties in conveying the power and authority of tipping points.

Furthermore, we may be experiencing in the emerging decade a new kind of geopolitics. There is the prospect of a radically different world order, a period of increasing instability for a growing number in unpopular dictatorships, of unprecedented growth of middle-class consumption in the emerging economies of China, India and Brazil, of massive social costs of ageing and concomitant under-representation of support workers, and, in recent times, an unusual and possible dangerous decline of accustomed affluence for many households in nations with established democracies. The ever-widening gaps between economic and social privilege and disadvantage, and the consequent deep democratic frustration combined with widespread sense of impotence – surely unwelcome hallmarks of this decade – will add to this instability (Turchin 2011).

Lying behind our contemplation of tipping points could just possibly be the most turbulent prospect facing the global human community in its existence, as covered in Part 8. The futures hinted in the discourses of tipping points could cover peaceful survival, completely new forms of learning and understanding, quite radical forms of communicating, and very different modes of enterprise and betterment for the whole of the human family. Laurence Freeman in Chapter 5.1 introduces *contemplative consciousness* as a means for combining wholeness with detachment, belief and faith, science with ethics. He offers a simple but powerful meditative framework for positive transitions.

On thresholds and bifurcations

For almost 200 years, classical physics, mathematics, and social sciences seemed to accept that change was smooth. Yet underlying the notion of continuity and positive readjustment, were formulations of exponential growth, with its characteristics of doubling times and rapid alteration. Mathematicians call the outcome a 'singularity', namely a point where the equations give results that tend to infinity. This too has become a metaphor for a grand tipping point, that imagined by Kurzweil (2005) as the transformation of human society and economy by mid-century through what he takes to be exponential advances in technology, data-processing power and artificial intelligence. The patterns of both smooth change and disruptive discontinuity create unstable rhythms where the characteristics of the system in question become radically different in function and structure.

When a state departs from its predicted path, on to some other trajectory, it is said to 'bifurcate'. This notion has been used in chaos theory to show that small shifts in initiating conditions, which may not even be observable, can lead to radically different outcomes. Earth system dynamics, such as those dictating monsoonal patterns, locations and timing, or abrupt changes in forest water availability and drought-induced burning – all these express disequilibrium, with hierarchies of dynamics and outcomes which can be modelled, but where the modelling also requires large doses of creative intelligence.

In ecological systems, such thresholds can be depicted as points, or as zones of interruption in a prolonged transition. The 'point' notion is more common, since there are many examples of sudden shifts in ecological conditions arising from very small additional changes. One oft-quoted example lies in nutrient enrichment or eutrophication of shallow lakes, where a pattern of low-nutrient status with particular plant diversity can switch abruptly to a high-nutrient low-diversity pattern. Many more examples of ecological tipping points can be found in the recent literature (Barnosky *et al.* 2012; UNEP 2012) and the Resilience Alliance and Santa Fe Institute thresholds database (Resilience Alliance 2004).

'Hysteresis' is a term reflecting the level of dependence of any system state on its history. It is possible for a change to be reversible, but the return to the original state will almost always be at a very different point from the initiating conditions of change. Thus coastal salt marsh, removed due to the squeezing of the coastline caused by a combination of rising sea levels and the construction of tide-protecting seawalls, is proving extremely difficult to re-create. This is one of the factors behind the economics of sharing with nature, namely the potentially huge cost of restoring lost eco-functions, either by human-made arrangements or lengthy and expensive repair.

'Panarchy' is one characterization of the relationship between thresholds in natural states and adjustments in human management arrangements (Gunderson and Holling 2002). Toby Gardner (4.3) considers how the lengthening dry season in the Amazon rainforest could result in whole new patterns of water resource care and reforestation, just to ensure that the rainforest communities have sufficient water for human and commercial consumption in the years to come. Meanwhile in the boreal forest, warming and drying weakens the natural resistance of trees, rendering them susceptible to pest infections. Pests are strengthened and more dispersed due in part to climate change. These are instances of combinational thresholds, which place special strains on the adaptive capabilities of human response.

There is much interest amongst ecosystem modellers over the changing rates of return to earlier population states following some disruption, such

11

as drought or cold, or loss of feeding availability. It is possible to measure patterns of 'loss of resilience' in some of these adjustments so that early indicators of incipient stress can be identified and monitored. This is part of the bifurcation approach to modelling, which relies on precursors to possible thresholds of altered conditions. Research on the drying of the Amazon rainforest, and associated incidence of ground-litter fires, is making use of this approach, as Toby Gardner (4.3) notes. However, the metaphor allusion is still relevant, as the range of data over time and space may not be sufficient for reliable measurements to be made meaningful, except through the metaphor process.

More attention needs to be paid to inter-linkages, to much more interdisciplinarity between physical and ecological processes and human interpretation and behaviour, and to localness of action. This is the message of the Amazonian drying and burning, as pointed out by Toby Gardner (4.3) and Patricia Howard (4.2). It is a function of accumulating local decisions, connected to regional climate change effects, and it can best be addressed through connecting local initiatives which are comfortable to local cultures, even though the whole response needs to have the form and shape of joint regional cohesion. Such arrangements are not easy to put into effect, but will be given expression in our final chapter (8.1).

On appropriate metaphors for social transformation

It is by no means so easy to follow the threshold/bifurcation metaphor for social systems. Paul Ekins (6.2), Sara Parkin (6.3) and Tim Lang and John Ingram (4.1) adopt this position. Social changes are not readily characterized by flows and patterns, as they are so infused with histories of culture, power and institutional rigidities. Despite the wish of policymakers and chief executives to imagine a world where it would be possible to predict an outcome from a given set of causal agents and behavioural variables, this is not in the socio-economic purview. (For a qualified defence of the case for prediction in social science based on such modelling of agents and variables, see Turchin 2011.) And there is no model of mass action which can show that if sufficient people change their behaviour in a certain way, then a predicable outcome, say for carbon reduction, or household water consumption, will follow. This suggests that the tipping point metaphor is inescapably qualitative, at least given our current and prospective knowledge of ecosystems, economies and societal evolution, and thus unsuitable for serious adaptation in governance, and all too dependent on creative imagining and empathy. Such characteristics do not commend themselves to policymakers and business leaders, who prefer quantitative models, no matter how ill-founded or even bogus, with some estimation of riskiness.

In the socio-ecological systems realm, therefore, it is naive to visualize any possible transitional condition, or possible precursor bifurcation, as having some kind of objective independent existence. Social phenomena are shot through with learning and forgetting, commitments to existing power and decisional arrangements, and plain cussedness. There is therefore a deep conceptual weakness in the translation of ecosystem analysis of threshold metaphors to governance generally, and to human behaviour more typically.

Resilience seems to be a concept more attuned to ecosystems functioning. To transfer it to governing arrangements and social systems brings in all manner of non-measurable phenomena such as equity, foresight, learning capabilities, scales of action, path determinacy of previous institutional commitments and 'mindsets', and wilful denial. Business and market mindsets, and the political realities of grappling with 'wicked problems', where the 'boxes are too difficult to tick' (see Charles Clarke (6.7)), lead to insecure action and to mindful delay. Nevertheless, we live in a coupled world of human–nature interrelationships (Ostrom 2009), so there is still merit in assessing just how human aspirations in favour of manageable survival and reduction of avoidable threat can be channelled on to the threshold metaphor.

It is possible that the second group of tipping points (induced vulnerabilities) is beginning to accelerate and amplify the onset and severity of the first (unintended worsening). If so, human resilience and acquired adaptive capabilities may not be sufficiently robust and flexible to cope. Tim Lang and John Ingram (4.1), for example, in their exploration of food security and attendant ecological ills, point out that the tipping point metaphor is less apposite than studies of raw power: of huge unaccountable corporations with limited foresight capacity; of complex governing rules and regulations which disguise and promote over-consumption; of misappropriated production, and chaotic pricing patterns; and where affordability and availability are working at cross purposes. In their analysis, tipping points are not metaphors but dysfunctional system conditions. Emily Boyd (7.2) echoes this dysfunctionality of system states. The economic/business/governance analysts led by Paul Ekins

13

(6.2) also acknowledge the evident and pervasive failure to foresee the foreseeable.

What emerges here is the notion of technological 'lock-in'. This is the tying down of technology and market forces into self-reinforcing patterns of continuation, a syndrome of 'path dependency' based on sunk costs, fear of stranded assets and unwillingness or inability to invest in major infrastructural change. This is very evident in the failure to remove carbon from the global economy, and in myriads of tiny decisions, from exploitation of new oil reserves in the warming Arctic, to the 'fracking' of shale-based oil and gas, to the enormous difficulty in achieving electric/hydrogen filling points for more ubiquitous low-carbon fuel availability. The obverse of techno-lock is 'social-unlocking' – the scope for benign transformation, rooted in changes in values and social organization, as addressed in our final chapter (8.1).

More attention needs to be paid to the polycentric nature of responses beyond the level of the nation state (alone or in concert) (Ostrom 2009a). We need many kinds of sub-national and cross-sectoral responses, on the basis of a number of nations and other actors, such as city governments, NGOs, and corporations combining forces, creating the basis for networks of action on many different timescales and levels (Carley and Christie 2000). Addressing the 'governing region' in the evolving metaphor of tipping points requires much more attention than is now the case. This would apply to China and India and Brazil as well as the 'soon to be water-poor' neighbours of shrinking montane glaciers.

There may be an even greater need for preparing for tipping thresholds in this combinational form at very local levels. This is the focus of Part 8. There is much interest in the determinants of human behaviour and in the scope for cultural shifts in both habit formation and group outlooks and action. If we are eventually to get anywhere with adaptation and resilience to such groupings of tipping points, then these seemingly intractable arenas of imperfect learning and responsiveness will need to be addressed. As Laurence Freeman observes in Chapter 5.1, 'The virtue of hope is not putting the best spin on bad news or fiddling while the planet burns. It is a conviction that because of, and not despite the human element, an eventually positive outcome is always possible.'

On resilience, adaptation and adjusting to the unfamiliar

If we can work through the various metaphors of thresholds, bifurcation, and convulsion, we need to address the complementary thresholds of adaptation, accommodation, and adjustment to the unfamiliar. In the climate change world, the Intergovernmental Panel on Climate Change regarded adaptation as having three purposes: to reduce exposure to known or possible hazard; to develop a capacity to cope with unavoidable damage (the costs which cannot be removed by reduced exposure); and to take advantage of new forms of living and governing so as to seek to redesign hazard or threat out of the system. The process of adaptation can be spontaneous, namely autonomous and reactive; or planned and managed through deliberate policy decisions and investments based on reasonable precaution or prediction; or anticipatory, in that there is a long-term process of accommodation of human activity and behaviour.

Emily Boyd (7.2) adopts the notion of four phases to adaptation in an adaptive cycle (Gunderson and Holling 2002):

- *rapid growth* (r) typically characterized by pioneer species, innovators or entrepreneurs;
- *conservation* (K) where resources are increasingly available and locked up in existing structures;
- *release* (omega) often triggered by a disturbance (e.g. fire, flood, disease) that exceeds the systems' capacity for resilience;
- *reorganization and renewal* (alpha) where invention, experimentation and re-assortment are common.

According to Boyd, the adaptive cycle has two opposing ways of operating. The rapid growth and conservation phases operate together as the 'front loop', while the release and reorganization phases form the 'back loop'. The front loop characterizes the development phase, and features activities such as the accumulation of capital, stability, accommodation and improvement. Empirical studies of complex adaptive systems often focus on gradual change, such as forest conservation operating on the front loop. Tipping points work is looking at the back loops, where systems that are undergoing shock may result in a reorganization that maintains the essential character of the original system within the desired state, yet shifts thinking to new ways of framing, adapting to and governing climate shocks. Toby Gardner (4.3) on the drying of the Amazon provides an example here.

15

Of interest here is the scope for merging the metaphors of thresholds with those of adjustment and anticipation. In almost all cases there is little institutional clarity for any meaningful and comprehensive approach to adaptation and the removal of vulnerability. Human patterns which rely on large settlements, now the dominant norm, are thus vulnerable to the confrontation of sheer inertia with the need for rapid adjustment. The possibility of parts of the West Antarctic ice sheet collapsing over a period of decades, with concomitant rises of sea level of a metre or more (unlikely but not unimaginable) would place megacities such as Shanghai, Dhaka, Jakarta and Mumbai in an adaptation crisis. There is at present no institutional machinery for dealing with the provision of food, fresh water, transport, or waste, to say nothing of relocation of many millions of people in many forms of supportive or fragmented community structures, in the timescale of a couple of decades. And to seek to do so whilst aiming at giving everyone the opportunity of adopting sustainable livelihoods is almost unimaginable.

The literature on collapse of earlier human settlement seems to focus on the role of adverse events (even when predictable); the excessive size of collapsing settlements; rapid population growth; competition for scarce privilege amongst elites; and evidence of over-exploitation of resource use immediately before catastrophic 'system failures'. All of this suggests that the metaphor of adjustment, either through planning/management, or by anticipation and pro-activity, may be very difficult to implement for resource-intensive, high-density, rapidly developing, increasingly unequal, and information-technology-dependent societies. Yet these are the very conditions being replicated on a daily basis.

So it is possible that we are creating the very elements of destabilizing bifurcations in our maladjusted adaptive responses which carry within them the seeds of tipping thresholds. The very act of simplification may be leading to emergent conditions of behaviour (for example, denial or resistance to innovation) which may lead to new unstable system states, and which profoundly affect the connections with other adaptive systems. This may be happening with the 'green growth' scenarios, where investments may not give rise to many new jobs because too many of the current unemployed are not suitably trained for such employment. We return to this in our final chapter (8.1).

On social construction and opportunism

The third framing device we can use for approaching tipping points is that of social construction, the meaning and purpose of entertaining the concept at all. Here we enter the world of creative imagination and of new forms of constructing social relations and outlooks. Giles Foden (3.1) reminds us that stories are segments cut into the flow of time, sections of continuity which convey order and structure into what otherwise is chaos. This helps to bring the dimensions of space and time and causality to tipping points.

So another way to consider the metaphor is to think of tipping landscapes – of terrain where many different explorations of possible future states can take place, and where creativity and not just modelling from datasets can be fused with rational enquiry. This would require more training and exposure to many different models of learning. Game-playing, storytelling, scenario-exploring, new forms of measuring betterment, justice, and adaptation will be needed in the design of business management, public service training, and schooling. Being more comfortable with the unfamiliar will become very important, as will cooperating in groups under circumstances of the unexpected and the removal of bias associated with sunk costs dependencies.

This will require a new approach to communicating future conditions. If people can begin to have the tools to imagine 'beneficial tipping landscapes' which reveal the strength of change and adaptation, but which are also underpinned by empathy, compassion, and virtuous responsibility (see Tim O'Riordan (6.1) and Joe Smith (7.1)), we may begin to create cultures of communication over tipping point metaphors which offer the incentive of hope, and hence the incentive for creative change.

This transformation may not be possible in present arrangements of social existence and economic development. Maybe current models of governing, of power relationships, of path dependency and of markets, convey inbuilt structures which critically impede such transformational narratives (Rist 2011). For us to be sure, we need to uncover the essence of governance and of markets, of cultures, and of diversity of living patterns, which can reveal just what bifurcations can be anticipated and designed, at least experimentally, just to see what is possible even in a world of impossibilities. These aspects are addressed in Part 6, both from a philosophical viewpoint of market immoralities, and from the hard-headed pragmatics of the business and political worlds.

This will require leadership of quite an unusual kind. Leadership which is deviant from normal managing styles, where social enterprise of the more imaginative and experimental kind is permitted to emerge and to be tested and supported. Sara Parkin (6.3), Amanda Long (6.4) and John Elkington (6.6) give this aspect prominence in their contributions. Leadership means a willingness to accept the learning and adaptiveness of failure, both on an individual and collective level. This means making much more use of the modern communicating technologies of social networking so that people can talk to each other with inventiveness, imagination and experimentation, as suggested by Matthew Taylor (3.2). It is just possible that the technology of the emerging age will enable 'localism' within mega-structures to flourish, so that communities can design their capabilities and renewal in the spaces of their familiarity and comfort zones. The 'urban village' could come of age.

Good news stories

In all our consideration of the threats, risks and foreboding inherent in the study of tipping points, we may lose sight of the myriad 'good news stories' which are shining beacons across the face of the planet. We certainly need to hear of these and to learn from their successes and capacities for furtherance and repetition. Businesses are learning and responding, and we need to know more of these adventures. Communities are managing under the most amazingly adverse circumstances to create economic, ecological, and social resilience, and we need to know more of their achievements and why they persevere.

One such example is the aftermath of the 2010 Pakistan floods which afflicted over 20 million people and some 1.7 million homes. Emily Boyd (7.2) reveals the huge challenges of combining many aid and relief efforts with infrastructure and social capital investments on a vast scale. She concludes that there is no guarantee that even the combined weight of the international development banks, the various aid streams, and the resources of the aid charities can bring about sustainable livelihoods in the coming years. Responses in the aftermath of disaster may inform us more of better preparedness for adaptation to tipping points.

One optimistic arena is the emergence of the social entrepreneur with the capacity to make profit from socially and ecologically sustaining business. We certainly need to hear more about such entrepreneurs and what forms of governing and market conditions, on a suitable geographical and cultural basis, might offer the best scope for their flourishing. John Elkington (6.6) has made a specialization of studying and advocating for this fascinating business niche. This in turn suggests a discussion on the appropriate models for businesses in facing tipping points/thresholds, again in a regional/local setting. There may well be a case for a more integrated approach to public/private/civil connections in future business models, with appropriate regulatory incentives to support them.

Laurence Freeman (5.1) reminds us that we are fearful of our mortality, that we do care about contributing knowingly to calamity, and that we can connect to the long term through devices such as meditation and opening of the mind. The ultimate metaphor may be what Freeman terms the 'inner eye'. This is the element of our imagination and awareness which transcends our normal reasoning. Triggering the inner eye may be the precursor to triggering the benign elements of addressing tipping points. This is a profound feature of anticipation, of alertness, and of recognizing the scale of the complexities before us.

Humble meditation may offer the beginning of visualizing the new horizons. Anthony Seldon (2011), Master of Winchester College, has initiated a period of stillness throughout his school for all beginnings of classes and meals. He regards stillness as a means to help young people to avoid responding to impulses. Pupils see immediate gains, but not the long-term consequences of their choices. Learning to be still, to cultivate mindfulness – and to think before acting – is thus not only a desirable, but also a key responsibility for education.

We cannot cope with tipping points with the outer eyes we use every day. Paul Ekins (6.2) shares this view. The markets and the financial arrangements do not appear to have an inner eye. Keith Clarke (6.5), speaking from a business perspective, says there is no far-sight in business unless it is regulated for. The critical elements of the modern economy do not yet contain this critical inner eye. Amanda Long (6.4), also a chief executive, is more optimistic. There is a glimmer of the creative visioning of the inner eye in the best of business leadership. Such 'good news stories' should be discovered and amplified. There is still just enough time to do this, as we explore in our final chapter (8.1).

So we begin our journey. Arguably critical thresholds are what spur us on. There is a long history of belief in catastrophic convulsions and ecological 'die-outs' in the planetary evolutionary journey. And the science of risk is peppered with associations of learning from hazard and precaution. So we may have to experience the onset of tipping points simply to be 'shocked and awed'. This should not stop us right now from at least recognizing our follies and our institutional deficiencies. This is the context in which the chapters and commentaries unfold.

References

Barnosky, A.D., Hadly, E.A., Bascompte, J., Berlow, E.L., Brown, J.H., Fortelius, M., *et al.* (2012), 'Approaching a State Shift in Earth's Biosphere', *Nature*, 486 (7401): 52–58.

Carley, M. and Christie, I. (2000), *Managing Sustainable Development* (London: Earthscan).

Duarte Santos, F. (2011), *Humans on Earth: From Origins to Possible Futures* (New York: Springer).

Gunderson, L.H. and Holling, C.S. (eds) (2002), *Panarchy: Understanding Transformations in Human and Natural Systems* (New York: Island Press).

Kurzweil, R. (2005), *The Singularity is Near* (New York: Viking).

Lenton, T.M. and Watson, A.J. (2011), *Revolutions That Made the Earth* (Oxford: Oxford University Press).

Ostrom, E. (2009), 'A General Framework for Analyzing Sustainability of Social-Ecological Systems', *Science*, 325: 419–23.

Ostrom, E. (2009a), *A Polycentric Approach for Coping with Climate Change* (Washington DC: World Bank Policy Research Working Paper No. 5095).

Resilience Alliance (2004), 'Thresholds and Alternate States in Ecological and Social-Ecological Systems', http://www.resalliance.org/index.php/thresholds_database.

Rist, G. (2011), *The Delusions of Economics: The Misguided Certainties of a Hazardous Science* (London: Zed Books).

Scheffer, M. (2009), *Critical Transitions in Nature and Society* (Princeton, NJ: Princeton University Press).

Seldon, A. (2011), 'Stillness in Schools', *Resurgence*, 269: 18–20.

Turchin, P. (2011), 'Social Tipping Points and Trend Reversals: A Historical Approach' (Mt Pilatus, Switzerland: Tipping Points Workshop, http://clio dynamics.info).

Turchin, P. and Nefedov, S. (2009), *Secular Cycles* (Princeton, NJ: Princeton University Press).

UNEP (2012), *Geo-5: Global Environment Outlook: Environment for the Future We Want* (Nairobi: United Nations Environment Programme).

PART 2
EARTH SYSTEM TIPPING POINTS

2.1
Tipping elements from a global perspective

TIM LENTON

The aim of this chapter is to provide an overview of potential tipping points in the Earth system, which we may cross this century, due to our collective impact on the planet interacting with its natural patterns of variability. I take a risk-assessment approach, summarizing existing information on the likelihood and impacts of tipping different elements of the Earth system, and using that information to produce a tentative assessment of the relative risks that they pose. Then I consider the prospects for early warning of approaching tipping points, as a means of helping manage the risks. The chapter is structured around a series of simple questions about Earth system tipping points: What are they? Where are they? How close are they? Which carry the greatest impacts? What is the worst case scenario? What early warning signs should we be looking for? When can we get reliable predictions? How should we respond?

At the start let me pin my colours to the mast, and defend my use of the term 'tipping point'. Distaste regarding it seems to stem from two main concerns. One is the over-liberal or uncritical application of such physical science concepts to social systems, containing actors with an element of both free will and reflection, who continually shape and reshape the systems of which they are a part. I can sidestep this, because my primary focus here is on our planet and its physical sub-systems, and I have no qualms about applying physical theories there. The definition I propose below is intended for physical systems, and I do not claim that it can be applied to social ones.

The second concern is psychological; talking about damaging tipping points is perceived as alarmist and likely to breed hedonism, despair or other maladaptive responses in the population. This line of argument I find morally challenging, because as a scientist I am trained to 'tell it like it is', as clearly as I can. The argument that the evidence and modelling I will discuss carry distasteful messages, and therefore their presentation should be adjusted, is not one I can accept. (That said, I realize we live in an era of 'post-normal' science, in which the objective and the subjective are always entwined (Stirling 2003).)

What and where are tipping points?

Little things can (sometimes) make a big difference, as Malcolm Gladwell's book that popularized societal tipping points argues (Gladwell 2000). Mathematicians, with their concept of a bifurcation point, have known this for centuries, as have physicists fascinated by phase changes of matter. More recently ecologists have borrowed from bifurcation theory to describe 'regime shifts' in ecosystems. Gladwell takes his cues from epidemiology, and the theory of infection spread, which has different underlying mathematics. Dynamical systems theory encompasses these and other classes of physical phenomena, which all share a common feature: a small change within, or from outside, a system can cause a large change in its future state. It seems natural to me to use the term 'tipping point' to describe this group of phenomena, and to communicate about them to non-scientists.

Thus, a *tipping point* is a critical threshold at which the future state of a system can be qualitatively altered by a small change in forcing (Lenton *et al.* 2008). Tipping points can conceivably occur in any spatial scale of system which has strong non-linearity in its internal dynamics. Here I focus on large-scale tipping points in the physical, chemical, and biological make-up of our planet. A *tipping element* is a part of the Earth system (at least sub-continental in scale) that has a tipping point (Lenton *et al.* 2008). Policy-relevant tipping elements are those that could be forced past a tipping point this century by human activities. In the language of the Intergovernmental Panel on Climate Change (IPCC), they are called 'large-scale discontinuities' (Smith *et al.* 2009), and are one type of dangerous anthropogenic interference in the climate system. *Abrupt climate change* is a subset of tipping point change which occurs faster than its cause (Rahmstorf 2001). Tipping point change also includes transitions that are slower than their cause (in both cases the rate is determined by the system itself). In either case the change in state may be reversible or irreversible. *Reversible* means that when the forcing is returned below the tipping point the system recovers its original state (either abruptly or gradually). *Irreversible* means that it does not (it takes a larger change in forcing to recover). Reversibility in principle does not mean that changes will be reversible in practice.

Previous work (Lenton *et al.* 2008) has identified a shortlist of nine potential policy-relevant tipping elements in the climate system that could pass a tipping point this century and undergo a transition this millennium under projected climate change. These are shown with some other candidates in Figure 2.1, where the tipping elements are grouped into those that involve ice melting, those that involve changes in the circulation of the ocean or atmosphere, and those that involve the loss of major biomes.

We should be most concerned about those tipping points that are nearest (least avoidable) and those that have the largest negative impacts. Generally, the more rapid and less reversible a transition is, the greater its impacts. Additionally, any amplification of global climate change may increase concern, as can interactions whereby tipping one element encourages tipping another, potentially leading to 'domino dynamics'. The leading candidates are now briefly summarized, with an emphasis on recent behaviour, and what the nature of the underlying mechanisms means for the reversibility and rapidity of any future transitions (for more details, see recent reviews (Lenton *et al.* 2008; Lenton 2012)). In later sections, the proximity of individual tipping points and their impacts are expanded upon.

Ice melting

The *Arctic sea-ice* underwent a new record summer loss of area in 2012, breaking the previous record set in 2007 and reaching around half of the area it had in the summers of the late 1970s, when the satellite record began. Projections are for the complete loss of ice in summer within decades. Whether this will involve an underlying bifurcation is debated (Abbot *et al.* 2011; Eisenman and Wettlaufer 2009) because ice re-grows in each dark polar winter, i.e. the loss is reversible in principle (Notz 2009). But already the changing ice cover is changing atmospheric circulation patterns (Overland and Wang 2010; Wu and Zhang 2010), with knock-on effects that extend to mid-latitudes, including contributing to cold winter extremes over Europe (Petoukhov and Semenov 2010).

The *Greenland ice sheet* (GIS) may be nearing a tipping point where it is committed to shrink (Kriegler *et al.* 2009; Lenton *et al.* 2008). Record seasonal melting occurred in summer 2012, probably associated with record

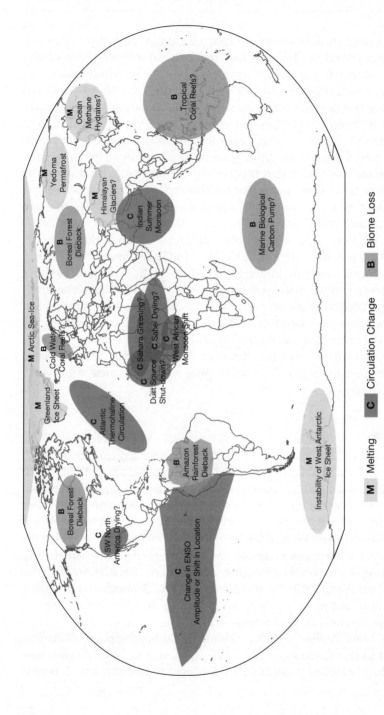

Figure 2.1 Map of potential policy-relevant tipping elements in the Earth's climate system. Question marks indicate systems whose status as tipping elements is particularly uncertain (Lenton 2012).

Arctic sea-ice loss, as it was in 2007 (Mote 2007). Extraordinary warmth around 12 July 2012 saw thawing across almost the entire ice sheet surface, which would have lowered the albedo (reflectivity), further amplifying the melt (Box *et al.* 2012). Once underway the transition to a smaller ice cap will have low reversibility, although it is likely to take several centuries (and is therefore not abrupt). The impacts via sea-level rise will ultimately be large (around 7 m) and global, but will depend on the rate of ice sheet shrinkage. There may be several stable states for ice volume, with the first transition involving retreat of the ice sheet on to land and around 1.5 m of sea-level rise (Ridley *et al.* 2010), up to 50 cm of which could occur this century (Pfeffer *et al.* 2008).

The *West Antarctic ice sheet* (WAIS) is currently assessed to be further from a tipping point than the GIS, but this is more uncertain (Kriegler *et al.* 2009; Lenton *et al.* 2008). Recent work (Schoof 2007) has shown that multiple stable states can exist for the grounding line of the WAIS, and that it has collapsed repeatedly in the past (Naish *et al.* 2009; Pollard and DeConto 2009). It has the potential for more rapid change and hence greater impacts than the GIS. Current models (Pollard and DeConto 2009) put the threshold for WAIS collapse when the surrounding ocean warms by around 5°C, and expert elicitation concurs that if global warming exceeds 4°C, it is more likely than not that the WAIS will collapse (Kriegler *et al.* 2009). The WAIS has the potential to cause sea-level rise of the order of 1 m per century and 3–4 m in total.

The *Yedoma permafrost* (perennially frozen soil), in north-eastern Siberia (150–168°E and 63–70°N), has an extremely high carbon content (2–5 per cent) and may contain up to 500 PgC (billion tonnes of carbon) (Zimov *et al.* 2006). It could tip into irreversible, self-sustaining collapse, due to an internally generated source of heat released by biochemical decomposition of the carbon, triggering further melting in a runaway positive feedback (Khvorostyanov *et al.* 2008a; Khvorostyanov *et al.* 2008b). This would produce emissions of 2–3 PgC yr^{-1} (equivalent to about a third of current fossil fuel burning). Tipping this system requires an estimated >9°C of regional warming (Khvorostyanov *et al.* 2008a), and may also be rate sensitive (Wieczorek *et al.* 2011). Although this seems far off, during the sea-ice retreat of 2007, Arctic land temperatures jumped (Lawrence *et al.* 2008) around 3°C.

Ocean methane hydrates may store up to 2000 PgC beneath the seafloor (Archer *et al.* 2009), and as the deep ocean warms, this reservoir of frozen methane could be destabilized, perhaps triggering submarine landslides

(Kayen and Lee 1991). However, an abrupt massive release of methane into the atmosphere is very unlikely (Archer 2007).

The *Himalayan glaciers* could lose much of their mass this century (Ramanathan and Feng 2008), and this will likely involve self-amplifying processes whereby dust accumulation and the exposure of bare ground lower the surface albedo and accelerate melt (Oerlemans *et al.* 2009; Pepin and Lundquist 2008). However, it is unclear whether there is a large-scale tipping point for this particular montane ice melt.

Biome loss

The *Amazon rainforest* experienced widespread droughts in 2005 and 2010, which turned the region from a sink to a source of carbon (0.6–0.8 PgC yr^{-1}) (Phillips *et al.* 2009). If anthropogenic-forced (Vecchi *et al.* 2006) lengthening of the dry season continues, and droughts increase in frequency or severity (Cox *et al.* 2008), the rainforest could reach a tipping point resulting in dieback of up to 80 per cent of trees (Cook and Vizy 2008; Cox *et al.* 2004; Salazar *et al.* 2007; Scholze *et al.* 2006), and its replacement by seasonal forest (Malhi *et al.* 2009) or savannah. This could take a few decades, would have low reversibility, large regional impacts, and knock-on effects far away. Widespread dieback is expected in a >4°C warmer world (Kriegler *et al.* 2009), and it could be committed to at a lower global temperature, long before it begins to be observed (Jones *et al.* 2009). Toby Gardner (4.3) considers the social and economic implications of these forecasts for the region.

The *boreal forest* in Western Canada is currently suffering from an invasion of mountain pine beetle that has caused widespread tree mortality (Kurz *et al.* 2008a) and has turned the nation's forests from a carbon sink to a carbon source (Kurz *et al.* 2008b). More widespread future dieback has been predicted at >3°C global warming (Kriegler *et al.* 2009; Lucht *et al.* 2006) (7°C regional warming), through a mixture of heat stress, increased vulnerability to disease, decreased reproduction rates and more frequent fires, all increasing mortality. The forest could be replaced by open woodlands or grasslands, in turn amplifying summer warming, drying and fire frequency.

Tropical *coral reefs* have recently experienced widespread and detrimental bleaching events as the ocean warms, and may be nearing a 'point of no return' (Veron *et al.* 2009). Ocean acidification (due to rising atmospheric CO_2) may also contribute to threshold-like changes (Riebesell *et al.*

2009) particularly for cold-water corals that grow down to 3000 m depth. Up to 70 per cent of them could be in corrosive waters by the end of this century (Guinotte *et al.* 2006). However, it is unclear whether there is a large-scale tipping point in the offing.

Circulation change

The *Atlantic thermohaline circulation* (THC) could be shut down if sufficient freshwater enters the North Atlantic to halt density-driven deep water formation there (Hofmann and Rahmstorf 2009; Peng 1995; Stommel 1961). This probably needs >4°C warming this century (Kriegler *et al.* 2009), although existing models are systematically biased towards a stable THC (Drijfhout *et al.* 2011). Still, as the THC weakens (IPCC 2007) it may pass a nearer tipping point in which deep water stops forming in the Labrador Sea region (to the west of Greenland) and switches to only occurring in the Greenland-Iceland-Norwegian Seas (to the east of Greenland) (Born and Levermann 2010; Levermann and Born 2007). This would increase sea level down the north-eastern seaboard of the USA by around 25 cm (in addition to a rise in global mean sea level) (Yin *et al.* 2009).

The *Sahel and the West African Monsoon* (WAM) have experienced rapid but reversible changes in the past, including devastating drought from the late 1960s through to the 1980s. Forecast future weakening of the THC contributing to 'Atlantic Niño' conditions, including strong warming in the Gulf of Guinea (Cook and Vizy 2006), could disrupt the seasonal onset of the WAM (Chang *et al.* 2008) and its later 'jump' northwards (Hagos and Cook 2007) into the Sahel. Whilst this might be expected to dry the Sahel, models give conflicting results. In one, if the WAM circulation collapses, this leads to wetting of parts of the Sahel as moist air is drawn in from the Atlantic to the west (Cook and Vizy 2006; Patricola and Cook 2008), greening the region in a rare example of a positive tipping point.

The *Indian Summer Monsoon* (ISM) is already being disrupted (Meehl *et al.* 2008; Ramanathan *et al.* 2005) and rice harvests impaired (Auffhammer *et al.* 2006) by an atmospheric brown cloud (ABC) haze that sits over the sub-continent and, to a lesser degree, the Indian Ocean. The ABC haze comprises a mixture of soot, which absorbs sunlight, and some reflecting sulphate. It causes heating of the atmosphere rather than the land surface, weakening the seasonal establishment of a land–ocean temperature gradient which triggers monsoon onset (Ramanathan *et al.* 2005). Conversely, greenhouse gas forcing is acting to strengthen the monsoon as it warms the northern land masses faster than the ocean to the south. In some future projections, ABC forcing could double the drought frequency within a decade (Ramanathan *et al.* 2005) with large impacts, although it should be highly reversible.

The *El Niño–Southern Oscillation* (ENSO) has recently produced severe El Niño events (e.g. in 1983 and 1998), and their pattern has arguably changed towards 'Modiki' events where the warm pool shifts from the west to the middle (rather than the east) of the equatorial Pacific (Ashok and Yamagata 2009; Yeh *et al.* 2009). Models disagree over the sign of future changes in El Niño amplitude (Collins *et al.* 2010) but generally give no change in frequency. Some models simulate increased El Niño amplitude in future (Collins *et al.* 2010; Guilyardi 2006), but ENSO is unlikely to either vanish or become overly strong this century (Kriegler *et al.* 2009; Latif and Keenlyside 2009). Whether there is any underlying tipping point is highly uncertain.

Southwest North America (land within 125–95°W, 25–40°N) is probably already in transition to a drier state 'unlike any . . . we have seen in the instrumental record' (Seager *et al.* 2007), which may link to increased flooding in the Great Plains (Cook *et al.* 2008). However, a tipping point is again unclear.

Other stressors

Of course human activities could trigger large-scale tipping points that are unrelated to climate change. Humans are stressing the planet in a variety of ways, including profound changes in land-use, an order-of-magnitude increase in soil erosion rates (and associated sedimentation in marine margins) and widespread reductions in biodiversity. As humans progressively eliminate the links in complex food webs, and introduce new links in the form of invasive species, there will likely come points at which the underlying network structures and the functioning of the corresponding ecosystems must be fundamentally altered. Meanwhile the widespread erosion of the soils is depleting stores of essential nutrients and the storage capacity for water, upon which ecosystems (including agricultural ones) depend. The transfer of fertilizer nutrient inputs and eroded soil to the ocean, either washed through freshwaters, or carried in dust and gases through the atmosphere, then tends to fuel the depletion of oxygen in coastal waters, and ultimately the open ocean. Toxic algal blooms can be triggered in coastal waters. In the open ocean, oxygen minimum zones (or 'dead zones') at depth are already spreading (Stramma *et al.* 2008) and causing essential nutrients to be released from the sediments, in a positive feedback loop that is thought to have driven much of the ocean anoxic in intervals of Earth's past (Handoh and Lenton 2003).

Risk assessment

The prospect of having to deal with high-impact but uncertain events, including a strong element of unpredictability, is not new. Think of earth-quakes or hurricanes making landfall. Systems exist for dealing with such events, and they hinge around a risk management approach. Although these are relatively short-timescale 'events', some of the risk management principles may be usefully mapped over to climate tipping points. Risk, in the formal sense, is the product of the likelihood (or probability) of something happening and its (negative) impact. So a meaningful risk assessment of tipping elements would demand careful assessment of the likelihood of passing various tipping points (under different forcing scenarios), as well as the associated impacts.

How close are tipping points?

It is natural to try to locate tipping points in terms of global mean temperature change ('global warming'), although the connection is always indirect, often difficult to make, and sometimes not meaningful. Recent efforts suggest that 1°C global warming (above the 1980–1999 mean) could be dangerous as there are 'moderately significant' (Smith *et al.* 2009) risks of large-scale discontinuities (i.e. tipping points). Also, Arctic sea-ice and possibly the Greenland ice sheet would be threatened (Hansen *et al.* 2007; Lenton *et al.* 2008). Warming of 3°C is clearly dangerous as risks of large-scale discontinuities are 'substantial or severe' (Smith *et al.* 2009), and several tipping elements could be threatened (Lenton *et al.* 2008). Under a 2–4°C committed warming, expert elicitation (Kriegler *et al.* 2009) gives a >16 per cent probability of crossing at least one of five tipping points, which rises to a >56 per cent probability (i.e. more likely than not) for a >4°C committed warming. Considering a longer list of nine potential tipping elements, Figure 2.2 summarizes recent information on the likelihood of tipping them, under the IPCC range of projected global warming this century.

31

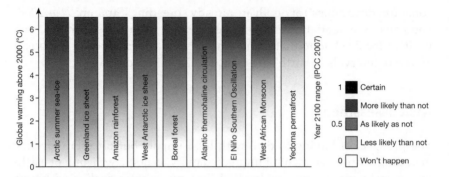

Figure 2.2 The likelihood of tipping different elements under different degrees of global warming (Lenton and Schellnhuber 2007), updated, based on expert elicitation results (Kriegler *et al.* 2009) and recent literature.

Current assessments suggest that Arctic tipping points involving ice melting are probably most vulnerable, with the least uncertainty surrounding this (Lenton *et al.* 2008). However, the greater uncertainty surrounding other tipping points allows for the possibility that some of them may be close as well. More detailed information can be found in the expert elicitation results (Kriegler *et al.* 2009).

Which tipping points carry the greatest impacts?

Passing a climate tipping point is generally expected to have large negative impacts, but these have only begun to be quantified for some elements and scenarios (Lenton *et al.* 2009a), notably a collapse of the THC (Arnell *et al.* 2005; Higgins and Vellinga 2004; Link and Tol 2004), where questionable (Shearer 2005) extrapolations have been made to national security concerns (Schwartz and Randall 2003). To translate climate tipping points into societal impacts typically involves several intervening steps and variables. Underestimation problems arise because studies tend to only consider a subset of consequences or impacted sectors (e.g. insurance (Lenton *et al.* 2009a)). Still, estimated impacts are already large for several tipping points (Lenton *et al.* 2009a). For a THC collapse this has been contested (Link and Tol 2004), although one is tempted to quip that only an economist could come to the conclusion that rearranging the large-scale ocean circulation would be beneficial to societies. Such disagreement (Arnell *et al.* 2005; Link and Tol 2004) is to be expected, as impacts depend on human responses and are thus more epistemologically contested than assigning likelihoods to events (Stirling 2003).

With these caveats in mind, a 'straw-man' tipping point risk matrix is presented (Figure 2.3). Here tipping elements from the original shortlist (Lenton *et al.* 2008) where a threshold can be meaningfully linked to global temperature change are considered (thus excluding the Indian Summer Monsoon). Relative likelihoods and impacts are assessed on a five-point scale: low, low-medium, medium, medium-high, and high. Information on likelihood is taken from review of the literature (Lenton and Schellnhuber 2007; Lenton *et al.* 2008; Lenton 2012) and expert elicitation (Kriegler *et al.* 2009). Impacts are considered in relative terms, based on limited research (Lenton *et al.* 2009a) and my subjective judgement. The bold ring indicates the one system where impacts have been considered in several studies (Arnell *et al.* 2005; Higgins and Vellinga 2004; Lenton *et al.* 2009a; Link and Tol 2004), which thus forms a reference point. Impacts depend on timescale and here the full 'ethical time horizon' of 1000 years is considered (Lenton

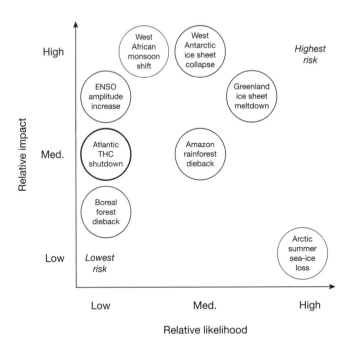

Figure 2.3 A 'straw-man' risk matrix for climate tipping points (Lenton 2011).

33

et al. 2008) assuming minimal discounting of impacts on future generations. (Note that if placed on an absolute scale compared to other climate eventualities most tipping point impacts would be high.)

This risk matrix illustrates some familiar dilemmas for the would-be risk manager: 'relatively high impact–low probability' events, such as West African monsoon shift, come out with a similar risk to 'relatively lower impact–high probability' events, such as Arctic summer sea-ice loss. However, what stand out are the 'high impact–high-probability' scenarios as a priority for risk management effort: in this case Greenland ice sheet meltdown and West Antarctic ice sheet collapse. I emphasize that this straw-man assessment could be spectacularly wrong, especially on the impact axis. The point is to inspire a more scientifically credible and socially legitimate assessment of the risks, which in turn demands the engagement of a wider team of experts and relevant stakeholders (Stirling 2003).

The effort to translate climate tipping points into impacts inevitably leads down to regional, local and individual scales where the impacts will be felt. Whilst the Earth system scientist tries to gaze omnisciently at the planet from the top down, an alternative approach would be to define tipping points in impacts from the bottom up. The bottom-up approach would doubtless lead to the identification of some different threats, not least because some nations may experience tipping points as a result of entirely smooth changes in climate. For example, even a smooth movement in latitude of the jet streams, relative to island nations that are fixed in location underneath, can cause tipping point changes. The 2007 summer flooding in the UK is a seasonal example of the effects of a southward-straying polar jet. For Australia, the future depends crucially on whether the subtropical jet, which has been weakening, drifts away from the continent.

Having taken a risk-assessment approach, where the tipping points are treated independently, it is also worth considering a worst case scenario, which includes potential interactions between them. The aim of such horizon scanning is to be braced for all possible eventualities.

What is the worst case scenario?

By 2100, the worst case would be to be locked on to a trajectory to a hotter, higher sea-level, low-ice state for the planet, with qualitatively different patterns of atmospheric and oceanic circulation, different modes of internal variability, diminished carbon stores on land, and major changes in biomes – in short, a structural change in the Earth system. In this worst case scenario, unmitigated radiative forcing and high climate sensitivity trigger 'domino dynamics', in which tipping one element of the Earth system significantly increases the probability of tipping another, and so on. Worryingly, from the limited information (Kriegler *et al.* 2009) that exists on the causal relations between different individual tipping events, the majority of connections do reinforce one another. Furthermore, the palaeo-record shows us that the Earth system 'prefers' particular states from time to time and tends to switch between them. On several occasions in the past, the planet was radically reorganized without there being any sign of a particularly large forcing perturbation (e.g. at the end of the last ice age).

This scenario might go something like this. The loss of Arctic summer sea-ice accelerates warming on the neighbouring land surfaces. The Greenland ice sheet is already in a state of irreversible shrinkage, and sea-ice loss accelerates its contribution to sea-level rise. The West Antarctic ice sheet starts to collapse and the rate of sea-level rise exceeds 1 metre per century (upper limit 2 metres by 2100 (Pfeffer *et al.* 2008)). The Atlantic overturning circulation weakens and deep water formation shifts in location, leading to regionally enhanced sea-level rise along the north-east cost of North America (Yin *et al.* 2009). Weakening of the overturning contributes to strong warming in the tropical Atlantic and a collapse of the West African monsoon (Chang *et al.* 2008). Meanwhile the monsoon in Southeast Asia shows enhanced inter-annual variability and Himalayan glaciers shrink, first increasing and later reducing dry season river flow. El Niño events become stronger and droughts afflicting the Amazon cause rainforest dieback mid-century. Some regions of unfreezing tundra lose their carbon abruptly (Khvorostyanov *et al.* 2008a), and large areas of boreal forest dieback (Lucht *et al.* 2006), releasing yet more carbon. Arctic sea-ice is lost year-round at the end of the century (Eisenman and Wettlaufer 2009), contributing to further reorganization of atmospheric and ocean circulation patterns.

This is an apocalyptic storyline, which should not be viewed as a prediction or projection. In its totality, the scenario is highly unlikely to transpire. However, the impacts are so great that from a risk-management point of view, it deserves consideration. Furthermore, parts of the scenario may become more likely than not (Kriegler *et al.* 2009) if we are heading into a >4°C warmer world.

What early warning signs should we be looking for?

Faced with the risk of unpleasant climate surprises, perhaps the most useful information that science could provide to help societies cope is some early warning of an approaching tipping point. Early warning information can take several forms, ranging from the knowledge that a threshold change could occur, through qualitative assessment that it is becoming more likely, to a forecast of its timing. For several rapid onset natural hazards, e.g. hurricanes (Willoughby *et al.* 2007) and tsunamis (Titov *et al.* 2005), quite sophisticated early warning systems are already in place (Sorensen 2000), whilst for some slower onset hazards, e.g. drought (Verdin *et al.* 2005) and malaria outbreaks (Thomson *et al.* 2006), seasonal forecasting skill is beginning to be used in early warning. The United Nations (2006) has called for the development of a globally comprehensive early warning system, but this has yet to consider early warning of climate tipping points.

There are encouraging signs that we can directly extract some information on the present stability (or otherwise) of different tipping elements. Recent progress has been made in identifying and testing generic early warning indicators of an approaching tipping point (Dakos *et al.* 2008; Lenton *et al.* 2008; Lenton *et al.* 2009b; Livina and Lenton 2007; Scheffer *et al.* 2009). In particular, slowing down in response to perturbation is a nearly universal property of systems approaching various types of tipping point (Dakos *et al.* 2008; Scheffer *et al.* 2009; Wissel 1984). To visualize this, picture the present state of a system as a ball in a curved potential well (attractor) that is being nudged around by some stochastic (random) noise process, e.g. weather (Figure 2.4). The ball continually tends to roll back towards the bottom of the well – its lowest potential energy state – and the rate at which it rolls back is determined by the curvature of the potential well. As the system is forced towards a bifurcation point, the potential well becomes flatter. Hence the ball will roll back ever more sluggishly. At the bifurcation point, the potential becomes flat and the ball is destined to roll off into some other state (alternative potential well).

Slowing down can be detected as increasing temporal or spatial correlation in data, increasing memory, or a shift to greater fluctuations at lower frequencies. Such signals have been successfully detected in past climate records approaching different transitions (Dakos *et al.* 2008; Lenton *et al.* 2012a; Lenton *et al.* 2012b; Livina and Lenton 2007), and in model experiments (Dakos *et al.* 2008; Held and Kleinen 2004; Kleinen *et al.* 2003; Lenton *et al.* 2009b; Lenton *et al.* 2012b; Livina and Lenton 2007). This offers the prospect of probabilistic forecasting of some conceivable future climate

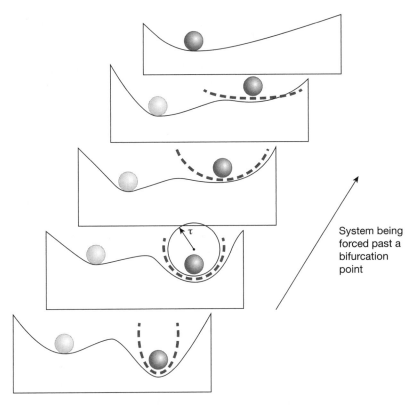

Figure 2.4 Schematic representation of a system being forced past a bifurcation point. The system's response time to small perturbations is related to the growing radius of the potential well (Lenton *et al.* 2008).

tipping points (Lenton *et al.* 2008), especially if such statistical early warning indicators can be combined with dynamical models. However, critics have questioned the statistical robustness of proposed early warning signals (Ditlevsen and Johnsen 2010), and have noted that some types of abrupt transition carry no early warning signals (Ditlevsen and Johnsen 2010; Hastings and Wysham 2010).

Other early warning indicators that have been explored for ecological tipping points include increasing variance (Biggs *et al.* 2009), skewed responses (Biggs *et al.* 2009; Guttal and Jayaprakash 2008), and their spatial equivalents (Guttal and Jayaprakash 2009). Successful tests on ecological models (Dakos *et al.* 2010) suggest it would be worth looking for increasing spatial correlation as an early warning indicator in climate data and models. Also, increasing variability is beginning to be applied to anticipating climate tipping points (Ditlevsen and Johnsen 2010). For climate sub-systems subject to a high degree of short timescale variability ('noise'), flickering between states may occur prior to a more permanent transition (Bakke *et al.* 2009). For such cases, we have recently developed a method of deducing the number of states (or 'modes') being sampled by a system, their relative stability (or otherwise), and changes in these properties over time (Livina *et al.* 2010).

Looking ahead, there is a need for much better targeted monitoring of tipping elements and their leading indicators of vulnerability. In many cases, model-based research is needed to establish which variables best indicate underlying vulnerability (and can be readily monitored). Then direct or remote-sensing-based monitoring can be designed and implemented (for example, much recent effort has been invested in directly monitoring (Cunningham *et al.* 2007) the overturning strength of the Atlantic at 26.5°N).

When can we get reliable predictions?

Whilst the prospects for early warning are encouraging, the very nature of Earth system dynamics is such that we can never have complete predictability of tipping points: a mixture of deterministic and stochastic processes will always be at work. We can work to better constrain the deterministic components, and to get a measure of the nature, level and influence of the 'noise'. But there will always be the potential for a random fluctuation to tip a vulnerable system at a time that cannot be precisely predicted. This is a kind of 'irreducible uncertainty'. It means that any tipping point early warning system has the potential for missed alarms.

Still, by 2030, if we continue to clean up our aerosol pollution, then we may get a much better measure of the sensitivity of global temperature to radiative forcing. The reason is that the direct and indirect effects of aerosols (especially on cloud properties) are currently having a cooling effect, but the size of that effect is by far the most poorly constrained term in the equation determining global temperature. By removing the aerosols we will learn how much cooling effect they have been imparting. This will greatly improve our upper limit on how warm it could get by the end of the century, and hence which tipping elements are vulnerable.

How should we respond?

Once an early warning of an approaching climate tipping point has been obtained and effectively communicated, risk can be reduced by trying to minimize the likelihood of passing a tipping point, or by trying to minimize the impacts of passing it. Corresponding risk-reduction strategies need to be considered and evaluated (Keller *et al.* 2008). Conceivably, for some climate tipping points, warning could be early enough to allow aversive action by mitigation of short-lived radiative forcing agents (Jackson 2009), or by geo-engineering to reduce incoming sunlight (Lenton and Vaughan 2009). However, the multiple sources of inertia in the climate system, and in human response systems, make this proposition questionable. An analogous problem of avoiding an approaching tipping point in an ecological system – a fishery (Biggs *et al.* 2009) – shows that once there is a reliable early warning of an approaching tipping point, it is too late for slow intervention methods to avoid it. Even where a tipping point is unavoidable, mitigation action may still help. For example, the rate of Greenland ice sheet melt and corresponding sea-level rise, even when committed to irreversible meltdown, depends on the extent to which this threshold has been exceeded (Huybrechts and De Wolde 1999). Still, adaptation to minimize impacts is likely to be the dominant response when faced with most tipping point early warnings. Appropriate adaptation action will clearly depend on the particular tipping point, but in the worst case it could involve intentional resettlement of populations before their home region becomes uninhabitable. As a general rule, early warning information is only useful if the warning recipients are empowered to act effectively on the information (Patt and Gwata 2002).

References

Abbot, D.S., Silber, M., and Pierrehumbert, R.T. (2011), 'Bifurcations Leading to Summer Arctic Sea Ice Loss', *Journal of Geophysical Research*, 116: D19120.

Archer, D. (2007), 'Methane Hydrate Stability and Anthropogenic Climate Change', *Biogeosciences*, 4: 993–1057.

Archer, D., Buffett, B., and Brovkin, V. (2009), 'Ocean Methane Hydrates as a Slow Tipping Point in the Global Carbon Cycle', *Proceedings of the National Academy of Sciences USA*, 106: 20596–601.

Arnell, N., Tompkins, E., Adger, N., and Delaney, K. (2005), 'Vulnerability to Abrupt Climate Change in Europe' (Technical Report 34: Tyndall Centre for Climate Change Research).

Ashok, K. and Yamagata, T. (2009), 'Climate Change: The El Nino with a Difference', *Nature*, 461 (7263): 481–84.

Auffhammer, M., Ramanathan, V., and Vincent, J.R. (2006), 'Integrated Model Shows That Atmospheric Brown Clouds and Greenhouse Gases Have Reduced Rice Harvests in India', *Proceedings of the National Academy of Sciences USA*, 103 (52): 19668–72.

Bakke, J., Lie, O., Heegaard, E., Dokken, T., Haug, G.H., Birks, H.H., *et al.* (2009), 'Rapid Oceanic and Atmospheric Changes During the Younger Dryas Cold Period', *Nature Geoscience*, 2: 202–05.

Biggs, R., Carpenter, S.R., and Brock, W.A. (2009), 'Turning Back from the Brink: Detecting an Impending Regime Shift in Time to Avert It', *Proceedings of the National Academy of Sciences USA*, 106 (3): 826–31.

Born, A. and Levermann, A. (2010), 'The 8.2 Ka Event: Abrupt Transition of the Subpolar Gyre toward a Modern North Atlantic Circulation', *Geochemistry Geophysics Geosystems*, 11 (6): Q06011.

Box, J.E., Fettweis, X., Stroeve, J.C., Tedesco, M., Hall, D.K., and Steffen, K. (2012), 'Greenland Ice Sheet Albedo Feedback: Thermodynamics and Atmospheric Drivers', *The Cryosphere*, 6 (4): 821–39.

Chang, P., Zhang, R., Hazeleger, W., Wen, C., Wan, X., Ji, L., *et al.* (2008), 'Oceanic Link between Abrupt Change in the North Atlantic Ocean and the African Monsoon', *Nature Geoscience*, 1: 444–48.

Collins, M., An, S.-I., Cai, W., Ganachaud, A., Guilyardi, E., Jin, F.-F., *et al.* (2010), 'The Impact of Global Warming on the Tropical Pacific Ocean and El Nino', *Nature Geoscience*, 3 (6): 391–97.

Cook, K.H. and Vizy, E.K. (2006), 'Coupled Model Simulations of the West African Monsoon System: Twentieth- and Twenty-First-Century Simulations', *Journal of Climate*, 19: 3681–703.

Cook, K.H. and Vizy, E.K. (2008), 'Effects of Twenty-First-Century Climate Change on the Amazon Rain Forest', *Journal of Climate*, 21: 542–60.

Cook, K.H., Vizy, E.K., Launer, Z.S., and Patricola, C.M. (2008), 'Springtime Intensification of the Great Plains Low-Level Jet and Midwest Precipitation in GCM Simulations of the Twenty-First Century', *Journal of Climate*, 21: 6321–40.

Cox, P.M., Betts, R.A., Collins, M., Harris, P.P., Huntingford, C., and Jones, C.D. (2004), 'Amazonian Forest Dieback under Climate-Carbon Cycle Projections for the 21st Century', *Theoretical and Applied Climatology*, 78: 137–56.

Cox, P.M., Harris, P.P., Huntingford, C., Betts, R.A., Collins, M., Jones, C.D., *et al.* (2008), 'Increasing Risk of Amazonian Drought Due to Decreasing Aerosol Pollution', *Nature*, 453: 212–15.

Cunningham, S.A., Kanzow, T., Rayner, D., Baringer, M.O., Johns, W.E., Marotzke, J., *et al.* (2007), 'Temporal Variability of the Atlantic Meridional Overturning Circulation at 26.5°N', *Science*, 317 (5840): 935–38.

Dakos, V., Scheffer, M., van Nes, E.H., Brovkin, V., Petoukhov, V., and Held, H. (2008), 'Slowing Down as an Early Warning Signal for Abrupt Climate Change', *Proceedings of the National Academy of Sciences USA*, 105 (38): 14308–12.

Dakos, V., van Nes, E., Donangelo, R., Fort, H., and Scheffer, M. (2010), 'Spatial Correlation as Leading Indicator of Catastrophic Shifts', *Theoretical Ecology*, 3 (3): 163–74.

Ditlevsen, P.D. and Johnsen, S.J. (2010), 'Tipping Points: Early Warning and Wishful Thinking', *Geophysical Research Letters*, 37: L19703.

Drijfhout, S., Weber, S., and van der Swaluw, E. (2011), 'The Stability of the MOC as Diagnosed from Model Projections for Pre-Industrial, Present and Future Climates', *Climate Dynamics*, 37 (7–8): 1575–86.

Eisenman, I. and Wettlaufer, J.S. (2009), 'Nonlinear Threshold Behavior During the Loss of Arctic Sea Ice', *Proceedings of the National Academy of Sciences USA*, 106 (1): 28–32.

Gladwell, M. (2000), *The Tipping Point: How Little Things Can Make a Big Difference* (New York: Little Brown).

Guilyardi, E. (2006), 'El Nino–Mean State–Seasonal Cycle Interactions in a Multi-Model Ensemble', *Climate Dynamics*, 26: 329–48.

Guinotte, J.M., Orr, J., Cairns, S., Freiwald, A., Morgan, L., and George, R. (2006), 'Will Human-Induced Changes in Seawater Chemistry Alter the Distribution of Deep-Sea Scleractinian Corals?', *Frontiers in Ecology and the Environment*, 4: 141–46.

Guttal, V. and Jayaprakash, C. (2008), 'Changing Skewness: An Early Warning Signal of Regime Shifts in Ecosystems', *Ecology Letters*, 11: 450–60.

Guttal, V. and Jayaprakash, C. (2009), 'Spatial Variance and Spatial Skewness: Leading Indicators of Regime Shifts in Spatial Ecological Systems', *Theoretical Ecology*, 2: 3–12.

Hagos, S.M. and Cook, K.H. (2007), 'Dynamics of the West African Monsoon Jump', *Journal of Climate*, 20: 5264–84.

Handoh, I.C. and Lenton, T.M. (2003), 'Periodic Mid-Cretaceous Oceanic Anoxic Events Linked by Oscillations of the Phosphorus and Oxygen Biogeochemical Cycles', *Global Biogeochemical Cycles*, 17 (4): 1092 10.29/2003GB002039.

Hansen, J., Sato, M., Ruedy, R., Kharecha, P., Lacis, A., Miller, R., *et al.* (2007), 'Dangerous Human-Made Interference with Climate: A Giss Modele Study', *Atmospheric Chemistry and Physics*, 7 (9): 2287–312.

Hastings, A. and Wysham, D.B. (2010), 'Regime Shifts in Ecological Systems Can Occur with No Warning', *Ecology Letters*, 13 (4): 464–72.

Held, H. and Kleinen, T. (2004), 'Detection of Climate System Bifurcations by Degenerate Fingerprinting', *Geophysical Research Letters*, 31: L23207.

Higgins, P. and Vellinga, M. (2004), 'Ecosystem Responses to Abrupt Climate Change: Teleconnections, Scale and the Hydrological Cycle', *Climatic Change*, 64 (1): 127–42.

Hofmann, M. and Rahmstorf, S. (2009), 'On the Stability of the Atlantic Meridional Overturning Circulation', *Proceedings of the National Academy of Sciences USA*, 106: 20584–89.

Huybrechts, P. and De Wolde, J. (1999), 'The Dynamic Response of the Greenland and Antarctic Ice Sheets to Multiple-Century Climatic Warming', *Journal of Climate*, 12: 2169–88.

IPCC (2007), *Climate Change 2007: The Physical Science Basis* (Cambridge: Cambridge University Press).

Jackson, S.C. (2009), 'Parallel Pursuit of Near-Term and Long-Term Climate Mitigation', *Science*, 326 (5952): 526–27.

Jones, C., Lowe, J., Liddicoat, S., and Betts, R. (2009), 'Committed Ecosystem Change Due to Climate Change', *Nature Geoscience*, 2: 484–87.

Kayen, R.E. and Lee, H.J. (1991), 'Pleistocene Slope Instability of Gas Hydrate-Laden Sediment of Beaufort Sea Margin', *Marine Geotechnology*, 10: 125–41.

Keller, K., Yohe, G., and Schlesinger, M. (2008), 'Managing the Risks of Climate Thresholds: Uncertainties and Information Needs', *Climatic Change*, 91 (1): 5–10.

Khvorostyanov, D.V., Ciais, P., Krinner, G., and Zimov, S.A. (2008a), 'Vulnerability of East Siberia's Frozen Carbon Stores to Future Warming', *Geophysical Research Letters*, 35: L10703.

Khvorostyanov, D.V., Krinner, G., Ciais, P., Heimann, M., and Zimov, S.A. (2008b), 'Vulnerability of Permafrost Carbon to Global Warming. Part I: Model Description and the Role of Heat Generated by Organic Matter Decomposition', *Tellus B*, 60B: 250–64.

Kleinen, T., Held, H., and Petschel-Held, G. (2003), 'The Potential Role of Spectral Properties in Detecting Thresholds in the Earth System: Application to the Thermohaline Circulation', *Ocean Dynamics*, 53: 53–63.

Kriegler, E., Hall, J.W., Held, H., Dawson, R., and Schellnhuber, H.J. (2009), 'Imprecise Probability Assessment of Tipping Points in the Climate System', *Proceedings of the National Academy of Sciences USA*, 106 (13): 5041–46.

Kurz, W.A., Dymond, C.C., Stinson, G., Rampley, G.J., Neilson, E.T., Carroll, A.L., *et al.* (2008a), 'Mountain Pine Beetle and Forest Carbon Feedback to Climate Change', *Nature*, 452: 987–90.

Kurz, W.A., Stinson, G., Rampley, G.J., Dymond, C.C., and Neilson, E.T. (2008b), 'Risk of Natural Disturbances Makes Future Contribution of Canada's Forests to the Global Carbon Cycle Highly Uncertain', *Proceedings of the National Academy of Sciences USA*, 105 (5): 1551–55.

Latif, M. and Keenlyside, N.S. (2009), 'El Nino/Southern Oscillation Response to Global Warming', *Proceedings of the National Academy of Sciences USA*, 106: 20578–83.

Lawrence, D.M., Slater, A.G., Tomas, R.A., Holland, M.M., and Deser, C. (2008), 'Accelerated Arctic Land Warming and Permafrost Degradation During Rapid Sea Ice Loss', *Geophysical Research Letters*, 35: L11506.

Lenton, T.M. (2011), 'Early Warning of Climate Tipping Points', *Nature Climate Change*, 1: 201–09.

Lenton, T.M. (2012), 'Future Climate Surprises', in A. Henderson-Sellers and K. McGuffie (eds), *The Future of the World's Climate* (Oxford: Elsevier), 489–507.

Lenton, T.M. and Schellnhuber, H.J. (2007), 'Tipping the Scales', *Nature Reports Climate Change*, 1: 97–98.

Lenton, T.M. and Vaughan, N.E. (2009), 'The Radiative Forcing Potential of Different Climate Geoengineering Options', *Atmospheric Chemistry and Physics*, 9: 5539–61.

Lenton, T.M., Held, H., Kriegler, E., Hall, J., Lucht, W., Rahmstorf, S., and Schellnhuber, H.J. (2008), 'Tipping Elements in the Earth's Climate System', *Proceedings of the National Academy of Sciences USA*, 105 (6): 1786–93.

Lenton, T.M., Footitt, A., and Dlugolecki, A. (2009a), 'Major Tipping Points in the Earth's Climate System and Consequences for the Insurance Sector' (Tyndall Centre for Climate Change Research).

Lenton, T.M., Myerscough, R.J., Marsh, R., Livina, V.N., Price, A.R., Cox, S.J., and the GENIE team (2009b), 'Using GENIE to Study a Tipping Point in the Climate System', *Philosophical Transactions of the Royal Society A: Mathematical, Physical and Engineering Sciences*, 367 (1890): 871–84.

Lenton, T.M., Livina, V.N., Dakos, V., and Scheffer, M. (2012a), 'Climate Bifurcation During the Last Deglaciation?', *Climate of the Past*, 8: 1127–39.

Lenton, T.M., Livina, V.N., Dakos, V., van Nes, E.H., and Scheffer, M. (2012b), 'Early Warning of Climate Tipping Points from Critical Slowing Down: Comparing Methods to Improve Robustness', *Philosophical Transactions of the Royal Society A: Mathematical, Physical and Engineering Sciences*, 370 (1962): 1185–204.

Levermann, A. and Born, A. (2007), 'Bistability of the Atlantic Subpolar Gyre in a Coarse-Resolution Climate Model', *Geophysical Research Letters*, 34: L24605.

Link, P.M. and Tol, R.S.J. (2004), 'Possible Economic Impacts of a Shutdown of the Thermohaline Circulation: An Application of FUND', *Portuguese Economic Journal*, 3 (2): 99–114.

Livina, V.N. and Lenton, T.M. (2007), 'A Modified Method for Detecting Incipient Bifurcations in a Dynamical System', *Geophysical Research Letters*, 34: L03712.

Livina, V.N., Kwasniok, F., and Lenton, T.M. (2010), 'Potential Analysis Reveals Changing Number of Climate States During the Last 60 Kyr', *Climate of the Past*, 6 (1): 77–82.

Lucht, W., Schaphoff, S., Erbrecht, T., Heyder, U., and Cramer, W. (2006), 'Terrestrial Vegetation Redistribution and Carbon Balance under Climate Change', *Carbon Balance and Management*, 1: 6.

Malhi, Y., Aragao, L.E.O.C., Galbraith, D., Huntingford, C., Fisher, R., Zelazowski, P., *et al.* (2009), 'Exploring the Likelihood and Mechanism of a Climate-Change-Induced Dieback of the Amazon Rainforest', *Proceedings of the National Academy of Sciences USA*, 106: 20610–15.

Meehl, G.A., Arblaster, J.M., and Collins, W.D. (2008), 'Effects of Black Carbon Aerosols on the Indian Monsoon', *Journal of Climate*, 21: 2869–82.

Mote, T.L. (2007), 'Greenland Surface Melt Trends 1973–2007: Evidence of a Large Increase in 2007', *Geophysical Research Letters*, 34: L22507.

Naish, T., Powell, R., Levy, R., Wilson, G., Scherer, R., Talarico, F., *et al.* (2009), 'Obliquity-Paced Pliocene West Antarctic Ice Sheet Oscillations', *Nature*, 458 (7236): 322–28.

Notz, D. (2009), 'The Future of Ice Sheets and Sea Ice: Between Reversible Retreat and Unstoppable Loss', *Proceedings of the National Academy of Sciences USA*, 106: 20590–95.

Oerlemans, J., Giesen, R.H., and van den Broeke, M.R. (2009), 'Retreating Alpine Glaciers: Increased Melt Rates Due to Accumulation of Dust (Vadret Da Morteratsch, Switzerland)', *Journal of Glaciology*, 55: 729–36.

Overland, J.E. and Wang, M. (2010), 'Large-Scale Atmospheric Circulation Changes Are Associated with the Recent Loss of Arctic Sea Ice', *Tellus A*, 62 (1): 1–9.

Patricola, C.M. and Cook, K.H. (2008), 'Atmosphere/Vegetation Feedbacks: A Mechanism for Abrupt Climate Change over Northern Africa', *Journal of Geophysical Research (Atmospheres)*, 113: D18102.

Patt, A. and Gwata, C. (2002), 'Effective Seasonal Climate Forecast Applications: Examining Constraints for Subsistence Farmers in Zimbabwe', *Global Environmental Change*, 12 (3): 185–95.

Peng, T.H. (1995), 'Future Climate Surprises', in A. Henderson-Sellers (ed.), *Future Climates of the World: A Modelling Perspective* (Oxford: Elsevier), 517–35.

Pepin, N.C. and Lundquist, J.D. (2008), 'Temperature Trends at High Elevations: Patterns across the Globe', *Geophysical Research Letters*, 35 (14): L14701.

Petoukhov, V. and Semenov, V.A. (2010), 'A Link between Reduced Barents-Kara Sea Ice and Cold Winter Extremes over Northern Continents', *Journal of Geophysical Research*, 115 (D21): D21111.

Pfeffer, W.T., Harper, J.T., and O'Neel, S. (2008), 'Kinematic Constraints on Glacier Contributions to 21st-Century Sea-Level Rise', *Science*, 321: 1340–43.

Phillips, O.L., Aragao, L.E.O.C., Lewis, S.L., Fisher, J.B., Lloyd, J., Lopez-Gonzalez, G., *et al.* (2009), 'Drought Sensitivity of the Amazon Rainforest', *Science*, 323 (5919): 1344–47.

Pollard, D. and DeConto, R.M. (2009), 'Modelling West Antarctic Ice Sheet Growth and Collapse through the Past Five Million Years', *Nature*, 458: 329–32.

Rahmstorf, S. (2001), 'Abrupt Climate Change', in J. Steele, S. Thorpe, and K. Turekian (eds), *Encyclopedia of Ocean Sciences* (London: Academic Press), 1–6.

Ramanathan, V. and Feng, Y. (2008), 'On Avoiding Dangerous Anthropogenic Interference with the Climate System: Formidable Challenges Ahead', *Proceedings of the National Academy of Sciences USA*, 105 (38): 14245–50.

Ramanathan, V., Chung, C., Kim, D., Bettge, T., Buja, L., Kiehl, J.T., *et al.* (2005), 'Atmospheric Brown Clouds: Impacts on South Asian Climate and Hydrological Cycle', *Proceedings of the National Academy of Sciences USA*, 102 (15): 5326–33.

Ridley, J., Gregory, J., Huybrechts, P., and Lowe, J. (2010), 'Thresholds for Irreversible Decline of the Greenland Ice Sheet', *Climate Dynamics*, 35: 1065–73.

Riebesell, U., Körtzinger, A., and Oschlies, A. (2009), 'Sensitivities of Marine Carbon Fluxes to Ocean Change', *Proceedings of the National Academy of Sciences*, 106: 20602–09.

Salazar, L.F., Nobre, C.A., and Oyama, M.D. (2007), 'Climate Change Consequences on the Biome Distribution in Tropical South America', *Geophysical Research Letters*, 34: L09708.

Scheffer, M., Bacompte, J., Brock, W.A., Brovkin, V., Carpenter, S.R., Dakos, V., *et al.* (2009), 'Early Warning Signals for Critical Transitions', *Nature*, 461: 53–59.

Scholze, M., Knorr, W., Arnell, N.W., and Prentice, I.C. (2006), 'A Climate-Change Risk Analysis for World Ecosystems', *Proceedings of the National Academy of Sciences USA*, 103 (35): 13116–20.

Schoof, C. (2007), 'Ice Sheet Grounding Line Dynamics: Steady States, Stability, and Hysteresis', *Journal of Geophysical Research*, 112: F03S28.

Schwartz, P. and Randall, D. (2003), 'An Abrupt Climate Change Scenario and Its Implications for United States National Security' (Emeryville, CA: Global Business Network).

Seager, R., Ting, M., Held, I., Kushnir, Y., Lu, J., Vecchi, G., *et al.* (2007), 'Model Projections of an Imminent Transition to a More Arid Climate in Southwestern North America', *Science*, 316: 1181–84.

Shearer, A.W. (2005), 'Whether the Weather: Comments on: "An Abrupt Climate Change Scenario and Its Implications for United States National Security"', *Futures*, 37: 445–63.

Smith, J.B., Schneider, S.H., Oppenheimer, M., Yohe, G.W., Hare, W., Mastrandrea, M.D., *et al.* (2009), 'Assessing Dangerous Climate Change through an Update of the Intergovernmental Panel on Climate Change (IPCC) "Reasons for Concern"', *Proceedings of the National Academy of Sciences USA*, 106 (11): 4133–37.

Sorensen, J.H. (2000), 'Hazard Warning Systems: Review of 20 Years of Progress', *Natural Hazards Review*, 1 (2): 119–25.

Stirling, A. (2003), 'Risk, Uncertainty and Precaution: Some Instrumental Implications from the Social Sciences', in I. Scoones, M. Leach, and F. Berkhout (eds), *Negotiating Change: Perspectives in Environmental Social Science* (London: Edward Elgar), 33–76.

Stommel, H. (1961), 'Thermohaline Convection with Two Stable Regimes of Flow', *Tellus*, 13: 224–30.

Stramma, L., Johnson, G.C., Sprintall, J., and Mohrholz, V. (2008), 'Expanding Oxygen-Minimum Zones in the Tropical Oceans', *Science*, 320 (5876): 655–58.

Thomson, M.C., Doblas-Reyes, F.J., Mason, S.J., Hagedorn, R., Connor, S.J., Phindela, T., *et al.* (2006), 'Malaria Early Warnings Based on Seasonal Climate Forecasts from Multi-Model Ensembles', *Nature*, 439 (7076): 576–79.

Titov, V.V., Gonzalez, F.I., Bernard, E.N., Eble, M.C., Mofjeld, H.O., Newman, J.C., and Venturato, A.J. (2005), 'Real-Time Tsunami Forecasting: Challenges and Solutions', *Natural Hazards*, 35 (1): 35–41.

UN (2006), 'Global Survey of Early Warning Systems: An Assessment of Capacities, Gaps and Opportunities Towards Building a Comprehensive Global Early Warning System for All Natural Hazards' (United Nations).

Vecchi, G.A., Soden, B.J., Wittenberg, A.T., Held, I.M., Leetmaa, A., and Harrison, M.J. (2006), 'Weakening of Tropical Pacific Atmospheric Circulation Due to Anthropogenic Forcing', *Nature*, 441: 73–76.

Verdin, J., Funk, C., Senay, G., and Choularton, R. (2005), 'Climate Science and Famine Early Warning', *Philosophical Transactions of the Royal Society B: Biological Sciences*, 360 (1463): 2155–68.

Veron, J.E.N., Hoegh-Guldberg, O., Lenton, T.M., Lough, J.M., Obura, D.O., Pearce-Kelly, P., *et al.* (2009), 'The Coral Reef Crisis: The Critical Importance of <350ppm CO_2', *Marine Pollution Bulletin*, 58: 1428–37.

Wieczorek, S., Ashwin, P., Luke, C.M., and Cox, P.M. (2011), 'Excitability in Ramped Systems: The Compost-Bomb Instability', *Proceedings of the Royal Society A: Mathematical, Physical and Engineering Science*, 467 (2129): 1243–69.

Willoughby, H.E., Rappaport, E.N., and Marks, F.D. (2007), 'Hurricane Forecasting: The State of the Art', *Natural Hazards Review*, 8 (3): 45–49.

Wissel, C. (1984), 'A Universal Law of the Characteristic Return Time Near Thresholds', *Oecologia*, 65 (1): 101–07.

Wu, Q. and Zhang, X. (2010), 'Observed Forcing-Feedback Processes between Northern Hemisphere Atmospheric Circulation and Arctic Sea Ice Coverage', *Journal of Geophysical Research*, 115 (D14): D14119.

Yeh, S.-W., Kug, J.-S., Dewitte, B., Kwon, M.-H., Kirtman, B.P., and Jin, F.-F. (2009), 'El Nino in a Changing Climate', *Nature*, 461 (7263): 511–14.

Yin, J., Schlesinger, M.E., and Stouffer, R.J. (2009), 'Model Projections of Rapid Sea-Level Rise on the Northeast Coast of the United States', *Nature Geoscience*, 2: 262–66.

Zimov, S.A., Schuur, E.A.G., and Chapin, F.S. (2006), 'Permafrost and the Global Carbon Budget', *Science*, 312: 1612–13.

PART 3
THE CULTURE DIMENSIONS

One of the purposes of the Kavli conference was to place together contrasting perspectives on the tipping points theme. This is particularly true of the relationship between the two contributions of this Part in the context of the science-based Chapter 2.1. Tim Lenton is well aware of science–policy relationships, so he frames his analysis both from the perspective of evidentiary science and the organized prognoses of informed commentators. Giles Foden, who is a writer, but also a student of complex systems and indeterminacy, offers (3.1) the framing of metaphor and narrative for providing another insight into the reading of tipping points. He recognizes the power of bringing together contradictory and novel information to kick-start revelation as fresh ways of creating understanding. He sees the notion of 'tipping' as being both a tap or a hit, and the transformation of the object or process which is struck or tilted. This allows for the joining up of analysis and interpretation on the one hand, and narrative and scenario on the other, where the process of speculating about the future is one of both storytelling and prognosis. In this way, Tim Lenton's prognoses depicted in Figure 2.2 are but one version of the metaphor process offered by Foden.

What we discern here is the mixing of three sets of observation which perhaps lie at the core of this book. One is the longevity of the concept of abrupt change in the lexicon of language and metaphor. So 'tipping points' may be a relatively recently coined phrase, but the notion of tip and travel (or transformation caused by some form of hitting or forcing) is well settled in the linguistic tradition.

A second concept is the bringing together of many ideas and perspectives which cause some form of fresh outlooks, or revelation, of 'contemplative consciousness' to use the phrase offered by Laurence Freeman in

Chapter 5.1. Here may lurk the devices for the kinds of transformative beginnings we search for in Part 8.

The third view is that provided by Matthew Taylor in this section (3.2) and by Camilla Toulmin (7.4). This is the scope for enabling individuals and groups to be confident about letting go of the interpretations of rapid and convulsive change as these perspectives are influenced by peer pressure and by personal mindsets, and to have the opportunity and courage to explore new ways forward, both for personal behaviour as well as for collective resilience.

Giles Foden had provided the spark for this scope for transformative action, and Laurence Freeman offers the spiritual and meditative under-pinning for the process to evolve without internal intellectual crises or external stress. We are very grateful to both of these authors for initiating this vital perspective on tipping points in such a rich interdisciplinary manner, and to their companion commentators Matthew Taylor (3.2) and David Atkinson (5.2) for reinforcing their contributions. Tipping points are as turbulent for the mind as they are for the planet.

3.1
Skittles

The story of the tipping point metaphor
and its relation to new realities

GILES FODEN

Let us assume, for the context of the present discussion, a situation in which 'global coordination for sustainable outcomes is needed to an extent that existing institutions are clearly unable to provide' (Foden 2009: 1). This would not necessarily mean that we need new institutions – but it would at least mean that existing institutions must find novel ways to disengage from linear, 'locked-in' modes of thinking. The proposed challenge is genuinely multidimensional and definitively transdisciplinary. It involves from the outset a need for clarity about who the 'we' is, and an accompanying effort of inclusion and flexibility. It would therefore seem likely that systems theory is a framework in which radical new approaches might be taken.

As it is now commonly encountered in models of complex systems, the metaphor of the tipping point seems a good place to begin a systems-based encounter with metaphor. Metaphor and its close cousin narrative can offer pathways to a higher-order management of complexity. This can aid decision-making, policy formulation, and communication. All this is already to hand: what lies further from our grasp, beckoning from times ahead, is a kind of benign tipping point for all, a shift in global consciousness that will allow us to face the future with excitement and purpose. Inevitably that process will involve us separating ourselves mentally from those modes of thinking and habits of behaviour which have put us in abeyance as regards the world to come.

A new paradigm

One of the functions of metaphor is to open up unmeasured domains and potential channels of action. This is necessary at a time when our models of the world and consequent plans for action are underdetermined by our scientific observations and overdetermined by our past experiences (Van der Leeuw 2004; Atlan 1992). We make policies on a deficit of knowledge, effectively seeding future crisis into socio-economic systems, with correlate damage to Earth systems.

Our current plight relates to global society's inability to process a wide range of signals, suggesting that multiple systems have either failed or are on the point of failure. We can see it happening, despite inadequate data, but we don't seem to be able to do anything. We appear paralysed by our modes of thought, as if viewing multiple images of ourselves in mirrored postures of rictus. One way out could involve a new engagement of science, technology, humanities, and the creative arts. This would begin by acknowledging both general indeterminacy and the particular interrelations of systems/groups, and then move forward to new states, through a linked understanding of relativity and metaphoricity. We need to design the future from a range of narrative options rather than accept it as it comes to us: metaphor gives us the frames with which to begin doing that.

Metaphor and science

At the very least, commitment to the study and practice of metaphor is a useful supplement to traditional scientific activity, offering a different type of future-oriented knowledge that can provide a platform for decisive action. The combinations of metaphor are anyway bound up with the semi-intuitive aspect of science as it relates to language and the unconscious. Metaphor is of a type with 'the combinations which present themselves to the mind in a kind of sudden illumination' identified by Poincaré (1914: 58), who was extremely alert to the mutual transformations of mathematical and verbal concepts, and how verbal analogies can stimulate both research and public understanding. (It was also Poincaré, of course, who developed the modern conceptions of stability on the foundations laid by the eighteenth-century mathematicians mentioned below.)

Long before publication of Malcolm Gladwell's (2000) famous book, the phrase 'tipping point' existed in interrelated areas of ecology and environmental science. In these fields, tipping points often have the status of discretely understood academic and physical realities: they are 'literal', to use the appropriate linguistic term, rather than 'figurative'. Frequently these apparently non-metaphorical tipping points have already established different scientific understandings through discipline and paradigm, so that 'tipping point' *means* something different as well as *being* something different.

In general it appears that these scientific users are not, at least not consciously, committing the useful error of metaphoric expression. When encountering a word or phrase somewhat at odds with its expected conceptual context within a language system, interpreters seek out – through perceived resemblances between the tenor (underlying idea A) and vehicle (the metaphorical word or phrase B) of a metaphor – the perceived semantic intention (C), according to a particular discourse. As we will see, such interpretation is not without risk of failure: it is not necessarily a given that (C) is more easily or instantly grasped, or even that more creative communication is the underlying purpose of metaphors. Metaphor is creative in the sense that fire is creative: it jumps from roof to roof, opening up new ground, and fresh arrays of positional information, according to how the burnt sticks fall.

Between conceptual context, discourse situation, and models of a language system in general, are various philosophical traps: each of those interrelated contextual domains is a shifting field of uncertainty.

Tripping, tumbling – tipping – into one of these traps and suddenly understanding the problem, otherwise well-intentioned scientists might find they had, in fact, been using metaphors without having realized they were doing so. It would be a specific instance of Jakobson's observation (1960: 356) that like Molière's M. Jourdain we all 'practice metalanguage without realizing the metalingual character of our operations'.

This recognition would be in the nature of a tipping point in itself, as the notionally solid footing of the phrase within a particular scientific discipline could then be impeached. And then, as if a line of marching soldiers were to trip in succession, the ankles of one having been entangled in the bolas of a guerrilla rhetorician, why not the next term and the next?

Yet as we will see, if metaphorical slippage is itself recalibrated as offering a visionary half-glimpse of quantum realities, what was a problem becomes a novel opportunity.

What does metaphor do?

Metaphor offers a displacement of information: it dynamically makes other linguistic contexts present, subjecting the pre-existing understanding (A) to a shift or substitution (B), which process may summon a composite or third value (C) that asks to observed and understood in turn. It is important to consider that while A and C operate over longer time series (forward and backwards in time – see Figure 3.1 below), B's union or equivalence with A is instantiated in a single transformative moment.[1] It is a kind of new beginning: a 'tipping point', as we may say, a place where or moment when new types of being are begun, born of the couplings of language in a particular context.

Metaphor's moment of conjecture ('throwing together') invites us on a voyage towards future conclusions, taking us on a new tack in the direction of other final states than those we might otherwise have envisaged. As Mason (1987: 245) has it, 'Metaphor gives us a new, unthought-for equation, an infusion of meaning from outside customary domains.'

For decision-makers, the appearance of these new potentialities within the bounds of conception implies at least an optional possibility of actualization. Whether the decision was not at all possible before (because the mental conditions for it had not been created until the conjecture had taken place) is an arguable philosophical point. The issue is bound up with ideas about time and the ways in which humanity deals with continuous and discrete phenomena. In open systems, tipping points remain a critical change but the separateness of the pre- and post-tip point moment is challenged: by feedback and feedforward issues, by activity at the edge of the system, by disappearances from it, and by the new values brought into being by the emergent situation. It is in these areas that our best hopes lie: by simultaneously inculcating a sense of a developing present,[2] revising past projections, and envisioning new possibilities, we can ourselves

---

[1] However, the equivalence may be perpetuated over longer time series through repeated motifs and artistic concinnity. This is Roland Barthes' point about a 'syntagmatized paradigm'. It is worth bearing in mind, as Čermák (1997) shows, that synchrony and diachrony are much debated terms in linguistics.

[2] Some related temporal aspects of dynamical narratives are addressed from a literary perspective in Mark Currie's 'The Novel and the Moving Now' (2009), which considers the fictional novel as a model of time, specifically for a *nunc movens* (moving now) conception of time. Links to narrative are briefly addressed at the end of this chapter.

become resilient. Elsewhere I consider some ways of addressing ourselves to that ideal practically (Foden 2010).

Metaphor plays a key role in what literature knows, as well as in its poetic effects. It is also something that users of language in general 'do' or 'perform', consciously or unconsciously. Rhetoric (traditionally the native ground of metaphor as a practice) provides language-based heuristics for various purposes, while in linguistics metaphorology is a distinct branch of objective study. From Aristotle to Hegel, to Derrida and beyond, philosophers of language have tried to grasp metaphor, either within a total rationale, or in passing while focused on other matters.

The slipperiest of fishes, metaphor won't be in fact governed by any one of these disciplines or types of activity. This is why systems theory is a good environment in which to think about it, though we should not be complacent about the ability of any discipline or practice to contain metaphor. Engaging with metaphors we leap across logical and hierarchical divisions, making category errors that overturn the authority structures embedded in linguistic and philosophical systems. As Paul de Man (1979: 10) suggests: 'Rhetoric radically suspends logic and opens up vertiginous possibilities of referential aberration.'

To see metaphor as a form of knowledge is to acknowledge its errant behaviour (broadly, its positing of A as B against contextual expectation) as useful. At the same time, we must equally acknowledge the unruliness of metaphor's transformative power. This is to recognize metaphor as 'the unsystemizable, transcendent centre of language' (Coetzee 1979: 28). The best we can hope for is that since metaphors summon their newly observed values from other contexts, these new values contain the possibility of greater social utility than that which obtained with old values. Of course, the reverse is also true: this is the secondary risk of metaphor, the first being that you simply are not understood (see the commentary by Matthew Taylor which follows).

There are no doubt complicated reasons in the social psyche for metaphor's double life as a communicative civil servant and a tramping outcast. The essential relation of metaphor to positional information (and 'context' in general) means that polarity just offered (A = B) can never be relied upon. Sometimes metaphors fail and then 'irony comes in to save the day when the world turns upside down on consciousness, when the old certainties become uncertainties, and there is no new standard to put in place of the old' (Mason 1987: 245).

Interdisciplinary problems and opportunities

Many scientists, rightly seeking to be exact about phenomena, struggle with the concept that all language is subject to metaphoric slippage; yet to not believe so would come close to being a *trahison des clercs* in the humanities. At the same time, humanities people make little effort to make an accommodation with scientific models and methodologies about and around uncertainty, in particular those

> system dynamics that have been generalized by advances in mathematical, scientific and technological research over the past 50 years, together with new approaches to the use of data and ICT.
>
> (Hunt *et al.* 2012: 1)

Though the idea of mimesis is well developed in the humanities, it is not adequately linked with the scientific idea of a model: that needs to happen if a truly transdisciplinary moment is to occur.

There have, however, been a number of attempts to link systems theory with linguistics (such as Rogers 1987–88). There have also been significant attempts by creative writers to admit systems theory. Some of these are charted in Tom Leclair's groundbreaking *In the Loop: Don DeLillo and the Systems Novel* (Leclair 1988), one of few attempts to bring systems theory into literary hermeneutics.[3]

Scientific and humanities conceptions of uncertainty and indeterminacy need, in any large systems model, to be brought into yoked harness if a higher-order field of enquiry and decision-making is to be established. Part of this will involve further transfer to formal logic and mathematics of philosophical concepts. While that has long been a direction of some aspects of Anglo-American philosophy, it seems to have happened much less with the French and German philosophers whose work is concerned with, indeed is often based on, uncertainty and indeterminacy. This process would need to recognize the objection made by Coetzee (1979: 28) to '*any* scheme that has recourse to analogy . . . If rules are to be rules, they must be well-defined. The relation "to be like" must be defined.' (The occluded context of Coetzee's observation is the system of political apartheid in South Africa.)

---

[3] I myself write not as a specialist of metaphor within linguistics but as a creative writer who stumbled into the world of complexity while writing a novel. *Turbulence* (2009), which is about the D-Day weather forecast, invokes the paradigm of turbulent fluid motions across multiple systems to address issues of uncertainty.

The idea of metaphors (and narratives) as vehicles across dimensionality and between groups or sets, in a mathematical sense and in the wider field of information processing, does not seem to have been adequately explored. It may in the future be possible to develop an ICT-enabled spatial (or topological) conceptualization of a lexicon that exploits the ability of metaphors to 'travel' across experiences that are usually demarcated. But as de Beaugrande observes:

> the concept of 'dimensionality' is meaningful only if we assume that any particular observed value belongs within a range of alternative values of 'the same' dimension. In that sense, the observed value rests on the interference pattern of other possible values.
>
> (de Beaugrande 1989: 23)

Nonetheless, as a subject for information processing (as something which offers instantaneous communication between cognitive categories or linguistic events), metaphor might helpfully be understood as an interference phenomenon on this basis, with the pattern developing from the new value-system that is in the process of emerging when metaphorization takes place.

The problem, of course, is that we don't know the limits and correlations of the emergent structure, so it is not fully logical or intelligible. But this is also the opportunity of metaphor as a pointing tool to orientate evolving structures.

Semantics, discourse analysis and related areas of the social sciences have evolved many useful modes of analysis that could act as a bridging mechanism between humanities and science, but these seem to be rarely deployed in the service of global systems science, despite the current importance placed on metaphor, narrative and communication in general by scientists and policymakers.

There is, however, some background for treating tipping points as metaphors with respect to an analogous discussion of the related term 'resilience' within the literature of adaptation within socio-environmental systems:

> When applied to people and their environments, resilience is fundamentally a metaphor. With roots in the sciences of physics and mathematics, the term originally was used to describe the capacity of a material or system to return to equilibrium after a displacement. A resilient material, for example, bends and bounces back, rather than breaks, when stressed (Gordon 1978; Bodin and Wiman 2004). In physics, resilience is not a matter of how large the initial displacement is or even how severe the oscillations are but is more precisely

the speed with which homeostasis is achieved. The image is a compelling one, capable of sparking human imagination, as it clearly did for Holling (1973) in his original and influential thesis about 'ecological resilience'.

(Norris *et al.* 2008: 127)

The two terms, 'resilience' and 'tipping point', are extremely significant in current socio-environmental discourse, and that they come from the domain of physics (demonstrably so in the case of resilience, more tentatively with the tipping point phrase – see the quotation from Bernoulli below), should probably be being treated as significant information in itself, i.e. the figurative dimension of these words says something about the disciplines in which they are being used; and this should not really be that surprising at all, as linguistic developments are systemic signals just as valid as ocean temperature data.

For now, and for that reason, we will proceed on the basis that tipping points are both metaphors and physical realities, as if a convergence of discursive and physical systems has taken place, a collapse between the multidisciplinary usage of the term 'tipping point' in a major world language and the interdependent actualization of tipping points in different socio-environmental systems. If that is indeed the case, it would be an extremely worrying development.

Theories of metaphor

As is well known to humanities scholars, the origin of the word 'metaphor' in many European languages is the Greek *meta-pherein*, a carrying over from one realm to another, a 'transference'. The word relates to a wider conception of 'transport' deeply embedded in ancient Greek thought. This carrying over is more specifically defined as the transport of a linguistic entity from one category, discipline or paradigm to another. It relates to classical theories of groups, and in respect of the interference patterns mentioned above it is worth remarking that mathematical/physical and philosophical group theory comes from the same fundamental classical sources.

When a metaphor is made, a process of mapping takes place between literal and figurative. Already, however, in the notion of a map we see an example of metaphorical usage conditioning our everyday language. This conditioning explodes the dichotomy between literal and figurative on which more basic metaphor theory depends, which is one reason why the simplistic appeal to analogy between A and B cannot be maintained philosophically.

Partly for this reason, the theory of metaphor has since classical times been one of the most contentious subjects in philosophy, literary criticism and linguistics. We cannot hope to cover all that bloody ground here but, arming ourselves with patience, we shall try to sow a few dragon's teeth that might spring up in the service of systems thinking generally, rather than fomenting disputes.

We might begin with understanding what class of concept metaphor is within rhetoric. While there have been many philosophical challenges to the classification, within literary study metaphor is commonly treated as an example of a 'trope' or 'figure' whereby there has been a divergence from a proper or literal use, thus also 'error', as in *err* (wander), an important concept in literary study.

There may well be a link to the systems idea of the non-linear or dynamic reaction in Bahti's well-founded observation that:

> the general insistence on trope's and figure's divergence from a quasi-naturalistic or basic norm is apparently preserved in the terms themselves, trope being from the Gr. *tropein*, 'to turn', 'to swerve', figure from the Lat. *figura*, 'the made', 'the shaped'.
>
> (Bahti 1993: 410)

This suggests that the preceding linguistic context constitutes a system input from which the emerging metaphor is the unpredicted output. The idea of trope is at base sensuous and organic while the opposite is true of *figura*, where the emphasis is on construction: the distinction is significant in metaphorology but little observed.

The most commonly deployed theory of metaphor, from Aristotle to Jakobson and beyond, through various modulations, involves a substitution. A = B, again (though of course the conditions are always different). Hitherto, this diachronic moment of substitution has been opposed, graphically and conceptually, with a related synchronic structure of signification: that is to say, the structure of metonymy in which concepts are either categorically related or contiguously linked by syntax.

In a famous paper concerned primarily to identify the empirical linguistic function of poetry, Jakobson (1960) argues that any utterance is a function of two axes: the metaphoric (the axis of selection/substitution) and the metonymic (the axis of combination). Communication takes place at the intersection of the axes, in a joint process (see Figure 3.1):

The selection is produced on the base of equivalence, similarity and dissimilarity, synonymity and antonymity, while the combination, the buildup of the sequence, is based on contiguity. The poetic function projects the principle of equivalence from the axis of selection into the axis of combination.

(Jakobson 1960: 358)

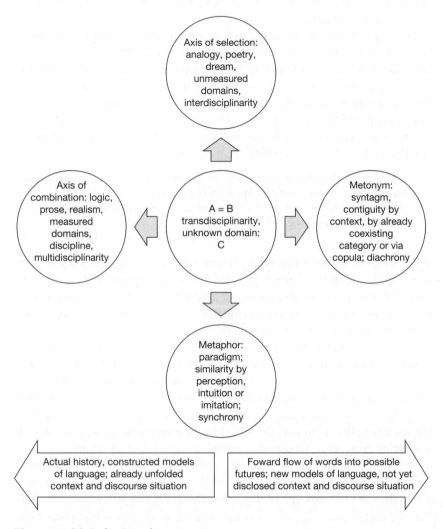

Figure 3.1 Metaphoric and metonymic axes

Figure 3.1 is a customized version of a graphic crux that has dominated the study of linguistics and literature, emphasizing (to put it in systems terms) the linearity of grammar and a language system and the non-linearity of metaphoric reference (and to a larger degree signification in general, for the conditioning reasons I have explained); all linguistic activity is involved with both axes. In linguistics and cultural study, as Jayne (2005) has concisely shown, this binarism originated with Saussure's 'axis of simultaneities' and 'axis of successions' within language, then rapidly propagated through twentieth-century thought in modulated and disputed forms. It is worth stressing again that the linearity of models of language systems is an idealization: in reality, of course, language-in-use reflects all manner of variations and fluctuations across time and space, which are flattened by models of language.

One key issue in these developments involves the direction of travel of information between the two axes, and the related choice of ground into which the projection of equivalence is made. As Barthes puts it:

> Any metaphoric series is a syntagmatized paradigm, and any metonymy a syntagm which is frozen and absorbed in a system; in metaphor, selection becomes contiguity, and in metonymy contiguity becomes a field to select from. It therefore seems that it is always on the frontiers of the two planes that creation has a chance to occur.
>
> (Barthes 1968: 88)

There are many related versions of this point in the semiotic literature and it clearly also relates to aspects of group theory and relativity in mathematics and physics; it is within this intersection that a sensible new space between the sciences and humanities might be opened up (see Favre *et al.* 1995). Derrida (1982: 207–71) explores the problematic play of metaphor across groups and categories from the perspective of philosophy and the wider humanities.

In this context it might be useful to think of the relationship between metaphor and metonymy as itself being a tipping point (see Figure 3.2). Of course, the diagram could equally be rearranged laterally, or with a different balance, and this is rather the point. There is a problem or (depending how you look at it) an opportunity of indeterminacy and perspective. For certain: one of the problems is the challenge this presents to the computation of language. To speculate: the opportunity could concern aspects of quantum computation. As de Beaugrande has it:

> A willingness to acknowledge indeterminacy should allow us to gain a more determinate grasp of complex issues and of potential relations among them.

59

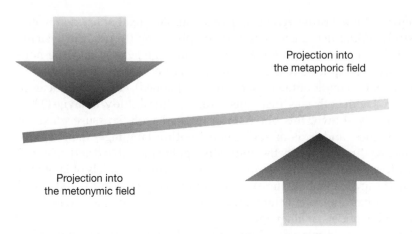

Figure 3.2 The relationship between metaphor and metonymy

> Ideally, this result could greatly expand human perception by revealing the model character of quantum reality for numerous modes of access to classical reality.
>
> (de Beaugrande 1989: 46)

Versions of the substitution theory of metaphor remain the method in working pedagogical use in most of the humanities. For many decades, however, those working in literary semantics and other areas on the margins of philosophy, as well as related groups working in cognitive psychology, have challenged substitution theory. Despite their differences, many of the other theories hold that:

> rather than simply substituting one word for another, or comparing two things, metaphor invokes a transaction between words and things, after which words, things and thoughts are not quite the same. Metaphor, from these perspectives, is not a decorative figure, but a transformed literalism, meaning precisely what it says.
>
> (Martin 1993: 761)

In this precision, we may say, the ground is prepared for a limited recovery from aberrance of metaphor, turning its propensity to induce a *mise en abîme* of signification into a useful capacity within systems science – as a vehicle for communicating information about inaugural states of affairs, systemic developments, or hypothetical conceptual relationships. We need to start thinking about other metaphors that shed light on the future arrangements implied by tipping points.

Connecting all this with hard science is not easy. As we have discussed, the limitation arises because metaphoricity resists finite quantities and discrete categories. Derrida (1982: 219–29) demonstrates the paradoxical impossibility of total schematics for a metaphorics of philosophy:

> Each time that a rhetoric defines metaphor, not only is *a* philosophy implied, but also a conceptual network in which philosophy *itself* has been constituted. Moreover, each thread in this network forms a *turn*, or one might say a metaphor . . . What is defined, therefore, is implied in the defining of the definition.
>
> (Derrida 1982: 230)

It follows that an intrinsic metaphorology of any delimited domain of human experience is similarly circumscribed. In other words, the effective metaphoric intervention is always a paradigmatic intervention. Metaphor is, in terms of models of language, again itself a tipping point, since the very idea of 'other words' always comes into play, along with challenges to the limits of underlying groups or sets.

Metaphor and complexity

The idea that metaphor teeters on a seesaw of intelligibility/unintelligibility is one of the links between metaphorology and complexity science. The complex system 'organizes within the space placed at the edge of chaos, where an activity arises that produces a maximal information processing' (Longa 2001: 5). In this way metaphors might be seen as both an approximation of chaos and as attractors which capture emergent aspects of the language system 'forcing it to abandon the territory of chaos thus entering into an ordered pattern' (Longa, 2001: 6). As Longa shows, the space of possibilities is not constrained by historical possibilities but by the attractors themselves. They constitute the informational conditions of the new situation.

None of this should deter scientists from listening, on a simple and practicable level, to their inner metaphor meter as they present their findings. The temptation or need to metaphorize is probably itself a signal that a paradigmatic shift is involved with their work and that some alteration of theory must be made to catch up with the new information. The rhetoric itself is part of that information, projecting itself on to the grammar of the ostensibly scientific work as a kind of feedback effect.

'Catching up with the new information' – this is rather in the nature of dynamical systems, both in their interpretation and in terms of the systems themselves, as they process information. As Hunt *et al.* (2012) reveal, a mismatch between the speed at which a system operates and the speed at which it processes information is often the cause of crisis.

Martin (1993: 762) points out, citing Brooke-Rose (1958), that verbal forms of metaphor ('the dying year'; 'the tipping point') are more common than 'the nominal "A is B" equation'. In systems terms, the use of the verbal form would equate to the dynamical aspects of non-linearity, and a wider sense that something unpredictable is in the process of happening, that may or may not involve a typological change or contextual turbulence.

Richards's (1936) idea of metaphor as a 'transaction between contexts' was developed by others to draw out the idea of an apparent contradiction which causes us to seek out an emergent meaning. Black's (1962) interaction theory distinguished the *frame* (the verbal unit in which a metaphor occurs) and the *focus* of a metaphor (the figurative expression itself), with the focus bringing into being a 'system of associated commonplaces' that 'interacts with its frame to produce implications that can be shared by a speech community' (Martin 1993: 764).

Metaphor as risk

The risk of metaphor, and it is the risk currently being run by users of the tipping point metaphor in the context of Earth systems, is that these implications are not understood or acted upon. As well as within systems theory, it might be possible to consider metaphor within a framework of risk, but for the time being we shall keep within the domain of linguistics (not least because ideas about risk differ radically across different disciplines and practices).

In their seminal paper, Nair *et al.* (1988: 20–40) explore metaphor with reference to the notions that (1) 'metaphor can usefully be seen as a kind of risk-taking in the interests of richer interpersonal communication (hence a risk with rewards)'; and (2) that there is the possibility of a 'cline of metaphoricity associated by speakers with items in the lexicon'.

To expand, the implication of the second point is that makers and interpreters of metaphors construe what is normal in context-determined language-in-use (rather than simply the lexicon) and discern degrees of anomalous difference away from that as they create and interpret metaphors:

This could be cast as a continuum with familiar standard language use at one end of the scale and the nearly indecipherable at the other end. Between these two poles lies the usage we are interested in, involving degrees of individual and creative risk-taking.

(Nair *et al.* 1988: 35)

As these authors recognize, understanding of these clines of difference is fraught with problems, because of context dependence and other questions. However, their most important point for our purposes relates to their speculation that there is a 'roughly delimitable set of core, productive and culturally salient vocabulary items that predominate in conventional and creative metaphors'. These are the frames the past is built upon; somehow they must also serve as the foundations, the good Earth, for the new core metaphors of the future.

With core metaphors, the metaphor has become so embedded and widespread in particular cultural formations across time that the meta-phorized concept itself shapes discourse and thought, for example, 'life is a journey', 'argument is war'. The definitive statement on this is the work of Lakoff and Johnson (1978), though there have been many advances since. It is possible that the widespread use of tipping point across disciplines indicates its adoption as a core metaphor.

Tipping: an emergent core metaphor?

The set of core metaphors derives from basic-level concepts: that is, 'the most vividly grasped, most discriminable, most usefully differentiated items in our taxonomies' where instances of a category are judged to have many attributes in common (i.e. wings and feathers but rarely fur in birds). The suggestion is that the commonest, most effective, most rewarding metaphors are those which project an equivalence of attributes from one set to another and that that projection is understood and absorbed by interpreters. These metaphors then become extended by analogy and become institutionalized.

Whether this means we are now to take 'tipping' as an emergent basic-level concept across multiple systems is a speculation too far, but it is certainly the case that 'tipping point' is a phrase being used across a very wide range of instances, and within certain disciplines it is institutionalized. That multi-projection of tipping attributes across different domains is in itself significant.

63

Metaphor and separation

'It is quite true what philosophy says; that life must be understood backwards. But then one forgets the other principle: that it must be lived forwards.' Kierkegaard's conundrum (1966 [1843]: 63, 161) invites us to apply a folk form of Bayesian probability as a way of dealing with tipping point problems, in that to face them we must actively reconsider the fixities of our previous beliefs in the light of new data and new needs. Metaphor can help memory in this work. There is a long tradition in European philosophy whereby the relative roles of dialectic and metaphor, in consciousness and in culture generally, offer a revivifying new connection based on a recollection of (and therefore separation from) previous states of being. Chief arbiter of this tradition is Hegel who integrated these dual processes in the structure of his *Phenomenology*. As Jeffrey Mason writes:

> The employment, supercession and transformation of metaphors in the *Phenomenology* are part of a rhetorical strategy of recollection. The way consciousness moves through its permutations is based on need and lack. That need and lack in turn depend on the recognition of their existence by consciousness. And that recognition itself depends upon recollection. Only when consciousness can say 'that is what I was, but I am no longer it' has it moved beyond its former position. The dialectic is the liberation of consciousness from its own creations, its images and pictures.
>
> (Mason 1987: 245)

Mason's characterization of metaphors as 'the stepping stones of speculative thought, which never stops on any one stone but without them could not move' (1987: 247) is itself a useful metaphor with which to progress to the next stage of my own argument, which concerns the relation of metaphors to the body and, by extension, all the living systems currently under threat.

Metaphor and the sensuous

To recollect the brief and incomplete survey of metaphorology above, which left unsaid the recognition that much else has been said on the topic, one must also consider the relation of metaphors to living things.

It has become a commonplace in systems circles to think of narratives, metaphors and models (in the sense of computer models) as idealized representations of experience. But the direction of some key metaphors (and the metaphor of the key might be one of them, being to hand) seems to be explicitly anti-idealist, sending us back in the direction of the sensuous body. Fusion theorists within linguistics argue that metaphors unify the sensual and the conceptual and/or the concrete and the abstract in a single universal. This surely relates to the appeal of the tipping point metaphor across multiple disciplines, within a total concept of Earth and socio-economic systems. From the side of the philosophers, Nowell-Smith shows,[4] Heidegger's view is that metaphor's transference is dependent on division of sensuous and non-sensuous realms. The best metaphors bear back on the body, and the forbidding power of 'tipping point' as a phrase is that it seems to ask: is it me, or is it my body, that is falling?

The etymology of the tipping point metaphor

When we try to understand what that means – is it me that is tipping? – the differentiations of social and national groups come into play,[5] as does the historical usage of the tipping point phrase. Employment of the phrase carries through a whole host of meanings from previous usage.

As Lang and Ingram observe in Chapter 4.1, the phrase was itself tipped into mass usage by the publication of Malcolm Gladwell's book, *The Tipping Point: How Little Things Make a Big Difference* (2000), which sought to explain sudden changes, dramatizing tipping point narratives over a range of disciplines and paradigms. While the original scientific usage on which Gladwell largely draws is actually from the world of epidemiology, the current popular definition (and the only definition in the *Oxford English Dictionary*) is:

> The prevalence of a social phenomenon sufficient to set in motion a process of rapid change; the moment when such a change begins to occur.

[4] 'Heidegger's Figures', *Textual Practice*, 26: 5 (November 2012). This essay focuses on Heidegger's insistence that the import of metaphor for philosophy and poetry lies in its structural dependence, as *meta-pherein* or *Über-tragung* (carrying-over), on the dualism between sensuous and nonsensuous realms. In this, the critique opens on to a far more developed thinking on the relation between bodily experience and linguistic cognition, and in particular an attempt to think of the body as a site for an 'articulation' of language anterior to any opposition of sound and sense. The relation of this articulation to resilience could bear further examination.
[5] Writing an article on global climate change for a national broadsheet, I received the following communication from the editor: 'But what does it mean for Britain?'

This definition is likely to be a consequence of the popularity of Gladwell's book and does not reflect a wider diversity of uses in academic discourse.

Its first recorded emergence in the context of urban racial balance seems to have been in *Scientific American* in 1957:

> White residents who will tolerate a few Negroes as neighbors . . . begin to move out when the proportion of Negroes in the neighborhood or apartment building passes a certain critical point. This 'tip point' varies from city to city and from neighborhood to neighborhood.

Instinctively, this seems wrong as a base origin for tipping points. The source is much more likely to be concrete, embedded in everyday life (see 'Skittles' below), and intellectually related to the history of the physics of stability. For example we can hear the emergent tipping point rhetoric in this 1738 quotation from Bernoulli:

> a minimal arbitrary force makes a body – although put in firm equilibrium – nod a little, but when the force has been undergone [i.e. ceases to act], the body tends again to its natural position, unless the nodding would have exceeded certain bounds.
>
> (Bernoulli 1738: 148, cited in Leine 2009: 175)

Investigation shows that across all its senses the origins of tip and those words with which they seem likely to be cognate are obscure. However, we can identify the following verbal forms for tip in these edited and adapted extracts from the historical thesaurus of the OED:

Verb form 1 [V1]
a. To strike or hit smartly but lightly; to give a slight blow, knock, or touch to; to tap noiselessly.
[The remainder of the entries for V1 need not delay us further.]

Verb form 2 [V2]
Transitive senses:
a. To overthrow, knock, or cast down, cause to fall or tumble; to overturn, upset; to throw down by effort or accidentally.
b. **Skittles**. In the older game, said of a pin. To knock down another skittle by falling or rolling against it, as distinguished from the direct action of the bowl. 1801: 'In playing at skittles, there is a double exertion; one by bowling, and the other by tipping.' [This meaning seems highly relevant to the interaction of tipping points across different systems. Though one is only asserting rather than proving this, it feels as if skittles might be the genuine origin of tipping point as a phrase, sometime in the mid-to-late 1700s, coming at roughly the same period as physicists such as Bernoulli,

Euler and Lagrange were working out the effect of small disturbances on stability (see Leine 2009).]

c. To cause to assume a slanting or sloping position; to raise, push, or move into such a position; to incline, tilt.

d. *to tip the scales*: to tilt or depress the scale of a balance by excess of weight; to turn the scale.

e. *to tip one's hand*: to disclose one's intentions inadvertently. 1979: 'Mr Hunt will not tip his hand on the price at which he will buy more bullion.' [This meaning probably comes from card play.]

f. To empty out (a wagon, cart, truck, or the like, or its contents) by tilting it up; to dump.

g. To dispose of or kill (a person). 1928: 'Jake's sort o' done me a good turn, getting himself tipped off.'

Intransitive senses:

a. To be overthrown, to fall.

b. To fall by overbalancing; to be overturned or upset; to tumble or topple over.

c. To assume a slanting or sloping position; to incline, tilt; e.g. of a balance.

d. To be drunk, intoxicated, unsteady.

e. *to tip off*, *also simply to tip, or tip the perch*: to die.

V2 may be related (but not necessarily) to V1. If so, this would suggest a link between smart or slight blows and severe effects, and clearly this is relevant to tipping points. V1 in turn seems likely to be cognate with 'tip' (noun form 1) as in 'point' or 'top', but this cannot be fully established:

Noun form 1 [N1]
The slender extremity or top of a thing; *esp.* the pointed or rounded end of anything long and slender; the top, summit, apex, very end.

We can see already how all these meanings further feed into our current understanding of tipping points. Yet there is a further etymology which seems relevant, which is the root of N1 but also (demonstrably) of the word 'type' in its taxonomical, representative sense, as in a typical situation, norm or pattern.

'Type' comes from the Greek τύπος [*tuptein*] which connotes both a blow, and, more commonly, things produced by means of a blow or pressure; and hence, the means by which one can reproduce craft objects by moulding, imprinting, etc. (such as seals, which is a primary technological usage; it was also used for engraving, making dots on dice, or other kinds of carving). Over time, *tuptein* became a primary way of thinking about replicating, figuring and modelling in more abstract ways, too. Some meanings of *tuptein* can be listed as follows:

1. A blow, pressing
2. The results of a blow: mark, impression
3. Mark, figure, image, outline
4. General character of a thing: sort, type
5. Text, content
6. Pattern, example, model
7. Summoning.

A relevant early verbal sense of 'type' in English was 'to prefigure or foreshadow as a type; to represent in prophetic similitude', i.e. according to the aforesaid pattern or paradigm.

Overall, one begins to build a picture of a related set of words in which there is a semantic collapse between:

1. A smart blow
2. Deleterious falling
3. Slanting with a sense of the imminent possibility of fall
4. The communication or 'summoning' of information about an emergent phenomenon (also there in tip as in a stock market or betting tip)
5. The end or top of something
6. And, much more vaguely and tendentiously, a replicable 'type' within a category, something designed according to a paradigm.

Obviously different contexts imply different separate historical usages but the widest sense of tipping point which one might infer – the reasonable bundle of connotations – is of an unstable phenomenon which faces two ways in time, doubly summoning information from past (because of the historical push into tipping) and future (because tipping initiates new states). This is anyway cohered in its grammatical dual state as a compound noun (a complex category). The emphasis on 'tipping' rather than 'point' in pronunciation (cf. compounds such as 'bath-house' and 'greenhouse' in contrast with 'bath bun' and 'a green house') allows some room for manoeuvring the concept in a positive direction, i.e. we haven't tipped yet, we are only tilting. But the primary scientific use seems to place the emphasis on point, i.e. the point at which an irreversible critical change has taken place.

The parallels between the past/future conjectures of tipping points and metaphor itself are stimulating to consider, opening up the possibility of a cognitive tipping point in which human beings are able to pursue a higher-level systems-oriented approach to solving complex problems by 'stretching the present' of their subjectivity to consider future humans and other species. This 'extended body' is the necessary condition of a solution to climate change: to follow the elusive etymological trail, we need to find the new 'type' of being hidden in 'tip'.

The new condition may well involve a turn away from mechanistic (linear) conceptions of world systems to more dynamical frames of thought that account for indeterminacy. This would amount to a shift in cultural consciousness, as we respond to a dialectic whereby tipping events become a recognized norm (but a norm which is always challenging its own normativity). Many people in the world already live this kind of precarious life already: it is us in the insulated West who should change our future outlook. We need to find ourselves a new story.

Metaphor and narrative

Metaphors frame narratives in so far as they condition the worldviews which narratives propose. In storytelling the author or speaker solicits the reader or listener into a story world through a direction ('Imagine that . . .') or declaration ('It must have been about nine that the postman rang . . .') with a relativistic orientation to ordinary time and being.

This is a form of the illocutionary act, in which fictional world A (often with its *nunc movens*) is proposed to supplant or suspend real world B in which time is irreversible. The story often remains dimensionally indeterminate, so 'A is B' is more like a proposition or option than a linear equation; at least it is optional until what is metaphoric/narrative has become syntagmatic, an intelligible but fixed 'fact' institutionally.

The ability to see the syntagmatic possibilities of the metaphoric, to follow through from the frame to a possible story, which is akin to prediction, is surely part of human risk management. It is there in the brain's reading of perceptions according to particular frames of reference. It is in this area that we need to work hardest to find our new stories, sifting possible futures.

One sees all this very clearly when one hears one's children successively propose in a role-playing game, 'Pretend that . . .'. The rapidity with which children are able to run through the narrative options, shuttling between optional possibilities, fills one with hope for humankind; but why does this ability to shuttle between metaphoric frames/narratives ossify so quickly? How to prevent that is a useful research question in itself, but for the time being some metaphorical and narrative equivalent of physical education might be usefully dispensed to Western adults.

Shell and other companies already do versions of this with scenario writing, as do some government departments, but the process needs to be extended and embedded in society so that, co-creating a better future, we can all become agents of 'the broader genre of declarative illocutions whose function is to inaugurate a new state of affairs' (Genette 1993: 42). In this sense the story of the metaphor of the tipping point is always waiting to be told again, since the context for that retelling always already exists, in the ultimate ground of each individual consciousness.

References

Atlan, H. (1992), 'Self-organizing Networks: Weak, Strong and Intentional: The Role of Their Underdetermination', *La Nuova Critica*, N.S. 19–20: 51–70.

Bahti, T. (1993), 'Figure, Scheme, Trope', in A. Premingerand and T.V.F. Brogan (eds), *The New Princeton Encyclopedia of Poetry and Poetics* (Princeton, NJ: Princeton University Press), 409–12.

Barthes, R. (1968), *Elements of Semiology* (New York: Hill & Wang).

Bernoulli, D. (1738) (1747), *Commentationes de statu aequilibrii corporum humido insidentium. Comment. Acad. Scient. Imp. Petrop. X,* 147–63. As cited in Leine (2009).

Black, M. (1962), *Models and Metaphors* (Ithaca, NY: Cornell University Press).

Bodin, P. and Wiman, B. (2004), 'Resilience and Other Stability Concepts in Ecology: Notes on Their Origin, Validity, and Usefulness', *ESS Bulletin*, 2: 33–43.

Brooke-Rose, C. (1958), *A Grammar of Metaphor* (London: Secker & Warburg).

Čermák, F. (1997), 'Synchrony and Diachrony Revisited: Was R. Jakobson and the Prague Circle Right in Their Criticism of de Saussure?', *Folia Linguistica Historica* XVII/1–2: 29–40.

Coetzee, J. (1979), 'Surreal Metaphors and Random Processes', *Journal of Literary Semantics*, 8: 22–30.

Currie, M. (2009), 'The Novel and the Moving Now', *Novel: A Forum on Fiction*, 42 (2): 318–26.

De Beaugrande, R. (1989), 'Quantum Aspects of Perceived Reality: A New Engagement of Science and Art', *Journal of Literary Semantics*, 18: 1–49.

De Man, P. (1979), *Allegories of Reading: Figural Language in Rousseau, Nietzsche, Rilke and Proust*, ch. 1, 'Semiology and Rhetoric' (New Haven, CT: Yale University Press).

Derrida, J. (1982), 'White Mythology: Metaphor in the Text of Philosophy', collected in *Margins of Philosophy* (Brighton: Harvester Press), 207–71.

Favre, A., Guitton, H., Guitton, J., Lichnerowicz, A. and Wolff, E. (1995), *Chaos and Determinism: Turbulence as a Paradigm for Complex Systems Converging Towards Final States* (Baltimore: Johns Hopkins University Press).

Foden, G. (2009), 'Towards a Science of Global Systems', a report on a workshop organized by the European Commission's coordination action Global Systems Dynamics (Brussels: DGINFSO, EC) http://cordis.europa.eu/fp7/ict/fet-open/docs/2009-12-global-systems-workshop.pdf.

Foden, G. (2009), *Turbulence* (London: Faber & Faber).

Foden, G. (2010), 'Designing Together to Unshock the New', a workshop on Future Technology and Society organized by the European Commission (DGINFSO). http://cordis.europa.eu/fp7/ict/fet-open/docs/2010-11-19-designing-together-to-unshock-the-new.pdf. The full set of presentations for the workshop can be viewed at http://cordis.europa.eu/fp7/ict/fet-open/events-future-technology-and-society_en.html.

Genette, G. (1993), *Fiction and Diction* (Ithaca, NY: Cornell University Press).

Gladwell, M. (2000), *The Tipping Point: How Little Things Make a Big Difference* (New York: Little, Brown).

Gordon, J. (1978), *Structures* (Harmondsworth: Penguin).

Holling, C.S. (1973), 'Resilience and Stability of Ecological Systems', *Annual Review of Ecology and Systematics*, 4: 1–23.

Hunt, J.C.R., Timoshkina, Y., Baudains, P.J., and Bishop, S.R. (2012), 'System Dynamics Applied to Operations and Policy Decisions', *European Review*, 20: 324–42.

Jakobson R. (1960), 'Closing Statement: Linguistics and Poetics', in T. Sebeok (ed.), *Style in Language* (Cambridge, MA: MIT Press), 350–77.

Jayne, E. (2005), 'The Metaphor-Metonymy Binarism', http://www.edwardjayne.com/critical/metonymy.html.

Kierkegaard, S. (1966 [1843]), *Journals* IV A 164, in *Kierkegaard: Papers and Journals*, translated by Alastair Hannay (London: Penguin).

Lakoff, G. and Johnson, M. (1978), *Metaphors We Live By* (Chicago: University of Chicago Press).

Leclair, T. (1988), *In the Loop: Don DeLillo and the Systems Novel* (Urbana: University of Illinois Press).

Leine, R.I. (2009), 'The Historical Development of Classical Stability Concepts: Lagrange, Poisson and Lyapunov Stability', *Nonlinear Dynamics*, 59: 175.

Longa, V.M. (2001), 'Sciences of Complexity and Language Origins: An Alternative to Natural Selection', *Journal of Literary Semantics*, 30: 1–17.

Martin, W. (1993), 'Metaphor', in A. Preminger and T.V.F. Brogan (eds), *The New Princeton Encyclopedia of Poetry and Poetics* (Princeton, NJ: Princeton University Press), 760-66. [This encyclopaedia entry constitutes a good short introduction to the topic.]

Mason, J. (1987), Review of Donald A. Verene, *Hegel's Recollection: A Study of Images in the Phenomenology of Spirit* (1985), *Journal of Literary Semantics*, 16: 242–47.

Nair, R.B., Carter, R., and Toolan, M. (1988) 'Clines of Metaphoricity, and Creative Metaphors as Situated Risk-taking', *Journal of Literary Semantics*, 17: 20–40.

Norris F.H., Stevens, S.P., Pfefferbaum, B., Karen F., Wyche, K.F., and Pfefferbaum, R.L. (2008), 'Community Resilience as a Metaphor, Theory, Set of Capacities, and Strategy for Disaster Readiness', *American Journal of Community Psychology*, 41: 127–50.

Poincaré, H. (1914), *Science and Method*, ch. 3, 'Mathematical Discovery' (London: Nelson).

Richards, I.A. (1936), *The Philosophy of Rhetoric* (New York and London: Oxford University Press).

Rogers, R. (1987–88), 'General Systems Theory and Literary Texts', *Journal of Literary Semantics*, 16–17, Part I (16): 94–112, Part II (17): 182–99.

Van der Leeuw, S. (2004), 'Why Model?', *Cybernetics and Systems: An International Journal*, 35: 117–28.

Van der Leeuw, S. (2010), 'Information Processing: A Long-Term Perspective', a presentation within the workshop Future Technology and Society organized by the European Commission (DGINFSO). http://cordis.europa.eu/fp7/ict/fet-open/docs/2010-11-19-designing-together-to-unshock-the-new.pdf (see Foden (2010) above).

Commentary 3.2

Aligning contrasting perspectives of tipping points

MATTHEW TAYLOR

It is illuminating to explore the ideas of tipping points through the prism of the theories of plural rationality. Of these perhaps the most developed is the unhelpfully named 'cultural theory', based broadly on the research of anthropologist Mary Douglas (Douglas and Wildavsky 1982) and often used as a way of thinking about risk.

Cultural theory argues that there are four basic and distinct ways of thinking about change – both descriptively and prescriptively. As the anthropologist and systems thinker Michael Thompson has described, each of these perspectives is associated with a different underlying model of nature as a system (Thompson *et al.* 1990). These models can be represented by four images in which a healthy natural system is portrayed as a ball, along the lines introduced by Tim Lenton in Chapter 2.1 (see Figure 2.4, page 37).

The *hierarchical* perspective sees nature as volatile but manageable. This perspective sees tipping points as real phenomena, but also as something that can be predicted and managed through the right combination of expertise and leadership.

The *individualistic* perspective sees nature as highly resilient and adaptive. This perspective leads either to scepticism about tipping points or a faith in nature and its human stewards to avoid catastrophe by adapting to change to achieve a new and better equilibrium. (In the words of Richard Sears, 'the Stone Age didn't end because we ran out of stones'.)

The *egalitarian* perspective sees nature in the modern world as fundamentally unstable and vulnerable. Our management of the environment needs to take account of the basic fragility of natural systems. From this perspective, tipping points have a powerful resonance both as descriptions of concrete reality but also as a kind of morality tale about the dire consequences of our cavalier treatment of natural systems.

Finally, there is the *fatalistic* perspective that, in as much as it believes at all in tipping points, sees them as inevitable and malign. Nature in this view is capricious and liable to threaten human interests. Fatalists will tend to see tipping points either as a propaganda tool to justify interference by those with other perspectives, or simply another example of the unhappy vagaries of life.

Cultural theory therefore has a warning for those seeking to use the concept of tipping points as a way of enhancing public awareness of, and engagement in, issues relating to sustainability (broadly defined). The very idea of tipping points will tend to be seen in some quarters as a concept intimately bound up with a particular worldview (egalitarianism) and the political and ethical positions associated with it.

In the hierarchical position of being a Downing Street adviser some years ago, I noticed that it was almost taken for granted that interest groups lobbying government would offer apparently credible evidence that the sector or people they represented were about to face catastrophe without some form of intervention. Given how jaded we advisers became, there is a danger that the idea of a tipping point comes to be seen as simply a new pseudo-scientific form of special interest 'shroud-waving'. Indeed, given Whitehall's predisposition towards seeing the world as predictable and manageable, a weakly made argument for a tipping point could even be seen as an admission of an inability to make a case in terms of a more conventional incremental change process.

The current Coalition government has shown some interest in ideas of discontinuous change, particularly in their enthusiasm for the 'Black Swan' thesis of Nassim Nicholas Taleb (2010). Taleb touches on the argument of Giles Foden here in visualizing a 'black swan event' as an outlier, something which reconfigures thought, a process which allows reflective explanation in the wake of its occurrence. Black swan events are an outcome of selective blindness, influenced by patterns of outlook and uncontested thought.

As we observe in the United States, the free market (individualist) right tends to portray environmental 'alarmism' as simply the latest ruse deployed by apologists for state interference over enterprise. The point from cultural theory is that, in as much as other worldviews can accommodate the idea, there will be a profound difference between their interpretations of the significance of tipping points and what they imply, if anything, for policy. This perspective reflects the argument of Dan Kahan (2012: 255) who contends that views on highly polarized interpretations tend to be channelled towards what one's social and cultural reference group contends, and not to any objective weighing of the evidence.

So far, so pessimistic: but culture theory also provides some ideas about how to make debate more constructive and inclusive. In debates over risk – particularly risks associated with the environment – protagonists can expend a great deal of energy in the generally futile process of beating each other around the head with evidence. To start by recognizing that we each bring certain predispositions to the table can provide a more constructive context based on mutual recognition.

For example, in talking to school students I have found it useful to ask them to choose between four different responses to climate change, the paradigmatic example of threat regarding catastrophic tipping points. The four responses are these:

- Climate change should be addressed through global treaties drawn up by experts and leaders (hierarchical).
- The threat to nature and global justice require us in the West fundamentally to change our lifestyles (egalitarian).
- Technology and markets are most likely to solve the problem (individualist).
- Man-made climate change is either all made up or it is a real phenomenon that we cannot cope with, and therefore we are doomed (fatalist).

Managing to find agreement about what it is people disagree about can be a powerful way of opening up debate (see also Mike Hulme (2010) in this regard). I have found that when the young people with whom I have spoken feel their position is being fairly represented, they are less resistant to recognizing the virtues of other views – and even the frailties within their own.

While we may not find it easy to agree about the nature of tipping points, this doesn't mean we can't combine perspectives to produce what cultural theorists such as Thompson *et al.* (1990) call 'clumsy' solutions – approaches to policy that ensure that all the perspectives are brought to bear and that voices representing all of them are heard.

What tends to emerge from the conversations I have just described is agreement that we need a combination of leadership, social responsibility and invention to reduce carbon emissions. 'Clumsiness' in the design of deliberations can then turn the discussion from a loser-inducing argument over whether there is a problem at all to a positive debate about the relative contributions that representatives of each perspective can make. Conversation can also explore the inherent strengths and weaknesses in each approach, marshalling the combined insights and techniques of hierarchy (while resisting its tendency to be controlling), egalitarianism (while resisting its tendency to be alarmist), and individualism (while resisting its tendency toward complacency) – always bearing in mind the allure of fatalism.

The concept of the tipping point is rich and valuable on many levels. It can help us understand the world, the way we think about the world and why, and also why social power as it is currently configured may be unable to respond to extreme and rapid change. But if our aim is for the tipping point idea to open up new debate and challenge deeply held assumptions, we should be aware that the very concept and how it is used can be perceived as betraying strong ideological preconceptions. Cultural theory provides tools and processes, the art of designing 'clumsy' solutions, to help overcome the barriers to dialogue that our values and predispositions can set up.

References

Douglas, M. and Wildavsky, A. (1982), *Risk and Culture: An Essay on the Selection of Technical and Environmental Dangers* (Berkeley, CA: University of California Press).

Hulme, M. (2010), *Why We Disagree About Climate Change* (Cambridge: Cambridge University Press).

Kahan, D. (2012), 'Why We Are Poles Apart on Climate Change', *Nature*, 488: 255.

Taleb, N.N. (2010), *The Black Swan: The Impact of the Highly Improbable* (2nd edn) (London: Penguin).

Thompson, M., Ellis, R., and Wildavsky, A. (1990), *Cultural Theory* (Boulder, CO: Westview Press).

PART 4
FOOD SECURITY, BIODIVERSITY, AND ECOSYSTEMS DEGRADATION

In the first eight months of 2012 the price of fish oil rose from $1500 to $2000 per tonne, and fish meal from $1300 to $1700 per tonne (Neate 2012: 33). The causes connect across space and society. Storms off the Peruvian coast reduced anchovy populations; diversion of drought-diminished corn output in the USA in favour of ethanol production (required by climate change mitigation rules) left a huge gap in animal feed supplies; and a surge in Omega 3 pills usage amongst wealthy health-conscious consumers across the world combined to guarantee high prices for oily fish products. It is not surprising that financial investment firms took an interest in anchovy fishery companies, and that the lucrative prospect of rising prices of farmed fish and beef was also of interest to speculators. Neate (2012: 33) also explores the impact of warming seawater on farmed salmon growth, probably one outcome of global climate change. Balmier waters have increased the metabolisms of the salmon, leading to more demand for fish meal and lower prices as stocks increase. Consequently consumers are acquiring a taste for what was previously considered a luxury, but also a basis of bodily and mental health.

As Tim Lang and John Ingram explore in this Part, the food industry is both global and predatory. It makes sincere reference to sustainability, as we see from the commentary by Thomas Lingard (6.8), but at its heart it is unsustainable. The former Government Chief Scientist, John Beddington (2009), likened the combination of a 33 per cent rise in population, a 50 per cent growth in energy and food requirements, and a 30 per cent increase in water usage as producing the 'perfect storm' of what we termed in our introductory chapter as 'combinational tipping points'.

We believe that there is a powerful mutually propulsive set of forces – lying between a changing climate, aided in part by increasing agriculturally based emissions of nitrous oxides and methane; urbanization with over 60 per cent of the world's population in cities by 2050 (UN Habitat 2011); changing diets in favour of more meat and fish; losses of biodiversity and ecosystem life-support functions; and the near impossible challenge of producing large amounts of healthy food from new genetic technologies and ecologically adaptive farming methods – which will combine to bear out Beddington's prognoses.

Lang and Ingram (4.1) assert that the global food industry aggressively markets foods which encourage ill health and overeating by both poor and rich. The industry is one of the most sophisticated lobbies in an arena of oppressive business bias, acting well beyond the reach of national governments. Indeed, according to Action Aid, these lobbies control the international trading bodies:

> *Under the Influence* reveals a worldwide explosion of corporate lobbying which contributes to unfair trade rules that undermine the fight against poverty. The report highlights examples of privileged corporate access to, and excessive influence over, the WTO [World Trade Organization] policy-making process. In the EU alone, there are 15,000 lobbyists based in Brussels – around one for every official in the European Commission. Annual corporate lobbying expenditure in Brussels is estimated at €750 million to €1 billion. In the US, 17,000 lobbyists work in Washington DC – outnumbering US Congress lawmakers by 30 to one. Meanwhile, the pharmaceutical industry is reported to have spent over $1 billion lobbying in the US in 2004.
> (Action Aid 2012: 2)

Lang and Ingram do not offer any easy or reliable resolution. They see tensions between political and commercial priorities (for example in the increasingly troublesome conflict between biofuels and food needs), between all levels of competing governments (rendering them easy to pick off), and awesome overlapping complexities of governing organizations. If sustainability was to be shared as the overriding objective, there would be a chance of shifting to lower and healthier food and drink consumption, of building adaptive resilience in food-producing societies and economies, and of sharing food and water use with the natural world before its inherent diversity is irrecoverably lost.

Patricia Howard (4.2) documents the losses of both natural and cultural biodiversity. She concludes that the declines and extinctions of highly interconnected and interdependent natural species will be magnified by the removal of long-established cultural restraints which were designed to safeguard against the dangerous narrowing of the historical range of food plant species. She is concerned over the disruption of the cultural trans-mission of language and farming practices which are needed to accumulate social and ecological resilience. She also sees a failure of governing leadership, and the meddling of corporates and lobbies as contributing to what may become the sixth mass extinction of the global evolutionary journey. In this human-induced case there will be no prolonged, largely stress-free period of restoration and reconstitution as was available in past biodiversity recoveries and transformations.

Munang *et al.* (2011) point to emerging experiments in ecosystem-based adaptation (EbA) in African agriculture as an exciting opportunity for redesigning farming and biodiversity:

> Ecosystem-based adaptation is the use of biodiversity and ecosystem services as part of an overall adaptation strategy to help people and communities adapt to the negative effects of climate change at local, national, regional and global levels. EbA provides many other benefits to communities including food security (from fisheries to agro-forestry), sustainable water management and livelihood diversification (through increasing resource-used options).
>
> (Munang *et al.* 2011)

But such positive schemes rely on robust and extended leadership, investments in transport and marketing arrangements, and integrative behaviour by farmers and food suppliers/distributors protected from the volatilities of the international food markets. This is a tall order. But it could be met if honourable experiments are carefully monitored for their fairness, community well-being, and ecosystem integrity. The outcome could result in better land care and public health, improved incomes and community security, and avoidance of the perfect storm.

Toby Gardner (4.3) offers a genuinely interdisciplinary analysis of one of the more immediate tipping points. This is the insidious drying of the Amazon rainforest, the hugely debilitating subsurface slow-burning fires, and the self-reinforcing perverse climate changes caused by loss of forest to cattle and soya production to feed the new meat cultures of Brazilian megalopolises and further afield. Gardner provides the scientific bases for prognoses and the hope of new approaches to forest management and regeneration which will require global financial support. The loss of the rainforest has global as well as regional repercussions. If paying for eco-system services has any meaning, then the nearby urban populations, which are experiencing periodic but severe water shortages, should be investing in forest replanting which mixes the triumphs of ecosystem restorative cultures with the best of applied sustainability science.

Gardner also points to the instabilities of Amazonian land use futures. Variations in the US Dollar/Brazilian Real exchange rate can have huge and sudden impacts on soya production and resulting forest loss or recovery. If the prices offered for stewarding the carbon and biodiversity of the virgin rainforest biomes are not adjustable to highly variable food prices, then the best laid plans of carbon sequestration could fail to achieve their intended sustainability outcomes. And if the long-established forest safeguarding cultures of the Amazon are forced to migrate in the face of drought and savannah incursion, then Patricia Howard's anxieties may be fulfilled. Tipping points may be metaphors. But they can point to unsettling and deeply destabilizing interconnecting processes with no obvious entry points and no clear pathways for guidance and proactive intervention.

References

Action Aid (2012), *Under the Influence: Exposing Undue Corporate Influence over Policy Making at the World Trade Organization* (London: Action Aid).

Beddington, J. (2009), 'Food, Energy, Water and the Climate: A Perfect Storm of Global Events' (London: Government Office for Science).

Munang, R., Thiaw, I., and Rivington, M. (2011), 'Ecosystem Management: Tomorrow's Approach to Enhancing Food Security Under a Changing Climate', *Sustainability*, 3: 937–54.

Neate, R. (2012), 'Fish Price Leap Has Food Chain Reaction', *Guardian*, 25 August: 33.

UN Habitat (2011), *State of the World's Cities, 2010–2011* (Geneva: UN Habitat).

4.1
Food security twists and turns

Why food systems need complex governance

TIM LANG AND JOHN INGRAM

A note of caution about Mr Gladwell's metaphor

The language and theory of tipping points have become popular in academic, political and everyday discourse since Malcolm Gladwell's book of the same name was published (Gladwell 2000). We are well aware of the arguments advanced around the association with metaphors in the introductory chapter to this book (1.1). But while metaphors and analogies are useful (and beloved of the human mind as well as culture) we believe some caution is necessary. Gladwell's popular book is a pot-pourri of ideas, an intelligent journalist's interpretation of insights from psychology, sociology and, above all, his reading of epidemiology. That he is a journalist is not a criticism. We offer it as a comment on how fissured modern academia and the sciences are. As is suggested by Giles Foden (3.1), Joe Smith (7.1), and Paul Brown (7.3), it is often left to brilliant journalists and science writers to offer overviews or narratives that inform our lives and outlooks, especially where there is no solid evidentiary ground.

Gladwell's thesis is attractively simple. It filled a vacuum: how to interpret threats in a language that suits a political era infused (some say made) by the sound-bite. His concern is for change and whether there are points at which internal dynamics can go haywire. From epidemiology, for example, he takes the notion that we need to understand how diseases 'tip' from minorities to the masses. This is a deeply rooted and fearful notion, the age-old threat of contagion as superior force, and an unstoppable set of sequences and consequences, which can overwhelm human existence. The 'tipping points' metaphor thus can lead to deep pessimism, if not fatalism. History gives this some legitimacy, of course. There is a vast human experience of viruses, boiling points, catastrophe, and plagues. No wonder the 'tipping points' metaphor features so much in science fiction and sci-fi films. But Gladwell's is a very American book in its inherent optimism. You can turn crisis into opportunity. You can make a difference. In this he is on a par with another popular metaphor now given credence in an era which favours light-touch government – 'nudge' theory (Thaler and Sunstein 2008; and Dobson (8.2)).

Although we are wary of the consequences of politicians believing their favoured metaphors, this chapter is not a critique of Gladwell's metaphor per se. Rather, it suggests that policymakers need more subtle analyses and metaphors if, in the case of food security, they are to begin to address the complexities of the real problems. Metaphors are useful if they help funnel activity in appropriate directions. They become dangerous if they encourage decision-makers to pursue single 'triggers' or tension points. In food security, the best contemporary analyses suggest the need for multi-layered, systemic approaches to ensure availability and affordability of food. On a positive note, Gladwell himself has acknowledged that the real question is to ask what generates change, not the characteristics of tipping points. Our chapter tries to stay true to that wider task. Policy needs to be better informed by an understanding of the dynamics, drivers and challenges that shape or ought to shape food demand and supply ahead. The goal ought to be a world where societies are able to feed all people equitably, healthily, and in ways which enhance rather than destroy the habitability of the planet.

That is clearly not the case at present. There is a troubling but not unfamiliar gap between evidence and policy. And looking ahead, unless the vast majority of forecasting is wrong, humanity faces awesome challenges in this first half of the twenty-first century. It will have to adapt food systems to improve food resilience. Already, climate change is upon us; water stress too; and biodiversity loss (as Patricia Howard (4.2) and Toby Gardiner (4.3) cover in their companion chapters) endemic. The parameters of such environmental pressures have begun to be outlined by science and are impinging on the attention of policymakers. Less attention, however, is being given to the two other nodes of sustainable develop-ment's triangle – society and economy – yet the social and economic implications of coming environmental change for food are considerable: threats of social dislocation, price volatility, and speculation. Over the last half-century, modes of consuming food have become normalized in the

West which are unsustainable but profitable. The lock-in to unsustainability is tight. If food insecurity is to be tackled, innovative thinking which integrates environment, society and economy will be required from institutions and governance. This is currently not the case, and it is a failure not just of government, but of commerce and consumer culture.

Food security and food systems

Like tipping points, 'food security' is a term with much baggage, used in many ways and with many different meanings (Maxwell 2001). Nonetheless a cluster of meanings dominates contemporary discourse (see examples in Table 4.1). In public policy, the notion of food security centres on the pursuit of a situation where everyone is fed or could be fed adequately, appropriately, affordably and regularly. The key issues are often described as three As: Availability, Access and Affordability. Analyses have tended to assume that insecurity stems from insufficiency of production or dislocation of supply. Yet from the 1970s, just as the term 'food security' came into policy discourse, the old awareness that hunger and insecurity can occur despite there being sufficient food on the planet to feed everyone had been reasserted by Drèze, Sen, and others (Drèze *et al.* 1999). Sen's own argument stressed the role of entitlements as a key factor in famines. A deciding factor in whether famine takes hold is the social expression of rights and demand for food; it makes or breaks political demands to resolve or ride out harvest failure. Such analyses of food security stress the need for not just sustainable production, but equitable distribution and sensitive culture change. Why is it that some people are well fed (and now over-fed) while many others are not?

In mainstream policy, the conventional definition of food security is that offered by the Food and Agriculture Organisation (FAO). Morally based on the articulation of rights in the 1948 Universal Declaration of Human Rights, and voiced loudly at the 1974 World Food Conference (FAO 1974), a definition of food security emerged which, by the 1996 World Food Summit, saw it as a state when:

> all people, at all times, have physical and economic access to sufficient, safe, and nutritious food to meet their dietary needs and food preferences for an active and healthy life.
>
> (FAO 1996)

This definition suggests a broader notion than just the three As. But some key words, such as 'food production' and 'agriculture' – which might have been expected in such a definition – are *not* included. Most formal discussions of food security, therefore, recognize that it sits in a web of issues

Table 4.1 Strands in the food security discourse

Term	Focus	Comment
Food security	The extent to which food systems can deliver adequate, affordable, accessible supplies, at many levels	Currently this does not connect with the sustainability agenda. Security implies food systems which are 'likely to continue or remain safe' (OED).
Food nationalism	Policy priority to food from national resources and land	May range from general desire for more self-sufficiency to autarky
Food control	Actions of state or other power sources to shape food systems	Top-down control systems; rationing, at the most extreme
Food defence	Feeding in extreme emergencies	Assessment of minimum requirements for survival
Food resilience	Capacity to withstand and recover from shock	Used widely in food security discourse with ecological roots but appeals elsewhere, e.g. insurance, military
Food risks	Factors which threaten food goals	Appeals to systems thinking and suggests need to identify, rate and prevent risks
Food entitlement	Citizens' sense of their rights to have access to adequate food	Articulated by Nobel Laureate Amartya Sen to explain why famines occur despite supply
Food sovereignty	Ensuring bottom-up societal control of primary production	Championed by small farmer movements and development NGOs
Food democracy	Social engagement and pressure for food rights	Emphasizes political processes within societal demands for adequate food
Food capacity	Capabilities and requirements for any system of food production	Environmental, economic and societal requirements for and limits to sustainable food systems
Community food security	Building local food systems	Mainly used in developed world to indicate locally led food provision. Tends to be used by organizations committed to sustainability frameworks.

Source: Adapted from Lang (2008)

including food production, distribution, demand, rights, environment and health, all shaped by actors whose moral buy-in is assumed or expected. Yet this is not the case. Hunger remains on a mass scale today. And this approach to food security barely acknowledges that mal-consumption and over-consumption might be factors in under-consumption. The discourse is pitched on welfarist terrain, with the developing world as supplicant or applicant and the developed world as donor (Lang *et al.* 2009).

The politics that this implies has a very long history. Arguably, the entire food security debate goes back centrally to Malthus's *Essay on the Principle of Population* (Malthus 1798). Malthus, like Gladwell two centuries later, worried about irresolvable forces and trends; above all he feared population rising faster than the potential to increase food supply. His core question – and why his writing remains so potent today – was partly philosophical, partly political: can humans escape the limits of nature? (Malthus 1815).

Malthus was not one to shirk the politics of food security, which is why in part Karl Marx later in the nineteenth century was so exercised with finding flaws in his arguments. Societal structures, particularly land ownership and capital distribution, were downplayed, when the potential lay to unleash technology which could remove the barriers to hunger. Ossified social structures, not Malthusian inevitabilities, create hunger, said Marx.

In the mid-twentieth century, science and technical advance were posited as value-neutral means through which the Malthusian spectre could be banished. The Green Revolution's plant breeding remains a prime example of that approach to food security; Norman Borlaug won the *Peace* Nobel Prize. By the end of the twentieth century, however, the social dimension of food (in)security was once more being reasserted. Even if technical change was needed, a social framework would be necessary to unlock its potential. A recent example of this more balanced approach was the World Bank's and FAO's evidence-based review published as the *International Assessment of Agricultural Science and Technology Development Knowledge* (IAASTD 2008). This assessment proposed that social support, particularly to small-scale farming and to women in Africa, would help them achieve large increases in output and create economic pathways by which food demand could be met. Other recent large-scale reviews of the global food system conducted by national scientific teams in Australia, France and the UK have concurred with the case for a more balanced mix of technical, social and economic improvements to deliver food security

(Foresight 2011; Paillard *et al.* 2011; PMSEIC (Australia) 2010). If this is the case, a framework of thinking based on systems analysis becomes almost inevitable. Food security has to blend multiple strands of issues – land, people, economics, social structures, environment, health, distribution – not reduce their complex interactions to one factor or favoured approach.

This is why policy discussion of food security inexorably dovetails into the challenge of wider sustainable development; indeed, food security is a microcosm of sustainable development. Equal attention to societal, economic and environmental drivers and outcomes is needed to ensure that food systems operate stably and adaptably.

The literature on food security amply justifies the necessity of such a systems analysis, pointing to critical stresses emerging for food supplies from:

- *Environmental forces,* such as climate change, water stress, soil, land use, biodiversity loss;
- *Economic forces,* such as inappropriate price signals and uncosted externalities, fossil fuel reliance, labour force reorganization, urbanization, and first regionalization and now globalization;
- *Social forces,* such as population demand, the nutrition transition (changed eating patterns), diet-based ill-health patterns, the triumph of choice culture, the continuation of high levels of food waste.

The challenge ahead is not just producing enough but changing expectations that everyone can and should aspire to eat like the USA or UK. To eat like the former implies a society consuming as though there are five planets, and the latter a mere three planets (Global Footprint Network 2010). How did such an extraordinary state of affairs come about?

The world of food policy

Throughout the twentieth century, while communist bloc politics were driving their experiments in one direction, the West was taking different routes. At the global level, food production kept ahead of rising population until relatively recently. Building on chemical, biological and transport advances, food production rose. 'Researchers turned policy advocates' such as John Boyd Orr, the first Director General of FAO, charted a pathway past the opposing poles of Malthus and Marx. More food could be produced, by applying science, technology and capital, working *with* rather than imposing on primary producers. Knowledge could be dispersed, for example via extension services, rather than enforced through social control. Science could unleash potential everywhere. It could also help prevent waste from poor storage and inefficient distribution techniques. Thus food costs would come down, and availability would increase, delivering general welfare and preventing ill health (Boyd Orr 1943; Boyd Orr and Lubbock 1953). This had been a powerful and dominant analysis of food security for most of the twentieth century (Vernon 2007). Termed variously the 'productivist' or 'productionist' analysis, it emphasized underproduction as the policy problem to be resolved. The environment was to be reshaped, mined, and indeed tamed, to meet core human needs. With variations, it has been the paradigm for food policy for the last 70 years; food policy sought a planet tailored for people.

Part of the rationale for the paradigm's adoption was the powerful evidence of hunger and mal-distribution of food in the West itself. Boyd Orr's book, *Food, Health and Income* – a study of food poverty in the UK – was enormously influential throughout the British Empire (Boyd Orr 1936; Ostry 2006). The institutional architecture created in and after the Second World War owed its existence to such arguments. In the crisis of wartime, they began to plan for better structures to share knowledge and food, while avoiding draconian USSR-type intervention. The evidence of poor social distribution within the capitalist West – hunger in the USA and UK being particularly cited – reminded political decision-makers of how under-consumption and unaffordability were core problems, not just under-production. Hence the visionary language of rights and possibilities in the 1943 Hot Springs Conference that spawned the FAO (Hot Springs Conference 1943), and the strand of 'Right to Food' legalism from the 1948 UN Declaration to the 1974 World Food Conference, to the creation of the UN's 'Special Rapporteur on the Right to Food' (Eide and Kracht 2005).

Recognition of the history of food security thinking clarifies why global and national institutions are as they are, and why they struggle to address food security as sustainability. They have adapted, of course, but they clearly struggle to face, let alone resolve, the complexity now emerging from multi-factorial analyses, such as from IAASTD and the Global Environmental Change and Food Systems project (IAASTD 2008; Liverman and Kapadia 2010). Even in its decades of success, much of the pressure on the productionist paradigm came from mounting evidence about environmental damage and externalities. Evidence grew about the complexity of ecosystems' infrastructure and about the impact of a runaway food culture based on untrammelled choice. Yet policy remained overwhelmingly productionist, with a welfarist safety net at global, but not always at national level (Shaw 2007).

In the twenty-first century, the world faces both old and new food dynamics. Today, for instance, hunger is again rising; after three decades of dropping as a proportion of world population, it is now back up to affecting a billion people. But this is outstripped by the 1.2 billion estimated to be overweight or obese (Gardner and Halweil 2000). Nowadays under-, over-, and mal-consumption of food co-exist. Loosened tastes and rampant consumerism have become major drivers of land use, as we see in the Amazon case study provided by Toby Gardner (4.3). Powerful global retailers and traders, not just national governments, dominate how food is grown, distributed, priced and consumed (Burch and Lawrence 2007). The marketing budget of one giant soft-drinks corporation exceeds the World Health Organization's bi-annual public health budget (Lang *et al.* 2006). Billions of people today eat as only kings and the rich ate in the past; more people are clinically obese or overweight than are malnourished (Gardner and Halweil 2000). Entire new structures and networks of food commodity routes have been created, aided by the age of oil. Cheap oil has fuelled both the nutrition and logistics revolutions. Neither is sustainable.

At the start of the twenty-first century, therefore, public policy over food security is in some turmoil. On the one hand, there is widespread specialist recognition that a structural reassessment is in order. On the other hand, there is institutional and consumer lifestyle 'lock-in' to productionism's inappropriate brilliance. This mismatch emerged clearly in 2006–08, when world political leaders began to realize something serious and new was facing the future of food and agriculture. In 2006, world agricultural commodity prices began to rise, and then rocketed in 2007–08. These peaked in 2008, but not before the FAO had won attention for the view that unless agriculture received more R&D investment and political support, the world would enter a neo-Malthusian crisis (FAO 2008). Neoliberal economists disagreed, arguing that price signals would reinvigorate production. As prices dropped and crop figures rose, it seemed they were right, only for the FAO Food Price Index to rise slowly again to the point where by 2011 prices had exceeded 2008 peak levels. Oil prices, too, exceeded $125 a barrel. This added weight to the structural analyses urging fundamental review. Although the seriousness of the situation helped trigger many national inquiries and processes, such as former French President Sarkozy's G20 inquiry into food price volatility, the fundamental 'blank sheet' rethink has not yet happened. Dominant thinking still centres on 'produce more' rather than 'consume less or differently', let alone radical redistributive politics.

The significance of this policy mess cannot be overestimated. There is much lock-in to the status quo. Who could not want to maintain a supermarket culture which offers 30,000 food items for the consumer to choose? But who takes seriously that, behind this astonishing feat, is an unsustainable reliance on oil? In the UK, for instance, one company sells a third of all food and drink consumed, one-quarter of all lorries on UK roads are food-related, and half travel empty. Vast investment has been expended on building the twentieth-century food infrastructure to enable this affront to sustainability. Yet policymakers continue to believe that somehow 'business as usual' is both possible and desirable; they are either in a state of denial or else believe that market dynamics will resolve the difficulties.

Meanwhile evidence that addressing greenhouse gas (GHG) emissions alone requires huge change in rich countries' food and lifestyles mounts (Audsley *et al.* 2010). Future challenges go further than just GHGs, of course. A 'one planet' food system must develop new relationships with not just oil, but water, carbon, land, climate and ecosystems support. The transition to sustainability and long-term food security will be rocky and requires culture change, not just a few products with 'lo carbon' or 'bird friendly' labels.

UK governments since the 1970s have championed liberal food policy analyses despite (sometimes because of) membership of the Common Agricultural Policy (HM Treasury and Defra 2005). Today, with home food production back down to 1950s proportions (after a high point in the 1980s), UK governments are acutely aware of their reliance on external sources, on how sterling levels shape food prices, and how reliance on big food retailers to lower food prices has its limits (Collingham 2011). Investment in sustainable food systems is a priority, yet consumers and retailers themselves are hooked on the pursuit of 'cheap food' rather than sustainable food. This tension began to surface in the UK, and across OECD economies more generally, when world agricultural commodity prices rocketed in the 2007–08 price spike.

Concerned, the UK set up a Cabinet Office review. The resulting *Food Matters* report in 2008 proposed a more integrated analysis and policy (Cabinet Office 2008). It suggested a new 'low carbon and healthy' framework for the UK and de facto EU food system. This new perspective suggested that equal emphasis needs to be given to supply and consumption;

to push and pull; to society, environment and production, not just production; to the interface of people, natural systems and socio-economic structures. It called for processes and institutions to manage change, and the need to acknowledge not just technical but socio-political options; to incorporate not just economic but cultural factors; to address not just farming but ever longer supply chains. The discourse thus began to move from mapping problems and their extent to what to do about it, and to scoping policy re-engagement with the world of investment, and better coordination between state, companies and consumerism. In short, what began to emerge from just one high level review of one relatively small country was a case for renewed integrated public policy, not just narrow 'market-think'. 'Leave it to Tesco *et al.*' is not a sustainable or sensible public policy, not least since big retailers and processors are only too aware of how coming crises might destabilize their own supply chains and market value – hence their creation of some interesting parallel processes such as the Sustainable Agriculture Initiative and GlobalGAP (GlobalGAP 2008; SAI 2008). These are company-specific rather than planetary global initiatives, but they are signs that even the powerful are nervous. Certainly, the undertow is that not just academics and analysts are voicing the question as to whether public food governance and institutions are 'fit for purpose'.

It is important not to lose sight of the enormous successes of twentieth-century agriculture. The impact of 150 years of research and field experimentation has delivered major advances in food production, most notably in food crops (and especially in the 'green revolution' in the 1960s and 1970s). There have also been significant advances in animal sciences and in understanding the population dynamics of fisheries. Globally, however, although food production has kept ahead of global demand, there are still marked regional differences in food security. And the fragility of the current global food system was illustrated by the immediate consequences of the 2008 price rises.

This is important in the context of tipping points. The 2006–08 food price spike propelled the broader notion of food security into the policy and public eye. Almost overnight, governments were issuing statements about food security (as opposed to food production) and the media were relaying these to civil society. A key consideration for the tipping points discussion is that many reasons were advanced for the 'food crisis' including not only poor harvests due to weather anomalies but also commodity price speculation, increased demand for grains, export bans on selected foodstuffs, inadequate grain stocks, higher oil prices and the use of crop lands for the production of biofuels (Gregrory and Ingram 2008).

The world of food policy now has to address a wide range of drivers. These are highly complex. While climate change could well accentuate the interaction of factors shaping access, affordability, and utilization, it is but one of several external stressors acting on the food system. Economic access to food, and hence livelihoods, is critically important. If policymakers are to consider future change successfully and based on evidence, they require understanding of the whole food system rather than just the production component. In this context we share the argument, advanced in Chapter 1.1, that tipping points could be better understood as combinations of intertwining factors.

Food systems, food security and food vulnerabilities

The Global Environmental Change and Food Systems (GECAFS) project is an example of a major research effort in the 2000s which ideally ought to have been central to this process of building integrated policy understanding. For GECAFS, Ericksen (2008) conceptually divided food security into three major components, each of which needs to be stable over time: *food availability* (which depends on food production, distribution and exchange), *food access* (which depends on food affordability, allocation and preference), and *food utilization* (which depends on nutritional value, social value, and food safety) (Ericksen 2008). These components are all *outcomes* of a number of *activities* of the 'food chain': (1) producing food; (2) processing food and packaging food; (3) distributing and retailing food; and (4) consuming food. Both the food systems activities and the consequences of these activities for food security (i.e. their outcomes) are influenced by global environmental change; and the activities have environmental feedbacks as well as food security implications.

These activities therefore lead to a number of outcomes, many of which contribute to food security, and others which relate to environmental and other social welfare concerns. The GECAFS food-system model attempted to capture this dynamic. Ingram (2011) details five contrasting examples where its application has helped focus research and policy formulation. Food security is compromised as and when any of the components of food security are diminished, as is usually the case when food-system activities are disrupted by any stress. While each activity is to some extent vulnerable to global environmental change, it is the combined vulnerability of the food system as a whole which is critically important for food security. This is what the Royal Institute for International Affairs (Chatham House) called the 'new fundamentals' for food policy (Ambler-Edwards *et al*. 2009). The massive floods in Pakistan in 2010 affected the whole food system: storing food, distributing food, retailing and consuming food, as well as severely disrupting production itself. Single issues affect all food-system activities, but are influenced by cultural and social capacities for accommodation and adjustment, as covered by Emily Boyd (7.2).

So what are the likely pressures for change in food systems which might lead to increased food insecurity? While climate change will undoubtedly be a major factor impacting food production in many regions, it is the combination of increasing demand for food, coupled with growing climate stress (combined with yet further environmental stresses such as reduced water availability or soil degradation), that will be critical. While producing food has kept ahead of food demand historically, global demand is now growing fast. Economic growth in countries such as China and India, coupled with urbanization and the increasing influence of the retailing sector, is pushing up the consumption of meat and dairy products, projected to increase by up to 2.4 per cent annually between 2007 and 2016 (Von Braun 2007). Goodland and Anhang (2009) suggest that the total contribution to global GHG emission could be as high as 51 per cent. This kind of analysis contributes to the lively debate for one meatless day per week.

Diets don't 'Westernize' by themselves. Very aggressive campaigns on the part of major corporations and Western governments to shift diets to Western patterns in poorer economies continue to have a very substantial impact, as have Western subsidies and 'dumping' of products – e.g. milk powder from the EU into China. Different policy discourses emerge from this picture. On the one hand some argue that this is progress; why shouldn't the Chinese or Indians eat more and differently? On the other hand, evidence from Western countries already suggests costly healthcare consequences from the nutrition transition. How can Mumbai afford its rocketing type 2 diabetes rate? Or China its rise of non-communicable disease as it consumes more fat? (Chen *et al*. 1991). Even the West has political difficulties with the health aspects of its unsustainable food footprint. One European Commission study, for instance, estimated that food accounts for 30 per cent of European consumers' environmental impact (Tukker *et al*. 2006). A study of UK food GHG emissions also estimated that food accounts for 30 per cent (Audsley *et al*. 2010). If GHGs are to be reduced, considerable changes in Western food consumption patterns will be crucial.

This is what troubles politicians. In developing countries, the rising middle classes would love to be able to eat like their counterparts in the West. In the developed world, companies and politicians are both nervous of weaning consumers off that lifestyle. Yet already policy decisions are being made which add further pressures to the already unsustainable mix. Commitments to increase and subsidise biofuel production are a case in point. On the supply side, the diversion of a significant proportion of the US maize crop to bio-ethanol production (25 per cent of the crop in 2007), coupled with poor harvests of wheat in Australia and parts of eastern Europe, reduced the amount of long-distance tradable grains at a time when global cereal stocks (about 400 million tonnes) were at their lowest levels since the early 1980s (Gregrory and Ingram 2008). Maize exports from the USA averaged 47 million tonnes per year from 2000 to 2005, but in 2007 80 million tonnes went to ethanol refineries. Oil prices have also risen leading to increased fertilizer, transport and distribution costs, and a growing realization that world cereal and energy prices are not independent (Von Braun 2007). This was realized in the early 1970s but was politically marginalized, ironically due to the success of the Green Revolution and the new political compact between the oil-rich Middle East and dependent OECD Western states (Green 1978). The linkage is clearly seen in wheat prices, which like oil tripled between January 2000 and July 2007, and in the doubling of maize and rice prices over the same period (Von Braun 2007).

The OECD and FAO have now acknowledged that the era of dropping agricultural commodity prices may well be over. While average food prices have declined, food prices for many of the poor have not dropped over time as a percentage of their disposable income. This may be good news for urbanized consumers and food processors, but troubling for primary producers (OECD and FAO 2008). Their joint *Agricultural Outlook* report predicts price rises in the 2010s. The lack of stocks may be a major factor in the short-term increase in grain prices, but while the current high prices are unlikely to be sustained as farmers increased production in 2008, they are likely to remain relatively high for the medium term. This will bring benefits to some producers but it poses problems for the poor, governments of low income countries, and aid agencies supplying food, although with the appropriate policies higher prices could provide incentives to produce local food and stimulate agriculture.

But how will the additional impacts of climate change, and its likely growing importance in the future as a factor affecting food systems, further complicate what is already a very complex situation? Gregory and Ingram (2008) reviewed the present knowledge of recorded impacts of climate change and variability on crop production, and estimated its contribution to the then current 'food crisis' (Gregrory and Ingram 2008). Such contributions might arise directly through the impact of existing climate change and/or climate variability on crop production, or arise indirectly through actions to mitigate or adapt to anticipated changes in climate. As they point out, the effect of increasing the mean temperature is relatively straightforward with the frequency distribution moved towards hotter and away from colder temperatures. However, increased variability of temperature becomes very important if crop biological responses are non-linear, and there are absolute thresholds for crop resilience.

Increasing variability of weather (and thus climate) may stem from three sources:

- Changes in the mean weather, such as an increase in annual mean temperature and/or precipitation;
- A change in the distribution of weather so that there are more frequent extreme weather events such as physiologically damaging temperatures or longer periods of drought;
- A combination of changes to the mean and its variability.

The consequences of the dry conditions on grain production and exports have been significant. Recent volatility in wheat prices has shown the impact of drought and seasonal fluctuation and has been a reminder that small variations in Australia, for example, can throw price predictions, open up opportunities for speculation and compound the effects of US and EU decisions to build biofuel production (Gregrory and Ingram 2008).

Environmental interactions with food systems

There is now a substantial body of work that shows how sensitive agricultural production is to climate change, water and energy inputs (e.g. IPCC 2007, Stern 2008). Agricultural systems could be thrown by weather extremes, such as a drought season (or successive droughts), thereby accelerating migration and urbanization which in turn stresses food distribution and labour markets.

While the impacts of environmental change on food production might be the most obvious issue, other food system activities are vulnerable to such stress. Food transport is one determinant of food availability; most people do not grow their own food and they rely on distribution systems to bring food to them. The world has now passed the point where a majority is urbanized. At a local level, food distribution might be stressed if a critical piece of distribution infrastructure (e.g. a railway or road bridge) is destroyed by a flood. In many cases a 'work around' can reduce its impact (by finding another route for example), but not always. Emily Boyd (7.2) takes this further, but relevant here are aspects of community response.

Concentrating on the vulnerability of distinct-level food systems to global environmental change in the Indo-Gangetic Plain, a GECAFS food-systems approach identified that the 'vulnerability points' were due to a number of interacting socio-economic and bio-geophysical factors; the context is fundamentally important (Aggarwal *et al.* 2004). In Ludhiana District of the Indian Punjab, for instance, where socio-economic development has led to a dependence on irrigation, the key vulnerability point is reduced irrigation supply due to lowering groundwater tables due to excessive extraction. This threatens crop productivity and overall production. In contrast, in the Ruhani Basin District, in the Nepali Terai, food security depends on moving food from village to village, especially in times of stress. Increased flooding due to glacier melt, coupled with more extreme weather, disrupts footpaths, bridges, and other vital food distribution infrastructure. Taking a food-system approach helped identify the vulnerability points in the two contrasting Districts in the Indian Punjab and the Nepali Terai and showed them to be quite different. They will need very different adaptation responses to reduce their respective vulnerabilities: agronomic in the Indian case, structural and policy in the Nepali case.

Climate change and other aspects of environmental change stress food systems in a number of ways which may lead to organized responses of the kinds described by Emily Boyd. But food-system activities feed back to environmental conditions, which may in turn exacerbate these stresses. From a food perspective, agriculture is usually thought of as the main culprit; 12–14 per cent of total GHG emissions are attributed to agriculture, and a further 18 per cent to land use change and forestry, much of which relates to clearing land for agriculture and pasture (Foresight 2011). While agriculture and associated activities clearly contribute substantially to

GHG emissions and other aspects of environmental degradation, all food-system activities lead to GHG emissions. Edwards and colleagues estimated that in the US food system 40 per cent of emissions are due to non-agricultural food-system activities (Edwards *et al.* 2009). But GHG emission is not the only environmental consequence of food systems. Impacts on biodiversity, on biogeochemical cycles, on fresh water resources, and on other environmental parameters are all in part caused by food-system activities.

An initial analysis by Ingram (2011) uses a matrix to indicate where the four sets of food-system activities contribute to crossing a number of 'planetary boundaries' (as identified by Rockstrom *et al.* 2009; see Table 4.2). Far from reducing the impacts attributed to agriculture, Table 4.2 provides examples in almost all cells of the matrix. Clearly mitigation opportunities exist across the food system. But it is also well worth noting that much of the GHG emission could be reduced across the whole food system if less food was wasted by consumers (Foresight 2011). Parfitt and colleagues report that 25 per cent of food purchased (by weight) is wasted in UK households, and that the 8.3 million tonnes of food and drink wasted each year in the UK has a carbon impact exceeding 20 million tonnes of CO_2-equivalent (Parfitt *et al.* 2010). Reducing food waste by only 25 per cent in the USA would reduce CO_2-equivalent by 65 million tonnes annually (Lyutse 2010).

The institutional challenge

The picture of food security sketched here is one whose complexity and global reach pose significant challenges for governance. In the mid-twentieth century, after the Second World War, governments were the drivers of reformed food policies designed principally to raise production. But, in the twenty-first century, power and influence lie in a new global configuration of vast companies alongside altered national governmental powers, along with consumer and environmental groups. This ill-coordinated patchwork of multilevel governance – part public, part private, part global, part national – has to address global to local capacities in order to feed an unprecedented combination of 9 billion people in 2050, in an era of climate change with changed economies, societal expectations and consumer cultures. Figure 4.1 provides a conceptual model of current food

Table 4.2 Examples of how food-chain activities (columns) affect key environmental variables (rows)

	Producing food	Processing and packaging food	Distributing and retailing food	Consuming food
Climate change	GHGs from fertilizers; changing albedo	GHGs from energy production	GHGs from transport and refrigeration systems	GHGs from cooking
Nitrogen cycle	Eutrophication and GHGs from fertilization	Effluent from processing and packaging plants	NOx emissions from transport	Food waste
Phosphorus cycle	P mining for fertilizers	Detergents from processing plants		Food waste
Fresh water use	Irrigation	Washing, heating, cooling		Cooking, cleaning
Land use change	Extensification and intensification	Deforestation for paper/card	Transport and retail infrastructure	
Biodiversity loss (including agro-biodiversity)	Land use change, pesticide and fertilizer pollution, overhunting, overfishing, crop homogenization, irrigation	Hydroelectricity dams for aluminium smelting	Invasive species	Consumer choices
Atmospheric aerosols	Smoke and dust from land use change		Emissions from shipping	
Chemical pollution	Pesticides	Effluent from processing and packaging plants	Transport emissions	Cooking, cleaning

Source: Ingram (2011)

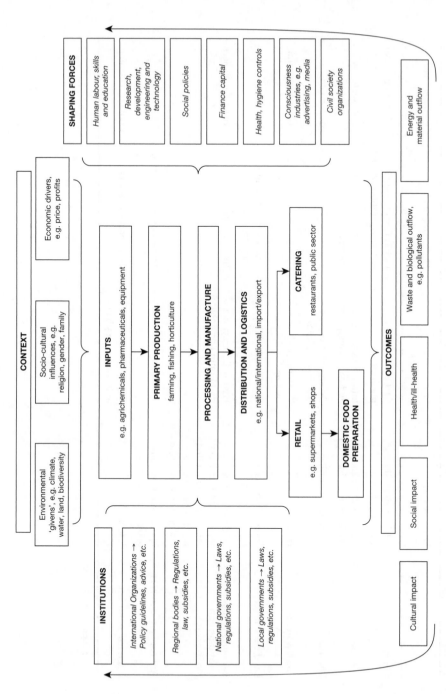

Figure 4.1 The food system, its external influences, and outcomes: a flowchart

systems. This conceives of food flowing down a supply chain, drawing upon natural, social and economic capital, with outputs and consequences which feed back on the system dynamics. Around this central flow, other forces operate. Multiple stresses and interactions are possible, whose direction is affected by institutions and governance.

The mid-twentieth-century policy model was more top-down than it is today, with government broadly shaping the relationship between supply-chain actors, consumers and civil society. That model has been frayed by new dynamics: regionalization and globalization, consumerism and the astonishing expansion of choice culture, and the spread and flow of information and other technologies. The result is that the activities of farmers and growers are largely dictated away from the land, even in the developing world, let alone in Western societies where more people are employed off than on the land. Farming and food production remain hugely important for food security, of course, not least because they are the largest employers on the planet, engaging nearly 400 million people.

It is primarily governments which have the legitimacy and policy potential to facilitate any transition to sustainable food systems for food security. Are governments able to do this? Attempts to create new policy frameworks, even in the area of trade (which governments almost universally state through the World Trade Organization is their top priority), have not successfully engaged with the challenge of sustainability. Trade rules have been framed around the pursuit of commerce rather than living within environmental limits. Yet, as we noted above, along with Amanda Long (6.4), some giant commercial companies now realize the urgency of sustainability, if only as threats to their brands and their own survival. The assumption is often made that food governance will inevitably be delivered by existing institutions, as though they are (a) functioning adequately, (b) have appropriate terms of reference, and (c) have a good understanding of how best to integrate environmental, social and economic policy demands for food systems.

These assumptions do not hold. And there are good reasons for why modern food governance is fraying. First, there are tensions over priorities – trade, environment, health, and consumers. Secondly, governance is inexorably multilevel, with competing pulls from local, sub-national, national, regional and global levels of democratic accountability. And thirdly, institutional complexity has been compounded by failure to restructure. At the UN level alone there is fragmentation among the big organizations. The FAO dwarfs the World Health Organization. Environmental issues are championed by the UN Environment Programme (UNEP), but are largely sidelined by the sole body which is supposed to arch across the UN, the old Administrative Committee on Co-ordination/Sub-Committee on Nutrition (ACC/SCN), now renamed the 'Standing Committee on Nutrition'.

No one champions an integrated approach to food policy per se. Food security de facto receives most policy attention from the World Food Programme, which has an overt crisis-mitigation role, but which is entirely dependent on donor beneficence. A welfarist backstop or safety net is essential, but prevention rather than crisis management is what is now required. In government, like commerce, institutional divisions are inevitable. What matters is cross-sectoral or ministerial coordination. And it is here that failures of governance have been most marked.

Happily, pressures to reform world food security governance have begun to emerge. In the UN, a Special Rapporteur on the Right to Food was created in the late 1990s. This office has become a remarkable voice for reformed governance through a series of powerful papers addressed to the Secretary General (www.srfood.org). In 2010, the Committee on World Food Security, created in 1974, was revamped and given new urgency. It remains to be seen whether the renewed body will get a grip of the new policy requirements, and drive action on prevention and the delivery of sustainable food systems.

Our recommendation is that more thought needs to be given to how global, regional, national, and local policy architecture could help the transition to sustainable food systems. Better coordination, thinking capacity and sharing of experimentation are clearly required. But where is the political will? For this to happen, policymakers need to give equal emphasis to all aspects of sustainability. History suggests that food shocks are not always anticipated. As Emily Boyd (7.2) suggests, resilience stems from building capacities, not assuming 'business as usual'.

References

Aggarwal, P.K., Joshi, P.K., Ingram, J.S.I., and Gupta, R.K. (2004), 'Adapting Food Systems of the Indo-Gangetic Plains to Global Environmental Change: Key Information Needs to Improve Policy Formulation', *Environmental Science and Policy*, 7: 487–98.

Ambler-Edwards, S., Bailey, K., Kiff, A., Lang, T., Lee, R., Marsden, T., *et al.* (2009), 'Food Futures: Rethinking UK Strategy', *Chatham House Report* (London: Royal Institute of International Affairs (Chatham House)).

Audsley, E., Brander, M., Chatterton, J., Murphy-Bokern, D., Webster, C., and Williams, A. (2010), 'How Low Can We Go? An Assessment of Greenhouse Gas Emissions from the UK Food System and the Scope for Reduction by 2050' (Godalming, Surrey: FCRN and WWF).

Boyd Orr, J. (1936), *Food, Health and Income: Report on Adequacy of Diet in Relation to Income* (London: Macmillan).

Boyd Orr, J. (1943), *Food and the People* (Target for Tomorrow No. 3), (London: Pilot Press).

Boyd Orr, J. and Lubbock, D. (1953), *The White Man's Dilemma* (London: George Allen & Unwin), 124.

Burch, D. and Lawrence, G. (eds) (2007), *Supermarkets and Agri-Food Supply Chains* (Cheltenham: Edward Elgar).

Cabinet Office (2008), *Food Matters: Towards a Strategy for the 21st Century* (London: Cabinet Office Strategy Unit), http://webarchive.nationalarchives.gov.uk/200808 04124019/http://www.cabinetoffice.gov.uk/strategy/work_areas/food_policy. aspx (accessed 3 April 2012).

Chen, J., Campbell, T.C., Li, J., and Peto, R. (1991), *Diet, Life-Style and Mortality in China: A Study of the Characteristics of 65 Chinese Counties* (Oxford/Ithaca, NY/Beijing: Oxford University Press/Cornell University Press/People's Medical Publishing House).

Collingham, L. (2011), *Taste of War: World War Two and the Battle for Food* (London: Allen Lane).

Drèze, J., Sen, A.K., and Hussain, A. (1999), *The Political Economy of Hunger: Selected Essays* (New Delhi/Oxford: Oxford India Paperbacks/Oxford University Press).

Edwards, J., Kleinschmit, J., and Schoonover, H. (2009), 'Identifying Our Climate "Foodprint": Assessing and Reducing the Global Warming Impacts of Food and Agriculture in the U.S.' (Minneapolis: Institute for Agriculture and Trade Policy).

Eide, W.B. and Kracht, U. (eds) (2005), *Food and Human Rights in Development, Volume I: Legal and Institutional Dimensions and Selected Topics* (Antwerp: Intersentia).

Ericksen, P.J. (2008), 'Conceptualizing Food Systems for Global Environmental Change Research', *Global Environmental Change*, 18: 234–45.

FAO (1974), 'Report of the World Food Conference, Rome, 5–16 November 1974' (Rome: Food and Agriculture Organisation).

FAO (1996), 'Rome Declaration on World Food Security and World Food Summit Plan of Action (World Food Summit, 13–17 November 1996)' (Rome: Food and Agriculture Organisation).

FAO (2008), 'Declaration of the High-Level Conference on World Food Security: The Challenges of Climate Change and Bioenergy, June 3–5 2008' (Rome: Food and Agriculture Organisation), http://www.fao.org/fileadmin/user_upload/ foodclimate/HLCdocs/declaration-E.pdf (accessed 3 April 2012).

Foresight (2011), 'The Future of Food and Farming: Final Project Report' (London: Government Office for Science).

Gardner, G. and Halweil, B. (2000), 'Underfed and Overfed: The Global Epidemic of Malnutrition', *Worldwatch Paper 15* (Washington DC: Worldwatch Institute).

Gladwell, M. (2000), *The Tipping Point: How Little Things Can Make a Big Difference* (London: Abacus).

Global Footprint Network (2010), 'Living Planet Report 2010: Biodiversity, Biocapacity and Development' (Gland/London/Oakland, CA: WWF/Institute of Zoology/Global Footprint Network).

GlobalGAP (2008), 'What Is Globalgap?' http://www.globalgap.org/ (accessed 15 June 2008).

Goodland, R. and Anhang, J. (2009), 'Livestock and Climate Change: What if the Key Actors in Climate Change Are – Cows, Pigs, and Chickens?', *World Watch*, Nov./Dec.: 10–19.

Green, B.M. (1978), *Eating Oil: Energy Use in Food Production* (Boulder, CO: Westview Press).

Gregrory, P.J. and Ingram, J.S.I. (2008), 'Climate Change and the Current "Food Crisis"', *CAB Reviews: Perspectives in Agriculture, Veterinary Science, Nutrition and Natural Resources*, 3 (99): 1–10.

HM Treasury and Defra (2005), 'A Vision for the Common Agricultural Policy' (London: HM Treasury and the Department for Environment, Food and Rural Affairs).

Hot Springs Conference (1943), 'Final Act of the Hot Springs [VA] Conference, 18 May–3 June 1943', http://www.worldfooddayusa.org/?Id=16367 (accessed 3 April 2012).

IAASTD (2008), 'Global Report and Synthesis Report' (London: International Assessment of Agricultural Science and Technology Development Knowledge).

Ingram, J.S.I. (2011), 'A Food Systems Approach to Researching Interactions between Food Security and Global Environmental Change', *Food Security*, 3: 417–31.

IPCC (2007), *Intergovernmental Panel on Climate Change Fourth Assessment Report: Climate Change 2007: The Physical Science Basis: Summary for Policymakers*, http://www.ipcc.ch/SPM2feb07.pdf (accessed 24 June 2008).

Lang, T. (2008), 'Food Security: Are We Sleep-Walking into a Crisis?' (London: City Leaders Lecture, City University), http://www.city.ac.uk/news/archive/2008/03_March/04032008_1.html (accessed 3 April 2012).

Lang, T., Rayner, G., and Kaelin, E. (2006), 'The Food Industry, Diet, Physical Activity and Health: A Review of Reported Commitments and Practice of 25 of the World's Largest Food Companies' (London: City University Centre for Food Policy).

Lang, T., Barling, D., and Caraher, M. (2009), *Food Policy: Integrating Health, Environment and Society* (Oxford: Oxford University Press).

Liverman, D. and Kapadia, K. (2010), 'Food Systems and the Global Environment: An Overview', in J. Ingram, P. Ericksen, and D. Liverman (eds), *Security and Global Environmental Change* (London: Earthscan).

Lyutse, S. (2010), 'The One Billion Ton Opportunity Cont'd, Part IV: Diet and Food Waste', *Switchboard: Natural Resources Defense Council Staff Blog* (Washington DC: Natural Resources Defense Council).

Malthus, T.R. (1798), *An Essay on the Principle of Population, as It Affects the Future Improvement of Society with Remarks on the Speculations of Mr. Godwin, M. Condorcet and Other Writers* (London: Printed for J. Johnson).

Malthus, T.R. (1815), *The Grounds of an Opinion on the Policy of Restricting the Importation of Foreign Corn: Intended as an Appendix to 'Observations on the Corn Law'* (London: John Murray & J. Johnson).

Maxwell, S. (2001), 'The Evolution of Thinking About Food Security', in S. Devereux and S. Maxwell (eds), *Food Security in Sub-Saharan Africa* (London: ITDG Publishing), 13–31.

OECD and FAO (2008), 'Agricultural Outlook 2008–2017' (Rome/Paris: Organisation for Economic Co-operation and Development/Food and Agriculture Organisation).

Ostry, A.S. (2006), *Nutrition Policy in Canada, 1870–1939* (Vancouver: UBC Press), 143.

Paillard, S., Treyer, S., and Dorin, B. (eds) (2011), *Agrimonde: Scenarios and Challenges for Feeding the World in 2050* (Paris: Editions Quae).

Parfitt, J., Barthel, M., and Macnaughton, S. (2010), 'Food Waste within Food Supply Chains: Quantification and Potential for Change to 2050', *Philosophical Transactions of the Royal Society B: Biological Sciences*, 365 (1554): 3065–81.

PMSEIC (Australia) (2010), 'Australia and Food Security in a Changing World' (Canberra: Science, Engineering and Innovation Council of Australia).

Rockström, J. *et al.* (2009), 'Planetary Boundaries: Exploring the Safe Operating Space for Humanity', *Ecology and Society*, 14 (2): 32, http://www.ecology andsociety.org/vol14/iss2/art32/ (accessed 3 April 2012).

SAI (2008), 'Sustainable Agriculture Initiative Platform' (Brussels: Sustainable Agriculture Initiative), http://www.saiplatform.org/ (accessed 3 April 2012).

Shaw, D.J. (2007), *World Food Security: A History since 1945* (London: Palgrave Macmillan).

Stern, N. (2008), *The Economics of Climate Change: The Stern Review* (Cambridge: Cambridge University Press).

Thaler, R. and Sunstein, C. (2008), *Nudge: Improving Decisions About Health, Wealth, and Happiness* (New Haven, CT: Yale University Press).

Tukker, A., Huppes, G., Guinée, J., Heijungs, R., de Koning, A., van Oers, L., *et al.* (2006), 'Environmental Impact of Products (Eipro): Analysis of the Life Cycle Environmental Impacts Related to the Final Consumption of the Eu-25. Eur 22284 En' (Brussels: European Commission Joint Research Centre).

Vernon, J. (2007), *Hunger: A Modern History* (Cambridge, MA: Harvard University Press).

Von Braun, J. (2007), 'The World Food Situation: New Driving Forces and Required Actions' (Washington DC: International Food Policy Research Institute).

4.2
Human resilience in the face of biodiversity tipping points at local and regional scales[1]

PATRICIA HOWARD

Perspective

Biodiversity, in its broadest sense, is life on Earth. It has been characterized as a 'concept, a measurable entity, and a social or political construct' (Jax 2010). In this last sense, biodiversity is charged with great religious, aesthetic, moral, and economic meanings that vary according to the observer. For ecologists, the broad definition includes genetic diversity, species diversity, and ecosystem diversity, whereas a common narrower definition is the diversity of species (on Earth, in biomes, in ecosystems). Its relevance for biologists and ecologists is usually cast in evolutionary terms or in terms of ecosystem functioning, which some economists refer to as ecosystem services. Ecosystem services are defined as the benefits that humans derive from ecosystem functions or processes. Thus, the relationship between biodiversity change, ecosystem functioning, and ecosystem services has become central to contemporary scientific understanding of biodiversity and human well-being, as well as to a multitude of policies that seek to assess and address human well-being, environmental degradation, and global environmental change. There is great debate and uncertainty about the relations between biodiversity and ecosystem functioning, about the significance of change in biodiversity for ecosystem

[1] This work is based on the 'Human Adaptation to Biodiversity Change' Project NE/1004122/1, which was partly funded with support from the Ecosystem Services for Poverty Alleviation (ESPA) programme. The ESPA programme is funded by the Department for International Development (DfID), the Economic and Social Research Council (ESRC) and the Natural Environment Research Council (NERC).

functioning, and indeed for evolution. This necessarily creates much uncertainty about the nature of the relationship between biodiversity and human well-being. In spite of such uncertainty, which affects all assessments of the actual and potential threats to human well-being from biodiversity change, there is broad agreement that the implications of current and projected levels of biodiversity change for human well-being are, in most instances, major and possibly dire, at local, regional, and global scales.

Most people across the globe will feel the direct impacts of local biodiversity change, but everyone is likely to feel the indirect impacts, since local changes can connect to create global repercussions. One set of such impacts arises from the rapid emergence and transmission of new infectious diseases and pests that threaten plants and animals (and thus the humans that depend upon them), as well as humans (see e.g. Chivian and Bernstein 2008; Pongsiri 2009; Keesing *et al.* 2010). A second set is presented by 'biodiversity tipping points' that may emerge at regional scale, such as the loss of the Amazon rainforest or the collapse of coral reefs, that will have extra-regional or even global repercussions not only due to the loss of species and ecosystems, but also due to the loss of ecosystem services that these provide at higher scales. A third set of impacts results from the reconfiguration of ecosystems (including tipping into alternative ecosystem states) resulting from changes in species range, phenology, and abundance, which in turn provoke changes in ecosystem functions and associated human benefits. It also includes the loss of single species in particular contexts, such as 'cultural keystone' species or ecological keystone, engineer, or framework species. An example is the threat posed by the loss of functional groups of species, such as pollinators (see e.g. Potts *et al.* 2010), which has major implications for ecosystem productivity and the provision of benefits such as food, fibre, and fuels. A fourth set of direct and indirect impacts arises from human maladaptation to any of these threats.

To adapt successfully to biodiversity tipping points requires major changes in values, priorities, and institutions, particularly economic institutions. Some of this change may be forthcoming but much is unlikely to happen quickly or profoundly enough. A first step is to recognize the implications of biodiversity change and potential tipping points for human welfare. A second is to take urgent measures to mitigate such change, and a third is to consider potential responses to early warnings. This chapter focuses on the first and the third of these options, principally in relation to societies that are directly and highly dependent on biodiversity, since it is these populations that are (a) most immediately vulnerable to such change, and (b) most important to preserving both the planet's biodiversity and humanity's adaptive capacity.

Types, magnitudes and drivers of biodiversity change

We find ourselves in a period when rates of species extinctions could range between 50 and 500 times background losses, which is the highest rate in the past 65 million years. The effects have been summarized as:

> Changes in species' geographic ranges, genetic risks of extinction, genetic assimilation, natural selection, mutation rates, the shortening of food chains, the increase in nutrient-enriched niches permitting the ascendancy of microbes, and the differential survival of ecological generalists. Rates of evolutionary processes will change in different groups, and speciation in the larger vertebrates is essentially over . . . Whether the biota will continue to provide the dependable ecological services humans take for granted is less clear . . . Our inability to make clearer predictions about the future of evolution has serious consequences for both biodiversity and humanity.
>
> (Woodruff 2001: 5471)

The consequences for biodiversity and humanity depend in part on the timescale. Some scientists argue that the Earth's sixth extinction has already arrived, where an estimated loss of over 75 per cent of species can be expected, possibly within 250 to 500 years (Barnosky *et al.* 2011). Others highlight the fact that projections of species extinction rates are controversial (Pereira *et al.* 2010). A mass extinction hardly bodes well for humans, given the changes in the biosphere, in biomes and ecosystems, the associated pest and disease outbreaks, etc. that are associated with the different drivers of biodiversity change, and the possible critical thresholds or tipping points discussed below and in other chapters presented here. Thus, the implications of what is laid out below are magnified manyfold and their effects become increasingly synergistic over time – 500 years is a very short period when we consider that *Homininae* appeared 8 million years ago, *Homo sapiens* 500,000 years ago, and modern humans 200,000 years ago. Were humans to have a council of elders to deliberate the impact of our activities on future generations, they would certainly be extraordinarily alarmed and calling for radical transformations, as, indeed, are many scientists today.

What is extraordinary about this possible sixth extinction of species is that, for the first time in the Earth's history, a species is actually in a position to change the course of evolution writ large (Western 2001; Pereira *et al.* 2010). This is reflected in the wide range of projected changes in biodiversity, because 'there are major opportunities to intervene through better policies, but also because of large uncertainties in projections' (Pereira *et al.* 2010: 1496).

The causes of species extinctions and related changes in biodiversity and ecosystem services can be characterized as synergistic stressors – climatic change coupled with 'abnormally high ecological stressors' and 'unusual interactions' (e.g. between human-induced climate change, habitat fragmentation, pollution, overharvesting, invasive species, pathogens and, some would add, the 'expanding human biomass' (Barnosky *et al.* 2011), although one could just as easily add 'expanding livestock biomass' or 'expanding biofuels production' (Steinfeld *et al.* 2010; Wise *et al.* 2009)). Beyond this, humans have had a massive impact on the productivity, composition, and diversity of terrestrial ecosystems by changing the rates of supply of major nutrients (nitrogen, phosphorus, and atmospheric CO_2), altering regional fire frequencies, and relaxing biogeographic barriers to species dispersal (Tilman and Lehman 2001). Many human-dominated ecosystems are characterized by high natural resource extraction, short food chains, food web simplification, habitat and landscape homogeneity, heavy use of petrochemicals and fossil fuels, convergent soil characteristics, modified hydrological cycles, reduced biotic and physical disturbance regimes, and global mobility of people, goods, and services (Western 2001).

A great concern to biologists and ecologists is the uneven ability of species to change their range, or distributions, in response to climate change (CBD 2007). If individual species are not able to change their range, they are likely to be lost (Root and Hughes 2005; Malcolm *et al.* 2005). It also highlights a second major concern, which is the break-up of species associations and communities, which will result in further extinctions and also in major ecological changes that occur as new species associations form and species richness potentially decreases. Meta-analyses indicate that temperature rises in the twentieth century have led to shifts in species' range toward the poles that average 6.1 km per decade (Williams *et al.* 2007). Species with high dispersal capabilities may migrate at the rate of one kilometre per year or more, so that these species, together with climatically tolerant species, are likely to dominate many of the Earth's ecosystems. Scientists also argue that species are less able to adapt to climate warming today than at any other period in the last 10,000 years, due to the faster pace of change and to human-induced ecosystem changes, especially habitat change, which limit the possibilities for species to migrate and to adapt (Thomas *et al.* 2004). Both biodiversity losses and changes in species range can have multiple repercussions on ecosystems, in part due to changing species composition and richness.

Biodiversity-related tipping points

The tipping points (or critical threshold) concept has only quite recently been directly linked to the term 'biodiversity'. The concept of biodiversity tipping points is generally closely allied to an ecosystems perspective, where it is thought that there are a number of key variables and dynamics that have a determining role in the organization of an ecosystem. Within any given system, there are alternative stable states (or 'stability regimes'). For example, shallow lakes may be at one equilibrium with clear water and aquatic plants in place, or at another equilibrium where turbid water and a lack of vegetation persist (Scheffer *et al.* 2001). Beyond some limit, if there are even minor changes in the system, it can move over a threshold (or 'tipping point') into an alternative stable state that may be desirable or undesirable from the standpoint of the goods and services that it provides.

Not all ecosystem tipping points are closely related to biodiversity. But it appears that a large majority are, even though it is not always species diversity that plays a key role – it may be species abundance or only a few functionally important species. Scheffer's (2009) work on critical transitions addresses lakes, oceans, and terrestrial ecosystems as case studies. Table 4.3 presents examples from terrestrial ecosystems where biodiversity change is central to the dynamics. In such cases, there are three types of relations that can be discerned where biodiversity change is related to tipping points in ecosystems:

1. Biodiversity change is driven by exogenous driver(s) (e.g. climate change).
2. There are feedbacks between biodiversity change and an exogenous driver (e.g. climate change–vegetation feedbacks).
3. Biodiversity change is the direct driver of change leading to tipping points.

An example of the first dynamic is change in species' phenology due to warming or changes in precipitation that lead to changes in species' range or outbreaks of pests and diseases and thus reorganization of ecosystems. Examples of the second dynamic are the climate–vegetation feedbacks indicated in Table 4.3. Examples of the third are deforestation leading to changes in albedo, overhunting of large predators leading to the collapse of a trophic level, or certain 'self-organizing' effects of particular species. While each of these dynamics can lead to tipping points, in many cases all three may be occurring simultaneously and acting in synergy or antagonistically at different scales, but generally synergies between them lead to the highest probability of reaching tipping points.

A recent assessment of the vulnerability of Australian ecosystems to tipping points (Laurance *et al.* 2011) classified them into three sets according to the 'severity' of the tipping point: 'tipping' ecosystems, which are 'likely to experience profound regime changes across most or all of their geographic range'; 'dipping' ecosystems, which experience such profound change but in geographically limited areas; and 'stripping' ecosystems which are 'being stripped of important ecosystem components, such as their small mammal, amphibian, or large predator fauna, but such changes are more insidious and less visually apparent than major regime changes'. Laurance *et al.* identified a number of intrinsic features of what they considered to be the ten most vulnerable ecosystems, as well as the major environmental threats. Of the seven intrinsic features identified, four relate directly to the species composition of these ecosystems: the history of habitat fragmentation; reliance on ecosystem engineers; reliance on framework species; and reliance on predators or keystone mutualists. Of the environmental threats, five (or six, depending on the causes of salinization) are related to climate change, one to pollution, and the rest to biodiversity change (habitat reduction, habitat fragmentation, changed fire regimes, invasives, overexploitation, and pests and pathogens). They found that most vulnerable ecosystems are threatened by multiple drivers, where synergies between drivers are pervasive and directly contribute to the likelihood of tipping points.

Recently, potential biodiversity-related tipping points have been identified that are seen to have larger-scale regional effects, where such effects are of great concern not only because of the implications these have for large numbers of smaller-scale ecosystems and the people who inhabit them, but also for global biodiversity per se, and for their potential contributions to other Earth systems tipping points. Leadley *et al.* (2010: 8) concluded that major biodiversity transformations will occur at levels near or below a low level of only 2°C global warming, including 'widespread

Table 4.3 Examples of 'biodiversity' tipping points in terrestrial ecosystems (derived from Scheffer 2009: 216–39)

Dynamic	Ecosystem examples	Alternative states
Climate–vegetation feedbacks through albedo effects	Drylands – Sahel-Sahara – decrease in temperature contrast between ocean and land, weakening monsoon circulation	From wet vegetation state to desert state – drier conditions and loss of vegetation drove transition
Climate–vegetation feedbacks through transpiration	Amazon – deforestation decreases local moisture recycling	From wet forested state to dry savannah, and semi-desert, with expansion of tropical forest northward
Small-scale transitions in semi-arid vegetation	Herbivore mortality events trigger forest expansion	African savannah – Rinderpest epidemic reduced ungulate numbers allowing large-scale woodland expansion, then human-induced fire eliminated woodlands, and the open landscape again maintained by large herbivores
	Rare extreme weather events may trigger woodland expansion	Newly established vegetation may maintain itself through diverse mechanisms
	Self-organized vegetation patterns – transport of nutrients and water from barren land to vegetation patches	Loss of vegetation patches leads to desertic conditions devoid of perennial vegetation
	Alpine tree lines and lowland tree islands – sharp natural boundaries maintained through microclimates and soils	

Forest–climate feedback in boreal regions	Boreal forest deforestation increases albedo effect, leading to cooling; global warming may promote forest expansion	Regional amplifier of global warming; terrestrial vegetation can affect ocean circulation patterns
	Lichen woodlands – closed lichen mat prevents tree recruitment	Quebec – shift from forest to lichen woodlands provoked by spruce budworm and fire
	Insect outbreaks – warm dry weather gives boost to spruce budworms	Cycles between spruce/fir-dominated to aspen/birch dominance, with moose browsing leading to shift back to spruce
Formation of raised bogs	Form in wet climates when shallow open waters are filled with organic matter – peat mosses achieve dominance	Semi-terrestrial states become bogs; atmospheric nitrogen input and drainage lead to vascular plant-dominated system
Species extinction in fragmented landscapes	Allee effect – e.g. positive feedback between meta-population size and local population size	Meta-population goes extinct through excessive fragmentation, may have cascading effects, e.g. loss of fish leading to switch in turbidity to clear state in ponds and lakes
Epidemics	Epidemics occur only beyond critical thresholds of population density and eventually vanish, but system tips	Transformation of boreal forest to lichen plains from spruce budworm; collapse of Caribbean coral reefs from disease in sea urchins

coral reef degradation, large shifts in marine plankton community structure especially in the Arctic ocean, extensive invasion of tundra by boreal forest, destruction of many coastal ecosystems, etc.' They found that 'the risk of catastrophic biodiversity loss . . . has been substantially underestimated in previous global biodiversity assessments . . . Most of the biodiversity tipping points that we have identified will be accompanied by large negative regional or global scale impacts on ecosystem services and human well-being.' The main regional tipping points they identified are presented in the box below.

Possible regional tipping points with global repercussions (from Leadley *et al.* 2010)

The Amazon Forest 'due to the interaction of deforestation, fire and climate change, undergoes a widespread dieback, changing from rainforest to savanna or seasonal forest over wide areas, especially in the East and South of the biome. The forest could move into a self-perpetuating cycle in which fires become more frequent, drought more intense and dieback accelerates. Dieback of the Amazon will have global impacts through increased carbon emissions, accelerating climate change. It will also lead to regional rainfall reductions that could compromise the sustainability of regional agriculture' (p. 24). See also Toby Gardiner (4.3).

The African Sahel: 'under pressure from climate change and over-use of limited land resources, [the Sahel] shifts to alternative, degraded states, further driving desertification. Severe impacts on biodiversity and agricultural productivity result. Continued degradation of the Sahel has caused and could continue to cause loss of biodiversity and shortages of food, fibre and water in Western Africa' (p. 24). See Emily Boyd (7.2).

Island Ecosystems 'are afflicted by a cascading set of extinctions and ecosystem instabilities, due to the impact of invasive alien species . . . As the invaded communities become increasingly altered and impoverished, vulnerability to new invasions may increase . . . Because islands are the global hotspot for endemic species local

---

eliminations often constitute global extinctions . . . [There are also] large negative impacts of many invasive species on ecosystem services such as plant productivity, nutrient cycling, water supply, etc.' (p. 23).

The Tundra: 'boreal forests will permanently replace tundra eco-systems if current trends of greenhouse gas emissions persist . . . These changes in tundra systems substantially increase climate warming in many models. Permafrost melting and changes in game availability have already heavily impacted some indigenous popu-lations and these impacts are likely to become widespread and severe over the coming decades . . . The invasion of tundra by boreal forests can have a profound impact on global temperatures since low surface albedo from boreal forests during the winter season warms climate compared to tundra' (p. 53).

Coastal Terrestrial Systems and Sea-level rise of 20–60 cm or more by 2100 are likely and will continue for many centuries, with greatest impacts on coastal wetlands where sediment elevations are reduced, and where species migration landward is prohibited due to physio-graphic setting or urban development. Biodiversity impacts are large due to habitat loss and ecosystem area loss and degradation will increase 'coastal hazards to human settlements, reduce coastal water quality, release large quantities of stored carbon, etc.' (p. 25).

Marine Fisheries: The tipping point consists of changes in the composition of marine communities, where large predator popu-lations collapse and communities are dominated by organisms lower in the food chain where, in addition to overfishing, ocean warming and acidification are additional threats to marine biodiversity. 'Allowing global ocean fisheries to reach a tipping-point will not only affect marine biodiversity but it will also undermine life on the planet because of the immense importance of the global ocean to biogeochemical cycles . . . Total fish catch in the global ocean may be reduced to up to a tenth of its peak amount by 2048. This will result in significant negative economic and social effects, especially on some of the world's most vulnerable human communities' (p. 117).

Tropical Coral Reefs: These global biodiversity hotspots 'provide a broad range of ecosystems services with high socio-economic value: tourism, fisheries (food and employment), nutrient cycling, climate regulation, protection of the shoreline and other ecosystems (e.g. mangroves), and constitute the habitat for a wide range of species', but rising CO_2 concentrations will lead to levels of acidification that severely impede calcium carbonate accretion, while global warming leads to coral bleaching. 'If current trends continue coral reef ecosystems may undergo regime shifts from coral to sponge or algae dominated habitats. The tipping point for this phase shift is estimated to be a sea-surface temperature increase of 2°C and/or atmospheric CO_2 concentrations above 480 ppm (estimated to occur by 2050)' (p. 125).

Not all scientists agree with the projections about potential tipping points. For example, Willis *et al.* (2010) argue that fossil records covering intervals of time when magnitudes and rates of climate change were similar to those projected for the twenty-first century show that these were not associated with large-scale biodiversity extinctions. They note that one of the most biodiverse periods in the neotropics occurred during the Eocene Climatic Optimum (53–51 million years ago), when atmospheric CO_2 exceeded 1200 ppmv and tropical temperatures were 5–10 degrees warmer than now. The tropical forest biome extended to mid-latitudes in the northern and southern hemisphere and there was no ice at the poles. They note that models presume less ecological tolerance of species than is likely and that finer-grained resolution models predict far lower extinction rates than grosser resolution models. However, a World Bank report (Vergara and Scholtz 2011) also models CO_2 effects and concludes that the synergies between climate change, deforestation, and forest fires could well lead to major impacts as soon as 2025.

Regional level biodiversity tipping points and human resilience

There is a pressing need to begin to assess the vulnerabilities of different groups of people to the pain and suffering, and loss of livelihoods (and

114

indeed of life) associated with potential and real biodiversity-related tipping points. As a case in point, some scientists predict that much of the Amazon basin region could surpass a tipping point described in the box above, with some of it 'flipping' to savannah. A World Bank-sponsored modelling exercise that assessed this threat found that, with the interacting effects of climate change, deforestation, and fire, 'Substantial impacts are already projected by 2025 and the situation worsens by 2050. The effect of climate change alone would contribute to reduce the extent of the rainforest biome by one third by the end of the century' (Vergara and Scholtz 2011). Vergara presented a qualitative assessment of the likely implications:

> Direct economic losses . . . include yields and areas for specific crops in tropical areas . . . as temperatures increase and rainfall patterns are modified, and the ideal areas for different crops shift . . . dieback may reduce rainfall in agricultural areas in southern Brazil . . . Sustainable forestry would also be affected . . . [and the] magnitude of the carbon sink would likewise be diminished. In addition, weather extremes, longer dry periods, disappearance or reduction of dry-period rainfalls and increased intensity during rainy periods would all affect stream-flow regulation. This would have an impact on the firm capacity of existing hydropower plants and on the water storage capacity of future investments.
>
> (Vergara 2010: 74–75)

The 2011 report called for 'a full account of losses . . . a better valuation of the financial and natural capital represented by the Amazon ecosystem is required as well as a more comprehensive assessment of the economic implications of its potential dieback' (Vergara and Scholtz 2011: 63). The concern, however, is not for the impacts on human beings, but for 'economic losses', 'financial and natural capital', 'yields', and so forth. What, then, might be anticipated for human well-being in the region? Toby Gardiner (4.3) looks at this, but here are some possible outcomes that might be derived from the World Bank study:

- The livelihoods base of many indigenous forest peoples (perhaps a majority of the 349 ethnic groups) might collapse, which might lead to their virtual disappearance.
- There would be loss of much non-indigenous agriculture, fisheries, and forest industries and thus loss or collapse of self-sufficient production as well as rural employment in the areas worst affected.
- Rural populations would be regionally displaced in order to continue to fish, farm, and harvest forests.
- Rural–urban migration would occur on a mass scale.

- There would be chronic water, food, and energy shortages in urban areas, affecting nearly all populations but particularly the majority, who are poor.
- High unemployment in urban areas would result from direct and indirect loss of economic activities, including tourism.
- National and regional level economic crises would result from loss of export revenues, rising social insecurity, and attempts to substitute for lost ecosystem services.
- There would be increasing conflict, violence, and social instability at sub-national, national, and even inter-basin levels.
- Unemployment and displacement would result in high levels of migration to other nations and continents.

The implications for human welfare beyond the region might not be limited to the ramifications for downstream and upstream markets and employment (e.g. timber, soya, meat, minerals, etc.) and the regional and global financial system, or to the effects of international migration flows or national and regional conflicts. As the Amazon tips from a net greenhouse gas absorber to a net source of greenhouse gases, it will be extremely difficult to avoid exceeding 'dangerous' levels of global warming even if CO_2 reductions in other areas are achieved (Cox *et al.* 2003), with all of the implications that this has for humanity's efforts at climate change mitigation and adaptation.

Whether or not such scenarios closely or remotely reflect our possible futures, there are very strong reasons to develop them carefully and systematically based upon our best current knowledge, and for policymakers and for the public to pay close attention. Had scientists neglected to make clear the potential consequences of nuclear war for humanity and the types of devastation that were implied, it is possible that such a war would not have been averted until now. Knowing the implications for human suffering and for the future of the human species (e.g. from a possible nuclear winter) has been of inestimable importance in mobilizing public and political support on all sides of the political spectrum to limit nuclear weapons and avoid even limited nuclear warfare.

At the same time, there are very important measures that we must begin to take with equal seriousness at local scales. Adaptation to local-scale tipping points can have very major repercussions not only for regional and global level environmental change and equity, but also for human resilience in the face of local, regional, and global tipping points of all sorts.

Bio-cultural diversity and resilience

Humans have substantially altered some 77 per cent of the Earth's ice-free land, half of which is in agricultural or urban use (Ellis and Ramankutty 2008). Throughout much of human existence, humans have altered eco-systems and the biodiversity that these contain in the effort to ensure liveli-hoods and cultural integrity across generations. In the process, humans have often intentionally increased the biodiversity that is useful to them for food, fibre, fodder, fuel, medicinal uses, cash, and other cultural purposes, and this has modified landscapes in ways that support a multitude of other life forms. Most of the world's terrestrial biodiversity exists outside of protected areas in biologically and ecologically complex human-dominated landscapes.

Biodiversity constitutes the principal form of wealth for a large part of humanity. This includes about 2.8 billion people who live in rural areas of the least developed countries, 2.4 billion of whom subsist from agriculture. They constitute nearly 35 per cent of the world's population (FAO 2004), and feed a considerably larger proportion of the world's population. About half of the world's farmers rely on no- or low-input agroforestry farming systems ('traditional agriculture') (World Bank 2002), which generally tend to be biodiversity-rich polycultures (Vandermeer 2002). Nearly 250 million people live in forests and depend on them to a high degree, while some 60 million indigenous people are almost wholly dependent on forest bio-diversity for their livelihoods (World Bank 2002). Another 50 million people in developing countries depend on small-scale fisheries (ICLARM 2001).

It is estimated that about a billion people regularly consume wild foods (Sunderland 2011: 266, citing Pimentel *et al.* 1997). While there is no global inventory of all plant species that have direct-use values for humans, PROSEA (Plant Resources of South-East Asia)[2] recorded nearly 6000 species that are used in that region, which Heywood (1999) extrapolated to some 18,000–25,000 species for the tropics as a whole – excluding the 25,000 species that are herbal medicines.[3] The FAO Global Databank on Animal

---

[2] See http://www.prosea.nl/.

[3] Heywood (1999) noted that the Andres Bello Convention (involving Bolivia, Colombia, Chile, Ecuador, Spain, Panama, Peru, and Venezuela) has identified over a thousand native species that have 'not been extensively domesticated, are underutilised, or little known but with eco-nomic potential'. 'Another major source of agro-biodiversity is the tens of thousands of species that are grown in a pre- or semi-domesticated state on home gardens or similar polycultures . . . many thousands more are harvested wild to supplement farm household incomes . . . [but] our knowledge of their most basic biology and agronomy is virtually non-existent and we must depend on knowledge developed over long periods by local farming societies.'

Genetic Resources (covering 182 countries) contains a total of 14,017 live-stock breeds (FAO 2007), and it is estimated that humans consume around 1200 insect species (DeFoliart 2012). It is not only tropical biodiversity that directly supports humans – even in the Arctic, people consume in excess of a hundred local species, which represent the traditional and nutritionally rich components of their diets (Kuhnlein and Receveur 1996). About 1.3 billion people live from 'environmentally fragile' lands (World Bank 2003), where environmental disturbances and disequilibria are the rule rather than the exception, and people must be adapted to living with environmental hazard, risk, and extremes. Biological resources constitute the foundations of these people's cultural and material heritage, and the substance of the knowledge and practices that they pass on to future generations (Balée and Erickson 2006; Salick and Byg 2007).

Some small-scale societies are heavily dependent on only a few species, and some of these are located in areas that are relatively poor in biological diversity, as is the case with Touareg camel pastoralists in the Sahara, Inuit caribou hunters in northern Canada, and date palm (*Phoenix dactylifera* L.) farmers in the Arabian Peninsula. Even small changes in local biodiversity can present major threats to these populations' food supply and to the availability of fuel, medicine, fibre, construction materials, and other plant- and animal-derived resources. Some live in areas that are very rich in biological diversity – such as the Nuaulu of Seram who depend on sago palm (*Metroxylon sagu*), Amerindian swidden gardeners who exchange cassava (*Manihot esculenta*) in Amazonia, or Ethiopian Aari ensete (*E. ventricosum*) producers. Such species are considered to be 'cultural keystones', so important are they to livelihoods, social organization, and cultural identity (Christancho and Vining 2004; Garabaldi and Turner 2004). These species have ecological and cultural functions that are not readily substitutable, which renders the populations that depend on them more vulnerable to abrupt change. The loss of such species, or of the species that these same species depend upon (e.g. pasture grasses that camels consume), or an outbreak of a pest or disease that seriously affects the productivity of these species, could create many adverse effects not only for livelihoods, but also for social organization and demographics. Nevertheless, global biodiversity assessments focus on ecological keystone species while ignoring such cultural keystones. Accordingly, the vulnerability of populations that are dependent on a few species when facing biodiversity change is as yet largely unexplored, so their vulnerability is unrecorded.

Yet highly biodiversity-dependent societies may offer better prospects for continued evolution given biodiversity tipping points in comparison with systems that are highly dependent on external inputs (e.g. fossil fuels, chemicals, irrigation) and markets, with high population densities and high demands on natural resources and ecosystem services close to ecosystem thresholds. Adapting intensive systems to biodiversity change generally implies even greater intensification. Pest outbreaks, for example, are fought with higher levels of pesticide use, weed invasions with more herbicides, and soil biodiversity loss leads to higher levels of fertilizer use, which are likely to further compound the negative consequences of biodiversity change, price increases, etc. (see e.g. Lal 2007; IFDC 2008; Pimentel and Pimentel 2008; Smil 2008). Tim Lang and John Ingram discussed the context in Chapter 4.1.

Dobson *et al.* (2006) provided a general framework for understanding the ecological consequences of species and population losses for a partial collapse of ecosystems that they relate to habitat loss, but that may also be seen as applicable in relation to other drivers of change. They note that decreases in biodiversity should lead to reductions in ecosystem functioning, but this depends in part on the order in which species are lost or gained. If only a few species provide a function or service, decline in the service may be rapid if these species decline or disappear. Other services may be provided by functionally redundant competing species, so decline in one species is compensated by the increase in another. When habitats degrade, species at higher trophic levels are usually lost more rapidly than those at lower levels, and species at different trophic levels perform different ecosystem functions, so 'we might expect to see a predictable hierarchical loss of ecosystem services as habitats are eroded' (p. 1917).

The loss of some species at a specific trophic level may occur slowly and be compensated by the remaining species, until a point is reached through further species loss when a drastic decrease in ecosystem services occurs. At the other extreme, if the trophic level consists of a few rare or fragile species, then small changes in species biodiversity may result in large and rapid changes in ecosystem services. Most ecosystems will fall somewhere between these two boundaries, where 'a linear decrease in the service [follows] as each species is lost . . . in essence, the loss of each individual species results in the loss of a "unit" of ecosystem service' (p. 1918). Dobson *et al.* provide a table (Table 1, p. 1919) that relates the susceptibility of different ecosystem functions to species loss for different ecosystems. Their model suggests that 'the collapse of ecosystem services will be determined by a hierarchical series of nested thresholds, or breakpoints, whose magnitude will occur at different levels of decline in overall species abundance' where the most resilient species are at the bottom, and the least at the top, of the food chain (acknowledging that there are exceptions). They conclude that:

> because different ecosystem services tend to be undertaken by species at different trophic levels and because trophic webs will tend first to thin and then collapse from top to bottom, we would expect to see a predictable hierarchical and sequential loss of the economic goods and services by natural ecosystems as they become eroded and degraded by anthropogenic activities.
> (Dobson *et al.* 2006: 1925)

They warn that current dis-attention to the goods and services provided by species at different trophic levels means that there is also limited incentive to conserve these species.

The first requirement of any analysis of biodiversity change must be to characterize and understand the types of dependencies, or inter-dependencies, that different human population groups have with: rare or fragile species; cultural, ecosystem or economic keystone species; specific trophic levels; specific functional groups; and specific ecosystem services. The second is to deal with the question of how people are likely to adapt or maladapt to such phenomena. Tipping points do not occur overnight. Many ecosystems, trophic levels, etc. are already crossing thresholds towards alternative states; others are manifesting 'early warnings' (e.g. slower recovery from perturbations, increasing variance, increasing autocorrelation, flickering, and increased spatial coherence) (Scheffer 2009; Scheffer *et al.* 2009). Early warnings related to biodiversity loss have already been identified (e.g. for invasive species, see EEA 2010; for biodiversity change in general, see the indicators used in the Swiss Biodiversity Monitoring System[4]), and there is now a very interesting attempt to identify early warning indicators of biodiversity change in relation to local livelihoods in small island developing states in relation to the vulnerability of the rural poor, the status of resources important to nutrition, for food and medicine, and for access and benefit sharing, among others (Teelucksingh and Perrings 2010).

It is no coincidence that the globe's sixth extinction of species is occurring together with an unprecedented extinction of human cultures, where both are driven by similar underlying phenomena, and thus the current biodiversity crisis should be reconceived as a crisis of 'bio-cultural

---

[4] http://www.biodiversitymonitoring.ch/english/aktuell/portal.php.

diversity' (e.g. Sutherland 2003; Maffi 2005; Rozzi 2012). Half of the globe's cultures/languages are likely to be lost by the end of this century; at least as high a proportion of many rural subsistence socio-ecological systems are likely to disappear, as is the case, for example, of the San Bushmen of the Kalahari (e.g. Hitchcock 2006), the Ifaguo of the Philippines (Guimbatan and Baguilat 2006), and the Hani in Southwest China (Xu *et al.* 2009). Campaigns for the preservation of endangered cultures are rare; in fact, such cultures are often portrayed as the cause of species' loss and the provokers of degradation of forests and other areas that are mistakenly considered by outsiders to be 'pristine' environments.[5]

Scientists and policymakers often think that our resilience as a species is based on science, technology, economic growth, accumulated wealth, and modern democratic institutions, whereas in fact it is more likely to be based on the more than 6700 cultures/languages[6] across the globe that have evolved vast knowledge, technologies, and a myriad of institutions that have managed largely to meet the human needs that these have culturally defined, most often without compromising, and usually by enhancing, their natural base of existence, at times over millennia. Prioritizing and supporting such rural subsistence societies could be seen as a global insurance policy, so that the cultures, biodiversity, agro-biodiversity and ecosystem services that are crucial to the world's future continue to exist. The study of such systems and the ways in which traditional peoples maintain and use biodiversity can speed the emergence of the agro-ecological principles which are urgently needed to develop more sustainable agro-ecosystems and agro-biodiversity conservation strategies both in industrial and developing countries (Denevan 1995).

If we are indeed to be able to negotiate tipping points and meet the unprecedented challenges that we face as a species, we must transform our

---

[5] In the West, even the term 'culture' is widely misunderstood (e.g. known in reference to the arts) or regarded with suspicion: it is not generally considered to be the subject of serious policy attention or scientific inquiry, and is conveniently bundled off into underfunded disciplines such as anthropology and sociology.

[6] The 6700 languages across the globe are not identical with cultures. However, language is considered as an acceptable proxy for cultures, where UNESCO notes: 'Languages are humankind's principal tools for interacting and for expressing ideas, emotions, knowledge, memories and values. Languages are also primary vehicles of cultural expressions and intangible cultural heritage, essential to the identity of individuals and groups. Safeguarding endangered languages is thus a crucial task in maintaining cultural diversity worldwide' (http://www.unesco.org/culture/ich/index.php?lg=ENandpg=00136).

ways of thinking about our own species, going beyond a simple awareness that places and things of great beauty, harmony, and intrinsic and monetary value are disappearing for ever. It will be necessary to realize that the human race must maintain its cultural and technological options in case our great experiment of 'development' fails.

At this moment, then, we are beginning seriously to wonder whether the 'end-point' of 'development' toward which we have been racing might indeed be the wrong one. Many are coming to realize that, in spite of our vast accumulated wealth of scientific knowledge, we still seem to know very little about how to live in and with the natural world. In fact, we are just beginning to realize that we must attempt to retain the tremendous adaptive capacity, knowledge, and cultural resilience that have allowed people to occupy and thrive in virtually every ecosystem on earth over a long period of time. It is no coincidence that, with biodiversity loss, we are losing the basis of our physical existence, at the same time that we are also losing the basis of our collective resilience with the mass loss of human cultures.

Current adaptation thinking is based on the assumption that adaptation can be rationally planned, funded, and managed or engineered, which downplays the significance of autonomous adaptation at local levels, which anthropological research shows is manifest in mobility, exchange, rationing, resource pooling, diversification, intensification, innovation, and revitalization (Thornton and Manasfi 2010). Such studies suggest that the most resilient and adaptive social unit over long periods may be the household rather than the community or state, and that adaptation must be viewed not as a singular strategy, but as a set of diverse, intersecting decision-making and behaviour-changing processes that may evolve autonomously or through planning in response to a multitude of interacting biotic and non-biotic stressors. Understanding adaptation necessitates understanding of the dynamic flows and feedbacks between natural processes and human intentions and actions. Indeed, the hope is that humans can manage to adapt their social-ecological systems in ways that mitigate biodiversity change, support ecosystem resilience, and ensure human well-being. Human maladaptation will surely spell human and ecological disaster. Supporting human adaptation research and policy-making can only be conducive to adaptation.

References

Balée, W. and Erickson, C. (2006), 'Time, Complexity and Historical Ecology', in W. Balée and C. Erickson (eds), *Time and Complexity in Historical Ecology: Studies in the Neotropical Lowlands* (New York: Columbia University Press), 1–17.

Barnosky, A.D., Matzke, N., Tomiya, S., Wogan, G.O.U., Swartz, B., Quental, T.B., *et al.* (2011), 'Has the Earth's Sixth Mass Extinction Already Arrived?', *Nature*, 471: 51–57.

Chivian, E. and Bernstein, A. (eds) (2008), *Sustaining Life: How Human Health Depends on Biodiversity* (Oxford: Oxford University Press).

Christancho, S. and Vining, J. (2004), 'Culturally Defined Keystone Species', *Human Ecology Review*, 11 (2): 153–64.

Convention on Biological Diversity (CBD), Secretariat (2010), *Global Biodiversity Outlook 3* (Montreal: CBC). Available online at: www.cbd.int/GBO3 (accessed 6 June 2012).

Cox, P.M., Betts, R.A., Collins, M., Harris, P., Huntingford, C., and Jones, C.D. (2003), *Amazon Dieback under Climate-Carbon Cycle Projections for the 21st Century*, Hadley Centre Technical Notes 42 (Exeter: Hadley Centre, Met Office).

DeFoliart, G. (2012), *The Human Use of Insects as a Food Resource: A Bibliographic Account in Progress* (Madison, WI: University of Wisconsin-Madison, Dept. of Entomology), e-book available through: http://www.food-insects.com/ (accessed 5 June 2012).

Denevan, W. (1995), 'Prehistoric Agricultural Methods as Models for Sustainability', *Advances in Plant Pathology*, 11: 21–43.

Dobson, A., Lodge, D., Alder, J., Cumming, G.S., Keymer, J., McGlade, J., *et al.* (2006), 'Habitat Loss, Trophic Collapse, and the Decline of Ecosystem Services', *Ecology*, 87 (8): 1915–24.

Ellis, E.C. and Ramankutty, N. (2008), 'Putting People in the Map: Anthropogenic Biomes of the World', *Frontiers in Ecology and the Environment*, 6 (8): 439–47.

FAO (2007), *The State of the World's Animal Genetic Resources for Food and Agriculture* (Rome: FAO).

Food and Agriculture Organization of the United Nations (2004), *The State of Food and Agriculture 2003–2004* (Rome: FAO).

Garabaldi, A. and Turner, N. (2004), 'Cultural Keystone Species: Implications for Ecological Conservation and Restoration', *Ecology and Society*, 9 (3): article 1.

Guimbatan, R. and Baguilat, T. (2006), 'Misunderstanding the Notion of Conservation in the Philippine Rice Terraces: Cultural Landscapes', *International Social Science Journal* (UNESCO), March: 59–67.

Heywood, V. (1999), 'Trends in Agricultural Biodiversity', in J. Janick (ed.), *Perspectives on New Crops and New Uses* (Alexandria, VA: ASHS Press), 2–14.

Hitchcock, R.K. (2006), '"We Are the Owners of the Land": The Struggle of the San for the Kalahari and Its Resources', in R.K. Hitchcock, K. Ikeya, M. Biesele and R.B. Lee (eds), *Updating the San: Image and Reality of an African People in the 21st Century*, Senri Ethnological Studies 70 (Osaka: National Museum of Ethnology), 229–56.

International Center for Living Aquatic Resources Management (ICLARM) (2001), *ICLARM Medium Term Plan 2002–2004* (Manila: ICLARM).

International Fertilizer Development Center (IFDC) (2008), 'World Fertilizer Prices Soar as Food and Fuel Economies Merge', *IFDC Report*, 33 (1): 1–3.

Jax, K. (2010), *Ecosystem Functioning* (Cambridge: Cambridge University Press).

Keesing, F., Belden, L.K., Daszak, P., Dobson, A., Harvell, C.D., Holt, R.D., *et al.* (2010), 'Impacts of Biodiversity on the Emergence and Transmission of Infectious Diseases', *Nature*, 468: 647–52.

Kuhnlein, H. and Receveur, O. (1996), 'Dietary Change and Traditional Food Systems of Indigenous Peoples', *Annual Review of Nutrition*, 16: 417–42.

Lal, R. (2007), 'Anthropogenic Influences on World Soils and Implications for Global Food Security', *Advances in Agronomy*, 93: 69–93.

Laurance, W.F., Dell, B., Turton, S.M., Lawes, M.J., Hutley, L.B., McCallum, H., *et al.* (2011), 'The 10 Australian Ecosystems Most Vulnerable to Tipping Points', *Biological Conservation*, 144 (5): 1472–80.

Leadley P., Pereira, H.M., Alkemade, R., Fernandez-Manjarrés, J.F., Proença, V., Scharlemann, J.P.W., and Walpole, M.J. (2010), *Biodiversity Scenarios: Projections of 21st Century Change in Biodiversity and Associated Ecosystem Services, Technical Series no. 50* (Montreal: Secretariat of the Convention on Biological Diversity).

Maffi, L. (2005), 'Linguistic, Cultural, and Biological Diversity', *Annual Review of Anthropology*, 34: 599–617.

Malcolm, J.R., Markham, A., Neilson, R.P., and Garaci, M. (2005), 'Migration of Vegetation Types in a Greenhouse World', in T. Lovejoy and L. Hannah (eds), *Climate Change and Biodiversity* (New Haven, CT, Yale University Press), 252–55.

Pereira, H.M., Leadley, P.W., Proença, V., Alkemade, R., Scharlemann, J.P.W., Fernandez-Manjarrés, J.F., *et al.* (2010), 'Scenarios for Global Biodiversity in the 21st Century', *Science*, 330: 1496–1502.

Pimentel, D. and Pimentel, M.H. (2008), *Food, Energy, and Society* (Boca Raton, FL: CRC Press).

Pimentel, D., McNair, M., Buck, L., Pimentel, M., and Kamil, J. (1997), 'The Value of Forests to World Food Security', *Human Ecology*, 25: 91–120.

Pongsiri, M.J., Roman, J., Ezenwa, V.O., Goldberg, T.L., Koren, H.S., Newbold, S.C., *et al.* (2009), 'Biodiversity Loss Affects Global Disease Ecology', *BioScience*, 59 (11): 945–54.

Potts, S.G., Biesmeijer, J.C., Kremen, C., Neumann, P., Schweiger, O., and Kunin, W.E. (2010), 'Global Pollinator Declines: Trends, Impacts and Drivers', *Trends in Ecology and Evolution*, 25 (6): 345–53.

Root, T.L. and Hughes, L. (2005), 'Changes in Phenology and Ecological Interactions', in T.E. Lovejoy and L. Hannah (eds), *Climate Change and Biodiversity* (New Haven, CT: Yale University Press), 61–69.

Rozzi, R. (2012), 'Biocultural Ethics: Recovering the Vital Links Between the Inhabitants, Their Habits, and Habitats', *Environmental Ethics*, 34 (1): 27–50.

Salick, J. and Byg, A. (eds) (2007), *Indigenous People and Climate Change, Report of Symposium 12–13 April 2007, Environmental Change Institute, Oxford* (Oxford:

Tyndall Centre for Climate Change Research). Available online at: http://www.
ecdgroup.com/docs/lib_004630823.pdf (accessed 6 June 2012).

Scheffer, M. (2009), *Critical Transitions in Nature and Society* (Princeton, NJ: Princeton University Press).

Scheffer, M., Westley, F., Brock, W., and Holmgren, M. (2001), 'Dynamic Interaction of Societies and Ecosystems: Linking Theories from Ecology, Economy and Sociology', in L.H. Gunderson and C.S. Holling (eds), *Panarchy: Understanding Transformations in Human and Natural Systems* (Washington DC: Island Press), 195–240.

Scheffer, M., Bascompte, J., Brock, W.A., Brovkin, V., Carpenter, S.R., Dakos, V., *et al.* (2009), 'Early-Warning Signals for Critical Transitions', *Nature*, 461: 53–59.

Smil, V. (2008), *Energy in Nature and Society* (Cambridge, MA: MIT Press).

Steinfeld, H., Mooney, H.A., Schneider, F., and Neville, L.E. (2010), *Livestock in a Changing Landscape, Vol. 1* (Washington DC: Island Press).

Sunderland, T.C.H. (2011), 'Food Security: Why Is Biodiversity Important?', *International Forestry Review*, 13 (3): 265–74.

Sutherland, W. (2003), 'Parallel Extinction Risk and Global Distribution of Languages and Species', *Nature*, 423: 276–79.

Teelucksingh, S.S. and Perrings, C. (2010), *Biodiversity Indicators, Ecosystem Services and Local Livelihoods in Small Island Developing States (SIDS): Early Warnings of Biodiversity Change* (Nairobi: UNEP).

Thomas, C.D., Cameron, A., Green, R.E., Bakkenes, M., Beaumont, L.J., Collingham, Y.C., *et al.* (2004), 'Extinction Risk from Climate Change', *Nature*, 427: 145–48.

Thornton, T.F. and Manasfi, N. (2010), 'Adaptation – Genuine and Spurious: Demystifying Adaptation Processes in Relation to Climate Change', *Environment and Society: Advances in Research*, 1: 132–55.

Tilman, D. and Lehman, C. (2001), 'Human-Caused Environmental Change: Impacts on Plant Diversity and Evolution', *Proceedings of the National Academy of Sciences USA*, 98 (10): 5433–40.

Vandermeer, J.H. (ed.) (2002), *Tropical Agroecosystems* (Boca Raton, FL: CRC Press).

Vergara, W. (ed.) (2010), *Assessment of the Risk of Amazon Dieback: Main Report, Environmentally and Socially Sustainable Development Department Latin America and Caribbean Region* (Washington DC: World Bank).

Vergara, W. and Scholz, S.M. (eds) (2011), *Assessment of the Risk of Amazon Dieback, World Bank Study* (Washington DC: World Bank).

Western, D. (2001), 'Human-Modified Ecosystems and Future Evolution', *Proceedings of the National Academy of Sciences USA*, 98 (10): 5458–65.

Williams, J.W., Jackson, S.T., and Kutzbach, J.E. (2007), 'Projected Distributions of Novel and Disappearing Climates by 2100 AD', *Proceedings of the National Academy of Sciences USA*, 104 (14): 5738–42.

Willis, K., Bennett, K.D., Bhagwat, S.A, and Birks, H.J.B. (2010), '4°C and Beyond: What Did This Mean for Biodiversity in the Past?', *Systematics and Biodiversity*, 8 (1): 3–9.

Wise, M., Calvin, K., Thomson, A., Clarke, L., Bon-Lamberty, B., Sands, R., *et al.* (2009), 'Implications of Limiting CO_2 Concentrations for Land Use and Energy', *Science*, 324: 1183–86.

Woodruff, D. (2001), 'Declines of Biomes and Biotas and the Future of Evolution', *Proceedings of the National Academy of Sciences USA*, 98 (10): 5471–76.

World Bank (2002), *A Revised Forest Strategy for the World Bank Group* (Washington DC: World Bank).

World Bank (2003), *World Development Report 2003 – Sustainable Development in a Dynamic World: Transforming Institutions, Growth, and Quality of Life* (Washington DC: World Bank).

Xu, J.C., Lebel, L., and Sturgeon, J. (2009), 'Functional Links Between Biodiversity, Livelihoods and Culture in a Hani Swidden Landscape in Southwest China', *Ecology and Society*, 14 (2): article 20.

4.3
The Amazon in transition

The challenge of transforming the world's largest tropical forest biome into a sustainable social-ecological system

TOBY GARDNER

Setting

This chapter considers the fate of the Amazon as an integrated social-ecological system that during the last half a century has undergone an unprecedented period of change and disruption. The Amazon is a biome of truly global significance. Its total area is approximately 6.9 million km^2 and encompasses nine countries (Barthem *et al.* 2004). While 69 per cent of the biome is within Brazil, the Amazon also makes up 66 per cent, 60 per cent and 47 per cent of the total landmass of Bolivia, Peru and Ecuador respectively (Barthem *et al.* 2004). The Amazon basin discharges approximately one-fifth of the world's fresh water, provides a home and resources for more than 31 million people, as well as hosting a significant proportion of the world's terrestrial biodiversity (FAO 2011). Indeed, the Amazon has been described as the ultimate 'ecoutility', providing critical ecosystem services on local to global scales (Trivedi *et al.* 2009). The total amount of carbon stored in remaining forests across all of Amazonia (120 ± 30 billion tonnes; Malhi *et al.* 2006) is approximately equivalent to a decade of accumulated human-induced carbon emissions for the entire planet (Canadell *et al.* 2007). Amazonian forests absorb vast amounts of solar energy through the cooling effect of annually releasing trillions of tonnes of water to the atmosphere. This drives atmospheric circulation across the tropics, as well as being responsible for recycling between one-quarter and one-half of the region's rainfall (Elthahir and Bras 1994; Marengo *et al.* 2011). In addition, the water vapour released by the Amazon also moderates regional weather conditions and supplies rainfall for southern Brazil and the La Plata Basin, the economic powerhouse of Latin America, on which US $1 trillion per year of agribusiness, hydropower, and industry depends (Marengo *et al.* 2011).

The fate of the Amazon is currently at a crossroads. The last four decades have witnessed widespread deforestation across the entire basin (Perz *et al.* 2005; Etter *et al.* 2008; FAO 2011), with some 775,000 km^2 of Amazon forests having already been cleared in Brazil alone since 1988 (www.inpe. gov.br). More recently, falling deforestation rates in Brazil since 2005 have generated considerable international praise, giving rise to the notion that Brazil may be one of the first countries to achieve the status of a major economic power without destroying most of its forests (Davidson *et al.* 2012). Set against this positive outlook, a burgeoning number of studies have raised the spectre of the Amazon system facing a regime shift or tipping point, whereby a combination of global warming, continued deforestation, an increased frequency of severe drought events, unsustainable timber extraction, and an increased prevalence of fire is set to drive a vicious, and potentially irreversible positive feedback loop, leading to the loss or degradation of a significant proportion of remaining forest (Davidson *et al.* 2012). Here I use research on the prospect of Amazonian forest dieback as an entry point to a broader discussion concerning the Amazon as a complex social-ecological system undergoing an unprecedented process of transition. Drawing on work from across the natural and social sciences, and my own personal experiences working in the eastern Amazon, I then consider how this evermore dynamic system presents particular challenges for societal, governmental and scientific efforts to develop a more environmentally sustainable and socially progressive model of development for the region.

Climate change, deforestation, and dieback of the Amazon forest

Variation in moisture availability affects the productivity and resilience of tropical ecosystems more profoundly than any other aspect of the climate (Meir and Woodward 2010), meaning that reductions in precipitation and increases in the frequency of severe drought represent a major threat to the future of tropical forests (Marengo *et al.* 2011). Because of the sheer size of the Amazon rainforest even small changes in forest dynamics can have a significant impact on atmospheric CO_2 concentrations, and therefore on the rate of climate change itself. Climate modelling work has suggested two mechanisms that have the potential to drive widespread declines in precipitation across the Amazon, raising the spectre of a potentially irreversible shift towards a system that is only capable of supporting an impoverished secondary or savannah-type vegetation state (Cox *et al.* 2004; Nobre and Borma 2009; Malhi *et al.* 2009; Marengo *et al.* 2011). First, while there is considerable uncertainty in the predictions of different global circulation models (GCMs) there is some evidence to suggest an increase in the likelihood of drought-like conditions for Eastern and Southern Amazonia following twenty-first-century warming (Betts *et al.* 2004; Jupp *et al.* 2010). Second, because the Amazon recycles as much as half of its own rainfall, if a sufficient area of forest is cleared, it may be unable to sustain itself in its current form. These models indicate that a threshold or tipping point could be reached via either mechanism, with a 3–4°C temperature rise or 30–40 per cent level of regional deforestation potentially being suffi-cient to precipitate large-scale vegetation dieback (Nobre and Borma 2009).

Despite the widespread scientific and media attention these predictions have attracted, confidence in our ability to identify such a threshold or tipping point is marred by uncertainty in both climate change predictions themselves (Jupp *et al.* 2010; Poulter *et al.* 2010) and ecosystem responses to changes in climatic conditions. Regarding ecosystem responses, con-siderable uncertainty exists in the potential for a compensation effect from CO_2 fertilization on plant growth, and water loss through transpiration (Rammig *et al.* 2010; Meir and Woodward 2010). However, irrespective of debates regarding the potential resilience of intact forests to long-term declines in rainfall (see Meir and Woodward 2010), the Amazon is clearly vulnerable to extreme drought events (Phillips *et al.* 2009; da Costa *et al.* 2010). The Amazon suffered from two of the severest drought events on record in 2005 and 2010 (driven by increases in high-Atlantic sea surface temperatures) which resulted in a total CO_2 impact from reduced growth and increased tree mortality that was estimated to be potentially equivalent to the net carbon uptake by intact Amazonian forests for the whole decade (Lewis *et al.* 2011). It is possible that these two droughts alone resulted in the biome shifting from a net sink (Phillips *et al.* 1998) to a net source of carbon dioxide (equating to c.4 billion tonnes of carbon; Phillips *et al.* 2009; Lewis *et al.* 2011).

Both short- and long-term changes in climatic conditions and moisture stress present major threats to the integrity of Amazon ecosystems. However, it is impossible to disentangle their impact from ongoing patterns of deforestation and forest degradation associated with the expansion of agriculture, roads, and timber harvesting across the basin (Malhi *et al.* 2009; Davidson *et al.* 2012). Indeed, it is now broadly accepted that the greatest threat of a positive feedback cycle capable of driving the widespread and near-term loss or degradation of the Amazon forest comes, not from global and continental-scale changes in climate, but from the interaction between changes in both climate and local human activity – and specifically a rise in the occurrence and intensity of forest fires (Nepstad *et al.* 2001, 2008; Aragão *et al.* 2008). Most tropical rainforest tree species are poorly adapted to fire stress, and even low-intensity surface fires can lead to significant levels of mortality among adult trees (Barlow *et al.* 2002), with repeat burns having the potential to drive an almost complete turnover in tree species composition (Barlow and Peres 2008).

Conditions across much of the Amazon are now approaching something of a 'perfect storm' for driving widespread forest degradation, with an increasingly large area subject to a combination of: high levels of tree mortality from drought, fire, fragmentation, and logging impacts; an increased risk of recurrent fires from the drier and more flammable fuel loads (including drier litter and an increased dominance of understory grasses) that characterize partially degraded forests; and an increase in the number and frequency of ignition sources from the expansion of agriculture and road networks (Nepstad *et al.* 2008).

Attempts to incorporate fire dynamics alongside climate and deforestation modelling suggest that 'business as usual' scenarios of regional development may lead to a doubling of forest fires outside of protected areas in years of extreme drought, and an expanding fire risk to much of the Amazon, including the currently isolated north-western Amazon, by the middle of this century (Golding and Betts 2008; Silvestrini *et al.* 2011). Once the process of forest degradation has started, multiple and reinforcing feedback effects can lead to: (1) a runaway cycle of increased forest vulnerability and impoverishment, driven by fires and repeated and unsustainable logging cycles at local scales, (2) the inhibition of regional rainfall patterns from ongoing forest clearance and increased atmospheric smoke, and (3) feedback effects of elevated CO_2 emissions on the global climate system, resulting in further increases in temperature and the likelihood of more frequent and severe drought events, with associated impacts on soil

130

respiration, tree mortality, and fire dynamics (Nepstad *et al.* 2001; Davidson *et al.* 2012). The type of vegetation that is capable of withstanding this unprecedented onslaught bears no resemblance to a species-rich closed-canopy rainforest. Instead it is better characterized by the young secondary forests that are commonly found on degraded pastures – dominated by pioneer species with low biomass and negligible economic value, and only capable of supporting a tiny fraction of the original forest biota.

Expanding the tipping point metaphor: the Amazon as a social-ecological system in transition

The notion of a tipping point has been very effective in drawing attention to the increasing vulnerability of the Amazon rainforest, and the close coupling between the forest and global climate systems (Nobre and Borma 2009). However, in keeping with what has been shown by research on the resilience of a wide range of social-ecological systems (Folke *et al.* 2010), it is clear that the fate of the Amazon does not depend on some threshold change in a key system variable (e.g. atmospheric temperature, precipitation, or accumulated forest loss), but rather on a complex interplay of drivers and positive feedback loops that operate at landscape, continental, and global scales. Indeed, an exaggerated policy focus on a precise numerical tipping point can be both distracting and misleading insofar as it suggests that an individual basin-wide driver can be responsible for a change in system state, that degradation below a certain level is 'safe', and that improvements beyond that level are of no value (Davidson *et al.* 2012).

Despite scientific uncertainty regarding natural hydrological and biogeochemical cycles, projections of climate and land use change, their interaction effects and ecosystem responses to changing conditions, an increasingly large proportion of the Amazon is affected by the combined effects of deforestation and forest degradation. This process of change has taken place against a backdrop of social, political and economic change that has transformed the Amazon as a place to live over the course of the last fifty years, with rapid increases in population and widespread migration underpinned by regional economic growth, agricultural expansion and diversification, exploration of new mineral, oil, and gas resources, major infrastructure projects, and political and legal reform (Barthem *et al.* 2004; Killeen 2007; FAO 2011).

131

Encouragingly, deforestation rates in the Brazilian Amazon dropped rapidly from 2006 to 2011, with a 56 per cent decline in the annual rate of forest loss in 2006–11 compared to 2001–05 (www.inpe.gov.br). This change has offered some hope that the ambitious deforestation reduction target to 20 per cent of baseline levels (1996–2005) by 2020, announced by former President Lula in the Copenhagen climate change summit as part of Brazil's national climate change action plan, is possible. Indeed, it has even prompted proposals that the end of deforestation is feasible within the same period (Nepstad *et al.* 2009). However, despite the attractiveness and tantalizing nature of this proposal there are a number of reasons why we cannot afford to be complacent about the future of the Amazon, and why a general shift towards a low-emission trajectory of rural development is far from assured (Nepstad *et al.* 2011).

Assessments of alternative scenarios for regional development require consideration of two characteristic features of recent social and ecological changes in system dynamics: (1) an acceleration in the speed of many processes of change, and (2) an increase in the interconnectedness of changes at local, landscape, and regional scales.

One of the most important and far-reaching changes in the Amazon has been the increase in human population. Often perceived as a space for absorbing the population and development problems of other regions, government resettlement and incentive schemes and infrastructure projects have all contributed towards a massive increase and redistribution of people across the basin during the last half a century. Between 1980 and 2000 alone the population of the Brazilian Legal Amazon approximately doubled from 12 to 21 million people, with increases of comparable magnitude in Bolivia, Colombia, Ecuador, and Peru (Perz *et al.* 2005), resulting in a regional population today that exceeds 31 million (FAO 2011). Whilst links between population growth and deforestation are complex (Perz *et al.* 2005; Hecht 2010) this dramatic change has driven increased demand for land and natural resources, as well as increased investment in infrastructure and energy projects, as regions of the Amazon have become increasingly connected with national and international markets (Nepstad *et al.* 2006; Killeen 2007; Lambin and Meyfroidt 2011). The majority of recent population growth in the Amazon has occurred in cities (Guedes *et al.* 2009), many of which have also witnessed rapid rates of economic growth. For example, between 1970 and 2000 the average rate of growth per decade of urban Gross Domestic Product per capita was 85 per cent for cities in the Brazilian Amazon, compared to only 76 per cent for the rest of the country (www.ibge.gov.br). Whilst urbanization and agricultural intensification have led to a partial decoupling of deforestation and population growth, continued increases in the size and consumption levels of urban populations have contributed towards the strengthening of rural–urban linkages, and rising demand for agricultural commodities, particularly beef (McAlpine *et al.* 2009).

Coupled with the increase in size and wealth of regional populations, as well as the increased connection with international commodity markets (Lambin and Meyfroidt 2011), one of the most important threats facing efforts to reduce deforestation and forest degradation comes from rising prices of agricultural commodities. Such price rises can make deforestation more profitable and may weaken the resolve of local, regional and state government actors to enforce or maintain strict environmental legislation. Evidence for such a change can be seen in the recent negotiations to revise the Brazilian forest code, the law that governs environmental protection on private land, in response to strong lobbying from the agribusiness sector. The potential for a reversal of falling deforestation rates due to future agricultural development and changes in international markets can be observed from the peak of forest loss that occurred between 2002 and 2004 during a rapid increase in the Amazonian cattle herd, and the first large-scale expansion of industrialized agriculture to many parts of the Brazilian Amazon, which resulted in the clearance of 75,000 km² of forest in Brazil alone – equivalent to 95 per cent of the total area of forest that has been cleared since (2005–2011) (www.inpe.gov.br). The fact that projected demands for both cattle and biofuels are set to exceed the area of land legally available for agricultural expansion by 2020 (Walker 2011) indicates that the system remains highly vulnerable to economic incentives. That said, recent evidence of deforestation rates becoming decoupled from soy production in southern Mato Grosso suggest that improvements in farming techniques and regulation of land use have the potential to dampen fluctuations in forest losses (Macedo *et al.* 2012).

Finally, the profit incentive to expand agriculture into remaining areas of forest may be exacerbated further if much-publicized incentives for forest conservation through carbon payments are not forthcoming, and current expectations are replaced by an erosion of credibility and increasing resentment within the agricultural and forestry sectors.

The sensitivity of Amazonian agriculture to short-term changes in market prices also underpins a high level of instability and non-linear behaviour in rural development trajectories (Rodrigues *et al.* 2009) as well as contributing towards a highly mobile rural population (Brondizio and Moran 2008; Carrero and Fearnside 2011). This population mobility results in a high turnover rate of farm managers and workers, lowering the capacity to adapt to novel circumstances (such as droughts and price fluctuations in particular crops) as newcomers invariably lack a nuanced understanding of local ecological systems and social or economic networks (Brondizio and Moran 2008). Intra-regional mixing of rural populations in areas that often lack any clear system of property rights can also give rise to so-called 'contentious' land use change, driven by antagonism and conflict within and between large landowners and the rural poor – a dynamic which can greatly exacerbate attempts to improve land management practices (Aldrich *et al.* 2012).

In addition to increases in the rate of change of demographic, economic and environmental variables, the second factor to cast uncertainty over the future development trajectories of the Amazon is an increased level of interconnectedness amongst system elements. Research in recent decades has revealed an increasing number of strong and cross-scale connections in the drivers of deforestation and land use change with resonance at global, national and regional scales.

Perhaps the most commonly cited example of a cross-scale connection exerting a powerful influence on the dynamics of rural development in the Amazon is the existence of so-called 'teleconnections': phenomena that appear to be coupled, but take place in geographically distant places on the planet. These include economic signals from other parts of the world – such as trade-bans on beef export by the European Union following the outbreak of foot and mouth disease or sky-rocketing demands for soybean imports by China – which can play a potentially important (Nepstad *et al.* 2006; Hargrave and Kis-Kato 2011), albeit complex role (Ewers *et al.* 2008) in determining rates of change in agricultural expansion and deforestation.

Another important (though less appreciated) economic signal to have emerged from an increasingly interconnected global commodities market is the fluctuation of exchange rates between the currencies of Amazon nations and the US dollar. For example, Richards *et al.* (2012) present evidence to suggest that the recent devaluation of the dollar and appreciation of the Brazilian real have counteracted a recent rise in global soybean prices, and in the process, spared an estimated 40,000 km^2 of new cropland in the Amazon region alone.

At the regional scale the process of indirect land use change, where the expansion of more profitable mechanized farming can displace existing cattle pastures and smallholder farmers to the deforestation frontier, has long been posited as a threat to the Amazon. Indeed, Arima *et al.* (2011) found that for the period 2003–2008 a 10 per cent reduction in the expansion of soy into previously colonized landscapes could have reduced deforestation by as much as 40 per cent in the heavily forested counties of the Brazilian Amazon. Sharp fluctuations in economic opportunity across the Amazon, driven in part by strong cross-scale interactions in the price of land and the profitability of farming, also contribute towards a highly dynamic human population. Although endogenous birth rates are now the primary driver of population growth in the Amazon region, in-migration is still continuing and there is a very high level of migratory circulation within the region itself (Perz *et al.* 2010a).

One consequence of recent increases in the speed and connectivity of land use changes across the Amazon is the increased likelihood of cascading effects, whether negative or positive, of a development stimulus or conservation intervention in one place having important ramifications elsewhere (Brondizio *et al.* 2009). Learning how to cope with such variability, and to identify how it can be used to leverage positive change, is one of the greatest challenges and opportunities facing both the management and science of sustainable development in the Amazon and elsewhere (Brondizio *et al.* 2009; Folke *et al.* 2011).

Challenges for governance in securing a sustainable future for the Amazon

Discussions and proposals concerning the future of the Amazon suffer from the same shortcomings as many other debates about issues of sustainability – they are often catch-all, lack clarity of purpose and local relevance, and are underpinned by levels of ambition and understanding that vary enormously depending on the group of actors concerned. The enduring legacy of the Brundtland Commission (1987) is that inter-generational equity lies at the heart of the goal of sustainable development – that is, development that can meet the needs of the present without compromising the ability of future generations to meet their own needs. Holling (2001) subsequently recast this overarching goal as the need to foster and maintain adaptive capacities whilst continuing to create new opportunities for continuing development. Faced with an unprecedented state of social and ecological transition, including widespread environmental degradation and social inequality, the challenge lies in identifying, protecting and restoring the social, environmental and economic values that support this adaptive capacity, and whose loss or degradation may be irreversible or extremely costly to restore. Aspects of this overarching goal are evident in some visions of development for the Amazon region, including the Brazilian government's Plano Amazônia Sustentável, which has a strong emphasis on promoting economic betterment and reduction of poverty, whilst respecting and ensuring compatibility with social and ecological values (Federal Republic of Brazil 2008).

At a broad level we already know the main elements of a combined strategy that is needed to set the Amazon on a more sustainable trajectory (Nepstad *et al.* 2009, 2011; Malhi *et al.* 2007; Trivedi *et al.* 2009; Davidson *et al.* 2012; Boyd (7.2)). These include the need to:

- limit deforestation beneath the threshold of 30–40 per cent losses that may precipitate basin-wide shifts in precipitation through reduced transpiration and accelerated climate change;
- strengthen and expand protected areas close to the deforestation frontier;
- deliver effective state- and municipality-level planning processes to facilitate sustainable intensification of agriculture, responsible forest management, and the protection of biological corridors across already degraded landscapes;
- support a shift towards fire-free livelihoods amongst Amazonian farmers, especially the approximately 400,000 smallholders that currently lack access to technology and resources;
- alongside efforts to promote sustainable management systems, invest in increasing the value of raw agricultural and forestry products using locally trained labour forces;
- expand the agricultural land that is responsibly managed through development of reliable and premium markets, including a diversification of opportunities for the use of degraded land (e.g. silviculture and biofuels);
- support the development of stronger community-led institutions that help build adaptive capacity locally and help plan for and adapt to change (Boyd (7.2));
- effectively leverage new finance from carbon markets and other forms of ecosystem service payments to help support all of the above.

Implementing this integrated set of proposals depends upon the consolidation and scaling up of successful pilot initiatives, and the maintenance of momentum against a backdrop of increasing human population and consumption, shifting market prices and the impacts of rising economic globalization, and unproven incentive systems and regulatory frameworks. There is no 'one size fits all' model. The types of governance responses that are needed to foster social and ecological sustainability vary depending on the location, the current social and ecological condition of the system, and the timescale of the specific set of problems being addressed. In presenting the concept of ecosystem stewardship as a framework for promoting sustainability in a rapidly changing planet, Chapin *et al.* (2010) identify three different levels of engagement or strategies that are necessary for developing a more nuanced and regionally appropriate set of policy approaches and incentives, namely: reduce vulnerability to risks, invest in resilience, and promote positive transformation.

The first challenge is to reduce vulnerability towards known risks. Given sufficient political will and resources, risk avoidance is relatively straight-forward, as has been demonstrated by the expansion of the protected-areas system and the role this has played in lowering rates of deforestation in the Brazilian Amazon (Soares-Filho *et al.* 2010).

The second challenge is to invest in proactive policies that can improve the resilience of desirable system properties (e.g. ecologically viable forest reserves in agricultural landscapes) in the face of ongoing change. This is much harder than simply reacting to observed problems and it requires maintaining and/or restoring a diversity of options (e.g. migration corridors for biodiversity, different farm management systems and approaches to capacity building and rural extension), enhancing social learning to facilitate adaptation (including transparent information systems, effective channels of communication across different levels of government), and building adaptive governance systems that provide insurance for policy implementation by not concentrating skills and resources inside specific, overburdened institutions. Undermining efforts towards achieving these goals in the Amazon, as elsewhere, is a common lack of awareness and capacity for dealing with the often bewilderingly fast and patchily implemented changes in legal regulations, and rapid changes in market and financial incentives that influence land use choices. The continuing revision of the Brazilian Forest Code, and the growth industry of international, governmental, and non-governmental initiatives relating to the UN policy of Reducing Emissions from Deforestation and Forest Degradation (REDD+) are two such examples. The asymmetries in capacity and understanding that emerge following these changes can lead to unjust biases in the distribution of both penalties and benefits, and a divergence in abilities of different stakeholder groups to respond to new threats and opportunities.

The biggest challenge for sustainability lies in transforming areas that have already undergone major changes, and which have achieved a high level of resilience around a maladaptive and inflexible system (Steffen *et al.* 2011; Boyd (7.2)). Berardi *et al.* (2011) suggest that an overemphasis on improvements in agricultural efficiency has already undermined adaptive capacity and led to such a trap in the US mechanized farming systems, with a loss of diversity in types of production and an inability to respond to unexpected shocks (such as hurricane Katrina). Achieving genuine transformation to a new development pathway is both difficult and not without risk. Plausible and desirable alternative trajectories or scenarios need to be identified, as well as identifying potential barriers to change. Approaches need to be developed for navigating and consolidating the transitional processes that maintain broad stakeholder participation and support, as well as for building sufficient resilience to ensure the viability of the new system state.

One early attempt to promote a social-ecological transformation in the Brazilian Amazon was through the 'payment for ecosystem service' scheme, Proambiente (Programme for the Socio-Environmental Development of Rural Family Production) (Hall 2008). Under the scheme, smallholder farmers

> would cease to be regarded merely as suppliers of primary produce but be valued for their multi-functional contributions to economic production, social inclusion and preservation of the environment . . . [facilitating] compensation for environmental services rendered to Brazil and the world.
>
> (Proambiente 2003: 2–6)

Specific environmental services in this context were defined as: (1) reduction or avoidance of deforestation; (2) carbon sequestration; (3) recuperation of ecosystem hydrological functions; (4) soil conservation; (5) preservation of biodiversity; and (6) reduction of forest fire risks (Hall 2008). Despite its admirable aims, Proambiente has thus far fallen short of expectations, being undermined in particular by the lack of a national legal framework to allow direct payment schemes, but also due to limited funding, reduced implementation capacity, poor cross-sector collaboration and incompatibility with existing regional development policies (Hall 2008).

By contrast, the Municipio Verde (Green County) initiative spearheaded by the municipality of Paragominas in the Brazilian Amazon has achieved more success in facilitating what may be seen as the start of a genuine social-ecological transformation (Guimarães *et al.* 2011).

Until the 1990s, Paragominas was a region of the Amazon notorious for lawlessness and land speculation, with rampant forest clearance and unregulated timber extraction. Following a change in local governance and the leadership of the farmers' union a key group of actors managed to turn a potential crisis situation (exclusion from access to rural credit due to high levels of past deforestation) into a positive news story (zero-deforestation pact and widespread voluntary registration of rural properties in the state environmental land register) with an associated growth in opportunities for rural development (including preferential investment by donors interested in supporting sustainability initiatives, including the Fundo Amazônia and Fundo Vale).

Nevertheless, much work remains to be completed. The majority of small-holder farmers have benefited little from the changes thus far, extensive low-yielding cattle farming still dominates much of the region, and remaining forests are highly degraded and vulnerable to continued threats from unsustainable logging and rampant fires in the dry season. It is also not yet clear how easily the relative success of Paragominas can be replicated to neighbouring municipalities that often have much weaker political leadership, and still exhibit high levels of deforestation and degradation.

Ultimately the challenge of achieving sustainability in the Amazon requires engaging with problems across all three of these levels, and working to reduce vulnerabilities and building resilience within a broader agenda of transformation towards a more sustainable social-ecological system. As always, sustainability, and sustainable development, should not be seen as a static blueprint for management action but as a mechanism for creating a continued sense of purpose, and a guiding vision for social and political discourse that can balance national and regional goals with local values and circumstances. Whilst it is all too easy to become paralysed by the complexity of the challenges that confront development in the Amazon it is important to resist oversimplification of both problems and management responses.

Perhaps the most common shortcoming of proposals to better protect vulnerable ecosystems by changing institutional rules of use and sets of incentives (e.g. REDD+) is that they frequently focus on one level of governance (Brondizio *et al.* 2009; Brondizio and Moran 2012). In the case of the Amazon this is often at the basin-wide scale. This can be of limited practical value as we have a poor understanding of the wider system, and the agency of most organizations and institutions to foster real change is at sub-regional, municipality, and community scales. A common response to policy failure has been to simplify governance boundaries and shift management responsibilities to higher or lower levels of public authority (Brondizio *et al.* 2009). However, higher level management can be undermined by ignorance amongst managers who are distant from the source of the problem, whilst local managers are often unaware of wider-scale connections, dependencies, and the long-term implications of their choices. The frequent disconnect and tension between state-level ecological-economic zoning processes and property-level regulations for environmental protection in Brazil is a good example of this imbalance.

Counteracting this problem of scale is not trivial and requires improving the capacity of state and local governments, and developing institutions that reach across multiple scales and actor groups (Perz *et al.* 2008; Brondizio *et al.* 2009; Boyd (7.2)). The emergence of the Governors' Climate and Forests Task Force (http://www.gcftaskforce.org/) – a multi-jurisdictional collaborative effort between states and provinces across the tropics and the USA to develop capabilities necessary for implementing the REDD+ programme – is a good example of improvements in cross-scale governance where significant progress has been made to strengthen the position of state-level actors in international forest policy. More such examples are needed at the sub-national level within Amazonian nations. The combination of state and non-state actors in such hybrid governance models can help reconfigure state–market–society relationships towards improved social and environmental outcomes (Brannstrom *et al.* 2012). However, a lot of care is needed to ensure that responsibilities and capacities are not excessively transferred to large non-governmental organizations which may in turn lead to unsustainable and politically unviable institutional dependencies.

Challenges for science in securing a sustainable future for the Amazon

Science has a critical role to play in developing and securing a transition towards a more sustainable future for the Amazon region. Whilst an impressive body of knowledge has already been generated (Barlow *et al.* 2010; Davidson *et al.* 2012), the scientific community is commonly criticized for failing to deliver the evidence that is most needed to foster this change.

A lot of applied research is often of a narrow disciplinary focus, addresses only a limited range of spatial scales, and is concerned largely with drawing attention to problems instead of developing and testing specific management and policy solutions (e.g. Ferreira *et al.* 2012). Renewed efforts are needed to develop a genuinely interdisciplinary science that can overcome these shortcomings and help steer the region on to a more sustainable pathway (Barlow *et al.* 2010; Perz *et al.* 2010b).

Social-ecological research in the Amazon, as elsewhere, has often failed to focus on the most relevant spatial scales for guiding the development of more sustainable land use strategies. Instead, a lot of work has been concentrated either on the entire Amazon basin, thereby obscuring important inter- and intra-regional processes and interactions (Brondizio and Moran 2012), or on a detailed understanding of a small number of well-known research sites, thereby capturing only a tiny fraction of the variability in key environmental and land use gradients that drive social and ecological change (e.g. as in the case of biodiversity research; Peres *et al.* 2010). Whilst both large- and small-scale research is necessary, much more work is needed at the mesoscale (i.e. 100s km). Perhaps most importantly, the mesoscale corresponds to the scale of municipalities or counties – the administrative unit which resonates most closely with local pressures on natural resources and social services, as well as being responsible for institutional linkages between local communities and regions or states (Brondizio and Moran 2012). In addition, focusing work at the mesoscale allows for a more meaningful cross-scale or nested analysis that can simultaneously draw on data and understanding regarding both local and regional processes in a way that research focused at either the smallest or largest scales cannot readily achieve.

Building effective interdisciplinary research programmes remains one of the most difficult challenges facing the development of sustainability science (Carpenter *et al.* 2009). In summarizing the status of scientific knowledge across fourteen different areas of research in the Amazon, Barlow *et al.* (2010) emphasize the benefits of a shared geographic focus in developing a more interactive and interdisciplinary research and learning environment. Indeed, accelerating the acquisition of reliable and contextualized knowledge about the fate of the Amazon is partly dependent on our ability to build research networks that can effectively exploit economies of scale in shared resources and technical expertise, recognize and make explicit interconnections and feedbacks among sub-disciplines, and increase the temporal and spatial scale of existing studies. Researchers

141

also need to conceptualize interdisciplinary research as being much more than a combination of different sets of skills and data, and rather an opportunity to compare and integrate what are often fundamentally different ways of thinking (Polasky *et al.* 2011).

Ultimately the success of any such research network depends on the active participation of local and regional stakeholders, alongside different scientific disciplines, in a co-designed approach to research and implementation (Future Earth 2012). Managing such networks is challenging, and requires capabilities and strategies that often go far beyond the remit of normal scientific training, including managing the politics of collaboration and cooperation and building functional redundancies across networks in order to withstand the possible loss of key individuals or institutions.

Conclusions

The introductory chapter of this book (1.1) expanded the tipping point metaphor beyond thinking about threshold shifts in a system state to a much broader heuristic device for conceptualizing the causes and consequences of unprecedented change across multiple social and ecological attributes. In doing so it urges both decision makers and scientists to be more imaginative in seeking to understand and address the challenges that face the development of more sustainable and socially progressive economies. The editors of this volume further propose that human societies are predisposed towards creating the conditions that may contribute towards tipping points in physical and social conditions, and also that efforts to adapt to such changes can often have an exacerbating effect. Some evidence of both propositions can be found in the Amazon which, in only a few decades, has undergone an unprecedented period of social and ecological change and disruption. The spectre of a clearly defined tipping point in the Amazon system, driven by a threshold change in regional deforestation and/or global temperature increases, remains poorly understood due to variability in predicted climate and land use changes as well as ecosystem responses. Nevertheless, and despite recent positive changes – including a dramatic reduction in the rate of deforestation in Brazil – the region currently stands at a crossroads, with the long-term integrity of Amazon forests threatened by positive feedbacks between land use and climate change that could lead to a widespread shift towards an impoverished and fire-prone system.

On a more positive note the editors also urged us all to think about the possibility of positive transformational tipping points where societal responses can turn-around trajectories of degradation and maladaptation to build institutions that are capable of restoring and maintaining sustainable social-ecological systems. It is reassuring to observe that, while far from dominant or secure, elements of this potential for transformation are emerging across the Amazon in the form of declining deforestation rates, changing land use practices, and the emergence of a critical mass of individuals and institutions committed to demonstrating the potential for positive change (Hecht 2011). Building upon and consolidating these changes ultimately requires adaptability in the responses of decision makers at all levels of governance, and the support of a solution-orientated and interactive scientific community.

Acknowledgements

I am very grateful to Jamila Haider, Joice Ferreira, Luke Parry, Patrick Meir, Emily Boyd, Luis Fernando Guedes Pinto, and Tim O'Riordan for insightful comments that helped greatly to improve the manuscript. I am grateful to the Natural Environment Research Council (NE/FO1614x/1) and the UK Government Darwin Initiative (17-023) for funding support while this work was completed. This is publication #7 in the Rede Amazônia Sustentável series.

References

Aldrich, S., Walker, R., Simmons, C., Caldas, M., and Perz, S. (2012), 'Contentious Land Change in the Amazon's Arc of Deforestation', *Annals of the Entomological Society of America*, 102: 37–41.
Aragão, L.E.O.C., Malhi, Y., Barbier, N., Lima, A., Shimabukuro, Y., Anderson, L., and Saatchi, S. (2008), 'Interactions Between Rainfall, Deforestation and Fires During Recent Years in the Brazilian Amazonia', *Philosophical Transactions of the Royal Society of London, Series B, Biological Sciences*, 363: 1779–85.
Arima, E.Y., Richards, P., Walker, R., and Caldas, M.M. (2011), 'Statistical Confirmation of Indirect Land Use Change in the Brazilian Amazon', *Environmental Research Letters*, 6: 024010.
Barlow, J. and Peres, C.A. (2008), 'Fire-mediated Dieback and Compositional Cascade in an Amazonian Forest', *Philosophical Transactions of the Royal Society of London, Series B, Biological Sciences*, 363: 1787–94.

143

Barlow, J., Peres, C.A., Lagan, B.O., and Haugaasen, T. (2002), 'Large Tree Mortality and the Decline of Forest Biomass following Amazonian Wildfires', *Ecology Letters*, 6: 6–8.

Barlow, J., Ewers, R.M., Anderson, L., Aragao, L.E.O.C., Baker, T.R., Boyd, E., *et al.* (2010), 'Using Learning Networks to Understand Complex Systems: A Case Study of Biological, Geophysical and Social Research in the Amazon', *Biological Reviews of the Cambridge Philosophical Society*, 86: 457–74.

Barthem, R.B., Charvet-Almeida, P., Montag, L.F.A., and Lanna, A.E. (2004), *Waters Assessment GIWA Regional Assessment 40b* (Kalmar, Sweden: United Nations Environment Program).

Berardi, G., Green, R., and Hammond, B. (2011), 'Stability, Sustainability, and Catastrophe: Applying Resilience Thinking to US Agriculture', *Human Ecology Review*, 18: 115–25.

Betts, R.A., Cox, P.M., Collins, M., Harris, P.P., Huntingford, C., and Jones, C.D. (2004), 'The Role of Ecosystem-Atmosphere Interactions in Simulated Amazonian Precipitation Decrease and Forest Dieback under Global Climate Warming', *Theoretical and Applied Climatology*, 78: 157–75.

Brannstrom, C., Rausch, L., Brown, J.C., de Andrade, R.M.T., and Miccolis, A. (2012), 'Compliance and Market Exclusion in Brazilian Agriculture: Analysis and Implications for "Soft" Governance', *Land Use Policy*, 29: 357–66.

Brondizio, E.S. and Moran, E.F. (2008), 'Human Dimensions of Climate Change: The Vulnerability of Small Farmers in the Amazon', *Philosophical Transactions of the Royal Society of London, Series B, Biological Sciences*, 363: 1803–09.

Brondizio, E.S. and Moran, E.F. (2012), 'Level-dependent Deforestation Trajectories in the Brazilian Amazon from 1970 to 2001', *Population and Environment*, DOI 10.1007/s11111-011-0159-8.

Brondizio, E.S., Ostrom, E., and Young, O.R. (2009), 'Connectivity and the Governance of Multilevel Social-Ecological Systems: The Role of Social Capital', *Annual Review of Environment and Resources*, 34: 253–78.

Canadell, J.G., Le Quéré, C., Raupach, M.R., Field, C.B., Buitenhuis, E.T., Ciais, P., *et al.* (2007), 'Contributions to Accelerating Atmospheric CO_2 Growth from Economic Activity, Carbon Intensity, and Efficiency of Natural Sinks', *Proceedings of the National Academy of Sciences of the United States of America*, 104: 18866–70.

Carpenter, S.R., Mooney, H.A., Agard, J., Capistrano, D., DeFries, R.S., Diaz, S., *et al.* (2009), 'Science for Managing Ecosystem Services: Beyond the Millennium Ecosystem Assessment', *Proceedings of the National Academy of Sciences*, 106: 1305–12.

Carrero, G.C. and Fearnside, P.M. (2011), 'Forest Clearing Dynamics and the Expansion of Landholdings in Apuí, a Deforestation Hotspot on Brazil's Transamazon Highway', *Ecology and Society*, 16: 26.

Chapin, F.S., Carpenter, S.R., Kofinas, G.P., Folke, C., Abel, N., Clark, W.C., *et al.* (2010), 'Ecosystem Stewardship: Sustainability Strategies for a Rapidly Changing Planet', *Trends in Ecology and Evolution*, 25: 241–49.

Cox, P.M., Betts, R.A., Collins, M., Harris, P.P., Huntingford, C., and Jones, C.D. (2004), 'Amazonian Forest Dieback Under Climate-Carbon Cycle Projections for the 21st Century', *Theoretical and Applied Climatology*, 78: 137–56.

da Costa, A.C.L., Galbraith, D., Almeida, S., Portela, B.T.T., da Costa, M., Silva Junior, J.D.A., *et al.* (2010), 'Effect of 7 yr of Experimental Drought on Vegetation Dynamics and Biomass Storage of an Eastern Amazonian Rainforest', *New Phytologist*, 187: 579–91.

Davidson, E.A., Artaxo, P., Balch, J.K., Brown, I.F., Bustamante, M.M.C., Arau, A.C.D., *et al.* (2012), 'The Amazon Basin in Transition', *Nature*, 481: 321–28.

Elthahir, E.A.B. and Bras, R.L. (1994), 'Sensitivity of Regional Climate to Deforestation in the Amazon Basin', *Advances in Water Resources*, 17: 101–15.

Etter, A., Mcalpine, C., and Possingham, H. (2008), 'Historical Patterns and Drivers of Landscape Change in Colombia Since 1500: A Regionalized Spatial Approach to Historical Patterns and Drivers of Landscape Change in Colombia Since 1500', *Annals of the Association of American Geographers*, 98: 2–23.

Ewers, R.M., Laurance, W.F., and Souza, C.M. (2008), 'Temporal Fluctuations in Amazonian Deforestation Rates', *Environmental Conservation*, 35: 303.

FAO (2011), *The State of Forests in the Amazon Basin, Congo Basin and Southeast Asia* (Rome: UN Food and Agriculture Administration).

Federal Government of Brazil (2008), *Plano Amazonia Sustentavel* (downloaded from http://portal.saude.gov.br/portal/arquivos/pdf/pas.pdf).

Ferreira, J., Pardini, R., Metzger, J.P., Fonseca, C.R., Pompeu, P.S., Sparovek, G. and Louzada, J. (2012), 'Towards Sustainable Agriculture in Brazil: Challenges and Opportunities for Applied Ecological Research', *Journal of Applied Ecology*, DOI: 10.1111/j.1365-2664.2012.02145.x.

Folke, C., Carpenter, S.R., Walker, B., Scheffer, M., Chapin, T., and Rockström, J. (2010), 'Resilience Thinking: Integrating Resilience, Adaptability and Transformation', *Ecology and Society*, 15: 20–28.

Folke, C., Jansson, Å., Rockström, J., Olsson, P., Carpenter, S.R., Chapin, F.S., *et al.* (2011), 'Reconnecting to the Biosphere', *Ambio*, 40: 719–38.

Future Earth (2012), *Future Earth: Research for Global Sustainability: A Framework Document by the Future Earth Transition Team* (downloaded from http://www.icsu.org/future-earth/relevant_publications/future-earth-framework-document).

Golding, N. and Betts, R. (2008), 'Fire Risk in Amazonia Due to Climate Change in the HadCM3 Climate Model: Potential Interactions with Deforestation', *Global Biogeochemical Cycles*, 22: 1–10.

Guedes, G., Costa, S., and Brondízio, E. (2009), 'Revisiting the Hierarchy of Urban Areas in the Brazilian Amazon: A Multilevel Approach', *Population and Environment*, 30: 159–92.

Guimarães, J., Verissimo, A., Amaral, P. and Demachki, A. (2011), *Municipios Verdes: Caminhos Para a Sustentabilidade* (Belém: IMAZON).

Hall, A. (2008), 'Better RED than Dead: Paying the People for Environmental Services in Amazonia', *Philosophical Transactions of the Royal Society of London, Series B, Biological Sciences*, 363: 1925–32.

Hargrave, J. and Kis-Katos, K. (2011), *Economic Causes of Deforestation in the Brazilian Amazon* (University of Freiburg Department of International Economic Policy Discussion Paper Series, No. 17).

Hecht, S. (2010), 'The New Rurality: Globalization, Peasants and the Paradoxes of Landscapes', *Land Use Policy*, 27: 161–69.

Hecht, S.B. (2011), 'From Eco-catastrophe to Zero Deforestation? Interdisciplinarities, Politics, Environmentalisms and Reduced Clearing in Amazonia', *Environmental Conservation*, 39: 4–19.

Holling, C.S. (2001), 'Understanding the Complexity of Economic, Ecological, and Social Systems', *Ecosystems*, 4: 390–405.

Jupp, T.E., Cox, P.M., Rammig, A., Thonicke, K., Lucht, W., and Cramer, W. (2010), 'Development of Probability Density Functions for Future South American Rainfall', *New Phytologist*, 187: 682–93.

Killeen, T.J. (2007), *A Perfect Storm in the Amazon Wilderness: Development and Conservation in the Context of the Initiative for the Integration of the Regional Infrastructure of South America (IIRSA)* (Arlington, VA: Conservation International).

Lambin, E.F. and Meyfroidt, P. (2011), 'Global Land Use Change, Economic Globalization, and the Looming Land Scarcity', *Proceedings of the National Academy of Sciences* 108: 3465–72.

Lewis, S.L., Brando, P.M., Phillips, O.L., van der Heijden, G.M.F., and Nepstad, D. (2011), 'The 2010 Amazon Drought', *Science*, 331: 554.

Macedo, M.N., Defries, R.S., Morton, D.C., Stickler, C.M., Galford, G.L., and Shimabukuro, Y.E. (2012), 'Decoupling of Deforestation and Soy Production in the Southern Amazon During the Late 2000s', *Proceedings of the National Academy of Sciences* 109: 1341–46.

Malhi, Y., Wood, D., Baker, T.R., Wright, J., Phillips, O.L., Cochrane, T., *et al.* (2006), 'The Regional Variation of Aboveground Live Biomass in Old-Growth Amazonian Forests', *Global Change Biology*, 12: 1107–38.

Malhi, Y., Roberts, J.T., Betts, R.A., Killeen, T.J., Li, W., and Nobre, C.A. (2007), 'Climate Change, Deforestation and the Fate of the Amazon', *Science*, 319: 169–72.

Malhi, Y., Aragao, L.E.O.C., Galbraith, D., Huntingford, C., Fisher, R., Zelazowski, P., *et al.* (2009), 'Exploring the Likelihood and Mechanism of a Climate-Change Induced Dieback of the Amazon Rainforest', *Proceedings of the National Academy of Sciences*, 106: 20610–15.

Marengo, J.A., Nobre, C.A., Sampaio, G., Salazar, L.F., and Borma, L.S. (2011), 'Climate Change in the Amazon Basin: Tipping Points, Changes in Extremes, and Impacts on Natural and Human Systems', in M.B. Bush, J.R. Flenley, and W.D. Gosling (eds), *Tropical Rainforest Responses to Climatic Change* (London: Springer), 259–78.

McAlpine, C.A., Etter, A., Fearnside, P.M., Seabrook, L., and Laurance, W.F. (2009), 'Increasing World Consumption of Beef as a Driver of Regional and Global Change: A Call for Policy Action Based on Evidence from Queensland (Australia), Colombia and Brazil', *Global Environmental Change*, 19: 21–33.

146

Meir, P. and Woodward, F.I. (2010), Editorial: 'Amazonian Rain Forests and Drought: Response and Vulnerability', *New Phytologist*, 187: 553–57.

Nepstad, D., Carvalho, G., Cristina, A., Alencar, A., Paulo, Ä., Bishop, J., *et al.* (2001), 'Road Paving, Fire Regime Feedbacks, and the Future of Amazon Forests', *Forest Ecology and Management*, 154: 395–407.

Nepstad, D.C., Stickler, C.M., and Almeida, O.T. (2006), 'Globalization of the Amazon Soy and Beef Industries: Opportunities for Conservation', *Conservation Biology*, 20: 1595–603.

Nepstad, D.C., Stickler, C.M., Filho, B.S., Merry, F., Soares-Filho, B., and Nin, E. (2008), 'Interactions Among Amazon Land Use, Forests and Climate: Prospects for a Near-Term Forest Tipping Point', *Philosophical Transactions of the Royal Society of London, Series B, Biological Sciences*, 363: 1737–46.

Nepstad, D., Soares-Filho, B.S., Merry, F., Lima, A., Moutinho, P., Carter, J., *et al.* (2009), 'The End of Deforestation in the Brazilian Amazon', *Science*, 326: 1350–51.

Nepstad, D.C., McGrath, D.G., and Soares-Filho, B. (2011), 'Systemic Conservation, REDD, and the Future of the Amazon Basin', *Conservation Biology*, 25: 1113–16.

Nobre, C.A. and Borma, L.D.S. (2009), '"Tipping Points" for the Amazon Forest', *Current Opinion in Environmental Sustainability*, 1: 28–36.

Peres, C.A., Gardner, T.A., Barlow, J., Jansen, J., Michalski, F., Lees, A.C., Vieira, I.C.G., *et al.* (2010), 'Biodiversity Conservation in Human-Modified Amazonian Forest Landscapes', *Biological Conservation*, 143: 2314–27.

Perz, S.G., Aramburú, C., and Bremner, J. (2005), 'Population, Land Use and Deforestation in the Pan Amazon Basin: A Comparison of Brazil, Bolivia, Colombia, Ecuador, Peru and Venezuela', *Environment, Development and Sustainability*, 7: 23–49.

Perz, S., Brilhante, S., Brown, F., Caldas, M., Ikeda, S., Mendoza, E., *et al.* (2008), 'Road Building, Land Use and Climate Change: Prospects for Environmental Governance in the Amazon', *Philosophical Transactions of the Royal Society of London, Series B, Biological Sciences*, 363: 1889–95.

Perz, S.G., Leite, F., Simmons, C., Walker, R., and Caldas, M. (2010a), 'Intraregional Migration , Direct Action Land Reform , and New Land Settlements in the Brazilian Amazon', *Bulletin of Latin American Research*, 29: 459–76.

Perz, S.G., Brilhante, S., Brown, I.F., Michaelsen, A.C., Mendoza, E., Passos, V., *et al.* (2010b), 'Crossing Boundaries for Environmental Science and Management: Combining Interdisciplinary, Interorganizational and International Collaboration', *Environmental Conservation*, 37: 419–31.

Phillips, O.L., Malhi, Y., Higuchi, N., Laurance, W., Nuñez, P., Vasquez, R., *et al.* (1998), 'Changes in the Carbon Balance of Tropical Forests: Evidence from Long-Term Plots', *Science*, 282: 439–42.

Phillips, O.L., Aragao, L., Lewis, S.L., Fisher, J.B., Lloyd, J., Lopez-Gonzalez, G., *et al.* (2009), 'Drought Sensitivity of the Amazon Rainforest', *Science*, 323: 1344–47.

Polasky, S., Carpenter, S.R., Folke, C., and Keeler, B. (2011), 'Decision-Making Under Great Uncertainty: Environmental Management in an Era of Global Change', *Trends in Ecology and Evolution*, 26: 398–404.

Poulter, B., Hattermann, F., Hawkins, E., Zaehle, S., Sitch, S., Restrepo-Coupe, N., *et al.* (2010), 'Robust Dynamics of Amazon Dieback to Climate Change with Perturbed Ecosystem Model Parameters', *Global Change Biology*, 16: 2476–95.

Proambiente (2003), *Proposta Definitiva da Sociedade Civil Organizada Entregue ao Governo Federal* (Bensenville, IL: Mimeo).

Rammig, A., Jupp, T., Thonicke, K., Tietjen, B., Heinke, J., Ostberg, S., *et al.* (2010), 'Estimating the Risk of Amazonian Forest Dieback', *New Phytologist*, 187: 694–706.

Richards, P.D., Myers, R.J., Swinton, S.M., and Walker, R.T. (2012), 'Exchange Rates, Soybean Supply Response, and Deforestation in South America', *Global Environmental Change*, 22: 454–62.

Rodrigues, A.S.L., Ewers, R.M., Parry, L. Jr, Veríssimo, A., and Balmford, A. (2009), 'Boom-and-Bust Development Deforestation Frontier', *Science*, 324: 1435–37.

Silvestrini, R., Soares-Filho, B.S., Nepstad, D.C., Coe, M., Rodrigues, H., and Assuncao, R. (2011), 'Simulating Fire Regimes in the Amazon in Response to Climate Change and Deforestation', *Ecological Applications*, 21: 1573–90.

Soares-Filho, B., Moutinho, P., Nepstad, D., Anderson, A., Rodrigues, H., Garcia, R., *et al.* (2010), 'Role of Brazilian Amazon Protected Areas in Climate Change Mitigation', *Proceedings of the National Academy of Sciences*, 107: 10821–26.

Steffen, W., Persson, A., Deutsch, L., Zalasiewicz, J., Williams, M., Richardson, K., *et al.* (2011), 'The Anthropocene: From Global Change to Planetary Stewardship', *Ambio*, 40: 739–61.

Trivedi, M.R., Mitchell, A.W., Mardas, N., Parker, C., Watson, J.E., and Nobre, A.D. (2009), 'REDD and PINC: A New Policy Framework to Fund Tropical Forests as Global "Eco-utilities"', *IOP Conference Series: Earth and Environmental Science*, 8: 012005.

Walker, R. (2011), 'The Impact of Brazilian Biofuel Production on Amazônia', *Annals of the Association of American Geographers*, 101: 929–38.

PART 5
THE SPIRITUAL DIMENSION

Laurence Freeman, in his thoughtful chapter (5.1), makes the telling observation that 'the "spiritual dimension" of a conversation is often placed at the end of a meeting with a full agenda'. We have heeded his playful comment and placed his contribution at the heart of this book.

We have done so because the architecture of the volume rests on the evolution from the dissection of the causes and outcomes of tipping points in Parts 1–4 to the scope for learning, forecasting and adapting to their onset in Parts 6–8. In harmony with Giles Foden, Laurence Freeman suggests that addressing tipping points offers immense scope for creative re-interpretation of our psyches and mind patterns. It is right that his ideas enter the complete discourse at this point in the volume. He asks pertinent questions of science, of contemplation, of deeper awarenesses, and of creative optimism. He offers the prospect of meeting in wholeness, of opening minds to other ideas and possibilities, and of sharing understanding so that fresh perspectives can be gained. He suggests that science can learn to be more humble in its moralizing, and in so being, it can gain more attention and respect. Without the bedrock of sustainability science, we have no firm platform on which to address tipping points.

Contemplative consciousness rests on silence, on meditation, and on joining up. It provides the kinds of purposeful judgements and confidence in proposed actions which any attempt to get to the transformational tipping points which dominate the contributions to come will require. The wonderful value of Freeman's chapter lies in his presumption that we can think and act differently from where we have thought and acted until now. It is one aim of this volume to place into juxtaposition a range of perspectives from many patterns of thought and evidence, which release histories of imprisoned outlooks in favour of liberated reconnections. One

149

role for tipping points, no matter how irritating the notion is for many, is that they demand rethinking along with fresh ways of measuring and valuing actions and outcomes. Freeman offers us the insights which Foden initiated in what are delightfully complementary contributions.

David Atkinson, a former Bishop of Thetford, writes not just for Christianity (5.2). He proclaims that all faiths establish moral certainties for human occupancy of a self-perpetuating planet. These relate to ideals which, though rarely attainable and certainly not met, nevertheless guide our consciences and deeper behaviours. Many of the initiatives of sustainable localism which are appearing all over the globe, even in the face of oppression and impoverishment, stem from the faith communities. Indeed many are sustained by faith and by the tenacity of recognizing that well-being and betterment have to be fought for and triumphed in the face of the many impediments of mindsets and institutions. If we are indeed to overcome the scourges of malign tipping points which currently beset both the planet and its human family, we will have to do so with faith, conviction, and compassion at our core.

These twin contributions offer the hope and the enlightenment that spirituality and transcendence can grant us, should we develop the antennae to sense them and the limbs to enact them. They also provide a springboard for the emergence of a sustainability science. This is the science of exploring, of dialogue, of learning and listening, and of partnerships and companionships. Sustainability science blossoms through the marriage of evidence and interpretation; of the capacity to 're-behave', beyond the confines of habit and social loyalties; and of the scope for reconnection and conviction with passion. Sustainability science grapples with wicked problems which cannot be solved without wholeness and stillness being part of their analysis. Sustainability science seeks the experience of experiments and trials, at all scales of human endeavour, so that companionships endure between partners who explore and share the same journey. The two contributions in this Part provide the intellectual and spiritual basis for the successful emergence of sustainability science, without which we doubt whether tipping points can ever fully and confidently be addressed.

5.1
Contemplative consciousness

LAURENCE FREEMAN

Contemplative consciousness is a term acceptable, I hope, to the spiritually, religiously, and scientifically inclined. It describes a way of knowledge as old as history. Where do we start in making it useful as a guide through our contemporary labyrinthine crises?

Let me examine this with regard to two interesting aspects of our tipping points conversation. Contemplative consciousness reflects a common openness to radically new approaches (new ways of seeing and judging). It also links quite different specialities, thus aspiring to a new kind of vantage point of perception and action which is integral, simple and, hopefully, wise. I seek to contribute to both of these lines of thought by suggesting that the scientific method needs to be practically complemented by contemplative consciousness. But how might this best be achieved? The connecting link is that scientists and spiritual leaders need to trust each other and work together better. The present media-fuelled debate about religion and atheism is largely irrelevant, and a distracting sideshow to this endeavour.

Generally, the tipping points strategy strikes me, in the right sense of the word, as prophetic. Unfortunately the prophetic cannot be predictive in a way that satisfies our longing to know what is going to happen next. Altruistically, the prophetic seeks radical insights into the present structure of things in order to see what they *mean* in terms of the greater truth and of the well-being of the people. Contemplative consciousness differs from the scientific method in that it specifically addresses the undeniable human need for meaning.

So, I suggest that we are at a tipping point not only physically in terms of Earth's systems, but consciously, too, with regard to human self-awareness. Self-knowledge, according to some early masters of my spiritual tradition, is more important than the ability to work miracles. Technology has made the miraculous part of our daily life. So, as usual, human beings look for more. Beyond the miraculous lies . . . what?

Memento mori

To the degree that we can be sure that serious change is coming, and that we don't know quite how to deal with it, reflecting on the crisis is a memento mori, a remembering that we are mortal. Mortality characterizes everything from the individual organism to all energy systems we can observe. Spiritual wisdom engages this unsettling truth and has, in fact, turned it into a method for enhancing consciousness and maximizing our potential for experiencing quality of life. Buddhism expresses it in terms of *anatta*, the no-self or 'empty' nature of all things. This is not nihilistic, as it may sound, but denotes the universal characteristics of impermanence and interdependence. Christian thought arrives at the same insight through its terms of 'creatureliness' and poverty of 'spirit'. This is as much descriptive and verifiable as it is dogmatic. *Annata* and *God* are often seen as opposite poles of ways of describing the nature of things and their meaning. Contemplative consciousness is good at reconciling opposites. Nicholas of Cusa said that God is the 'union of opposites'.

Research shows that most people in terminal illness, if they accept their condition and if their pain is managed and they are psychologically cared for, will say that they have never enjoyed a better quality of life. Little more proof is needed than this research result, which never ceases to surprise, namely that happiness does not depend primarily upon our material situation. Terror Management Theory research claims that the repression of the fear of death is our primary repression, greater than the sexual. So, becoming free of repression constitutes an important part of the journey to human well-being. Facing our death is a way to clarity of mind and happiness. 'Keep death always before your eyes', as St Benedict said: environmental scientists today would probably agree. Better to die free than live imprisoned by fears. Science and its particular method of knowing also help us face this reality of mortality dispassionately.

The work of everyone involved in understanding and preparing for the great coming changes on the Earth can – by itself – help to raise consciousness and contribute to a better quality of life. We are facing change on a scale that involves dying to the past. Many geographical, biological, and sociological species and patterns that we have become attached to will be lost even in our lifetimes. Extinction, however, is not the only form of death. We demonstrably survive many forms of death – the irretrievable loss of what we once enjoyed. Whether we survive the last form of biological and neurological death is not a relevant part of the discussion here.

When we face mortality and impermanence we soon see that death is part of life and is to be accepted at every level from the molecular to the social. We are not only remembering the predicted death of the cosmos, the second law of thermo-dynamics, but also the inevitable changes in human self-organization which make up history and which have rapidly accelerated in the modern period. The feeling of fast and radical mutation is a particularly modern anxiety. 'Everything that is solid melts into air', according to Marx. The fear of change is no doubt related to our fear of death even if change is often as much desired as feared. The panic comes when we realize we cannot control the change. There is, however, no going back to the safe place we come from. Wherever we run, death is waiting for us.

So, the awareness of mortality, which is integral to the contemplative consciousness, is already present in the conversation we have begun regarding the future of the planet.

The scientific method and contemplative consciousness

The 'spiritual dimension' of a conversation is often placed at the end of a meeting with a full agenda. This may be for a number of reasons: because the spiritual is supposed to sum up and integrate all the preceding contributions (or give a satisfying illusion of this); or that it is intellectually generous to admit its relevance to the conversation even if that relevance is not paid much attention; or that, as we don't know the answer, we scoop the leftovers into this category of the nebulous, the paradoxical, and apophatic until we can deal with them rationally. Perhaps, though, if it is there at all, the spiritual aspect of our discourse should be somewhere in the middle of the agenda so that it exerts a panoptic influence and invites response from every aspect of the conversation. This however may be asking too much of most meetings.

In any case, by 'contemplative' I mean a way of seeing and under-standing that integrates all possible perspectives and available information.

It is therefore sapiential rather than encyclopaedic. Many great scientists of our era, from Heisenberg to Eddington, have arrived at this way of seeing through the scientific method. Thomas Aquinas defined it pithily as the 'simple enjoyment of the truth'. Simplicity is not facile but the goal of all truth-seeking and problem-solving. Children's consciousness may be our clearest teacher here.

By 'contemplative consciousness' I also mean a state of mind which is detached and free of absolutizing any point of view or interpretation whether scientific, political, or religious. This non-attachment (which is also good scientific method) is the mind and heart of the spiritual dimension. This too can be partially true of prayer without a contemplative element – even when you are praying 'for' something like good weather, or a medical cure, or world peace. But it is most fully true when contemplative consciousness is in play in prayer or indeed in any other application of our capacity for attention.

To understand the relevance of contemplative consciousness it is helpful to see that faith and belief are two distinct ways of seeing: although of course they cohabit and tread on each other's toes all the time. Briefly, I would say that faith is our capacity for commitment, endurance, transcendence of self-interest, and for love. Belief is how we articulate the reasons and values for our acting in a particular way.

At the end of his life the disillusioned philosopher Martin Heidegger came to believe that philosophy was finished, and that in the age of the new 'technicity', only a god can save us. Contemplative consciousness dispels the grip of this kind of disillusion and the pessimism it engenders with clarity of mind grounded in a verifiable, if not easily measurable, experience that generates only realistic expectations. The knowledge that arises in contemplation is distinct from that achieved by the scientific method, but they are compatible, complementary, and as necessary to each other as the two hemispheres of the brain. Contemplative knowledge is 'advaitic', that is, non-dualistic, free from the subject–object category. At times therefore it looks nonsensical or flaky to the rational mind. But it is also silent, simple, loving, and personally fulfilling, and it makes us happy. These are all aspects that touch and move us at the deepest human level, as do things like family, compassion, and beauty.

154

The elements of contemplation

I would like to suggest that terms like silence, stillness, and simplicity – universal elements of contemplation – are worthy of a good scientist's or indeed a good politician's attention.

Simplicity is empirical and irreducible. Its focus is on the thing being paid attention to, not the observer's own sense of identity or self-interest. Once we have connected to it we can more confidently confront the complexities of our problems, together with diverse models and metaphors for their resolution. *Silence* can, of course, be psychologically negative – as in denial or repression. But the silence of contemplation is a positive level of consciousness often enhancing creativity. It empowers us to use in a detached but energetic way all the necessary – even if necessarily abstract – models of intellectual enquiry. It is not anti-intellectual but it is not thought, as we ordinarily understand it, either. If the contemplative mind has been developed we can think, measure, analyse, and in fact do everything in a contemplative way. *Stillness* protects detachment and keeps us centred and free from emotional attachments, though it does not repress or deny feeling. It keeps us creative even after we have started to test the models and theories of our research and come to see that they need to be revised. This means we remain healthily detached from our own questions and answers, and hence open to criticism and change even after we have begun to invest our reputation in them.

Open minds

Contemplative consciousness is more concrete than it may sound. It therefore helps us to repair the abstraction and axiological poverty of an unintegrated, unbalanced scientific method – the kind that puts science above morality or common sense. I don't mean that contemplation discovers or endorses a particular morality or particular values. In this sense it is more about faith than belief. It touches on moral ideas and values, however, in ways that the scientific method is not called to do. Contemplative consciousness thus helps us to develop the axiologies that are necessary and relevant for our time. It teaches us that we cannot live by fixed, unchangeable beliefs as humanity did in the pre-industrial world. But it also reminds us that it is not enough to live by the law of market forces, by entrepreneurial projects driven by financial interest – or by science alone.

155

This contemplative approach leads to the opening of the 'catholic' mind. Forget the denominational associations with the word because it means the opposite of the sectarian. The *mens catolicus* is open to all sources of information and processing. Its default response to something new or strange is to try to include, not exclude. This means it is prepared, even eager, to change and expand its own parameters of belief. This openness to change in the patterns in which our mind works, is captured in the word 'metanoia' (turning of mind), and is equally essential to scientific development and to moral and spiritual growth.

Sometimes we get unexpected breakthroughs through this open-mindedness in understanding. Unassociated things come together in a wonderfully clear and simple way. But contemplative consciousness is generally developed by incremental growth rather than sudden enlightenments. Spiritual practices, pre-eminently the practice of meditation, have this effect. It is comparable with other 'nonlinear transitions where small changes make big differences'. The world's mystical traditions, which are all expressions of the catholic mind, distinguish between temporary (reversible) and permanent (irreversible) change. *States* of mind come and go and may give fleeting insights into truth. *Stages* of development represent the testing and integration of an insight after which we have changed direction, once and for all, even if we have not yet arrived at the destination.

This illustrates, I hope, why the 'spiritual dimension' of the conversation needs to be in the middle, not at the end. Contemplative consciousness does not build the solution, but it does help to create an integrated consciousness that is both more humorous and more serious, more playful and less dogmatic. It is a clearer mind. It also develops personal temperaments of finer quality and depth. This is what I mean by 'being spiritual'. The experiments through which we try to 'save the world' or improve it, are shaped by this way of seeing because they change people involved from within, developing those qualities that are embodied in the personalities who are doing the work. How many international summits on economic or environmental questions stumble and fail to apply the obvious necessary remedies because these personal qualities are not steering the debate or rescuing it from prejudiced nationalism or short-term political self-interest?

The current environmental crisis illustrates how urgent is this process of metanoia, this change of mind. The goal is a common or catholic mind that respects the rights of both the global and the local, and balances them. To advance the goal all possible ways of entering the common ground of humanity should be employed. Science is clearly one portal. Art and sport are others. Cultural exchange especially opens young minds. Education, rather than just technical training for employment, is a basic pre-requisite of this personal development. Religion is also necessary. The totalitarian failures to destroy it in the last century show that, like art and science, it is an integral part of the human mix.

The embarrassment of religion: contemplative science

The divorce and distrust between religion and science in the modern period is out of date in an era that demands a new consciousness. However much religious institutions may embarrass or outrage, the contemplative is often carried and transmitted by them.

The contemporary British polemics in the media between scientific atheism and religious superstition is entertaining but quaint. It misses the spirit of the age. The twentieth-century prediction of the extinction of religion in the face of scientific advances has been disappointed. But despite the rise of religious fundamentalism – a modernist product of this divorce between religion and science – a new kind of global, contemplative religious consciousness is developing. Each religious tradition revolves around a contemplative sun and the awareness of this is growing stronger in them all as their followers mature. Contemplative religious consciousness understandably receives much less media attention but what if it represents a *stage* of development, not (as in the case of fundamentalism) just a passing *state* of mind? Inter-religious dialogue, scientifically engaged religious teachers like the Dalai Lama, and countless grassroots movements are advancing a global metanoia through religion. The secular worldview that has emerged in all cultures to differing degrees is not inherently anti-religious. It simply sees that religion occupies a new place in the world, particularly in relation to science and personal freedom. Religion can no longer claim special privileges and must meet the non-religious on a level playing field of reason and faith.

The goal of a generalized contemplative consciousness is not just abstract science. It is an effective implementation of the best science. (Similarly the goal is not a platonic, unfeeling religion but one actively engaged in addressing the material and spiritual needs of all humanity.) This kind of 'total (or contemplative) science' is prophetic. It can be

157

ridiculed and may be treated with suspicion in the academy; but it could also turn out to be the kind of science needed today, upheld by the most authentic and effective kind of scientific behaviour.

Science and contemplative religion in the global crisis are both concerned with advancing the deepest well-being for the greatest number while they follow different protocols. But they are complementary; and so real connections can be made if the time is given to identifying them. These connections will be manifestations of wisdom, good sense guided by simple human kindness, and clear thinking backed up by courageous risk-taking. In the Book of Wisdom it says that the 'hope for the salvation of the world lies in the greatest number of wise people'. Unfortunately it doesn't say how many are needed, but presumably more than we have at present.

I suggest thought be given as to how the connections can be made between scientists and spiritual practitioners operating within a contemplative, integrated framework. This connection could easily begin (and perhaps has begun already) by acknowledging the psychological and physical benefits of meditation. It stands that if these benefits are useful at the personal and interpersonal levels they will also help in resolving the crisis we all face. For example, the British National Health Service has recognized that meditation may be more effective and certainly less expensive than medication in addressing the problems of mental illness and promoting mental health.

I think this approach to developing the contemplative consciousness is well-researched and persuasive. I would push it further, however, beyond cholesterol levels and depression. Beyond these benefits lie, in the next realm, many spiritual fruits.

Relating the scientific method to contemplative consciousness promises a radical new approach to human problem-solving. We need intercultural and political agreements about the rules of living together in the future, but for these to be sustainable there is also a need for consensus about the role of wisdom itself. This agreement would evoke the axiological matrices from which specific moral values can be created inside diverse human cultures and also govern our innovative projects for improving quality of life worldwide. It is important, of course, that these ways of agreeing on values are not too specific, and in particular not too occidental.

It is now time in my argument to get down to a practical issue, the role of meditation in developing contemplative consciousness.

Meditation

Once religion has been set free from the sectarian instinct to convert, it is able to explore reality and to advance the integration of all forms of knowledge. Central to this venture is the practice of meditation.

Present in the 40,000-year-old aboriginal culture (*dadirri*) and first recorded in Indian philosophy about 1500 BC, meditation is a universal human wisdom and form of knowledge. It is global and it is locally present at the core of all the religious traditions. It is a gateway to humanity's common ground. Medical research over the past sixty years concludes that meditation is good for people at the physical and psychological levels. The NHS is currently adopting meditation as part of its cost-cutting mental health policy. Schools are widely introducing it into the classroom. Many financial and industrial institutions have designated meditation spaces and like it being taught to their staff to reduce stress and increase productivity. These *benefits* – stress-reduction, anger-control, immune system enhancement – are not incompatible with those spiritual *fruits* of meditation which are less easily measured but no less constitutive of human well-being – love, joy, peace, patience, kindness, goodness, fidelity, and self-control.

There are circumstances when a purely 'secular' approach to meditation works best. However the religious origin and spiritual significance of meditation should not be ignored, as there are distinct advantages in teaching meditation with a spiritual approach as well. For example, the practice of meditation is a discipline as well as a technique. Disciplines are best learned and sustained in learning groups – the sense of community and the local and global networks which meditation naturally engenders at transcultural and inter-religious levels.

If we are to think radically, I would suggest an approach to a strategy for dealing with tipping points that includes acknowledging the practice of meditation as a way of metanoia, seeing in a new way. It can also be recommended because it develops the best possible environment for communicating hard truths to the general public, such as that of keeping global warming to a moderated 2 per cent over pre-industrial levels. Scientific method, political policy and religious wisdom can 'meet' in meditation where the personal and the collective are harmonized. They need to meet; they don't need to merge.

I suggest thought be given as to how the connections can be made between scientists and spiritual leaders operating within a contemplative, integrated framework. This connection could begin with an acknow-ledgement of the value of meditation for resolving the crisis and the responsibility of religion to collaborate in the work. It would also help to disseminate the insights necessary to change public policy from the grassroots upwards. It would encourage political and economic leaders to think and act with a common mind.

Meditation, of course, is part of the most ancient wisdom of humanity and has been carried through history by religious traditions, especially the monastic lineages. Seen with the detached but not cold gaze of the contemplative consciousness, the benefits are attractive but the spiritual fruits also come into view – ranging from love to self-control. In the understanding of this contemplative practice (maybe a technique to the scientist, a discipline to the spiritual) a possible new relationship between techno-science and religion becomes imaginable.

Teaching meditation as a spiritual practice has convinced me it is relevant to the contemporary crisis. As a way of experiencing unity with those of different cultural, intellectual and religious backgrounds it is the most direct way to verify the common ground of humanity. In teaching children to meditate the teacher or parent is often amazed at how readily – and profitably – the child responds. Better learning, happier behavioural patterns, personal peace, and calmness quickly become evident results. The benefits are the measurable expressions of the spiritual.

Thinking about medium- to long-term responses to the crisis, the teaching of meditation to children on a global scale makes a sense that is hard to deny. Within twenty years it would ensure a generation more attuned to the contemplative consciousness than we might imagine. If we believe that the way we look at a problem is an indispensable part of its solution, what better, cheaper, and simpler way do we have to change the way humanity approaches itself and its situation? Recent figures say that the number of people on anti-depressants in the UK has increased in the past four years by 40 per cent. We also know that more than half of the cases of diagnosed mental illness in later life make their first appearance before the age of fourteen. And we know that meditation makes a sig-nificant and beneficial difference.

Crisis

This 'contemplative dimension' to the science, economics and politics of global warming will help the tipping point to ease from the malign to the benign.

Critical moments are good for developing contemplative consciousness. Historically, some of the most flourishing contemplative schools of wisdom have come to birth in times of social and economic breakdown – like the great English mystical school of the fourteenth century during the Black Death and the Hundred Years War. Contemplative consciousness provides intellectual depth and stability in practical problem solving. It operates with greater calmness and clarity in the midst of crisis because it is able to trust the basic goodness of human nature.

Trusting the goodness of people is necessary for the kind of managed change that does not infantalize society or tyrannize it. Contemplative consciousness – even when it has been developed in a small minority of people – exposes lies and the machinations of tyranny. It helps to shape policy and allow quick response in ways that are not excessive or over-controlling. In times of social breakdown, 'security' becomes a major concern but, if it becomes obsessive, it leads to a perilous and hard to reverse mass surrender of civil liberties such as occurred in Germany in the 1930s. The cardinal virtues of justice, moderation, prudence, and courage infiltrate the political and social ethos through the contemplative mind and determine good political and economic policy that applies the recommendations of science. These virtues that underlie civilized behaviour are demonstrably generated and developed in the contemplative experience.

Developing a contemplative consciousness in a time of crisis is the opposite of indoctrination. It may not be a mass movement, and political or religious institutions have a limited power to promote it. Yet all are capable of it and all are influenced by its development. There is a hunger – a market for this – and enlightened scientists can help promote it by their endorsement. The contemplative way of *seeing* manifests liberty at the deepest level. It can be taught but it cannot be imposed and must be learned through personal experience. As Plato's allegory of the cave illustrates, it will be only a few at first who venture out of the realm of shadows into the clear light of day and then urge their fellows to do the same. But we must start somewhere.

Expanding our notion of prayer to include the exercise of contemplative consciousness, this definition by Origen, a second-century Christian teacher, makes good sense for us today:

> We do not pray to get benefits from God but to become like God. Praying itself is good. It calms the mind, reduces sin and promotes good deeds.
>
> *(De Oratione)*

In crisis, vulnerability and uncertainty also expose us, not just to the truths of chaos theory but also to the graciousness of life, the pure givenness of reality and, at times, the goodness of human nature. We can be open on a global scale and simultaneously as never before to the richness of a silent and non-formulaic truth. The contemplative state of mind attunes to this purity of existence and to the silence of truth. It gives space for all kinds of existence and yet also frees our powers of clear discernment. We are then not confused by a multiplicity of choices, and do not worship choice as the exclusive mark of freedom.

Language and silence

Conversations easily get bogged down when too much time is given to defining terms. Tipping points is a readily understood and attractive image for understanding the problems of change and uncertainty we face. If it is true that we can be imprisoned or misled by our metaphors, we can also practice detachment from them in the silence of the contemplative mind.

Stories and narratives are as necessary and helpful, but also as tenuous, as individual terms and vocabularies. The 'parable' may be a more helpful term for the ways we narrate the story of our quest. It means literally a 'throwing alongside' and it is more than a moral story or an allegory. It is an invitation to integrate that which seems incompatible and therefore leads to wisdom, the union of opposites, and creative intelligence. Parables, like *koans*, tend to leave us a little in the air, not totally certain that the end has yet come. They are ideal teaching tools, therefore, because they instruct with interest but do not deliver dogmatic answers. They cultivate the contemplative consciousness because they focus on the next stage of the process of understanding rather than building a shrine to what you have reached so far.

Some conclusions

The consequence of tipping points can, malignantly, be catastrophic both environmentally and socially. Driven by panic, the virtue of justice and the practice of compassion towards the weakest can quickly be lost. The more leaders develop a personal level of contemplative consciousness, the less likely are any downward spirals of collapsing social values.

Tipping points are nonlinear and unpredictable. This can terrify the rational mind. But the fear factor inspired by uncertainty is mitigated by the 'apophatic' mind. This complements the 'kataphatic' because it recognizes that 'unknowing' is also a way of knowing. In the same way, the left- and right-hand hemispheres of the brain are in constant communication while operating in distinct modes.

There are ethical questions raised by the science of tipping points. The personal dimension or the dignity of individuals in a time of crisis must not be overridden by scientific knowledge or political considerations. Balancing the local and the global, the individual and the collective, demands a new way of seeing and knowing. It is not merely of academic or political interest. The contemplative dimension of consciousness allows for the integration of these complementary perspectives – at times, faced with impossible choices, with the 'wisdom of Solomon'.

There may be a good outcome from all this. Most certainly there can be, and it depends largely upon the individuals who are leading the way through the crisis. The virtue of hope is not putting the best spin on bad news or fiddling while the planet burns. It is a conviction that because of, and not despite the human element, an eventually positive outcome is always possible.

Is it too late? The contemplative consciousness is programmed to find meaning in the worst. With the experience of meaning our confidence in the fundamental goodness of human nature allows for resilience in the face of failure or defeat that always transforms despair into hope – and an unexpected, new way of seeing.

I appreciate this opportunity to contribute to the discussion, because of what I have learnt from it, and also because it helps to clarify in my own mind the particular tipping point – many such points make up the current global crisis – that religion itself is passing through. In one perspective this looks like failure and erosion. From another – what I call the contemplative – it is full of hope and wonder as a new kind of religious consciousness evolves in humanity, one which advances the satisfying experience of unity

163

without diminishing the richness of diversity. If this is true of one area of human experience during our time of transition, it might well be of hope and interest to many other areas of human life and knowledge that are also undergoing our present transformation. Each newly perceived connection between all the tipping points releases energy and yields new insight. And, to end on a practical note, meditation shows how it is possible to create a community of faith, leading to action, among people of different beliefs.

Commentary 5.2

Faith and tipping points

DAVID ATKINSON

There is an episode of *Yes Minister* in which Jim Hacker is discussing a document with Bernard: 'I know what it says . . . what does it mean?' He knew the facts; he did not have a narrative of meaning in which to locate them. The same is often true about climate change. The scientific consensus is increasingly confident on many of the basic facts, for all the many remaining uncertainties. But what do they mean? What story shall we tell in order to respond to them?

As the authors of these chapters and commentaries explain, the language of 'tipping points' can be used as a metaphor for interpreting uncertainty, complexity, unpredictability. And one of the ways the metaphor is used is through narrative, the art of storytelling. There are a number of stories being told in response to the questions posed for us by 'potentially convulsive' climate change. Questions about our relationship to the planet and to each other; about altruism and selfishness; about whether we are able to overcome mistrust and develop global cooperation; about the place of technology in causing and perhaps solving our problems. There are other questions about the nature of our primary values, hopes and goals; about whether it is possible to live sustainably within planetary limits; about how we should seek justice, especially for the most disadvantaged parts of the Earth; about our obligations to the future; about how we think about human life and destiny, cope with uncertainties; and about our vulnerabilities, hopes, and fears. There are moral dimensions – and, I would argue, spiritual dimensions – to each of these questions.

A number of narratives are being formulated in response. One is about management. The Earth is resilient; we can therefore exploit it as much as we need for our own good. Resource depletion is not something to be anxious about – technological discovery has always come to our aid in the past.

165

Another is about fear. The Earth system is actually very fragile and sensitive to climate and other change. We must be very worried about what we are doing to the planet. Be afraid: be very afraid.

There is a third narrative that we could say is about greed. We are a market-led society in which something called 'the market' rules. Finance trumps every other value. Everything, including the environment, becomes a commodity to be desired. The myth of limitless economic growth is a primary driver of climate disruption.

Alongside these, other narratives are being prepared by religious people and communities, narratives which have something fresh and potentially more creative to offer. The narrative of the Christian story (which is where I locate myself) is not about our management of the world: but about wonder and worship and recognizing that the whole created order comes to us as gift. There is *sacredness* about God's world, in which we can delight, but which requires the acknowledgement of more – much more – than a technical fix.

The Christian story is not about fear, but about a community discovering what it means to live in freedom. It is about a narrative which begins in God's creative love for the world, and ends in God's 'kingdom' of justice, which is the whole of creation healed. This is the basis for living in hope. Within this narrative, humanity has a special role under God for the cherishing and protection of the planet and for the well-being of all creatures with which we are interdependent. It is a story about the growth of a community marked by neighbour love and justice, especially for the most disadvantaged. It is not about the autonomy which destroys any sense of community and makes everything into a commodity. It is rather a story about mutual cooperation and responsibility in place of fear. It recognizes human and planetary values which cannot be reduced to a price – such as friendship and loyalty, creative work, beauty, and love.

The Christian narrative of the human experience and our place in the created order is not therefore about greed, but about gratitude for gift, shown in self-giving, respect, and compassionate concern for the well-being of others, for 'the flourishing of innate and learned qualities of virtue and goodness, and for the empathy of compassion and solidarity'.

The retelling of this story is what Christian liturgy is about, including space for meditative reflection on 'what it means' – 'visualizing new horizons'. Such stories and liturgies are not unique to the Christian tradition. Many faith communities, focused in worship, are called to express their community life in service for others and for the planet. And this has given rise to a host of small-scale local initiatives, based around churches, mosques, temples, or synagogues, in which people are trying to live more simply, more responsibly, and more aware of the possible 'convulsions' of tipping points on the horizon.

For example, the 'Sabbath' principle is about recognizing the rhythms of the Earth, and about living with sufficiency. The biblical concept of 'jubilee' supported the Jubilee 2000 campaign about reducing international debt. The Church of England, with its buildings, schools, land, offices, and numerous community initiatives, promotes a 'Shrinking the Footprint Campaign' to reduce carbon emissions, and a Seven Year Plan for environmental responsibility. Christian agencies such as Christian Aid and Tearfund see that their development agenda needs to be woven into the environmental agenda. Climate change is described by such organizations as an issue of justice. Many Christians are involved in the Transition Town movement. There are a variety of Christian-based organizations (A Rocha, Christian Ecology Link, Eco-congregations, Operation Noah) working at the practice of a Christian ecology. The John Ray Initiative promotes scholarly and practical engagement between environmental science and religion. Archbishop Rowan Williams, when he was Archbishop of Canterbury, among others, has promoted significant inter-faith dialogue on the environment.

So faith communities are among many others working for what Tim O'Riordan calls (in drafts for this volume) 'the beneficial outcomes of new states of living and valuing betterment for all, such as in health, security, in manageable scales of living and communicating, and of forming economic relationships on the local rather than the multinational scale'. They contribute to the myriad of 'good news' stories we are urged to listen to, and in some places are becoming small, fresh 'islands of transformation'. Maybe they could even become benign cultural and social 'tipping points' themselves.

PART 6
POLITICS, THE MARKETS, AND BUSINESS

In designing the contributions for this volume, we knew this would be a difficult Part to get right. It deals with the heart of addressing tipping points. This is the nexus of markets, politics, corporates, and social mores, all of which are meant to produce betterment for both the planet and all of its human family for all time. Lying within this challenging mixture are the powerful themes of the modern age: the social value of markets, the effectiveness of democracies, the benign intent of business, and the strength and clarity of leadership.

One pivotal chapter is that by Sara Parkin (6.3). She stresses that the economy, democracy, and politics are social systems designed for collective betterment so are not beyond human engagement and improvement. But she bemoans the intellectual failure to fuse social and environmental outcomes as the purpose of economics. She finds the denial and fear of politicians as they struggle to resuscitate conceptually and practically bank-rupt economies understandable, but questions the capability of leadership to reconfigure the environmental challenge as one of social and economic opportunity. Promise lies through new strategies to build confidence around a new logic for how the economy *could* work. A logic that has a good story to tell about the long term, can guide decisions in the near term, and which builds on the best of people. She is optimistic that multiple social tipping points could come about, but only if the guardians of all the intellectual and evidential elements – universities – concentrate effort on supporting this civilization-determining effort.

Chapter 6.1 grapples with what is inevitably a highly contentious issue. This is the effectiveness of the markets to foresee, to anticipate, to avoid, and to adapt to tipping points. There will be many readers who see in already well-regulated but essentially liberated markets the qualities for achieving this. They will extol the propulsiveness of creative competition, innovation, and enterprise. They will champion the scope for technology, communication, and rapid data processing at the touch of an interactive phone, to open up whole new vistas of prosperity and social betterment. This has been the way of the markets over the years.

Others will share the feelings expressed in Chapters 6.1, 6.2, and 6.3, namely that there is no guarantee of deep learning and transformation in modern markets and polities. Paul Ekins (6.2) sees the likelihood of repeat failures of financial markets, as the sobriety of contrition gives way to a false euphoria of renewed bonuses and hence repeated mistakes. We take the view that only the spectre of real economic trouble coupled to the continued costs of maintaining international security, national social order, and containing the scope for socially disrupting economic migration on a mass scale, will cause politicians to rethink, and local communities to regroup.

But we recognize that this is not a widely held perspective. So we asked a number of business leaders and commentators to offer their perspectives on the discussions of the contributions in the book as a whole, as well as the controversial interpretations of markets and politics outlined in Chapter 6.1. Their overall reaction was both positive and optimistic. Two former chief executives, Amanda Long (6.4) and Keith Clarke (6.5), offer the pragmatic necessities of short termism and of the need to hold on to valued employees and to feed their families, whilst creating real wealth. Both see the scope for transformation, Keith Clarke through enlightened regulation with equal opportunities for creative competition within agreed and monitored frameworks. Amanda Long and John Elkington (6.6) as well as Thomas Lingard (6.8) from a company perspective, all see the unleashing of a breakthrough revolution towards sustainable capitalism, as information is better organized as to the possible malign and benign outcomes of their actions on social and ecological well-being. They hold a vision of a new form of ecologically framed and socially improving capitalism which can indeed flourish as sustainability science offers better advice and guidance. It is vital that they are right.

The other pivotal commentary (6.7) in this collection is that by Charles Clarke, a former UK cabinet minister. With the wisdom of perspective he offers seven reasons why it is so difficult for governments to grapple with tipping points even when they are menacing on the horizon. He identifies the monumental struggles of analysing and articulating issues when they are not fully nested in the public and media mind. He points to the power of disenchanted lobbyists when their interests are threatened, and the ever-present meddling of oppositions, often with opportunism as their guide. He also emphasizes the need to respect international treaties and obligations, not least associated with the European Union. These slow down and often weaken the kinds of spearing initiatives which the challenge of tipping points often demands.

Charles Clarke calls for the same kinds of bold and determined leadership advocated by Sara Parkin, but echoed by all of the contributors to this Part. What is missing is the politics and economics of the long term, the ethics of the compassion for those generations to come who have no democratic voice at present, and the sensitivities and scientific scenarios for estimating the resilience of the planetary life-support processes in times to come, especially if actions are taken now which are unpopular and unwelcome. This is why there are moves in both polities and markets for better capacities for evaluating the well-being of ecosystems and societies in the trajectories of addressing tipping points. This could amount to formation of an 'ombudsman for the future', or for processes of policy evaluation which explicitly encompass resilience and restoration of both ecological and social well-being.

But such ideas lie mostly in the domains of political institutions and processes. They do not nestle in the hearts of business and the many collectivities of people we loosely refer to as 'society'. When a systematic care for a better interconnected ecological, social and economic future in the round becomes embedded in markets, polities, and a real fusing of the private, public, and civic sectors: maybe then, this will be seen as one test of successfully addressing tipping points.

6.1
Sustaining markets, establishing well-being, and promoting social virtue for transformational tipping points[1]

TIM O'RIORDAN

The chapters and commentaries which compose this Part are concerned with the social, political, and economic conditions that might be best able to identify, anticipate, and cope with tipping points. Part of this process is to consider the changing roles of markets and of the political structures in which they function.

In approaching this coupling, this chapter looks at the evolving linkages between markets, citizens, and politics as means of making decisions about the economy, via the uses of concepts such as 'prosperity', 'progress', and 'citizenship'. It ends with some suggestions for restructuring the relationships between markets, regulation, incentives, civic virtue, and responsible government for guiding us towards positively transformational tipping points. In doing so, this introductory chapter and Chapter 6.3 by Sara Parkin consider not only the strengths and weaknesses of markets as means of making economic decisions, but also the strengths and weaknesses of the many influences of political systems and cultures which are shaped by markets, as well as the appropriate role for individuals and groups of citizens.

These arrangements are, of course, always linked together in some way. Political institutions are always occupied in regulating and responding to the workings of the market. Markets develop within expressions of values and aspirational contexts created by the activities and cultural outlooks of

[1] This chapter greatly benefited from the ideas of Victor Anderson.

civil society and its political structures. Individuals, in their own lives and as citizens, both respond to and influence the market and politics. The ways in which the three currently combine give little attention to long-term sustainability. It is therefore vitally important to address their very basic deficiencies so that they function cooperatively to create the conditions for successfully addressing positively transformational tipping points.

Markets and the future

The 'market' is a mechanism for guiding behaviour and investment, for encouraging a constructive relationship between buyers and sellers and supply and demand, for promoting innovation, productivity, and competition so as to encourage efficiency and to minimize inflation, and to guide behaviour through prices, incentives, and other regulatory measures. Broadly there are three forms of markets:

- Markets which are open to exchange processes, via buying, selling, and bartering, essentially informal markets of huge variety, including 'black' markets;
- Markets which seek a more formal social contract between the economy and the citizen, through a combination of political and market processes, the socio-democratic markets;
- Markets which seek to free up exchange and innovation in a more unrestrained manner, the so-called 'neoliberal' markets.

Markets can act locally, or through national and multinational agreements, or globally. All markets are regulated to one degree or another, but none is regulated to ensure the sustainable long term, or, indeed, a socially fair and redistributive present. Markets currently consider the uncertain future in a number of ways, as outlined below.

1. Insurance and the spreading of risk

This is normally only tackled where profits are reasonably guaranteed. In general, this process is based on relatively short-term planning and calculation of returns. So very long-term notions, such as those connected to malign or benign tipping points, are not automatically included. Markets are just beginning to recognize that climate change will introduce a whole series of 'normal abnormal' weather-related events, such as droughts, floods, storms, and fires, which will have to be factored into costs and opportunities. This is a key role for the tipping points science offered by Tim Lenton in Chapter 2.1.

2. Futures contracts

Futures contracts, whereby prices are fixed in advance of goods and commodities being supplied, are also fairly short-term in perspective – for example, for periods of three months. Futures contracts do not normally take into account long-term tipping point considerations, even when there are some (admittedly imperfect) measures on offer. This point is made clearly from the perspective of a CEO of a global company, Keith Clarke, in his commentary (6.5).

3. Investment geared towards future returns

Investment geared towards future returns, provided reasonable guarantees are thrown in, is nearly always based on models of investment where there is a presumption of growth, innovation, and overall betterment of income. Indeed, these are important preconditions. Up until now investment for the future has always been predicated on a reasonable guarantee of future returns on the funds committed. In a world of unstable financial markets and diminishing ecosystem functioning, as well as growing social tension and increasing political distrust, it may no longer be possible to guarantee long-term payback from a given investment. Yet, as Dolphin and Nash (2011: 20–21) argue, there is no apparent shift in the prevailing economic paradigm to give attention to this danger. Indeed they go further. They argue that unless those who seek a more 'eco-centered' economics of the kind promoted by Tim Jackson (2011) apply their new paradigms to real-world evidence, their propositions will not be heard by top-table economists who prefer to tweak the more conventional approaches. We address this conundrum in Part 8.

4. Lending at interest, depending on positive interest rates

The charging of interest also depends on a critical basic assumption. This is that borrowers will normally have more money (even after taking the effect of inflation into account) when they come to repay the loan than they had when they took it out in the first place, enabling them to pay the interest as well as repaying the loan. On the scale of the economy as a whole, this depends on economic growth, and continuing investment. And

175

such growth in turn ultimately depends on stable amounts of available ecological and natural resources, as well as reliable social relationships and justice. If these two conditions are not met, or are not calculated in pricing and regulation, or are not monitored by markets, then interest rates cannot do their intended job. The discussion in the concluding chapter (8.1) over planetary boundaries and social floors is not apparently yet incorporated in any setting of interest rates, which currently are geared to the very short term.

The UK government has established a Natural Capital Committee, reporting to the Treasury, which is asked to report on the unsustainable trajectory of natural resources use, to offer procedures to halt such losses based on robust cost-effectiveness measures, and to encourage scientific research to buttress its work. If this Committee is allowed to do its work effectively, this will mark the beginning of an important shift in national economic accounting, which may be emulated elsewhere and hopefully by the UN. The test will lie in the length of the time-framing of the Committee's scenarios, and how much it will take into account the precursors of possible tipping points outlined in Chapters 1.1 and 2.1.

5. Trading in shares, commodities, and currencies

This is based on guesses about the future, in which 90 days appears as 'long-term', and trading is often within daily cycles and perturbations. The recent convulsions in global commodity and stock markets show that these are subject to speculation and manipulation, on confidence and despair, on top of the basic influences of supply and demand. Commodities appear to be a form of currency and not just a natural resource. This will be another test for the Natural Capital Committee to prove its spurs.

6. Self-interest and short-term objectives

The market consists largely of individuals attempting to secure self-interested and/or short-term objectives. So there is no inherent sense of the collective interest. Indeed, it can be argued from the events of the past few years, that 'markets' predominately expose an ideology favouring the greed of the shareholder and the boards of directors, not a fundamental concern for the wider and longer-term public interest or social fairness.

7. Undervaluing of future costs and benefits

Interest rates, and discount rates based largely on them, usually lead to an undervaluing of future costs and benefits by comparison with the short term. This point was graphically illustrated by the Stern Report (2007), which showed that delay in reducing greenhouse gas emissions would result in increasingly higher costs in the future. These costs would escalate both in the expenditures for removing the gases as well as for the consequences to societies and economies of greater climate change. In such a case, claimed Stern, discount rates should be lower than normal 'market' rates.

Konrad Ott (2003) notes that 'rationality' tends to dictate 'prudence' in discounting. This brings the maximization of the present value of net benefits to the fore. This is a prescription for short-termism, high interest rates and 'sure bets'. But Ott also notes that 'reason' may amend this perspective when the future of the quality of life is at stake. Furthermore, if a moral outcome (such as social justice and ecological resilience) is to be retained (sustained) then a zero-discounting process may be used. Hence discounting may have to be much more dependent on context, especially where huge uncertainties over the well-being of the unborn are involved. Paradoxically, the current commitment to very low interest rates may penalize the scope for investment for the betterment of future generations, as scarce investment funds are diverted to present gains rather than providing buffering funds for possible tipping point outcomes.

8. Externalities

'Externalities' are, by definition, factors the market does not take into account. These include some very important considerations from environment and sustainability perspectives. This is the essence of the new moves to incorporate natural capital accounting into mainstream economics (Kumar *et al.* 2010; HM Government 2011: 36). What some economists see as 'externalities' others see as 'cost-shifting successes', an outcome of an essentially political process in which firms, and some other economic actors, are able to shift costs away to someone else, and/or to the environment. As noted above, the possible pioneering reports of the newly formed Natural Capital Committee could open up exciting new approaches to long-term adaptation to avoid degradation of nature. It will have its work cut out. The very persistence of the term 'externality' suggests that such effects are regarded as essentially peripheral to the mainstream of prosperity formation.

9. Abrupt basic change

Abrupt basic change is difficult for markets to cope with because of their inherent lack of coordination, unless they either take the form of a highly organized monopoly or oligopoly, or depend on large-scale government intervention. This suggests that 'tipping points', or abrupt and reinforcing shifts in Earth system processes, are not readily handled by market procedures. As was outlined by Tim Lenton in Chapter 2.1, not only are tipping points highly uncertain, they are also potentially catastrophic in effect, over relatively short time periods. Markets at present contain few cushioning mechanisms for such eventualities.

What is particularly revealing is the current fixation with the short term, and the hedging against future uncertainty. A survey for the UN Environment Programme (2011) found that both the demands of the shareholders and the needs to ensure current profitability are seriously limiting both the ability for businesses to plan for sustainability, and to prepare for anything close to tipping points.

A global survey of 642 senior executives, campaigners, and academics conducted by consultancies GlobeScan and SustainAbility found that 88 per cent of respondents regarded pressure to deliver immediate financial results remained a significant barrier to firms' sustainability efforts.

Dolphin and Nash (2011: 16–18) offer an interesting perspective on this theme. They claim that the mainstream economists and their polity bedfellows have faith in technology and investment, that they put to one side climate change and resource limitations, believe that ecological economics has no firm deliverable foundation, and in any case cannot cope with the current fiscal and sovereign debt crises. So they see the economics of a regulated market as continuing well into the real crises to come.

Complexity economics seeks to understand how interactions at the micro level lead to particular macroeconomic outcomes. Change and adaptation at the individual level are viewed as the cause of emergent patterns that can only be seen at the macro level. Most non-economists would recognize this as a reasonable description of the real world and accept that 'without an adequate understanding of [the inherent dynamics and instability of economic systems] one is likely to miss the major factors that influence the economic sphere of our societies' (Colander *et al.* 2008: 3). They would be surprised, therefore, to discover that the vast majority of economists continue to cling to the orthodox or traditional neoclassical economic view of the world, which simply fails to provide for such an understanding.

How do polities deal with tipping points?

'Polities' rather than governments are the issue here. What we are concerned with is not simply governments themselves, but governments in the context of whole political systems, including the values and behaviours of citizens and organizations involved in those systems. This combination is what is referred to here as 'polity'.

Again, as with markets, there are both strengths and weaknesses. The strengths and weaknesses of a polity concern not only the merits of its institutions and their procedures, but also the political culture within which the institutions function. Political parties generally play an important part in shaping the culture, as well as the workings of the institutions. Polities consider the future in a number of ways:

- They generally exist for longer than the lifetime of an individual, and therefore can take a more long-term view.
- They can draw on senses of loyalty, identification, and idealism which favour long-term approaches – e.g. building up an industrial base at the expense of individual consumption, sacrifice in wartime for the good of the nation, the sense of a 'long march' of national or social progress, and perhaps 'environmentally virtuous' behaviour for the good of the planet.

However there are weaknesses:

- There is a constant temptation for politicians to prioritize short-term considerations – generally made worse by the behaviour of the mass media, but also often by the expectations of citizens as well, especially when in consuming mode.
- Many actors within political institutions are concerned with their own self-interest and/or short-term perspectives. Ministers do not easily arrange to promote multi-departmental initiatives where the gains may go to other departmental budgets. Yet such arrangements are often the

hallmark of sustainable investment. Virtually all tipping point issues, such as food and ecological security as revealed in Part 4, combine many aspects of government and economy, and hence departmental responsibilities. One outcome here is that crises may have ominously to rear up into attentive reality before avoiding action is taken.

The Commons' Public Administration Committee (PAC) bemoan the lack of capacity in government to create policy coherence for strategic vision:

> We have little confidence that Government policies are informed by a clear, coherent strategic approach, itself informed by a coherent assessment of the public's aspirations and their perceptions of the national interest. The Cabinet and its committees are made accountable for decisions, but there remains a critical unfulfilled role at the centre of Government in coordinating and reconciling priorities, to ensure that long-term and short-term goals are coherent across departments. Policy decisions are made for short-term reasons, little reflecting the longer-term interests of the nation. This has led to mistakes which are becoming evident in such areas as the Strategic Defence and Security Review (carrier policy), energy (electricity generation and renewables) and climate change, child poverty targets (which may not be achieved), and economic policy (lower economic growth than forecast).
>
> (Public Administration Committee 2012: 1)

Tim Jackson (2011: 183) argues convincingly that the building of social capital with an equivalent committee to the Natural Capital Committee, can only take place with the provision of a consistent policy framework for building resilient communities and supporting social cohesion. This should have been the broader message of the PAC. It is still not in the work of central government, where a long-term approach to building well-being is not yet in evidence. The nearest effort is being developed by the Department for Environment, Food and Rural Affairs, the department with a sustainability remit in government (see Figure 6.1).

Indeed this is the central message. It appears that the institutional lock-in effect, introduced in Chapter 1.1, may take us to a point of genuine crisis before transformation is even contemplated. As Dolphin and Nash conclude:

> Consequently, one might be inclined to presume that change will only come if it is driven from outside the profession by demands for economics to provide solutions to problems in the real world, rather than models of hypothetical worlds that bear little relation to reality.
>
> (Dolphin and Nash 2011: 21)

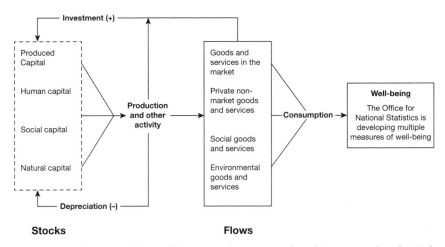

Stocks   **Flows**

Figure 6.1 The approach to well-being in the context of evolving natural and social capital (personal correspondence by Gemma Harper, 2012). Note that the links are not fully connected to social coherence and neighbourhood resilience.

Comparison of markets and polities

The essence of political decision-making is that it depends on conscious choice – so consideration for the future comes about only if that is what citizens and governments wish. Markets appear to operate more 'automatically', beyond the will of individuals. In reality they are the consequence of individual behaviour and decisions, but these are aggregated (in the form of 'supply' and 'demand' and various financial structures), rather than being developed or transcended through deliberation and conscious interchange of opinions (Lyotard 1984).

This is particularly true of 'free' markets, which provide the basis for pure market theory in neoclassical economics, and have often guided economic policy, especially in the USA and UK. There are, however, other types of markets, summarized at the outset, which differ from this. These are social markets and 'informal markets', in which free market principles are mixed in with the operation of social institutions and connections between people, principally the state in 'social markets' (e.g. through high levels of welfare provision or economic planning), and local communities in the case of 'informal markets'. These forms of market therefore incorporate some of the characteristics of a polity into the workings of the

181

marketplace. Where contrasts are drawn in this chapter between 'markets' and 'polities', they are therefore principally between polities and the 'free market'. There seems to be huge untapped scope for enabling more informal and socially framed markets to rise to the challenge of transformational tipping points as introduced in Chapter 1.1.

The notions of well-being, virtue citizenship, and virtue politics

The concept of 'well-being' raises many issues. The most central is the question of whether well-being can serve as the primary aim of policy, perhaps as a rival to GDP, or perhaps as one corner of a triangle in which GDP growth, well-being, and sustainability have equal status.

There is some scepticism about this. Rather than attempt to measure well-being in some overall way, it may be more reliable separately to investigate different 'domains of well-being' based on responses about what factors people feel affect their well-being. It would then be possible to monitor trends in these different sectors affecting well-being, monitoring each separately, although perhaps combining them into some overall index. Laurence Freeman addresses these matters in Chapter 5.1. The strands within 'well-being' include:

- self-esteem, self-respect, and personal awakening, built into a setting of social justice and civil rights;
- security of person, of safety, of income, of health, employment, and home, set in the context of a supportive community or neighbourhood;
- responsibility for others, for the future of the human family and for the betterment of the life-support functions of the planet, set in an empathetic, moral and spiritual context.

These three elements – esteem, security, responsibility – lie at the heart of virtue, the notion that existence is a matter of social obligation and not just personal gain.

In his treatise, *On the Theory of Moral Sentiments*, Adam Smith defined 'virtue' through a combination of four qualities as the basis for both virtue and well-being: *prudence,* careful planning and satisficing consumption (enough but not too much and guided by considerations of tempering indulgence); *justice,* the careful avoidance of knowable harm to others; *beneficence*, the unconditional giving to others to promote their happiness;

and *self-command*, the personal moderation of any excesses in behaviour or desire. The virtuous know by what means to reach satisfaction, and not to strive for everything, which only leads to dissatisfaction, and ultimately unhappiness. Laurence Freeman develops this theme in his examination of meditation and contemplative consciousness.

Nevertheless, virtue is a treacherous concept. For many it is a route to citizen compulsion, on the basis that altruism is not often voluntarily followed. For others, such as Michael Sandel, virtue is akin to searching out what is ultimately the common good:

> We can't decide any of the questions we argue about, without implicitly relying on certain ethical ideas, certain ideas of justice; certain ideas of common good. We can't be neutral on those questions even if we pretend to be.
>
> (Sandel 2012)

Virtue will remain argued over as it divides those who see it as an entry point to some form of regulated coercion, while others regard it as the basis of sustainable citizenship.

This leads to the role of citizens as individuals and members of families and other small units. Citizenship aims to bind sets of individual freedoms and responsibilities to a secure and safe human family and community. All societies combine rights and responsibilities.

Andrew Dobson (2009) (and 8.2) suggests that 'good' citizenship does not just stem from particular patterns of behaviour. It is spurred by profound values of care, compassion, and justice. Moreover, it requires a sympathetic and supportive form of representative government that extols such qualities and sets the examples for citizens to follow. So virtue in citizenship is promoted by virtue in governance. This combination is almost non-existent in such 'democracies' where 'government' is seen as synonymous with sleaze, deceit, or duplicity.

Dobson promotes the notion of a cosmopolitan citizen, outward-looking, somewhat independent of locality, nationhood and time dependency, yet in a zone of conflict over rights, civil care, ecological sensitivity, and spirituality. In essence, Dobson is looking at a new concept of political space – 'the space in which citizens move, and the space in which citizens' rights and obligations are noticed'. The notion of the safe operating space outlined in Parts 1, 2, and 8 means that nations as well as individuals are unavoidably confronted with the injustice and immorality of absorbing too much ecological and social space. This means knowingly reducing the

183

ecological-social space for today's impoverished peoples, and particularly for all future generations This is the essence of the Brundtland concept of sustainability, namely, enabling future citizens to be able to use the planet and meet their social requirements without being avoidably prohibited from doing so by our present actions and outlooks.

To get to benign tipping points, we need to address virtue through three primary concepts:

- *Autonomy*, criticality, rationality, awareness of self in a social and spiritual context. Freedom to choose, but to do so with care and understanding.
- *Responsibility* based on an extended notion of utility and satisfaction from being concerned about the general well-being of others. This includes building self-respect by taking greater responsibility for others' livelihoods. This also touches on human flourishing as a basis for living a good life; and fairness – ensuring that the interests of the self are also related to the interests of others.
- *Awareness and accountability* linked to better information and moral interpretation of the consequences of actions on others and on future societies and ecologies. The key here is moral sentiment as well as understanding and recognition of outcomes of any behaviour. Not just arriving at a judgement and then labelling accordingly, but also alerting the conscience.

All of this places an emphasis on the institutions and values that contribute to the shaping of individual choice and behaviour. 'Virtue' provides a concept of social transformation that better aligns the individual to the interests of others and to the natural world. This in turn breeds consideration and respect for the interests of others. This leads to a better 'wisdom' and a wish to be more active in participation for a better life for self and others.

The possible implications of virtue ethics and citizenship for effective democracy and for any shift towards transformational tipping points are these:

- Schools should be effective learning experiences for civic virtue and sustainable values. So all schools should live out virtue and sustainability. This is beginning to happen in the energy and climate change arenas, where responsible behaviour is being learned and rewarded, and where notions of good citizenship are being introduced to inculcate social and cultural tolerance.

184

- Every active citizen, emboldened by this school experience, should find, and be offered, opportunities to participate in the design and success of sustainable consumption and living (Hobson 2003). So the institutions of effective engagement in sustainable community design are central to the practicalities of virtue citizenship.
- Acting sustainably becomes acting virtuously. It is the sense of fairness and rightness about sustainable behaviour that adds to its energy. Thomas and Brown (2011: 18) encapsulate this in a new culture of learning where the bounds of conventional classroom teaching become transformed to open networks of fun, play, imagination, creativity, and open-ended exploration, but set within bounds of well-being and the safe operating space introduced here and in the introduction. Their exuberant analysis opens up learning to exchange, to all manner of networks face to face, forming communities, and across cyberspace. If we can get the framework right, this new culture of learning will pay mighty dividends.

There is a case for re-introducing the notion of governments co-evolving with virtuous citizens to shape a common virtue destiny. Governments should act to enhance the human aspects of human nature. This raises the issue of what is a 'political context' for being prepared for benign tipping points:

- Build a new trust between politics and citizens so that each sees the other as a part of the same quest for reliable and fair futures. At present this is a long shot, given the antipathy to politicians. But as we cover in Chapter 8.1, 'islands of hope' are being formed, which provide the confidence to others that there are successes out there.
- Establish a series of opportunities for civic engagement in the visualization, design, and content of creating a stepwise progression to a sustainable future.
- Enable citizens to effectively become part of the legislature by co-existing with elected representatives in interesting and novel coalitions. Again, this is a long shot at present. But as localism in governance begins to take hold, there is scope for creative incorporation here.

In order to change this model, political systems need to re-engage and activate citizens. Currently, governments tend either to follow public opinion through jerking to opinion polls, or to try to lead it through asserting political manifestos and campaigns. Because of this, political systems and markets feel constrained and directed by public demand. However, the whole point of positive transformational tipping points is that public demand can be harnessed in cooperation with government and business for positive, long-term benefits.

A genuine move towards a participative democracy, where government has a more open debate on complex issues with the public, is one of the key ways that can shift the emphasis away from consumerism to responsible citizenship; by using debate to construct a wider consensus, political space for more radical action can be created. Sadly all the signs are that in most democracies there is declining public faith in politics and political institutions, especially at the local level. So creating a more effective and willing participative democracy is, at present, a herculean task.

Of course there are still conflicting interests and competing points of view in any democracy, and it is healthy that there should be. But it is also healthy that this should be complemented by a developing sense of the common good, arising out of discussion, deliberation, and a willingness to listen to other people's opinions.

As global political institutions develop, and as citizens are increasingly brought to focus on long-term and global questions as a result of impending climate change and a possible collapse of the conventional economy, so this sense of the common good will need to shift from a purely national and short-term perspective – as in the notion of 'social partners' negotiating about wages and social benefits, for example – to a primary concern for the future of the planet and its human family.

The more successful the efforts at bringing about these shifts in focus are – from consumer to citizen, from self-interested to virtuous, from short-term to long-term, and from national to global – the more likely it is that political systems will be adapted so that they take action to contribute to long-term sustainability.

References

Colander, D., Föllmer, H., Haas, A., Goldberg, M., Juselius, K., Kirman, *et al.* (2008), *The Financial Crisis and the Systematic Failure of Academic Economics*, http://www.debtdeflation.com/blogs/wcontent/uploads/papers/Dahlem_Report_EconCrisis021809.pdf.

Dobson, A. (2009), 'Citizens, Citizenship and Governance for Sustainability', in N. Adger and A. Jordan (eds), *Governance for Sustainability* (Cambridge: Cambridge University Press), 125–41.

Dolphin, T. and Nash, D. (2011), *All Change: Will There Be a Revolution in Economic Thinking in the Next Few Years?* (London: Institute of Public Policy Research).

HM Government (2011), *The Natural Choice: Securing the Value of Nature* (London: Department for Environment, Food and Rural Affairs).

Hobson, K. (2003), 'Competing Discourses for Sustainable Consumption: Does the Rationalization of Lifestyles Make Sense?', *Environmental Politics* 11 (2), 95–120.

Jackson, T. (2011), *Prosperity Without Growth: Economics for a Finite Planet* (London: Earthscan Publications).

Kumar, P. *et al.* (2010), *The Economics of Ecosystems and Biodiversity* (London: Earthscan Publications).

Lyotard, J.- F. (1984), *The Postmodern Condition* (Manchester: Manchester University Press).

Ott, K. (2003), 'Reflections on Discounting: Some Philosophical Remarks', *International Journal of Sustainable Development* 6 (1): 50–58.

Public Administration Committee (2012), *Strategic Thinking in Government: Without National Strategy, Can Viable Government Strategy Emerge? (Twenty Fourth Report)* (London: Stationery Office).

Sandel, M. (2012) *What Money Can't Buy: The Moral Limits of the Markets* (New York: Macmillan).

Stern, N. (2007) *The Economics of Climate Change* (Cambridge: Cambridge University Press).

SustainAbility GlobeSpan (2011) 'Keys to Transformative Leadership' (London: SustainAbility), http://www.sustainability.com/library/keys-to-transformative-leadership.

Thomas, D. and Brown, J.S. (2011), *The New Culture of Learning: Cultivating the Imagination for a World of Constant Change* (self publication, ISBN-10: 1456-458884).

UN Environment Programme (2011), *Annual Report 2010* (Geneva: UNEP).

6.2
Some socio-economic thoughts

PAUL EKINS

In Chapter 2.1, Tim Lenton defines a tipping point as a 'critical threshold at which the future state of a system can be qualitatively altered by a small change in forcing'. I would suggest that this is a definition that works best for natural systems, especially those currently in a broadly stable condition but which could be shifted from that condition by some 'forcing' once the tipping point has been reached.

Socio-economic systems seem to be less amenable to tipping point analysis, as I think emerges from much of the sustainability analysis of the last two decades. All readers will be aware of the characterization of sustainable development as having three pillars or dimensions: the environmental, the economic, and the social. My perception is that it has been relatively straightforward to identify sustainability criteria and thresholds for the environmental dimension (even though the overall science remains incomplete), as is shown in Chapter 8.1 in the discussion of planetary boundaries, and these can be quite well represented by the tipping point metaphor. For both the economic and social dimensions, the sustainability criteria are quite well-defined, or at least may be hypothesized, but the threshold values for these criteria are much more difficult, or even impossible, to establish. This is well illustrated in the 'social floors' complement to the planetary boundaries debate.

To take the economic dimension first. In straight economic terms, the idea of sustainability has some fairly well-established principles, such as:

- Borrow systematically only to invest, not to consume;
- Keep money sound: control inflation, public borrowing, trade deficits, indebtedness;
- Establish transparent accounting systems that give realistic asset values;
- Maintain or increase stocks of capital.

However, as has become apparent since 2008, every one of these principles has been spectacularly broken over the last few years in both the financial sector and the mainstream money economy. The financial crash of that year could well have been a tipping point. But in fact it is not at all clear that a qualitative change in the global financial system has in fact been brought about by the crash. Rather it could be argued that the financial system has shown astonishing resilience in the face of breathtaking mismanagement, such that huge bonuses in the financial sector are again the order of the day. And there is no shortage of speculation that new asset bubbles are in the making (e.g. in the social networking sector) or have not been fully exploded (e.g. in the housing market). While it may be still too early to make a definitive judgement, I currently do not see the global financial system being fundamentally changed by the social and economic mayhem it has brought about.

In terms of threshold values it is not at all clear what the tipping point values of inflation, public borrowing, trade deficits or indebtedness might be. Clearly a lot depends on size, power and context. For example, any nation whose currency was not the global reserve currency could not run anything like the level of trade deficit of the USA for any length of time without its currency being assigned junk bond status. But the USA persists with both trade and fiscal deficits that seem to defy financial gravity. In contrast, the UK government clearly regards its fiscal deficit (in 2010 of similar per cent of GDP to that of the US) as some kind of potential tipping point. Yet UK personal indebtedness has been allowed to grow to exceed UK GDP, without seemingly anyone perceiving tipping points on the horizon.

Many of the same arguments apply to the social dimension. It is quite easy to identify issues that would seem to be important for social sustainability. For example, there must be limits to the levels of violence, crime and unemployment that any country can experience without social breakdown. But it is not at all clear what those limits are. Nor is it clear how such conditions are related to broader issues like inequality (if at all). The Wilkinson and Pickett (2009) correlations between inequality and various social evils say nothing at all about causation, so that it is not clear how long societies can go on becoming more unequal before they break down: perhaps for ever.

In fact, it is not even clear what 'social breakdown' is. Did Iraq experience 'social breakdown' following the most recent Iraq War. The tens of thousands of civilians who lost their lives, if they could speak, would probably say 'yes'. If they are right, is Iraq still experiencing social breakdown? If not, what would social breakdown have looked like, or when did Iraq stop experiencing it? Or was the Iraq War itself a tipping point that resulted in the qualitative regime change from that of Saddam Hussein to that of, now, Nouri al-Maliki?

In fact, around the world there are societies experiencing momentous qualitative change all the time. Certainly the end of the Cold War was one such change at a global level, but what was the tipping point? Would it be the election of Gorbachev as Russian president, or his announcement of perestroika? And how does one characterize the collapse of the Russian economy that followed its wholesale transfer into the ownership of the oligarchs? What were the tipping points for the recent and current upheavals in North Africa and the Middle East?

Then there is the issue of foresight or prediction. Tipping points in the world of natural science may be identified in principle through models of the relevant system, although in practice the tipping points of interest relate to such complex systems that the models cannot identify them with any degree of precision. This greatly reduces the usefulness of the tipping point concept and presumably is why we continue to refer to tipping points as metaphors. In the social sciences, including economics, the relevant 'laws' that might lead to tipping points are much less well-established, so that socio-economic tipping points are less easy to predict even in principle. Why did the Soviet Union collapse in 1989 and not in 1946? Why was the velvet revolution successful but not the Prague Spring? There are doubtless learned answers to these questions that fill the pages of foreign affairs journals, but they are partial and highly contested. Those who predict these changes tend to predict them far more often than they actually occur (and therefore they are sometimes right but much more often wrong), and they therefore tend not to be believed. E.P. Thompson predicted the end of the Soviet Union in 1985, a good four years before it actually occurred, but he was not believed even by many of those in the anti-nuclear movement from which he came. Those who predicted the financial crash before 2008 were either marginalized in their companies, which could not afford to get off the treadmill while it was turning, or sacked.

This leads me to the conclusion that it is quite impossible to do more than speculate, perhaps through scenarios of how the world's different socio-economies, all now highly connected, would respond were any of the tipping points in the natural world actually to come to pass. The Japanese people seem to have responded to their tsunami tragedy in a spirit of huge social solidarity and desire for constructive renewal. The associated meltdown at Fukushima has certainly provoked a re-think of nuclear policy in Germany and some other countries, as well of course as in Japan itself (see *The Economist* 2012). But it is doubtful that it will prove a tipping point for the global nuclear industry, or for energy policy, as a whole. Returning to natural (or human-amplified) disasters, their absence from the headlines suggests that the Pakistani people and Queenslanders have reacted in similar vein to the Japanese to their widespread flooding in 2010–11, as Emily Boyd considers in Chapter 7.2. How often would this have to happen before their society broke down or they migrated en masse? And where would they go? And how would they be received?

To take an extreme case, if with global warming of 5°C or more (above pre-industrial levels), the world will only support 1 billion people because of the ravages of climate change (as a result of a number of tipping points being reached), as John Schellnhuber suggested at the Copenhagen Climate Science meeting before the 2009 UNFCCC Conference,[1] and if this occurs by 2100, which some IPCC emissions scenarios indicate is possible,[2] what would the trajectory of 2050 (with 9 billion people) to 2100 (with 1 billion) look like? Is it possible to say any more than that the trajectory would almost certainly be very unpleasant, even for the 1 billion people who lived through it?

The conclusion of these initial thoughts is that in the socio-economic domain the idea of a tipping point is not even a metaphor, but merely an intellectual construct indicating the increasing likelihood of disruptive change. As such it is able to shed very little light on when the relevant forces will bring about that change or what the outcome of it will be. We are here deep in the territory of unknown unknowns. But humans have to cope with and provide for the unknown as best they can.

The first unknown is the current robustness of the global economic system, both in itself and in the context of economic and environmental challenges in coming decades, whether they be the result of the shift of global economic power to China and Asia more broadly, the demise of the

---

[1] Reuters reported the speech by writing 'Professor John Schellnhuber of the Potsdam Institute for Climate Impact Research . . . said a warming of five degrees would mean the planet could support less than 1 billion people' (see http://in.reuters.com/article/2009/03/12/us-climate-stern-idINTRE52B37Q20090312). Schellnhuber's presentation, showing the world's carrying capacity of humans stabilizing at below 1 billion people is at http://climatecongress.ku.dk/speakers/schellnhuber-plenaryspeaker-12march2009.pdf/.
[2] See http://www.ipcc.ch/publications_and_data/ar4/wg1/en/tssts-5-2.html.

US dollar as the global currency, or continuing instability in the major oil-producing regions.

Whatever the circumstances, we would undoubtedly do well to observe the basic principles of economic sustainability stated earlier. But the evidence of the last two hundred years suggests that, even if human societies are more inclined to observe them after economic crises such as the world has being going through since 2008, they become increasingly heedless of them once the crisis seems to have passed, thereby precipitating the next crisis. One unanswerable question is whether one such crisis might prove a real tipping point, and actually cause the fundamental structure and nature of the global economy to change from its current basically capitalist and market-driven mode of operation, and whether such a change would be for the better or worse, and for whom.

Specifically in respect of the environment, human societies would be well advised to try to take care to stay within what has been called the planet's 'safe operating space' (Rockstrom *et al.* 2009), as is introduced in Chapter 8.1. But clearly such advice amounts to little more than recommending the avoidance of tipping points. Its importance lies in the counselling of a far more precautionary approach to human economic and other activities than human societies have shown heretofore.

It is far from clear what system of governance of human societies would be likely to develop a more precautionary approach to their use of the natural world and its resources. Certainly the command economy of the former Soviet Union was an unmitigated environmental disaster, while the state-planning of China has also until quite recently paid little attention to the environmental consequences of its economic expansion. There are encouraging signs, however, that this is now changing, with China taking a technological lead in the development and deployment of both solar and wind technologies, but so far this is proving nothing like enough to halt its meteoric rise in carbon emissions.

More market-based governance systems could in principle foster radical environmental conservation through the price mechanism, and there have been many experiments in this direction, ranging from the European Union's Emission Trading System (EU ETS) to the carbon taxes and environmental tax reforms that have been implemented in a number of so far mainly European countries. However, such measures have to date proved impossible to implement at a federal level in the world's largest market-driven economy, the USA, and even in Europe the emissions reductions to which they are leading are not putting the continent on the required trajectory of an 80 per cent reduction in emissions (from the 1990 level) that is consistent with a majority chance of limiting global warming to 2 °C. And the first steps at globalizing the EU ETS, in the absence of meaningful global action, by including aviation emissions within it, are being fiercely resisted, despite the currently very low carbon permit price, by both the market-driven USA and state-led China.

It is clear that a new momentum for collaborative global governance, whatever the national economic dynamics, is required, if the chances of avoiding environmental tipping points, or responding to them constructively, are to be increased. But it is not at all clear where such new momentum is to come from. It was certainly not apparent in the preparations for the Rio+20 Conference in 2012, the danger of which is that rhetoric about 'green growth' will simply translate into the 'business as usual' of economic growth at any environmental cost, which will make the achievement of such growth evermore difficult as the century progresses.

Can a new global alliance between businesses and civil society push the policymakers into an adequate response to these global environmental challenges, so that the institutions that have been established, such as the UN Conventions on Climate Change and Biodiversity, begin to fulfil their potential of keeping humanity within the Earth's 'safe operating space'? The answer to this question is clearly 'yes' in principle. But principle needs to be turned into practice very much sooner than is apparent from current institutional developments.

References

The Economist (2012), *Special Report: Nuclear Energy* (*The Economist*, 10 March).
Rockström, J., Steffen, W., Noone, K., Persson, Å., Chapin III, F.S., Lambin, E.F., *et al.* (2009), 'A Safe Operating Space for Humanity', *Nature*, 461: 472–75.
Wilkinson, R. and Pickett, K. (2009), *The Spirit Level: Why More Equal Societies Almost Always Do Better* (London: Penguin).

6.3
Leadership for sustainability
The search for tipping points

SARA PARKIN

'The crisis is in implementation'
(Kofi Annan, 2002)

'The key challenge is implementation'
(Ban Ki-moon, 2012)

Despite the human preference for the 'quiet life', our lives are nevertheless action-packed, full of events (big and small) that may tip trends one way or another: in love affairs, business dealings, in government. It is the same in any system, be it environmental, human, or a complex mixture, as in how we get food, use energy, or manage finance. Those who see the world from an ecological systems perspective see negative global trends of such magnitude they portend catastrophe; those who don't (or don't want to) stay absorbed in the hiccoughs and bumps of everyday life.

I don't think it helps to muddle the metaphors of tipping points in the natural systems that sustain life on Earth with those in social or even psychological systems. Because if we hope to find benign ways to mitigate *environmental* tipping points, as discussed in the introductory and final chapters of this volume, then we have to find them in our human systems. The logic here is that as the creators of the institutions and processes (including economic ones) which enable people to live together happily and to thrive, we have the power to change them when they go wrong as well as benefit when we get them right. As evidence demonstrates things are going seriously awry, the question becomes how to intervene in order to steer, if not tip, human behaviour in a direction that has sustainability as an objective? That is the central question I address in this chapter.

First we need to understand why the concept of sustainability is proving so hard to put into practice. Although a larger discussion is merited here,

194

an important reason is that too many articulations of sustainability 'permit' interpreters (either innocently or wilfully) to maintain clinical levels of separation between its environmental, social and economic components. Yet sustainability, like resilience in social and natural systems, is about relationships, so the task, surely, is to achieve our environmental, social and economic goals *at the same time*. It is the 'at-the-same-timeness' that persistently eludes us. Establishing why economic outcomes consistently trump progress on the other goals will be key to understanding what needs to change.

We also need to reclaim the original meaning of some important words that have been kidnapped by economists to refer solely to money. For example, Tim Jackson (2009) points out that 'to prosper' means to succeed, to do well, to thrive or flourish.[1] The Anglo-Saxon root of the word 'wealth' has a meaning beyond abundance of resources (not just cash): *wela* also means bliss, welfare and well-being. And, although ubiquitously used as a synonym for finance, 'capital' means head (from the Latin *caput*), originally of livestock, but meaning a stock of any resource – as in natural, human or social capital.

This is not just pedantry. Tipping human behaviour, policy, and economic systems based remorselessly on the logic that has locked us into the worst-case scenario advertised by the 1972 MIT report *Limits to Growth* (Meadows *et al.* 1972)[2] will not disappear if sustainability is unable to propose a future that is prosperous and wealthy in the fullest meaning of those words. Nor will any effort to correct for limits emerge unless we stop behaving as if capitalism is a force akin to gravity and so beyond our control.

Can benign tipping points in human behaviour happen in the context of conventional economics?

The answer to this particular question – a necessary element to resolving the central question about how to manufacture multiple sustainability-

---

[1] Jackson, T. (2009), *Prosperity without Growth* (London: Earthscan).

[2] Meadows, D.H., Meadows, D.L., Randers, J., and Behrens III, W.W. (1972), *The Limits to Growth: A Report for the Club of Rome's Project on the Predicaments of Mankind* (London: Earth Island Press). See also Turner, G.M. (2008) 'A Comparison of *The Limits to Growth* with 30 Years of Reality', *Global Environmental Change*, 18: 397–411 for an update.

oriented interventions – lies in the intellectual chaos amongst economic theories and their policy implications. This chaos was exemplified in speeches on capitalism given by the three main UK political party leaders in January 2012. They more than fulfilled the old *canard* that you always get more definitions of capitalism than there are definers when, between them, Messrs Cameron, Clegg, and Miliband came up with nine sorts of capitalism: three they didn't like – crony, turbo, and irresponsible; and six they did – moral, responsible, popular, productive, balanced, and liberal. No leader considered that the capital behind the 'isms' might be anything but financial. All put growth and employment as an immediate priority, apparently unaware they were advocating more of the same as a route to something they wished to be different. Only Miliband mentioned a future with a new relationship between finance and the 'real' economy; but he did not elaborate much beyond saying it was a longer-term 'agenda that must be led'.[3]

It is paradoxical that ideas about how our economy might be different from its under-delivering present have ended up in an intellectual quicksand. It is not as if the observation that our dominant economic model has limits is a new one: an argument minted by modern subversive tree-huggers. As Robert Heilbronner (1986: 143–44) points out, all the great economists saw that whatever 'regime of capital' they promoted, every single one had limits:

> Adam Smith describes the system as reaching a plateau, where the accumulation of riches will be "complete", bringing about a deep and lengthy decline. John Stuart Mill expects the momentary arrival of a "stationary state" when accumulation will cease and capitalism will become the staging ground for a kind of associationalist socialism. Marx anticipates a sequence of worsening crises produced by the internal contradictions of accumulation ... Keynes thought the future would require a "somewhat comprehensive socialization of investment"; Schumpeter thought it would evolve into a managerial socialism.[4]

---

[3] The speeches can be seen at: Cameron: http://www.politics.co.uk/comment-analysis/2012/01/19/cameron-s-moral-capitalism-speech-in-full; Clegg: http://www.libdems.org.uk/latest_news_detail.aspx?title=Nick_Clegg_speech_on_responsible_capitalismandpPK=3659d490-82ef-412c-80e6-6dd5240659e0; and Miliband: http://www.labour.org.uk/ed-miliband-on-responsible-capitalism,2012-01-19.

[4] Heilbronner, R.L. (1985), *The Nature and Logic of Capitalism* (New York and London: W.W. Norton), 143–44.

So why, regardless of our political stripe or theoretical bias, is it still so difficult to contemplate the probability that our economic system – that which mediates the relationship between capital and people – might not have the capacity to continue, in its own terms, never mind from a sustainability perspective? That it may have reached the limits of its logic? Indeed, so grave have become the negative consequences of political inaction in the face of economic gazumping of the environment and people, that in 2008 the US National Intelligence Council (NIC) elevated the resources and services of the natural world into the heart of international geopolitics and diplomacy when it warned the incoming Obama administration to expect 'scarcity' to dominate US international relations over the coming 25 years – scarcity of land, oil, food, water, and air-space for GHG emissions. From the history of the twentieth century the NIC brought forward three lessons:

- Leaders and ideas matter.
- Economic volatility introduces major risks.
- Geopolitical rivalries trigger discontinuities more than does technological change.

'[T]he greatest of these is leadership' concluded the report: 'no trend is immutable, and . . . timely and well-informed intervention can decrease the likelihood and severity of negative developments and increase the likelihood of positive ones.'[5]

Without being naive about how power works – internationally and nationally – the positive news is that the way out of the mess we are in is not through thrashing around in rapidly sinking intellectual sands of different shades of conventional economics, but through the creation of a new logic for capitalism, one capable of providing firm ground for making sense of what to do next, and how to do it in a way that does have the capacity to continue.[6] As anyone who tries to implement sustainability-oriented solutions – intellectually, practically, or politically – knows, there are legions of ready-to-go ideas, policies, and projects capable of being

---

[5] US National Intelligence Council (2008) *Global Trends 2025: A Transformed World* (Washington DC: US Government Printing Office), 5, or online at www@dni.gov/nic.

[6] Although 'isms' like socialism and communism are conventionally figured as alternatives to capitalism, they are, in reality, just different views on the relationship between capital and people. In that they all consider capital's relationship to be primarily with people as labour and consumers, 'sideline' human well-being in a broader sense, and more or less ignore nature, I view them all as similarly 'conventional'.

brought to scale, but which are stuck in the slough of an economy that simultaneously asks for less resource use and more consumption.

A new logic within which to make sense of what to do next

So, starting with Ed Miliband's evocation of a future new relationship between finance and the 'real' economy as a leadership proposition, I would like to elaborate a new logic for capitalism. This is a logic that helps us all make sense of how to decide and act *in* the here and now as well as *for* the long term. And then I shall end by illustrating some ways leadership could work within the new logic to trigger multiple 'tipping points' via policy and other interventions.

Figure 6.2 offers an illustration of the relationships involved in conventional definitions of capitalism. The pale shaded 'CAPITAL' box shows

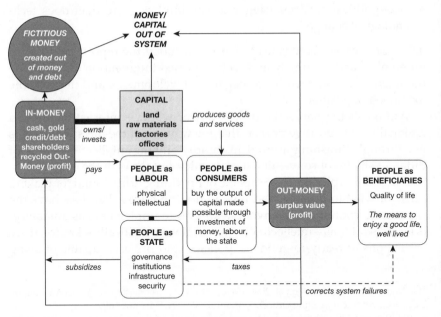

Figure 6.2 Conventional capitalism: model showing how the conventional economics sees the relationships between physical (natural) capital, people, and finance. Success is measured by a continual increase in (a) goods and services produced and consumed by people, and (b) the volume of financial capital.

the economically orthodox interpretation of physical capital. The lines and the dark shaded boxes show the circulatory and facilitating roles of finance. The white boxes and thick lines the various relationships people have with physical capital, showing the central relationships (as far as conventional notions of capitalism are concerned)[7] to be with people as labour and as consumers. The state is in close support of that central relationship, doing everything necessary to keep the productive and consuming activities increasing (i.e. growing). Illogically, the purpose of human economic activity – human quality of life, welfare, bliss even – is sidelined, with the state organized to compensate the worst consequences of this marginalization. So when Messrs Cameron, Clegg, and Miliband promise to secure growth and jobs, to restore markets and boost business, production, and consumption, they are trying to repair a capitalistic logic that stops short of serving human benefit (in its fullest sense). Instead they are concentrating on the shallower relationships capital has with people as only workers and consumers. Human well-being has been relegated to a sort of 'spin off' – nice to have but not essential to the success of the economy. Nature is nowhere.

It is only when considering a different 'regime for capital' that a new logic capable of tipping capitalism in a more sustainable direction emerges. In his revealing book, *The Mystery of Capital*, Hernando de Soto (2000: 61) points out that 'capital' originally meant the store of wealth represented by a herd of livestock. The endeavour of the stockman/woman is to keep the stock in good enough condition to maintain a flow of benefits (milk, blood, offspring, meat, hide), even in hard times.[8] The goal is resilience. By broadening the idea of capital to mean all natural capital, plus human and social capital, plus that represented in existing infrastructure and buildings, as Seregeldin and Steer, Ekins, and others have done, it is only a short step to seeing the flow of different types of benefits possible if all human activity were concentrated on repairing, maintaining and enhancing those capital stocks – at the same time[9] (Figure 6.3).

[7] See note 6.

[8] De Soto, H. (2000), *The Mystery of Capital* (New York: Basic Books), 41.

[9] Serageldin, I. and Steer, A. (eds) (1994), *Making Development Sustainable: From Concepts to Action (Environmentally Sustainable Development* (World Bank Occasional Paper Series, No. 2), epilogue. Ekins, P., Hillman, M., and Hutchinson, R. ([1992] 2000 edition), *Wealth Beyond Measure: An Atlas of New Economics* (London: Gaia Books). See also Ekins, P. (2000), *Economic Growth and Environmental Sustainability: The Prospects for Green Growth* (London and New York: Routledge). There is a hinterland of innovative thinking about the economy that should be acknowledged, including Daly, H.E. and Cobb, J. (1990), *For the Common Good: Redirecting the Economy Towards Community, the Environment and a Sustainable Future* (London: Greenprint); Schumacher, E.F. (1973), *Small is Beautiful* (London: Abacus, 1975 edition).

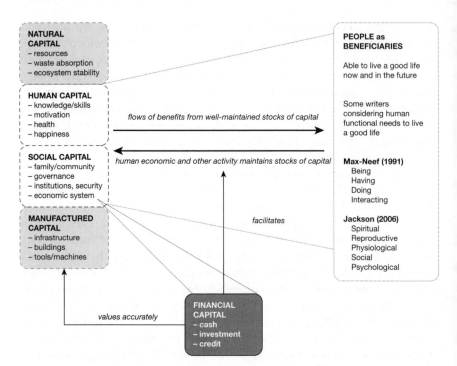

Figure 6.3 Sustainable capitalism: model for a sustainable regime for capital, showing how the relationship between physical (natural) capital, people, and finance would work. Success is measured by a continual increase in the *quality* of human and social capital and of physical capital (natural and manufactured). Finance facilitates rather than drives this model.

References: Manfred Max-Neef (1991) *Human Scale Development* (London and New York: Apex Press) pdf http://www.max-neef.cl/download/Max-neef_Human_Scale_development.pdf; Tim Jackson (2006) 'Consuming Paradise? Towards a Socio-Cultural Psychology of Sustainable Consumption', in Jackson, T. (ed.) *Earthscan Reader in Sustainable Consumption* (London: Earthscan).

Crucially, this new regime for capital restores the intimacy between capital and human well-being. As Figure 6.3 illustrates, the economy is no long conceptualized as some elemental force that intrudes between capital and human well-being, but as a feature of social capital which, like democracy, can add directly to the flow of benefit to people and be subject to continually improving processes. In the diagram, people as beneficiaries of a happy relationship with capital are seen as a 'pull out' of human and social capital (as is finance). The circle is thus virtuous and a new internally coherent logic is created in which the economic process is treated as social capital. Removed are the intellectual and practical barriers to seeing the purpose of life to be human well-being, flourishing, bliss, prosperity, wealth, health, and happiness. Also banished are the impediments to compre-hending that achieving those outcomes requires effort to be directed at building all the stocks of capitals to a good enough condition so they provide resilience in hard times and for the longest of times. The process may involve ownership, commerce, and markets, and making and exchanging stuff and services in different ways in different places, but not always and *never* as a moral or a quasi-scientific principle or theory, nor as the motor of the whole system, nor for ideological reasons. Finance flourishes in a facilitating role, instead of floundering in a 'real' capital-usurping role.

Change is in the system: leadership for sustainability

Nicholas Stern (2006) has said that climate change is the greatest market failure the world has seen.[10] He is wrong. As the US NIC (2008) report points out, the greatest failure is a leadership failure. Here I consider what leadership – intellectual and practical – could be doing to steer, hustle, tip human behaviour in a different direction, so that we mitigate the anticipated worst and set course for a sustainable future. Some ideas that 'make sense' from the perspective of the proposed new logic for capitalism are discussed here.

Leadership for sustainability means being able to work against the perverse logic of conventional capitalism and work within a new – internally coherent and timeless – logic for achieving sustainability

Gandhi urged people to be part of the change they wished to see in the world. Others have made the same point differently. For example, the late Vaclav Havel promoted 'living in truth' as the only way to live even under a communist regime, and American philosopher Susan Neiman (2009) argues that if the world is not what it should be, it is up to us to open our

[10] Stern, N. (2006), *The Economics of Climate Change* (London: HMSO).

eyes and close the gap between what is, and what ought to be. If we want moral clarity, we have to put it there.[11] Waiting for a new regime for capital to be installed is not an option; it will only happen if we act as if it were.

Thinking about how the future should be, in the shape of a flow of benefits from healthy stocks of all the capitals (see Figure 6.4) translates into the taking of decisions and subsequently acting in ways that contribute simultaneously to restoring or building healthy stocks of all capitals. Figure 6.4 forms a suitable framework for designing policies and projects, as well as analysing problems. This figure shows the headline stocks and related flow of benefits, and reveals interrelationships that have benefit-doubling potential. For example, squeezing waste out of the system makes the economic process more efficient, reduces the need for resource mobilization and concomitant pollution, improves human health, and builds local economies. More and better social organization and human interactions will lead to better governance, more resilient communities and local environments, improved mental health.[12]

There are implications of working for and within this new logic for scientific research and university teaching. While we need to track the potential ecological consequences of human impact on the environment, we run the risk of becoming the only species to have minutely monitored its own extinction. Far more resources need to be shifted into building 'sustainability literate' human capital. As Eugen Rosenstock-Heussy (1888–1973) said: 'the goal of education is to inform the citizen. And the citizen is a person who, if need be, can re-found his [sic] civilization.' The scale of change implied by sustainability is evidence that a re-founding moment for the human enterprise is overdue.

There are very many theories and models for organizational and other social change. Strip them back to their basics and they all involve three key steps:

(a) Understanding the need for certain (new) behaviours;
(b) Having the knowledge and skills to behave differently;

---

[11] Neiman, S. (2009), *Moral Clarity* (London: Bodley Head).

[12] Examples from Forum for the Future, see project with Technology Strategy Board for example: http://www.forumforthefuture.org/blog/getting-sustainable-innovation-heart-business, and Parkin, S. (2010), *The Positive Deviant: Sustainability Leadership in a Perverse World* (London: Earthscan).

Stock of capital (resource)	Flow of benefits (if stock in good condition)
Natural Renewable and non-renewable resources Services: climate, nitrogen, waste, other cycles	Food, energy, clean air and water, stable climate, beauty, inspiration, sustainable provision of resources, waste recycling
Human Health, knowledge, skills, motivation, spiritual ease	Adept at relationships and social participation, satisfying work, lifelong learning habits, personal creativity, recreation, healthy lifestyles
Social Organizations and associations for living together: families, communities, government, unions, voluntary groups	Trusted, accessible systems of justice, governance, economy, shared positive values, sense of common purpose, institutions promoting stewardship of natural and human capital
Manufactured All human fabricated 'infrastructure' already in existence: roads, rail, machines, buildings where people live and work, etc.	All infrastructure, technologies, and processes make minimal use of natural resources, maximum use of human innovation and skills
Financial Credit/debt, shares, banknotes, coins	Accurately represents value of natural, human, social, and manufactured capital. Facilitates the restoration, maintenance, and enhancement of those stocks

Figure 6.4 Capital stocks and benefit flows

(c) Having confidence that right behaviour is positively recognized and (sometimes at least) rewarded.[13]

As regards to sustainability there is arguably progress on (a), but few would contest that we are next to nowhere on achieving (b), never mind (c).

In the light of the government inaction noted by the US National Intelligence Council, the leadership role of universities gains consequence on a geopolitical level. This is an academic publication about tipping points, so readers are invited to imagine the almighty shove to social change that could come from a concerted effort by higher education. Given the magnitude of the challenge – and one that lies not in the environment, but with people – where else is the intellectual leadership to come from that will give others confidence to join in?

[13] See Kotter, J. (1996), *Leading Change* (Cambridge, MA: Harvard Business School Press), for just one example, and O'Toole, J. (1995), *Leading Change: The Argument for Values-Based Leadership* (San Francisco: Jossey-Bass), for another. O'Toole also looks at why people prefer things to remain more or less the same.

> It should be borne in mind that there is nothing more difficult to handle, more doubtful of success, and more dangerous to carry through, than initiating change.
>
> (Niccolò Machiavelli, *The Prince*, ch. 6)

Leadership for sustainability understands this is a social project – about how people behave – so is well versed in the psychological and sociological insights about how change happens – or not

The argument for putting the benefit of people as the purpose of sustainability is not to downgrade the primordial fact that if we do not have a life-supporting environment then we are dead. The point is that proclaiming this in various ways for decades has not encouraged any change in human behaviour sufficient to slow any major negative environmental trend, let alone tip it in the direction of sustainability. On the contrary, the arguments for protecting the environment are being recast as a case for putting people second, and increasingly used to support conventional economic theories and practices. Protagonists of this case range from climate naysayers to those who claim the environment movement is dead. Both are arguing within the logic of conventional economics, and neither gets practical about solutions that will benefit people and the environment *together*.[14] A new strategy is called for. One that puts human welfare (in the fullest sense) and an explicit compassion for people at its heart but which also makes it illogical for the environment to do anything but benefit too.

Compassion can start with the terrible mess that everyone – from scientists to campaigners to government to business – makes of communications around sustainability. Psychologists recognize the cognitive dissonance (and loss of personal agency) that arises from conflicting messages, such as simultaneous exhortations to consume more stuff for economic reasons, but to consume less for environmental ones. Clumsy campaigns also mix up opposing motivating value sets. For example, to say energy efficiency saves money taps into self-interest but also selfish-

---

[14] For a denier, see Lawson, N. (2008), *An Appeal to Reason: A Cool Look at Global Warming* (London: Duckworth Overlook). For environmentalists at war with one another, see the seminal 2004 article by Shellenberger, M. and Norhaus, E. (2011), *The Death of Environmentalism*, along with their 2011 follow-up at their website http://thebreakthrough.org/ (accessed 25 February 2012).

ness, while to say it is good for everyone taps into desires to belong, to share, and to be seen as caring.

Psychiatrist Elisabeth Kübler-Ross (1969) championed a cycle of grieving that, if amended, offers a way to identify different emotional and consequent practical responses to the huge implications of the sort of change we need to make to our lifestyles and the systems with which we live. For example, she notes that the most common response to hearing one has a terminal disease is *denial*. The next emotion on the way to acceptance is usually *fear*. Consider these two in relation to the response of governments to the idea we should transfer the way we secure the services of energy (heat, power, and light) from one that is centralized around fossil fuels to a system that is localized, hyper-efficient, and based on renewable sources. Despite the evidence of a dangerously changing climate there are deniers still. But many governments accept the evidence and reside uncomfortably at the fear stage. For example, the tax take from the big energy companies is huge, so big that subsidies are considered worthwhile. Can similar sums flow from decentralized systems? If so, how could they be collected? If not, where will they come from? Power and money mobilize strong emotions and behaviours, but fear of loss of control affects governments no less than a person contemplating their own mortality or that of a loved one.[15]

For years, the UK department responsible for sustainability, the Department for Environment, Food and Rural Affairs (Defra), was bamboozled by the gap between people's positive attitude to reducing their known environmental impacts and what they actually did (comparatively little). The belief–attitude–behaviour linear relationship was exemplified by Harry Triandis in 1977, with more recent writers exploring the intention/action gap and expanding on ideas about how to close it. For example, Elizabeth Shove (2003) underlines the importance of habits. The greater the habitual frequency of past behaviour (in, say, using a car or living in uniformly warm houses) the more difficult it is to change. Others point out that without clear 'facilitating conditions', however great the intention to change, adopting different behavioural practices is logistically – and maybe psychologically – impossible.

The relevant facilitating conditions are:

• Material (infrastructure);

[15] Kübler-Ross, E. (1969), *On Death and Dying* (New York: Scribner). For adaptation of the cycle for use in understanding human behaviour in relation to news about major environmental problems, see Parkin (2010: 216) (full reference note 25).

- Meaning (symbolism);
- Competencies (knowledge and skills).

The classic illustration is the making of a cup of tea. Material inputs include kettles, teapots, teabags, water and means of heating it, with a certain amount of pre-knowledge and skill required to create a satisfactory beverage. But most important is the pleasurable connotations around making and drinking a cup of tea – refreshment, break from work, convivial company – the things that enter people's minds when it is proposed. The Japanese have elevated the symbolism of tea drinking to ceremonial and artistic levels.[16] Apply these three facilitating conditions to behaviours associated with eating local or organic food, using public transport instead of a car, extreme energy efficiency, and it can be seen that the material infrastructure is not there for many people, nor is a level of knowledge and skills that make it easy to operate, even if it were. Consider the debates between the environmental impacts of local compared with long-distance food, whether wind-farms are a good idea or not. Such debates are continually confused by wilfully spread misinformation, government equivocation, and even disagreements between protagonists. Is it any wonder that it is hard to find a meaning embodying pleasure, belonging, or agency behind pro-environmental behaviour?

A comforting antidote is to be found in the growth, despite recessive economic times, of the market for Fairtrade products, though whether they are in addition to, or substituting for, non-fair-traded products, is not entirely clear. Nevertheless, the fact that big retailers are stocking, sometimes exclusively, Fairtrade staples like sugar, coffee, chocolate, and bananas, is evidence of change in the 'material infrastructure' which makes pro-sustainability consumption possible for more people.[17] Perhaps too it is evidence that the connections Fairtrade makes between consumers in countries like the UK and the benefits to people growing the products, *as well as* the environmental benefits, give a deeper meaning to the transaction. Organic cheerleaders, like the UK Soil Association, do make the link

---

[16] Triados, H.C. (1977), *Interpersonal Behaviour* (Monterey, CA: Brooks/Cole); see also Hargreaves, T. (2008), 'Making Pro-Environmental Behaviour Work: An Ethnographical Case Study of Practice, Process and Power in the Workplace' (Ph.D. thesis, Norwich: University of East Anglia); and Shove, E. (2003), *Comfort, Cleanliness and Convenience: The Organisation of Normality* (Oxford: Berg), and their bibliographies.

[17] http://www.guardian.co.uk/business/2011/feb/28/fairtrade-sales-rise-despite-recession (accessed 27 February 2012).

between the benefits to the environment and health of consumers. But the drop in the UK's organic food market share over the same period suggests that, in a world of enforced cost cutting, the benefit to the environment and personal health may not inspire the same depth of meaning as is associated with fairness to poor people through the purchase of Fairtrade products.[18]

Two related observations on the manner in which leadership can act to multiply the chances of benign behavioural tipping points derive from what Samuel Scheffler (2001) calls the 'infrastructure of responsibility', and the need for a more sophisticated approach to localism. Scheffler is neither alone nor recent in discussing how to be a moral agent when structures around you are amoral or immoral. At the most abstract level, he explores 'the capacity of liberal thought, and of the moral traditions on which it draws, to accommodate a variety of challenges posed by the changing circumstances of the modern world'.[19]

For ease of understanding the applicability of his arguments, I propose the unlikely metaphor of a dry stone wall – that is, a wall constructed without mortar and held together through careful positioning of the stones in relationship, one to another. It is the relationships between the stones that create the integrity of the wall – just like the relationships which make up a social system. As an individual member of society, understanding who we are is tightly caught up in the relationships we have with other people, other organizations, and with the rules and processes that govern how we behave, one to another. All our encounters – in shops, schools, golf clubs, concert venues, nightclubs, courtrooms, banks; with government local and national, news outlets, advertising – are structured to reinforce the message that our responsibility is to conventional capitalism as the mainstream, the normal, somewhere to which we unquestioningly belong.

There are examples of different types of relationships we could have (ethical banking, green energy firms, rambling clubs, Fairtrade, green theatres, social enterprises, time banks, one-to-one loans, ethical investment, and so forth), but they are not brought together and promoted in a way that inspires confidence that a wall – a whole society – built of them would be strong enough to become the 'new normal', a place where we very much want to belong.

---

[18] http://www.guardian.co.uk/business/2011/feb/28/fairtrade-sales-rise-despite-recession (accessed 1 March 2012).
[19] Scheffler, S. (2001), *Boundaries and Allegiances: Problems of Justice and Responsibility in Liberal Thought* (Oxford: Oxford University Press). See also Sandal, M. (2009), *Justice: What's the Right Thing to Do* (London: Allen Lane).

Figure 6.5 The infrastructure of responsibility: how individuals relate, one to another, to create a strong society.

My final point here is the need for a more sophisticated approach to *localism*. Environmentalists and social entrepreneurs alike laud the focus on local (usually small) initiatives as the bedrock for creating global change. They are right as far as they go, but a broader concept of the role of localism is needed, as is a deeper analysis of how relationships between the local and the global will have to work if resilience anywhere is to succeed. Emily Boyd takes this further in Chapter 7.2.

Take the example of the 'local to local' relationships that make Fairtrade popular with both the rich and the poor. The UK is promoting Local Enterprise Partnerships to promote local economic development. If local economic resilience is the goal, just what are the relevant proportions for locally traded goods and services, and those traded in the wider UK, or in Europe, or globally? Does 60:20:10:10 feel right, or would it be different for different products and different places? Who decides? For example, what are the ethics of Ghana becoming economically dependent on exports of pineapples to Europe, even if they are grown under Fairtrade rules? Should trade – at close and long distance – be governed by rules that support increased diversification as well as other social and environmental outcomes at *both* ends?[20]

[20] There is no indication of this sort of thinking in the UN briefing document on Trade and

Legally, local governments are considered potentially to be increasingly important actors in the emerging global order, not least because they are seen as 'prime vehicles for the dissemination of global capital, goods, work force, and images', and where policy and political ideas are put into practice.[21] Former UN Ambassador Jeremy Greenstock considers disillusionment with the capacity of the nation state's ability to deal with the major issues of our times ('culture, identity and politics are going local'), and points out that it is in local communities that the global challenges of terrorism, crime, or climate change will be addressed effectively.[22] For most people their locality is the place with which they identify most easily. Boil down the now extensive literature of what it is that makes people happy and/or satisfied with their lives and three things stand out: feeling good about oneself; having a knot of enjoyable relationships with other people; and feeling good about the place we live.[23]

Leadership aimed at stimulating the sort of social changes that will avoid the negative geopolitical consequences feared by the US NIC will need to take a less laissez-faire approach to localism, and how people feel about where they live, if global security (in its broadest sense) is to be constructed on an aggregate of resilient localities – which is the only sustainable option.

Leadership for sustainability means being able to use a broad canvas to diagnose and tackle the 'wicked' problems of unsustainability, and use measures of progress that anticipate (and therefore encourage) scale change

Keith Grint is not alone in pointing out that the job for twenty-first-century leadership is to prevent 'wicked problems' turning into critical ones. 'Tame'

the Green Economy published in the run-up to the 2012 Earth Summit in Rio de Janeiro, for example. See http://www.uncsd2012.org/rio20/index.php?page=viewandtype=400and nr=13andmenu=45.

[21] Blank, Y. (2006), 'Localism in the New Global Legal Order', *Harvard International Law Journal*, 37 (1): 264–81.

[22] Greenstock, J. (2008), 'Nations Have to Act Locally in a Globalised World', *Financial Times*, 16 May.

[23] For examples only of the extensive 'happiness literature' see Layard, R. (2005), *Happiness: Lessons from a New Science* (London: Penguin); Goleman, D. (2007), *Social Intelligence: The New Science of Social Relationships* (London: Arrow Books); Argyle, M. (second edition 2001), *The Psychology of Happiness* (Hove, East Sussex: Routledge).

problems are solvable; leaders will probably have met them before. 'Critical' problems are so bad that only a command and adjust strategy will do. 'Wicked' problems are complex, involve a high degree of uncertainty and don't appear to have clear solutions that avoid generating a new set of problems.[24]

Interventions to tip human behaviour towards sustainability fall largely into the 'wicked' category. There are ways, not of taming the wickedness (as many risk strategies try to do) but of increasing the chances that it does not degrade to a criticality. I offer some examples and further references elsewhere (Parkin 2010) though one pathway here is particularly relevant to thinking about tipping points in human behaviour.[25] That is to consider every problem in the broadest possible context. The larger canvas does not necessarily increase the complexity of the problem. On the contrary it can suggest other, perhaps more tangential but nevertheless effective, solutions. For example, the Co-Directors of Princeton University's Carbon Mitigation Institute offer a series of initiatives designed to stabilize emissions of CO_2 by 2060.[26] Only one is concerned with growing natural capital, the rest concern energy efficiency or technological shifts and innovations. None refers to the contribution of human or social capital building, despite the fact that without the participation of people any energy-focused solutions will be impossible to implement. To use one rarely mentioned contribution to mitigating any environmental impact as an example: providing contraceptives for women who say they want them but can't get them. Rich and poor countries alike report 40 per cent of pregnancies to be unplanned. Just meeting that need, without coercion, would mean that global population by 2060 could be 8 billion instead of the projected 10 billion. It would be a very inexpensive intervention to lower demand for the services of energy that also delivers significant

---

[24] Grint, K. (2000), *The Arts of Leadership* (Oxford: Oxford University Press).

[25] See Parkin, Sara (2010), *The Positive Deviant* (London: Earthscan), for examples of tools for thinking and deciding from a full sustainability perspective, including: Forum for the Future's Five Capitals decision-making; an expansion of the Impact on Nature = Population x Affluence x Technology (IPAT) to include human and social capital (based on Ekins, P. and Jacobs, M. (1995), 'Environmental Sustainability and the Growth of GDP: Conditions of Compatibility', in Bhaskar, V. and Glyn, A. (eds), *The North, the South and the Environment* (London: Earthscan); an adaptation of Pacala and Socolow 'wedges' (based on Pacala, S. and Socolow, R. (2004), 'Stabilization Wedges: Solving the Climate Problem for the Next 50 Years with Current Technologies', *Science*, 305: 968–72.

[26] Carbon Mitigation Institute, Princeton University, http://cmi.princeton.edu/about/ (accessed 27 February 2012).

benefits to the health and economic status of women and to the life chances of the children they do have.[27]

Last, but by no means least, the importance of being ready to take interventions to scale, either in size or through multiplication, is rarely seen in organizational or government planning. Preparations for disaster and recovery are there, but not preparations for quick and substantial success. And it is in this direction that social tipping points must go if environmental disaster is to be averted.

The tendency has been either to develop large complex methodologies for capturing data about how an organization is performing vis-à-vis its sustainability impacts, or to focus on just one element – such as CO_2 emissions.[28] Neither, however, is appropriate to systematic promotion of or response to a rapid shift to pro-sustainability behaviour – that is, speedy building of all capitals, including a full exploitation of positive interconnections between them.

Bearing in mind Einstein's mantra, 'not everything that can be counted, counts, and not everything that counts can be counted', three areas are identified where data (qualitative as well as quantitative) should be collected with an eye to stimulating improvement at scale while also tracking it:

1. Contribution to sustainability – What has been done to build stocks of capital (all of them)?
2. Ubiquity – How widespread is pro-sustainability practice (i.e. building stocks of capital) in the organization, government, etc.?
3. Influence – How significant has been the effort (of organization, individual) to influence change in others?

Using these three areas of organizational activity for evaluating progress also offers a good structure for telling a story from which others might learn. Unlike many existing evaluation models, they remain relevant in conditions where progress to sustainability is rapid and/or bumpy. Using the new interconnected logic for capitalism and measuring progress in an

---

[27] http://esa.un.org/unpd/wpp/unpp/p2k0data.asp (accessed 27 February 2012).

[28] Global Reporting Initiative, https://www.globalreporting.org/Pages/default.aspx, and Carbon Disclosure Project, https://www.cdproject.net/en-US/Pages/HomePage.aspx. This is not to criticize such initiatives, which are steps in the right direction, but to question whether, given the speed and scale of change implied by negative environmental trends, they are sufficient.

integrated manner sets reliable parameters within which leadership can allow thousands of initiatives and innovations to flourish – while being fairly confident that most of them will be headed in the right direction.

Inevitably, this section is only able to cover a few headline ideas about different models for and approaches to changing human behaviour. The intention is to demonstrate that seeking positive tipping points in human behaviour is a frontline strategy for avoiding negative environmental ones, and to signal areas where more research or trials can hasten change.

Conclusion

This chapter started as a short address to the Kavli seminar which opened by challenging the metaphor of tipping points, arguing (along with Joe Smith and Paul Brown in Part 7) that using fear of negative consequences from environmental degradation has clearly failed to change human behaviour so far. At the same time I promoted psychological and socio-logical insights into why people decide and act in certain ways, and proposed new strategies for putting human well-being as the lead motivation for pro-sustainability behaviour, along with a range of tools and techniques that leadership could deploy.

I have elaborated on the original talk here, but further argue that none of this will make a difference on the scale needed as long as environ-mentalist and sustainability scientists and activists argue and operate *within* the illogicalities of conventional notions of capitalism. Instead, by radically reinterpreting the relationship between capital and people, a new logic emerges that is not only internally coherent but also potentially timeless. One that means we all can use this new logic to decide and act straight-away, and so help create the way we want the world to be by acting as if it was so.

At our peril we underestimate the challenges inherent in galvanizing the magnitude and speed of change needed to avert environmental and human catastrophe(s). This places a huge onus on the current guardians of all the necessary intellectual and evidential elements – universities. How will they alter their own practice in order to tackle, *as a priority*, this 'wickedest' of problems – how to re-found human civilization in a way that is sustainable into the longest of terms? This is a mission of sustainability science that is explored in Part 8.

Commentary 6.4

Leadership by business for coping with transformational tipping thresholds

AMANDA LONG

We know that, in order to survive and thrive, we will all have to live and work in ways that are very different from those we have experienced in the past. As Sara Parkin introduced in Chapter 6.3, this presents a real leadership opportunity for transformational approaches to sustainable business.

Marcel Proust said: 'The real magic of discovery lies not in seeing new landscapes, but in having new eyes.' In providing leadership for coping with transformational tipping thresholds, I believe that it is essential to look with new eyes at our business models and our approaches to our customers, and to discover how can we catalyse and drive active partnerships for social good.

Business needs to embrace the reality of sustainable business. That it is not just an extension of corporate responsibility. It is about fundamental understanding of the interconnectedness of our world and the central role all business should play. Business needs to understand where and how it can make a positive difference and drive that change. Clarity and consensus in the boardroom are keys to success in developing a sustainable business.

Business needs to be open to innovative, creative, cross-societal forms of collaboration that engage public–private–civil connections in new ways and develop regulatory frameworks and incentives to support them. Indeed it is business which is taking the lead in seeking more reliable and appropriate regulations from governments (as commented by Keith Clarke (6.5)). This is a trend which will benefit from cooperation with the dynamic nature of third-sector organizations. So I see more formative alliance between these two surprisingly compatible sectors so long as their shared beliefs are synchronized.

In today's world, broadly speaking, our related shared beliefs are:

- The third sector are stewards of the community and people in need, but have to be enabled to fulfil their roles in today's difficult economic circumstances.
- The private sector's prime drive is making short-term money, at least for their shareholders, but its linked drive is for reliable continuity.
- The Big Society is an idea associated with David Cameron, UK Prime Minister and local volunteering, but has yet to catch on with community organizations because government has yet to offer the appropriate supporting regulations, cooperative funding, and effective communications.
- The main way that companies can help charities is by giving cash.
- Philanthropy is primarily about selfless giving to charity, though the benefits of doing so are also reputational and may be economically advantageous to the donor.
- Philanthropy helps fund charities who create interventions to support people in need.

We need to replace our old beliefs with new beliefs:

- We are all stewards of the future, so we cannot avoid a sense of virtue and responsibility as outlined in Chapter 6.1.
- Our shared focus should be on real social betterment and especially on ensuring that the circumstances for succeeding generations are not knowingly jeopardized.
- The only way to achieve that is through collaborative action, not just one-way giving.
- Sustainable business needs to be placed in a long-term context and is about nurturing society in a resilient nature.
- Our shared prime objective is to do whatever we can to help each of us help ourselves and help others.
- The public, private, and civil sectors should be working together to help companies achieve long-term success across the board for local communities and the economy.
- This is an age of continuous transformation; staying the same is not an option.
- Transformation requires game-changing thinking, so where we are currently at is not where we can continue to be.

214

New models for collaborative engagement will centre on co-ownership, new products and services, transformational philanthropy, community outreach, collaborative social marketing campaigns, and social action. Figure 6.6 sets out this transformational vision.

New approaches must also recognize the power of the market and how the necessary collaboration between business and customer behavioural change will play an important role in delivering positive outcomes for the future of the planet. We need to create new business norms – such as engaging social marketing or customer behavioural-change programmes in place of more traditional approaches to marketing and cause-related marketing. This will require collaborative engagement across business and with civil organizations, schools, and colleges, and working charitably with community organizations.

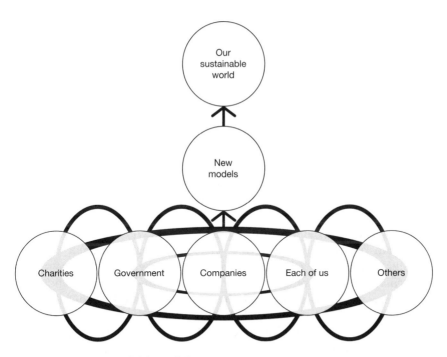

Figure 6.6 A new model for collaborative engagement

Source: Long and Drummond, Corporate Culture

Setting the tone

Some businesses are already engaging – coming out of the economic crisis and reinventing the way they think. Unilever's work (see Thomas Lingard (6.8)) on developing their Sustainable Living Programme and pioneering 'brand imprinting' sets the tone for a new approach from multinationals – still recognizing the commercial imperative but bringing the moral imperative into play too.

Post 'peak oil', post the 2008 economic crash, there is no uncertainty about the fact that the age of abundance is behind us. Wherever we look, tougher climate change regulation, stricter policies on forestry, and growing water shortages constitute a situation where food companies, for example, face a reduction in earnings – so even if a company's moral compass doesn't trigger action, economic interest highlights the necessity to act.

Defining a preferred future

The big question for business in this new world is – What is our preferred future operating environment and what do we need to do to bring it to life? I worked with Anglian Water to create the ambitious and holistic 'Love Every Drop' sustainable business programme. Its approach is designed to help to open eyes to the possibilities of a new definition of responsibility for business, where the real value of water as a gift from nature is recognized and water is no longer seen as a disposable commodity. Anglian Water wants to put water at the heart of a whole new way of living. This is not just about the company becoming sustainable, it is about the interconnectedness of the future of the business and the future of the region – Anglian Water is championing a sustainable region and encouraging sustainable living. To achieve this will demand a whole new engagement with customers. The company is investing in ground-breaking behaviour-change programmes which include some of the plethora of necessary interventions to drive sustained behaviour change.

Here is where collaboration with third-sector charities and social enterprises comes in, as one way forward is to develop sustainable water ambassadors who can work with households and neighbourhoods on new ways of conserving piped water and better ways of deploying the rain that falls on roofs and hard surfaces. Anglian Water is testing out the provision of home water butts to be linked to overall care for in-home water use, with community-based water ambassadors trained through funding partnerships.

Many of us do not get the opportunity to consider the true value of water as an intrinsic element of ecosystems functioning. We only realize how much we rely on it when our supply is disrupted in some way. Yet water is at the heart of everything we do. Every cup of coffee in the morning; shower after the gym; or clean shirt before a day's work. Water is such an inspiring, engaging product – ideal for the task at hand – to reach out across society and start to engage people to think differently about the resources we all consume.

Going large

There is a pressing need to push the development of new sustainable business models right up the agenda across the private sector. A decade ago, Business in The Community (BiTC) established 'Workplace, Marketplace, Community and Environment' as core to its Corporate Responsibility Index. Along with other organizations promoting sustainability in responsible business, this played an important role in engaging business to drive the agenda forward. To push for progress now, new approaches are needed to shape and facilitate new economic sustainable growth. It is important that 'corporate responsibility' reporting doesn't become a 'tick box' activity and in doing so act as a drag-anchor on innovation.

Embracing long-term timeframes and context greatly helps to improve business resilience and identify new business opportunities. Leadership by business in coping with transformational tipping thresholds can come when businesses engage in 'Big Picture' thinking. By taking the approach of highlighting business opportunities and new business models, businesses can consider the opportunities and issues they face and how they might overcome them.

We are now seeing a growing body of work which outlines visions and roadmaps out to 2050 (for example, the World Business Council for Sustainable Development Vision 2050). At its Responsible Business Convention in 2011, BiTC rolled out the first phase of its '2050 Vision for a Sustainable Future Project'. Through the provision of a series of visioning tools and cross-business collaboration, BiTC are seeking to stimulate businesses to develop shared positive visions of 2050 and a routemap to get there.

217

Going beyond 'shared value'

If we are going to accelerate progress and encourage leadership in business on the sustainability agenda there is a real need to open up the debate around going beyond 'shared value'. The concept of 'shared value', as set out by Porter and Kramer (2011), is a strong starting point for building the business case for sustainability: that long-term sustainability relates to business creating economic value in a way that also adds value for society by addressing its needs and challenges. The list of high or worthwhile achievers in this area is growing annually, which is good news. However, context is critical in this discussion. As austerity bites even deeper into society and resources become scarcer, the reality of the need to change fundamentally our approach to business in this age of transformation is ever more urgent. The focus for business needs increasingly to be on how business can help create more sustainable communities by making it easy for customers to live more sustainable lives, thereby helping to build stronger, more sustainable markets, with no separation between what is termed as 'business value' and 'social value'.

When Unilever CEO Paul Polman held the one-year review for its Sustainable Living Plan in April 2012, he talked of going beyond 'shared value' and responding more directly to the needs of a frugal resource-challenged society first. Some of the big players now understand that a real business model shift is required, although delivering on this in mainstream business is still 'work in progress'. GlaxoSmithKline, Centrica, General Electric, Kingfisher, and a handful of others, are all part of the picture of progress.

Sustainability must increasingly mean businesses focusing on what they can do to help customers live more sustainably and thereby contribute to creating stronger markets – a clear sense of long-term sustainable business success. Driving the creation of sustainable communities and sustainable living is core to creating sustainable markets within which to prosper. Businesses can no longer operate outside the context of a society with limited resources and hope for long-term sustainability. But when they work within that society, they can take advantage of the opportunities to become the life support of nations for the long term: for example, by moving from simply supplying food to helping people eat better and reduce waste.

There is a tangible sense of change within the private sector these days, as John Elkington (6.6) reinforces. However business needs to be much more proactive in stepping up to the challenges humankind faces with bold, mainstream 'at scale' solutions. To deliver on this in the long term will require the courage of leadership, the willingness to take some flak from shareholders, communicating more effectively the real value of sustainability to investors, and the need to seek collaboration with third-sector and social enterprises. It will require new approaches to how we all do business and an honest reassessment of the values that underpin why we do business and what business means to society. To make progress faster we need to face these big questions and respond with new business models and new approaches to sustainable economic activity. We need to be increasingly open to trialling creative and cooperative experiments and new approaches to sustainable economic growth.

Reference

Porter, M.E. and Kramer, M.R. (2011), 'Creating Shared Value', *Harvard Business Review*, 89, 1/2: 2–17.

Commentary 6.5

Private sector failure and risk management for tipping points

KEITH CLARKE

I used to run a global multinational company, with 10,000 employees to maintain and many shareholders to please. Ensuring a monthly payout and a stock market return are legally binding requirements on any chief executive. Tipping points have to be placed in context. Building up the corporate portfolio is the job description. If we are going to get anywhere we need to realign science, social science, regulation, and the markets in a fresh alliance with business, governments, and civil society organizations.

The introductory chapters to this book make a credible case that there are significant tipping points, which climate change and other Earth system adjustments are likely to trigger, which are system changes (arguably failures) that are abrupt and inevitably have unforeseen, and, to date, unforeseeable consequences on other systems. Not only are their consequences unpredictable, the prediction of when they may occur, or the criteria for showing that they have occurred, is effectively impossible to determine in the near term.

The private sector, composed of organizations that make things or provide services as a group, simply do not invest in avoiding system tipping points. The recent banking crisis has demonstrated this. Banks as global organizations that should arguably have seen system failure points, did not do so. History has shown repeated boom and subsequent bust of stock markets. The basic means for allocating capital in most economies has failed before, and all the evidence suggests that it will fail again.

There is one trend embedded in these failures. As economies become more connected and tend towards globalization, the highs and lows become more extreme, and their consequences increasingly unpredictable. Climate change has all of these characteristics. Individual companies do however manage risk with varying degrees of aggression and successful results. It is the variability of performance which is the basis of the private sector. Good markets attract more companies and more capital; well-managed companies do even better in any market. However, the essence is that poor markets cause disinvestment, and badly managed companies fail. This is basic economic theory: to rely on the private sector en masse to invest in mitigating the potential consequences of non-immediate tipping points and to do so effectively has, to put it mildly, no historical precedent.

Accepting these limitations, there is a role that the market can and should play. The best companies do anticipate demand, and do create products prior to the demand being evident, and do so within the bounds of imperfectly functioning markets. To prepare for future events outside of the known operating parameters cannot be left to individual companies. It is a collective responsibility to explore the edges of the 'system'. This anticipatory work should provide an understanding of how potential failures are occurring, something that did not occur in the Great Depression, nor in the recent financial collapse. Both were relatively simple system failures compared to any of the currently identified climate-change-induced tipping points. Markets do not and will not manage risk or anticipate risk in a politically, socially, or environmentally effective manner.

So here I turn to the power of regulation. Businesses can work with targets and structures which can be implemented on reasonable timescales and where there is reliable and consistent government leadership and legislative commitment. For addressing tipping points, the process of regulation is flawed as it tends to lie in the hands of particular interests, and is often controlled by the whims of political expediency. Where we need to go lies in the field of co-implementation; this involves bringing in a wider group of players.

In this simplistic view there are two other parties; academia and government. But they also have severe limitations on how they can influence the management of tipping points. Academic research is fundamentally important to the progression of knowledge and tells its story to a wider public in a language that is incomprehensible at best. Probability and risk are not items humans logically deal with, but much research is about likely outcomes. Without research we are a dead society, but it does not mean society can or should be changed because of better stories in the *Mail on Sunday*. Whilst the internet gives extraordinary access to information, it does not always lead to accurate knowledge dissemination. The percentage of US citizens who continue to believe their president is a Muslim is an interesting example. To convince, even with scientific evidence, that the melting of the permafrost is human-derived, that it is likely to cause a major global-wide problem, and that it will seriously affect their children's lives in a not particularly beneficial manner, is probably a stretch when it comes to US public opinion.

In recent years it has been the NGOs who have provided the link between science and society. They have the mission and the ability to synthesize research into an action agenda. The entities beginning to take note here are our professional institutions, The British Academy, The Royal Society, Confederation for British Industry, and the Institute for Civil Engineers. They not only have the ability to communicate meaningfully with government and the private sector, they can transcend the extraordinary tribalism in the academic world.

Governments globally have begun a change to commit to a decarbonized global economy. It is progress when for the first time governments collectively look to avoid a problem rather than mitigate the after-chain of its effects. The rate of change required in the next ten years is unprecedented; however, it is fair to assume no single world order will suddenly come to pass but we will continue with a whole gamut of political, social, and economic models.

The potential for both lessening the likelihood of reaching tipping points, or preparing for the consequences of when they occur, lies in the interface between academia, government, and companies. This means effective concentrations at the interface – not singular, but also not as hopelessly informal as exist today. NGOs provide the glue at this interface: they can change companies and governments. They started the decarbonizing revolution and provided stunning leadership in setting the question. To set the answers we need to supplement this glue.

Commentary 6.6

Creating a roadmap for sustainable, transformational change

JOHN ELKINGTON

One of my favourite quotations comes from the late Kurt Vonnegut, born some 90 years ago. 'We have to continually be jumping off cliffs', he said, 'and developing our wings on the way down.' I used it when kicking off our first Breakthrough Capitalism workshop, co-hosted by the Value Web,[1] in April 2012. The idea was to challenge the growing consensus among business leaders that they had already understood the sustainability agenda – and embedded the necessary responses in their organizations. My perspective on the nature of the challenge can be found in a *New York Times* op-ed published around the time of the UN Rio+20 Summit.[2] The content of the Breakthrough Capitalism initiative to date can be found on the dedicated website.[3] The richness of the discussion at the Breakthrough Capitalism Forum, which followed in May, is indicated by the sample of the Knowledge Wall (Figure 6.7).

Participants in that first workshop included some fifty people from companies (including Actis, Atkins, BP, Fenton, HP, SolarCentury), finance groups (Friends Provident, Goldman Sachs, Zouk Ventures), impact investment organizations (Big Issue Invest, Investors' Circle, Investing for Good, Social Finance, Tellus Mater), government (the Cabinet Office), social enterprises (More Associates, Polecat, the Social Stock Exchange), NGOs and think-tanks (Carbon Tracker, the Climate Group, Forum for the Future, the Foundation for Democracy and Sustainable Development,

---

[1] http://www.thevalueweb.org.
[2] http://www.nytimes.com/2012/06/22/opinion/global-agenda-magazine-going-green. html?pagewanted=all.
[3] http://www.breakthroughcapitalism.com.

Figure 6.7 A sample of the Knowledge Wall at the Breakthrough Capitalism Forum, London, May 2012

Source: Breakthrough Capitalism Forum/Yahoo Web 2012

SustainAbility, WWF), and networks like Green Mondays and the UK Youth Climate Coalition. The Breakthrough Capitalism Forum the following month attracted almost five times as many people, to hear nearly thirty speakers, with videos of the presentations available on the website.

The idea behind all of this is that even as competition helps drive change, it also gets in the way. So the time has come for the giant sustainability mash-up – to create a basic roadmap and toolkit for everyone investing in transformational change. Clearly, we don't expect to achieve the mash-up in one or two workshops, or even during the course of our Forum. Instead, our ambition is to catalyse a process many of us now know needs to happen – and help provide a sense of direction.

The workshop process, designed by Value Web/Innovation Arts and Volans, took participants through various stages, including a backcasting exercise from 2022. Then it dug into personal (and group) perceptions of the need for system change, the trajectories of breakthrough innovation – and the key barriers that stand in the way of progress. What was clear to participants was that we are at a key *inflection point*, that political leadership is often lacking, and new constellations of change agents are emerging. So we concluded that some form of leaderless revolution would be part of the way forward, offering better direction and support than is the case right now. But there was also a feeling that we need to get a better sense of what these constellations are doing, to avoid making them so big that they slow progress down, and to audit progress in key areas, as a means to better direct effort and resources.

A couple of breakout groups (out of eight) generated fairly dystopian scenarios for the future. There was a sense here that some form of meltdown (for example, a global pandemic that isn't put back in the bottle like SARS) would be needed to catalyse change of the nature and scale now needed. Among the identified brakes on breakthrough change, here are ten:

1. Many key people still do not feel the present system is broken – or 'broken enough'.
2. There is pervasive short-termism, fuelled by short electoral timescales and amplified by the economic crisis that began in 2007–08.
3. Intergenerational frictions cloud the picture.
4. Still-powerful incumbents are failing to adapt and lobby fiercely to block change.
5. The culture of ownership suppresses collaborative consumption.

6. There is competition between solution-providers (for example, we compete to develop our own language and are often unwilling to share that developed by others).
7. Transparency, accountability, and reporting mechanisms remain weak.
8. There are too many perverse incentives, including misdirected taxes and subsidies.
9. Our global governance mechanisms and institutions are precariously weak.
10. There is growing nationalism, protectionism, and xenophobia in some quarters.

Among the potential accelerators of breakthrough innovation and change we identified scores, but here are ten:

1. There is a collective sense that change is in the air – and that breakdown triggers breakthrough.
2. Some major companies and super brands are taking courageous leadership roles – and organizations like the World Business Council for Sustainable Development (WBCSD) are publishing interesting roadmaps identifying future risks and opportunities, in their case in the form of *Vision 2050*.[4]
3. New business models are emerging (e.g. B Corporations[5]), alongside the revival of co-ops and similar.
4. The right sort of corporate rating and ranking schemes can drive change.
5. There are encouraging emerging trends in design, including cradle-to-cradle and bio-mimicry, though they aren't yet viral.
6. We see a coming standardization of global sustainability-related standards.
7. There will be new forms of valuation, pricing and accounting.
8. There is energetic discussion of 'stranded assets', for example in CarbonTracker's work[6] and Generation Investment Management's white paper on 'Sustainable Capitalism'.[7]
9. The system is under creative pressure from new social movements (e.g. Arab Spring at its best, and Occupy).

---

[4] http://www.wbcsd.org/vision2050.aspx.
[5] http://www.bcorporation.net.
[6] http://www.carbontracker.org/news/environmental-stranded-assets.
[7] http://www.generationim.com/media/pdf-generation-sustainable-capitalism-v1.pdf.

10. There is interesting innovation taking place in such areas as behaviour change (take the example of Recyclebank's[8] relationship with Transport for London).

The workshop concluded with a brainstorm of some of the weak signals that are currently being overlooked or actively ignored. Here are ten of those:

1. A new paradigm is surfacing – with many of the apparently weak signals linking back to its emergence.
2. Technologies exist (or are in development) that can help solve many of our problems, if properly deployed, but are dismissed as unworkable or uneconomic.
3. There is new potential to tap into what Clay Shirky calls 'cognitive surplus'[9] – offering new ways of developing our 'Future Quotient'.[10]
4. New forms of communication, transparency, accountability, and reporting are evolving that promise to be crucial in driving and informing breakthrough change, but are adopted on a voluntary basis rather than regulated by governments.
5. Many governments are abdicating their responsibility to use the data and information that are already being produced to steer transformative change.
6. Under the radar, unusual partnerships are beginning to emerge (for example, sportswear and retail brands convening around a Zero Discharge of Hazardous Chemicals agenda, aiming to detoxify supply chains into China by 2020).[11]
7. There is often an obsessive focus on problems, when a more optimistic focus on solutions – a 'glass half-full' approach – could help switch on the unconverted. For example, Daniel Goleman encourages us to analyse not just the negative footprint of a business, but also its 'mindprint' and, at the potentially strongly positive end of the spectrum, its 'handprint'.[12]
8. The ageing trend is being investigated in terms of the implications for health care and pension provision, but not in terms of the potential for

[8] https://www.recyclebank.com.
[9] http://en.wikipedia.org/wiki/Cognitive_surplus.
[10] http://futurequotient.tumblr.com/report/.
[11] http://nikeinc.com/news/nike-roadmap-toward-zero-discharge-of-hazardous-chemicals.
[12] http://www.time.com/time/magazine/article/0,9171,2108015,00.html.

growing political conservatism among baby boomers – how do we counter that?

9. Young people (e.g. Generation Y) are often keen to be involved in transformative change, but could become deeply frustrated and/or angry where high levels of unemployment persist. So we need to discover from them how to engage with them before they disengage from us.

10. While we tend to avert our eyes from some of the areas of greatest current failure (e.g. Detroit or developing countries), their resilience may also turn out to become the sources and incubators of break-through solutions that could have a profound impact on the rest of the world, through what is now called 'reverse innovation'.[13]

Our aim is to use the insights we have captured so far, but also to create more, to generate an open-source Prospectus for Breakthrough Capitalism. Our latest book, *The Zeronauts: Breaking the Sustainability Barrier*, identifies fifty breakthrough innovators working in such areas as population growth, pandemics, poverty, pollution, and the proliferation of weapons of mass destruction.[14] We are not just sitting back and waiting for a 'leaderless revolution' on this front: a key aim is to identify, convene, and network leaders working in very different areas. And at a time when the mainstreaming of the sustainability agenda risks the dilution of ambition, we aim to triple distil the agenda, map the areas where 'the future is already here', and help jump innovation to the point where it drives truly transformative change.

---

[13] http://en.wikipedia.org/wiki/Reverse_innovation.
[14] http://www.zeronauts.com.

Commentary 6.7

Tipping points and 'Too Difficult Boxes'

CHARLES CLARKE

Analysing tipping points is both interesting and potentially illuminating. Amongst other things, such a process rightly respects the importance and practical significance of an enormous range of government decisions which, to varying degrees, certainly have an impact on the economic, social, and environmental conditions of billions of people.

Government is not the only player. Indeed you could argue that it is becoming less important over time; but it certainly is a major one, probably the most important. This vital fact immediately draws attention to the quality of government decisions. Do national governments properly address the magnitude of the challenges their country faces? At a global level, do governments have the capacity to work together to meet truly global challenges?

Where solutions cannot easily be identified and implemented, national governments often dispatch strategic problems to the 'Too Difficult Box'. This is not simply where there is rapid alternation of governments, though that makes things more difficult. Even longstanding governments, such as the eighteen Conservative years from 1979 to 1997 and the thirteen Labour years from 1997 to 2010, failed fully to address a wide range of important issues. These include climate change, the relationship of Britain to Europe, nuclear disarmament and terrorist threats, immigration control, regulation of the banks, social exclusion of certain groups, and the ageing society, including public sector pensions and long-term care for the elderly. There are many more.

In each of these cases, failure to grasp the nettle of change can bring the whole society closer to a tipping point which means that decisions finally have to be taken in an atmosphere of crisis or, worse, not taken at all.

What all of these subjects have in common is that change is needed, change is difficult, and time is not on our side. Moreover the solutions will

229

require at least some people to suffer some loss. And that means that in democracies change becomes difficult. Even longstanding governments have to face elections every four years or so.

All governments, whatever their electoral mandates, come to appreciate that it is indeed their responsibility to address the challenges I have described. They then need to establish how best to do that. They have to go through a series of stages. The starting point is to identify clearly the problem that needs to be addressed. This identification is itself not easy. The issues are themselves very complicated and intertwined. For example, the demands for energy sustainability and energy security, at one level entirely mutually compatible, can lead to quite different, even opposed, policy solutions.

Once the problem that needs to be addressed has been identified, government then needs to overcome seven further hurdles, any one of which can provide the obstacle which stops a government in its tracks.

First, the solution needs to be clearly identified. This will involve controversy, as honest people can differ about the best solution. Wherever possible, scientific analyses should offer better ways of addressing options than mixes of prejudice and media platitudes. Criticisms need to be properly dealt with, not ducked, by the scientists as much as anyone else.

Second, the challenges of implementation need to be understood. In some cases implementation is simple, in others very complex. It is rare that it is only a matter of decree, a simple stroke of the pen, even after a law is passed or an executive decision legally taken. Moreover the potential long-term advantages of change may well be outweighed by short-term disadvantages, which cause political problems.

Third, a variety of vested interests need to be placated or overcome. The vested interests who are losers will organize, and an iron rule of politics is that potential losers will organize against a change. Potential gainers will leave it to the government to make the case. The losers are likely to have at least some good arguments and they will maintain that their concern is actually the public interest, not their own. They will seek to undermine the overall argument for the proposed solution. They will often use pretty effective campaign techniques to mobilize hostile public opinion.

Fourth, a range of legal constraints, for example in international or European law, need to be circumnavigated. Ministers, rightly, have to act within the law. The United Kingdom is part of a wide range of international legal regimes, such as the European Convention on Human Rights. Many of these were established soon after 1945 in circumstances very different from those which govern our lives today, and they create a very real set of constraints within which Parliament and governments have to act. And renegotiating international agreements is a very difficult and time-consuming process.

Fifth, in many cases the international dimension of the problem has to be appreciated. This is particularly true in relation to the European Union, which is the main actor in relation to many areas of our national life, for example the environment, agriculture, competition policy, consumer protection, employment law, health and safety, and energy. The same is true, to a lesser extent, of our other international relationships and obligations, for example in the United Nations and the World Trade Organization.

Sixth, the political process is complex and its vicissitudes have to be overcome. Every policy proposal needs to be enacted. This is not just a question of a clear statement or speech, nor is it only a matter of determination. A law has to be passed, and at all points in the process political theatre will be present, parliamentary rebellions will happen, rethinks will go on, and retreats will take place. The Opposition will normally retreat to the opportunism of opposition. This is a real power: since in most Parliaments this is enough, together with rebellious sections of the governing party, to make votes tight in the Commons and to defeat government in the Lords.

And seventh, underlying everything, the government needs to sustain the political energy and creativity which is so essential if change is to be successfully accomplished. Divisions of ideology or ambition can make that difficult, as can the simple passage of time.

This is an impressive range of obstacles, which explains why governments, even with large majorities, have not been able to address comprehensively the problems which society faces.

When we turn to the problems of securing international cooperation, the problems become even greater, since definitions of common interest are so much more difficult to identify than at the level of the nation state. Even the European Union, the most sophisticated effort to do that in the last century, has found it very difficult to sustain itself against national preoccupations. The experience of the two World Wars led the whole world to try and create institutions which would express the common ambitions of all humanity. But they too have not found it easy to change in a way that reflects the wider changes in the world.

But, ultimately, it is simply not good enough to leave unsolved too many big and fundamental problems. The real-world problems are just too great, the pace of change too urgent. There are too many areas in which a tipping point approaches. Decision not to act, to delay, or to postpone are choices too, with their own consequences which may be very serious. It is now obvious that reform of the banking system, a classically difficult issue, was just such an example. Failure to reform across the world led to economic disaster which was far worse than it need have been. Inadequate government action meant that a tipping point was passed. The same may happen in the Eurozone. This is even more the case with some of the proposals discussed in this book. Climate change will not go away. Nor will nuclear proliferation or food insecurity.

It is important to emphasize that democracy offers the best means of making the necessary changes, though it also creates difficulties. Unlike authoritarian or dictatorial political methods, democracy seeks to take account of all aspects of society. But democratic politics has to face up to long-term problems. It has to be a long-term provider of solutions rather than a short-term scorer of political points. That is the message for politicians in both government and opposition, who have to show political courage and leadership in articulating that tough problems need to be addressed even if that means losing short-term popularity.

Commentary 6.8

It tips both ways

THOMAS LINGARD

Tipping points got us into this mess; tipping points will have to get us out. That, in a nutshell, is what I would like to argue in this commentary.

From a business perspective, tipping points are tricky. Management is essentially the art of making decisions based on imperfect information. Most information tells you that the future will be like the past. In fact, that assumption is so ingrained into how we think that most investment products are compelled by law to point out that this is not true.

> Please note that past performance is not a guide to the future. The value of investments and the income from them may go down as well as up.

It is probably fair to say that such warnings are now so ubiquitous as to make not a jot of difference, except to the lawyers who use them to fend off legal action.

For businesses, spotting and responding to fast-approaching tipping points in the ecological systems on which they depend is very hard. Responding to gradually increasing stresses on systems, even well before tipping points are reached, is hard enough. It is never clear that an emerging trend is indeed a trend until the trend is firmly established as normal. Businesses that fail to spot trends can sometimes catch their competitors up, but species that fail to adapt to tipping points in their environment tend to become extinct sooner than might otherwise have been necessary. Not existing makes catching up harder.

Fortunately, businesses are much better at responding to proxy indicators of approaching tipping points than to the tipping points themselves. This is because such proxies often bring shorter-term implications than the ecological tipping points themselves. Campaigning activities (about tipping point issues) by non-governmental organizations (NGOs), which threaten brand and reputation, can prompt rapid and helpful responses from companies. Regulatory and legislative interventions, or even the threat thereof, do indeed help to focus the mind of business executives.

But most influential of all is customer demand. A framing of opportunity and competitive advantage drives business action of several magnitudes beyond what is possible with a 'doom and gloom', doomsday scenario. The vaguest hint from consumers and customers that a concerted response to ecological issues will be rewarded with custom, brand preference, and loyalty is all that a well-intentioned business needs to change gear in its response. That is the power of the market. I had been working on sustainability issues in Unilever for five years when in 2007 Lee Scott, then CEO and President of Wal-Mart, Unilever's single largest global customer, gave the keynote speech at a high-level event hosted by the Prince of Wales's Business and Environment Programme. The next day it was as if someone had flicked a switch inside our organization. People understood that change was coming. It was a tipping point in a journey that had begun in the 1990s, when Unilever's sustainability programmes in water, agriculture, and fisheries were first established. People saw that the niche might just become the mainstream, even if they were not ready to admit that the people who had for a decade been pushing the idea of a more socially and environmentally responsible version of business were not simply conscience-troubled do-gooders but the early pioneers of a new way of doing business fit for a new century.

It is astonishing to think that no one was able to tweet anything from that speech. It is unlikely that anyone started a conversation about it even on Facebook. Few if any people in the audience were on LinkedIn, and the invitation to attend the event arrived in the post. In just five years there has been a complete transformation in how people collaborate, and an exponential change in the speed of conversation and the exchange and spread of ideas, thanks to the revolution in social media. If the challenge facing us was to find a way to radically raise awareness of the need for action, uncover the world's best insight into what action really works, and to make that action desirable, then the social media revolution is the single biggest gift for which we might have wished. Change leaders all over the world and in every sector have been handed a weapon for this fight, the power of which we have barely even begun to explore and understand. This is in my view a particularly inspiring tipping point, and we are right in the middle of it.

So far I have described tipping points in business cases and tipping points in communication. Many believe this will be enough to make the changes we need, on the scale we need them, in time to avert the other varieties of tipping points that haunt us in our darker moments, and which are described in Chapter 2.1. It is a view which is understandable, given the sheer force that both of these will unleash. But it is ultimately a view which I believe is wrong. This is because the inertia within the system dynamic is so far out of proportion with the forces pushing for change, that even if such transformational forces can rise to match it, I see no evidence that they will be able to overcome it completely.

This observation points to a third area where exponential change is necessary: the relationship between the public and private sectors. In John Elkington's commentary (6.6) he summarizes a number of blockers to breakthrough change identified at a recent workshop. Three of them are relevant to this challenge, and I have reordered them into the following narrative description of this problem:

- Our global governance mechanisms and institutions are precariously weak.
- There are too many perverse incentives, including misdirected taxes and subsidies.
- Still-powerful incumbents are failing to adapt and lobby fiercely to block change.

None of these insights is either particularly new, or contested. But what has been changing in the past few years is the growing realization that it is the combination of them that makes the situation particularly dangerous.

Global governance ought to resolve the issues of perverse incentives, yet at the United Nations Conference on Sustainable Development in Rio de Janiero in June 2012, governments largely ignored the major global campaign calling for an end to fossil fuel subsidies, acknowledging it only with a line, in paragraph 225 (of 283), reaffirming previous commitments to take action on this, but with no sense of a deadline, or indeed urgency of any kind. That is a simple failure of leadership.

Even without functioning global governance, perverse subsidies ought to be an attractive target for cost-cutting at the national level in times of global economic austerity, and yet the lobbying efforts of those powerful incumbents make this far less than straightforward. It is a painful irony that the direct and indirect subsidies afforded by governments to the fossil fuel industry are in part what ensures it remains cash-rich and able to

235

outspend the lobby efforts of more progressive business groups and NGOs who persuasively and painstakingly argue for transformational change in the system.

Even here, where it can seem we are far from where we need to be, I see evidence of positive tipping points. The World Economic Forum's report, *More with Less* (WEF 2012), argued that:

> Governments must act to shape demand for sustainable products and services directly through public procurement, and indirectly shape behaviours and attitudes through policy.

This is a direct plea for regulatory interventions to drive sustainability. The World Business Council for Sustainable Development, which for many years argued for progressive action on sustainability by business (rather than by government, as was some people's interpretation), saw a subtle but significant change in narrative at the Rio+20 Summit with the launch of *Changing Pace* (WBCSD 2012). This is a document whose primary purpose is to make it clear that transformational, scalable, and rapid change by business is only possible with the right policy frameworks, regulations and incentives. It felt like real progress, and time will tell whether it really was a tipping point in this critical global conversation.

I opened this commentary with the thought that tipping points got us into this mess and that tipping points are going to have to get us out. The triple tipping points of the new and real business cases, the social media explosion, and a change in discourse in the conversation between the businesses that create value for the world and the governments that we elect to create the rules by which they are required to operate; these three acting together give me great hope that the next great tipping point may be just around the corner.

References

World Business Council on Sustainable Development (2012), *Changing Pace* (Geneva: WBCSD).
World Economic Forum (2012), *More with Less* (Davos: WEF).

Commentary 6.9

Perspective of a global retailer

MIKE BARRY

Business is used to the idea of tipping points, insofar as it is exposed to the constant possibility of upheaval. From steam power to the computer, the financial Big Bang in the City of London to the internet, moments of transformational change have always happened in the world of business. We talk of 'game-changing' or 'disruptive' innovations. These might be the arrival of new technologies, of new ways of managing, of new market arrangements, or of radical changes in the operating environments of business. As ever, the strategic challenge to business leaders is to spot these moments before their implications undermine their position and prospects, or to respond nimbly to take advantage of the impacts of major change. In business as in other sectors, it is extraordinarily difficult to anticipate the onset of a transformational change and to assess the implications in a timely way, still more so to respond effectively.

Individual companies have always come and gone in the wake of such developments. Indeed whole sectors (think of manufacturing offshoring in Western economies in the 1980s) can go through seismic shifts. Are we facing such a profound shift now in the business world as a result of ecological and socio-economic 'tipping'? What makes the present moment different, why describe it as a time of tipping points rather than a period of 'business as usual' change?

I would contend that we are now entering a time in which several taken-for-granted fundamentals of business life are being undermined. They are assumptions, values, outlooks, and expectations that have become so embedded in business thinking – and far beyond business – that they are almost invisible. What are they?

- That 'the environment' would always be available as business's biggest 'factory', a constant 24/7 source of bountiful low cost 'inputs' (energy, water, raw materials) that business converts relentlessly into economic value whilst avoiding paying for any externalities.
- That Government would always be there as the 'backer of last resort', bailing out the financial sector that underpins the economy when things got tough, and a guarantor of progress and security when life was uncertain for business.
- That people would be content to coexist in separable lives as consumers, citizens, and employees, with the economic system sustaining order by giving them a little more of seemingly guaranteed comfort each year.

All these 'certainties' are now threatened.

Our bountiful environmental 'factory' is running out of capacity. Ecosystems are evidently unable to keep up with the need to provide resources or absorb wastes as global consumption relentlessly mounts. What has been obvious to environmentalists for many years is becoming a reality for businesses coping with high and volatile resource costs and the disruption caused by extreme weather events.

Although governments have stepped in to 'bail out' the banks during the economic crises of the last four years, many now can sense that political patience (not to mention financial reserves) is running out. Will the public sector reach its own tipping point in relation to dysfunctional banks and financial systems deemed 'too big to fail', and let them go under? More likely, governments will increasingly ask business to pick up the external costs of making and selling its products. This will not be done on the basis of some moral imperative. It will be because the state does not and will not have the cash to pay for the externalities of business practice – climate change, an obesity epidemic, etc. And governments have already sent a powerful signal that they are neither able nor willing to set a policy direction to tackle major environmental challenges such as climate change. A bickering multi-polar world just looks too daunting to corral. So businesses, relying on state action to organize a strategic and coordinated response to ecological disruption, are likely to be disappointed.

The Romans had 'bread and circuses' to keep the masses happy. We have strung along through rising income levels and the disarmingly ready availability of products to consume. But in many Western markets real disposable incomes are predicted to flat-line – at best. For many in the US middle and lower classes, real household wealth and income have been falling for years. The same story is being played out in the EU, as the Eurozone crisis and the impact of high personal debt levels make themselves felt at every level. The slogan 'We are the 99%' and the rise of the Occupy movements were signals that the basic compact between business and society is threatened.

No longer can business lazily assume that the griping will come from the edges, from the few who reject a consumerist life. Instead it will come from the mainstream, from citizens whose expectations of rising or at least stable income, wealth, and prospects are being dashed, for themselves and for their children. The disaffection probably won't manifest itself as violent revolution. Instead consumers will drift away from intense consumption, starting instead to select more carefully from whom they buy. Increasingly we will see people turning to a 'sharing economy' where goods are no longer possessed and disposed of in the classical sense. Rather they will be shared, bartered, rented, and exchanged in a parallel, not for profit, and often community-based economy.

Rising resource costs, the retreat of government, a re-definition of consumption collectively create an enormous visible tipping point for business. This is not to say that business as we know it will disappear, far from it. But it does mean that for today's incumbents the journey through the next decade will be that much harder and in all likelihood much more destructive of many more traditional business models. But seen another way, the next decade is incredibly exciting. New business models (not just businesses) will have to be developed, based on a much closer relationship with environment and society. They will be based on collaboration, not all-out competition. New technologies will emerge that offer fantastic rewards because they solve these enormous challenges. Tipping points offer opportunities as well as crises and threats. For the private sector, understanding the nature of these changes is a matter of life, death, and urgent adaptation.

PART 7
COMMUNICATING TIPPING POINTS AND RESILIENCE

Communicating tipping points is tough. The two chapters and four commentaries which follow cover the difficulties and the possibilities of using communications and media, as well as social networking, as a means for offering both the characteristics of convulsive change as well as the scope for telling the world about how to anticipate and to adapt. The real test, as Joe Smith (7.1) thoughtfully explains, is not to scare or to bore. In a world of constant bombardment, the possible dangers of ice melt, sea-level rise, extreme weather events, and human distress, even on a large scale, are easily lost in competing news stories, multiple distractions, the tedium of repetition, and the wish for peace and quiet.

The value of these contributions lies in their careful and intelligent approach to the ways in which good news can come out of possible threat and disruption. The power of this Part lies in the scope for anticipation and adaptation. This requires fresh approaches by the media as well as by governments and communities, as Emily Boyd (7.2) explains.

We need to say more about adaptation. In Chapter 2.1, Tim Lenton offers ways in which Earth-system tipping points may be addressed through early warnings. He especially points to the sluggishness of the manner in which a return to previous conditions following disturbance takes place, and the increasing randomness and unpredictability of reactions. This can be transported to the financial stage in the context of the capacity of banks to retain assets in the face of fluctuating stock markets and exchange rates as well as in increasingly demanding regulatory requirements for accessible capital to hedge against default or failure to bail out. In both cases there is a combination of randomness and sluggishness of response which is reminiscent of the early warnings scenarios.

What Emily Boyd reveals is the need for reliable warning of possible hazard, the capacity for delivering community-based civil defence in the face of flood or storm, the back-up of contingency measures (food, medical supplies, evacuation arrangements), and, above all, the resources and organizational abilities to restore a viable economy and functioning infrastructure. This is her heartening story of Mumbai in the wake of devastating floods, a city which also responded remarkably to two terrorist attacks.

What we cannot be sure about is how well really impoverished and ephemeral settlements can cope with prolonged and devastating after-effects. The 400,000 homeless in Haiti following the earthquakes of 2009 suffer all manner of deprivations, including tropical storms and almost unimaginable public health and security dangers. Yet somehow they survive, even though the conditions of survival must be dire. And much also depends on a vital combination of continuing aid and extraordinary personal courage. How such people build resilience in the face of vulnerability is very much part of what we need to know more about, and to learn from. As Emily Boyd notes, we are good at dealing with the aftermath, but still very weak at anticipating and designing in resilience for the 'foremath'.

The two commentaries by Paul Brown (7.3), a former environmental correspondent to the *Guardian* newspaper, and Jonathan Sinclair-Wilson (7.5), a former managing editor of Earthscan Publications, offer important suggestions. Brown is keen for analysts of tipping points to be very clear as to their prognoses and interpretations, as there is little room for getting it wrong initially, even if eventually proven right. Sinclair-Wilson is equally keen to begin a dialogue of mutual respect and understanding, the essence of sustainability science, to begin the search for anticipatory solutions, no matter how clumsy. He also argues we should not try to skirt around planetary boundaries and social floors, but address head on the bonds which tie us to a uniquely habitable Earth and to our progeny. All value the scope for tipping points to reveal our inadequacies of preparedness, our powers of creating irreversibility, and our inherent scope for redemption.

7.1
Media coverage of tipping points
Searching for a balanced story

JOE SMITH

Humanity tends to be fearful of change, yet change is our constant companion. What seems to be new about change is that climate science and linked policy research are indicating the possibility of abrupt and hazardous transformations. Yet change can be exhilarating if embraced with a spirit of creativity. In personal and working lives, and in business and public institutions, change is not just accepted, it is often actively sought. It is central to any notion of modernity. The media struggle to imagine or represent potential broad system changes, yet are constantly in search of apparently new 'stories'. This volume contains plenty of examples of the kinds of difficult new knowledge that climate research and other Earth-system adjustments are generating. Such alterations are novel threats and have, at times, generated fearful accounts of possible futures. However, there are also many ideas, innovations, and long-established practices that can permit human thriving, whatever may come its way. In this chapter I seek to cover both the media dilemma of how to inform and engage yet not panic, and the growing body of optimistic research which reveals how well humanity can cope.

Here I consider the ways in which the media might limit or enable learning and debate about the causes and consequences of climate change tipping points, and of ways of adapting to them. It is written during a period of widespread 'climate change fatigue' when cynicism and suspicion infect influential portions of the media and substantial minorities of public opinion. Yet it also takes place at a time when an unprecedented body of intellectual and creative effort is going into making sense of anticipating and responding to global environmental changes more generally. In short, humanity's relationship with the non-human natural world is being dramatically revised in a very short space of time. If that isn't a story – what is?

I begin with a summary of six distinct features of the cultural politics of climate change. These are the ground-conditions for media production and consumption. I subsequently consider the quality of media performance around these issues. This includes a discussion of the scope of media coverage about, and for, those people who are most vulnerable to the social and physical impacts of abrupt climate change. In this chapter I conclude with a discussion of how society might balance media accounts of potentially doom-laden environmental presents and futures which have been at the core of environmental politics in the past, with stories from the 'islands of hope' referred to in Chapter 8.1. This paves the way for Emily Boyd's chapter (7.2) which looks at the scope for exercising resilience in adaptation to extreme stresses in local and more distant factors affecting the quality of living for those who sometimes are termed (erroneously) as being 'vulnerable'. These experiences offer some insights to the 'islands of hope' which may benefit from more sensitive and full-hearted media coverage. Paul Brown's commentary that follows (7.3) muses on the possibilities for such coverage to become more relevant for the benign aspects of the tipping points debate.

Six elements of the cultural politics of climate change

> Beard sank into a gloom of inattention, not because the *planet* was in peril – that moronic word again – but because someone was telling him it was with such enthusiasm.
>
> (McEwan 2010: 36)

Ian McEwan's protagonist in his novel *Solar* (McEwan 2010), the Nobel physicist Michael Beard, summarizes how many people feel when at the receiving end of a lecture on climate change. Perhaps it shouldn't puzzle us that the promise of rapid environmental and social change is greeted with a 'gloom of inattention'. The topic introduces a novel cultural politics whose features have gone under-recognized and unresolved. The term 'cultural politics' is employed here to indicate the various ways in which values and meanings that underpin economic, political, and social discourses are generated and disputed. Much of the current discussion about climate change falls between the overstated rhetoric of jeopardy, which is now having a diminishing public impact, and more sober and open-ended discussions of risk and uncertainty, which are largely unreported because they do not readily fit media conventions.

Climate change has produced many unexpected responses, one of which resembles the 'Stockholm syndrome' – the phenomenon of hostages becoming emotionally attached to their captors:

> We are held captive by our own fears and misgivings and yet grateful for the small mercy of continued survival . . . Like the hostages in the 1973 bank robbery, we have started to show affection for the thing that is trapping us.
>
> (Tyszczuk 2011: 25)

A good deal of discussion about climate science and policy has an excited, even breathless tone as it conjures images of social and ecological jeopardy, wrapped up in sober scientific prediction. NGOs and commentators argue that devastation is inevitable unless action is taken in response to specific scientific diktats. For example, the website for the network '350.org' suggests that:

> 350 is the most important number in the world – it's what scientists say is the safe upper limit for carbon dioxide in the atmosphere . . . the planet face[s] both human and natural disaster if atmospheric concentrations of CO_2 [remain] above 350 parts per million.

Andrew Simms, who writes a monthly blog for the 'One Hundred Months' campaign, argues that time is 'fast running out to stop irreversible climate change . . . We have only 100 months to avoid disaster' (Simms 2008). Insistent arguments such as these have been allied to a very simplified representation of the state of climate science. Phrases such as 'the science is finished' or references to 'the IPCC consensus' have been used to foreclose debate, so that everyone has to move on to the next stage: taking action. Indeed the notion of a 'tipping point' often functions as a rhetorical trump card (Morton 2011: 86).

Giles Foden (3.1), whose novel, *Turbulence* (Foden 2011a), deals with the special significance of meteorology for the 1944 D-Day landings, suggests that there is 'a kind of hubris' in the reference to 'tipping points': 'it invests too much in human predictions of the nature and consequences and scope of the event'. He suggests that the doom-laden term might be replaced by other metaphors 'which are generative and work positively as an invitation to action'. Similarly, research suggests that taking shortcuts to public attention through dramatic disaster imagery – such as photos of drowning polar bears or drought-stricken children – delivers diminishing returns in terms of political engagement, as well as carrying other costs in terms of

245

the dignity of the subject and our relationship to it (see, for example, Cohen (2000) in relation to poverty, or Manzo (2010) on the iconography of climate change).

The phrase 'climate change' is put to work in complex ways, and the issue generates multi-layered cultural politics. This was demonstrated by the Climate Camp protestors objecting to a proposed third runway at Heathrow airport. They held up large-scale portraits of potential climate victims from around the world alongside a large banner stating: 'We are armed only with peer-reviewed science'. The banner was intended to underline the non-violent nature of their protest, but also sought to enrol climate science in their politically radical cause. In his pioneering examination of these issues, Mike Hulme suggests that climate change has become 'an idea that now travels well beyond its origins in the natural sciences. And as this idea meets new cultures on its travels . . . [it] takes on new meanings and serves new purposes' (Hulme 2009). Interpretation of those meanings and purposes is made easier by acknowledging the distinctiveness of the cultural politics of climate change. The novelty lies perhaps not in any one of the following six features, but in their combination.

The first distinguishing feature is *global pervasiveness*: climate change discussions get everywhere – from doorsteps to boardrooms – and pervade all layers of formal politics from parish and local councils to parliaments and international conference halls. Climate change reaches across the world and across generations in ways that no other public policy concern does – even more immediate, universal, and profound concerns such as poverty and injustice (though these prove to be intimately connected). The pervasiveness of the issue is frequently noted in both popular and professional contexts, but the quality of our anticipation of change would be helped by a more intent focus on how climate change poses unique ethical and political questions.

A second element is *uncertainty*, in both science and policy. Media representations in the past have more often than not failed to acknowledge that the sciences of global environmental change are not just 'unfinished' but 'unfinishable'. Climate change research is not unique in this respect, but it is a particularly dramatic and important example of what Funtowicz and Ravetz (1991) have termed 'post-normal science'. Climate change should not be responded to as a body of 'facts' to be acted upon (with the IPCC acting as prime arbiter). Instead it should be considered as a substantial and urgent collective risk-management problem. Projecting climate change as a risk problem rather than a communication-of-fact problem helpfully deflates 'debates' about whether climate change is or is not a scientific fact. Such an approach doesn't walk away from the science: rather it opens more possibilities for people to be tolerant of the unsettled, developing relations between climate science, policy, and politics.

Thirdly, knowledge of climate change emphasizes the *interdependencies* between human and non-human systems, both near and far. Acknowledgement of humanity's state of interdependence can be traced back at least as far as the depiction of city life as dependent on its rural hinterland in Virgil's *Eclogues*, written over two thousand years ago. There have been numerous invocations of interdependence across the last century in relation to, for example, food and farming, civil rights and biodiversity. However, climate change calls up interdependence both as a description of environmental processes (e.g. relating to the consequences of the release of anthropogenic greenhouse gases) and, inextricably, as a political problem (Smith *et al.* 2007).

The potential for substantial changes in Earth systems outlined in the introductory chapters of this book forces us to acknowledge that we live on a dynamic earth. It would be a mistake, nevertheless, to replace the hubristic assumption of human separateness from nature with an account of evenly balanced interdependence between the natural and the human. Acknowledging our new place in the world includes understanding and respecting the subtle differences between truly interdependent relations and those 'earthly imperatives' which might have huge consequence for humans, but not, ultimately, for nature.

A cultural politics that is rooted in a rich understanding of global environmental change is likely to look quite different from our current state. As Nigel Clark puts it:

> We are still a long way from the cosmopolitan thought we need, the kind that might point the way to forms of justice and hospitality fitting for a planet that rips away its support from time to time.
>
> (Clark 2010: 219)

Reportage of tsunamis and earthquakes in recent years starts to hint at how media production and consumption behaviour changes may allow for fuller telling of both interdependency and dynamism in the realms of Earth–human relationships.

It is also important to note that interdependency does not imply an uncomplicated convergence of interests around action. This leads to my fourth point: the cultural politics of climate change echoes a *post-colonial discourse*, by paying attention to histories of vulnerability and responsibility. The fossil-fuelled development of the last century shaped individual life chances and national opportunities for good and ill across the planet, but these chances were patterned by the pre-existing political economy of development. When Arctic Inuit assert their 'right to be cold', and Pacific Islanders argue for action to protect their land from rising sea levels, they do so in the knowledge that the threats they face have been generated by the rich world's exploitation and consumption of resources over centuries. These questions about ethics of responsibility and vulnerability serve to shift the boundaries of political community. Ultimately we are all in this together, whoever we are, and wherever/whenever we live. However, there is a danger of complacency in the assumption that climate change means 'there is no other way' and that we will inevitably 'form a global community with a set of shared beliefs', as Tim Flannery (2011) has suggested.

It seems likely that international climate change politics will become far more antagonistic in the future. The unevenness of the historical responsibility for and capability to adapt to climate change, and unevenness of experiences of environmental and social transitions (the latter introduced both by impacts and climate mitigation) seem certain to sharpen the intensity of climate change discourse. This need not halt progress on climate change action: indeed it may help to generate the 'real', honest and urgent politics that would permit climate change to feature in a more sustained way in mainstream media.

The fifth distinctive feature is the *interdisciplinary nature* of the knowledge upon which climate change science is founded. As one climate expert remarked in 1961:

> The fact that there are so many disciplines involved, as for instance meteorology, oceanography, geography, hydrology, geology and glaciology, plant ecology and vegetation history – to mention only some – has made it impossible to work . . . with common and well established definitions and methods.
>
> (quoted in Weart 2008: 33)

The IPCC process represents one of the most ambitious attempts at global peer review of a specific set of questions, and draws together a very broad body of scientific research. The panel's reports summarize an extraordinary body of intellectual achievement. However, even that process is limited by its failure to integrate adequately the social sciences, arts, and humanities with practical politics. This is all the more surprising given how heavily the processes of the IPCC, as well as of the United Nations Framework Convention on Climate Change, rely on 'scenarios', and hence involve acts of imagination about possible futures in human as well as natural systems. I acknowledge Giles Foden's important contribution to Part 3 in this regard. This raises the question of how the media can open up thinking about what it means to construct imagined futures, and the intellectual and creative work it might require.

The sixth distinctive feature of the cultural politics of climate change centres on the very particular mix of *representations of time*, and of the particular interests of other generations. Economists and policy specialists have sought ways to give future generations a voice in the present, albeit through very attenuated or clumsy proxies such as discount rates and policy targets (see 6.1). Past generations can also be heard: from our prehistoric ancestors, who coped with earlier changes in climate with doggedness, to the more recent ancestors who bequeathed inventions and discoveries that have resulted in changes both in climate and our understanding of it, such as the invention of steam engines or techniques for retrieving and interpreting ice cores. Although contemporary human interests are more audible than those of the past, this expanded ethical, political, and cultural community is increasingly present in our thoughts and actions. Mike Hulme says: the future 'is a place that we all live in, in our imaginations' (Hulme 2011: 76). This invites media experiments that allow for research, policy, and politics to play in new ways with time. Just as climate change prompts us to extend the boundaries of politics in space, so it also requires that we extend them in time.

These six features – global pervasiveness, uncertainty, interdependency, the reverberations of history, interdisciplinarity, and temporality – form the cultural foundation on which media engagement with climate change has developed and will continue to unfold. These are the conditions within which different media will absorb and re-present what we know about climate change, about future threats and our current and future capabilities for coping with them.

Climate change – media change

> What do we want? . . . Gradual change! . . . When do we want it? . . . In due course!
>
> (Armando Iannucci tweet, 5/4/2011)

249

Given the demanding components of the cultural politics of climate change it is perhaps surprising that the subject has achieved any media attention at all. The issue has emerged as a topic during a period of dramatic change in the nature of media consumption and production. Despite all this, the media have played a substantial role in establishing a global public imaginary concerning the capacity for everyday human actions to influence the functioning of Earth systems in hazardous ways. International polling shows a steady rise in concern about climate change in the developing world, and, albeit with some fluctuation, a stable body of opinion in the developed world. A Globescan (2011) poll, for example, shows 64 per cent in the developing world and 51 per cent in the developed world viewing climate change as 'very serious'. Within the EU, opinion polling in 2011 found that 89 per cent viewed climate change as very or fairly serious (Eurobarometer 2011).

James Painter's (2011) broad international study of the press coverage of science surrounding the Copenhagen climate conference of December 2009 showed a dramatic leap in coverage in the run-up to the meeting. This spike was particularly significant in the developing world and specifically emerging economies, with large press corps attending from China and India. Painter gathers evidence of a rebalancing of uneven global coverage at the conference:

> India and Bangladesh had more media representatives registered than Russia and South Korea; China and Brazil more than Italy, Spain and Australia. At the very least, the numbers suggest a re-evaluation of the widely held view that news consumers in the countries most vulnerable to the impacts of climate change always suffer an information deficit and have to depend on Western news agencies.
>
> (Painter 2011: 8)

Boykoff and Mansfield (2012) have been tracking newspaper stories featuring climate change internationally since 2004, and their graphs show a convergence over the 2006–11 period between developed and developing world coverage. Painter's study of climate scepticism has demonstrated that climate change science is currently represented more consistently in the developing world than the USA, UK and Australia. Indeed, developing world coverage is more firmly rooted in mainstream science and has far less tendency to report outlier views that take issue with, for example, the conclusions of the IPCC reports (Painter 2011).

Nevertheless, there is evidence that media coverage about adaptation and resilience is weakest and least frequent in the countries that are likely to experience the worst effects of possible climate change tipping points. Mike Shanahan (2009) has worked to support developing world journalists' engagement with climate change for many years, and has suggested that:

> It is a great irony that the countries, communities, and citizens that have contributed least to climate change will suffer most from its impacts. It is in these settings that the media is least prepared for the challenge.
>
> (Shanahan 2009: 157)

He has summarized the specific challenges for journalists seeking to tell climate change stories in the developing world media as: lack of training; unsupportive editors; limited access to information; and the biases of selecting and reporting interviewees. Shanahan (2009: 154) notes that while there is an increasing research base in relation to English-speaking and urban populations in the developing world 'there has been little study of how much reaches rural or non-literate people who depend more on radio and television, and on information in local languages'.

A notable exception is the evidence from a ten-country study of awareness of the topic in Africa. This work took an original approach to sharing interviews and research findings publicly in multimedia form (BBC 2010). Given the uneven distribution of the risks associated with tipping points in the climate system, weighted substantially against those already most exposed in terms of poverty and marginal environments, this is a critical area that calls for urgent attention from researchers as well as for investment in media training, bursaries, and knowledge exchange.

As with HIV/Aids, researchers found that the most vulnerable groups have the least access to appropriate information. One significant conclusion in the report is that climate change terminology is poorly understood and often does not have standard translations in African languages. 'Existing translations apparently do not clearly convey the concept' (BBC 2010: 3). Focus groups (both rural and urban) and interviews with opinion leaders showed considerable confusion about climate change science concepts, pointing to the need to 'build simple, correct mental models of how climate change works'. The report echoes research conducted in very different societies that emphasizes the need to 'be mindful of people's existing knowledge (e.g. in relation to trees, God, ozone depletion, pollution, and heat) which can function as a barrier or facilitator to effective climate change communication' (BBC 2010: 18). The researchers also concluded that communications should confirm the very wide experiences amongst African publics of changing weather patterns.

These researchers were exploring the state of understandings and experiences of climate change in the present. Preparing vulnerable societies, regions or groups for potential physical or related social tipping points adds a further layer to the communications challenge. However, there is relevant experience to draw upon in terms of research on information needs in the context of natural disasters. Assessments of humanitarian relief in the wake of the Asian tsunami of December 2004 and the Pakistan earthquakes of 2005 confirm that communications should be considered part and parcel of effective immediate post-disaster actions. A review of this field found that information is a 'critical and unmet need' (Wall and Robinson 2008: 3) and that international agencies should 'treat communication equipment as a lifesaver' (Wall and Robinson 2008: 6).

The oldest of broadcast media has continued to prove its simple merits in these situations: in Aceh, Indonesia an entire radio station was installed and made operational very rapidly in a converted shipping container. Radios can be distributed quickly and cheaply, and local shortwave radio can be produced at high speed in local languages. At the same time the almost universal distribution of mobile telephony has created very different but no less powerful two-way communications networks that are acutely well-tuned to community concerns. These examples of supporting populations facing sudden challenges and changes are not only pertinent to the task of responding to malign tipping points. They are also capable of supporting the free flow of knowledge, experience, and questions at a grassroots level that can multiply the number and forms of 'islands of hope' (see Chapter 8.1).

It is possible to gain some idea about the strengths and weaknesses of mainstream media by considering their coverage of disasters such as the Asian tsunami of 2004, the Pakistan earthquakes of 2005, and the Fukushima nuclear incident of 2011. In each of these instances, intense media coverage at the time of the event allowed global audiences to share some understanding of the experiences of the people facing threats. These focus on human interest and they struggle to communicate the wider context and complexities within the narrow communication spaces available within mainstream media. There is also the danger that these are shaped into spectacles that amount to a form of *terriblisma*; 'the strange, gratified awe one feels when beholding dreadful disasters and acts of God from afar' (Steffen 2003). Crucially, media attention tends to be short-lived, with perhaps some return to the locale or storyline at anniversaries. It is a curious but important fact that while these instances of intense media coverage do frequently seek to communicate human suffering, and point to means of its immediate alleviation (through fundraising appeals, or stories of triumph against adversity), there is a general failure to thread together experiences of such events in such a way as to support the pursuit of resilient or adaptable social systems and infrastructure. More sustained attention by the research and policy communities to storytelling, phrase-making and visual communication around resilience and adaptability promises to deliver substantial benefits in terms of public understanding and debate.

The media have already played a significant role in spreading awareness of climate change science and policy. This is despite the fact that the cultural politics of climate change present the media with one of their most demanding challenges. However, it is not sufficient that mainstream media communicate the possibility of 'malign tipping points'. They will need to play an equally substantial role in supporting social learning and imagination about what it is to inhabit the 'benign' equivalents. For media producers, consumers and, in the context of social media, producer-consumers to show any interest in these issues, the content will have to be as compelling as the disaster narratives of real or anticipated disasters that established environmentalism in the first place.

Imagining futures

> DIANE: . . . Stars are thick. Which star came up with the idea of using the energy stored in a lump of fossilized swamp to power the internet? Which star invented air travel, the internal combustion engine? Which star split the atom? The stars are God's mistakes. We are the miracle. Life: human intelligence: human innovation, creativity, inventions. That is why every night the stars gaze down on us in awe.
>
> (Bean 2011: 115)

In his play *The Heretic* (Bean 2011), Richard Bean deploys a sharp and funny provocateur in the form of earth scientist Diane to puncture the slack-jawed naivety of some prominent strands of environmentalist rhetoric. Diane's appeal for a celebration of human ingenuity at the close of the play can be understood as a riposte to those narratives. Faced as we are with the varied risks associated with the tipping points literature, her stance could be seen as a foolhardy over-correction. But there is something exhilarating – compelling – in her lines. To insist that mainstream media decision-makers show leadership, and 'move ahead' of the state of the political or public conversation, is to fail to understand their professional and cultural setting. To have any chance of enabling stories of adaptability and resilience, and of an imaginative preparedness for potentially sudden and devastating changes of state, requires that these become 'good stories' in the eyes of a journalist as much as in those of the policy analyst.

Giles Foden (2011a) proposes that: 'Effective narratives, which tend to have strong metaphors, dynamic human interest ("tension") and the ability to be abbreviated or simplified (so that they can be easily communicated), eventually begin to condition large parts of the total system.' He notes that art narratives 'can take a while to "open" into "ends" or become executive; and often the ends are counter-intuitive'. On this reading we might consider the 'set texts' of 1970s environmentalism, and the resonant iconography that they are associated with, as art narratives. Hence the blue marble images of the Earth and the T-shirts and posters featuring threatened charismatic megafauna are all the work of an imaginative and entrepreneurial movement that sought new narratives. They were trying to ask very demanding questions of a political economy that almost entirely failed to represent the interests of the non-human natural world and the interests of future generations and distant others.

Their impact has been impressive but, having had 'executive' consequences in terms of the greening of mainstream political and media discourses, it may now be having 'counter-intuitive' consequences. Most of environmentalism has done little new work in over a decade, and its tendency towards hyperbole, and its reliance on a narrow stock of fear-based narratives, appears to have left portions of the public apathetic and fateful, and others hostile. Moreover their inhabitation of the imaginative space around environmental change has to a significant degree inhibited others from introducing different kinds of narratives. The intermittent enthusiasm for 'solutions' stories does not amount to an antidote. Rather the problem–solution dualism that is implied narrows the public conversation to handfuls of actions by a generalized 'government', or 'business', or public. It may serve to reduce one of the most substantial revisions of humanity's understanding of its place in the world to a bland and forlorn exercise in social marketing.

Environmentalism has sought to win a working global majority around to one way of looking at the world. Yet Foden (2011b) argues that 'what is necessary in facing wickedly complex problems is not just one metaphor or story but many'. From a different starting point William Connolly (2002:

254

199) argues against 'thick universals' and in favour of 'a plural matrix of cosmopolitanisms'. This plural mix is an apt way of inviting people to engage with the range of scenarios generated by the tipping points literature. It also has integrity as a framework in which to hold the diverse human ideas, experiences, and institutional responses outlined by Boyd that are relevant to coping with, even flourishing in the face of, global environmental changes.

Changes in media culture, practice, and institutional forms carry pros and cons in terms of telling these stories. It is becoming harder for new stories to reach some audiences. Furthermore there is diminishing space and journalistic resource available in mainstream media outputs. Increased concentration of mainstream media outlets within fewer hands only intensifies this process, and public service media have to fight to maintain audience share. Corporate media's engagement in environmental change is fickle. For example, News Corporation can simultaneously sustain Fox News's assault on the legitimacy of mainstream climate science at the same time as running public engagement activities in other outlets and instituting ambitious carbon-reduction programmes within the business. At the same time, digital and social media are opening up new places for, and means of, storytelling. Although this is allowing interests and publics opposed to climate change science and policy to organize, and then feed content back into mainstream media, the opportunities presented by this 'cognitive surplus' (Shirky 2010) are resulting in substantial gains in terms of environmental understanding and action.

The opportunities won't be taken, however, unless a sense of entrepreneurialism, initiative, and imagination is applied to storytelling about the new knowledge that humanity is gaining at the messy intersections of economic, political, social, and environmental change. While environmental tipping points amount to important cautionary tales that people need to hear, they are difficult to act on, on their own account. Indeed it seems that they actually become disabling if they are the only story that people hear. There is a need for balancing narratives. In other words, the environmental research and policy community have tended to draw heavily on environmentalist 'beware of the wolf' stories that are driven by the fear of negative outcomes, and have done too little cultural work with what might be termed 'golden goose' arguments. The golden goose stories would emphasize the wisdom – indeed necessity – of recognizing the real underlying foundations of human flourishing.

255

There are examples of policy and economic documents that could underpin such stories. The UK Government's Stern Review on the economics of climate change (Stern 2006), and UN-sponsored reports on the economics of ecosystems and biodiversity (TEEB 2010) are prominent examples of carefully researched studies of the costs of environmental degradation and benefits of protection. They clearly demonstrate how the economy is founded on the functioning of a set of ecological systems that are barely represented in day-to-day decision-making. Media representations of this central piece of environmental knowledge remain too sparse. This is in large part because such thinking has not yet enjoyed the kinds of cultural investment that would see them amount to widely shared 'Tools for Change' (the strapline of the late 1960s Whole Earth Catalogs). These accounts need to be geographically and thematically diverse, and rooted in 'human interests', if they are to translate into a regular flow of media stories. It is helpful that Connolly's argument in favour of a 'plural matrix' maps neatly on to the characteristics and capabilities of contemporary media. The telling of diverse narratives of bold human ambition and capabilities, applied to the nurturing of humanity's 'golden goose', might move even *The Heretic*'s hard-nosed Diane.

References

BBC (2010), 'Africa Talks Climate', http://africatalksclimate.com/ (accessed 10 August 2012).

Bean, R. (2011), *The Heretic* (London: Oberon Modern Plays).

Boykoff, M. and Mansfield, M. (2012), 'Media Coverage of Climate Change/Global Warming', http://sciencepolicy.colorado.edu/media_coverage/ (accessed 10 August 2012).

Clark, D.N. (2010), *Inhuman Nature: Sociable Life on a Dynamic Planet* (London: Sage Publications).

Cohen, S. (2000), *States of Denial: Knowing About Atrocities and Suffering* (London: Polity Press).

Connolly, W.E. (2002), *Neuropolitics: Thinking, Culture, Speed* (Minneapolis: University of Minnesota Press).

Eurobarometer (2011), 'Special Eurobarometer 372: Climate Change' (Brussels: European Commission).

Flannery, T. (2011), 'We Will Form a Global Community with a Set of Shared Beliefs', *Guardian*, http://www.guardian.co.uk/commentisfree/video/2011/apr/04/tim-flannery-global-shared-beliefs-video.

Foden, G. (2011a), *Turbulence* (New York: Alfred Knopf).

Foden, G. (2011b) 'Narratives, Metaphors and Tipping Points', unpublished paper presented to the Tipping Points workshop, British Academy, January 2011.

Funtowicz, S.O. and Ravetz, J.R. (1991), 'A New Scientific Methodology for Global Environmental Issues', in R. Costanza (ed.), *Ecological Economics: The Science and Management of Sustainability* (New York: Columbia University Press), 137–52.

Globescan (2011), 'Greater Climate Concern in Developing Nations Persists', http://www.globescan.com/findings/?id=40 (accessed 10 August 2012).

Hulme, M. (2009), *Why We Disagree About Climate Change: Understanding Controversy, Inaction and Opportunity* (Cambridge: Cambridge University Press).

Hulme, M. (2011), 'Futures', in R. Butler *et al.* (eds), *Culture and Climate Change: Recordings* (Cambridge: Shed).

Manzo, K. (2010), 'Imaging Vulnerability: The Iconography of Climate Change', *Area*, 42 (1): 96–107.

McEwan, I. (2010), *Solar* (London: Jonathan Cape).

Morton, O. (2011), 'Futures', in R. Butler *et al.* (eds), *Culture and Climate Change: Recordings* (Cambridge: Shed).

Painter, J. (2011), 'Poles Apart: The International Reporting of Climate Scepticism' (Oxford: Reuters Institute for the Study of Journalism).

Shanahan, M. (2009), 'Time to Adapt? Media Coverage of Climate Change in Non-Industrialised Countries', in T. Boyce and J. Lewis (eds), *Climate Change in the Media* (London: Peter Lang).

Shirky, C. (2010), *Cognitive Surplus: Creativity and Generosity in a Connected Age* (London: Allen Lane).

Simms, A. (2008), 'The Final Countdown', *Guardian*, 1 August, http://www.guardian.co.uk/environment/2008/aug/01/climatechange.carbonemissions (accessed 15 February 2012).

Smith, J., Clark, N., and Yusoff, K. (2007), 'Interdependence', *Geography Compass*, 1 (3): 340–59.

Steffen, A. (2003), 'Terriblisma', *Worldchanging: Change Your Thinking*, http://www.worldchanging.com/archives/000089.html (accessed 10 August 2012).

Stern, N. (2006), *The Economics of Climate Change: The Stern Review* (Cambridge: Cambridge University Press).

TEEB (2010), 'The Economics of Ecosystems and Biodiversity: Mainstreaming the Economics of Nature: A Synthesis of the Approach, Conclusions and Recommendations of TEEB' (Nairobi: UNEP).

Tyszczuk, R. (2011), 'On Constructing for the Unforeseen', in R. Butler *et al.* (eds), *Culture and Climate Change: Recordings* (Cambridge: Shed).

Wall, I. and Robinson, L. (2008), 'Left in the Dark: The Unmet Need for Information in Emergency Response' (London: BBC World Service Trust).

Weart, S.R. (2008), *The Discovery of Global Warming* (Cambridge, MA: Harvard University Press).

7.2
Exploring adaptive governance for managing tipping points

EMILY BOYD

A tipping point – a process that starts off slowly and rapidly speeds up leading to cascading effects – was identified in the 1970s in the context of neighbourhood race relations and the spread of group behaviour through social networks. In more recent years the concept has gained traction in the frameworks of development planning, climate change, and ecological resilience. Resilience theory suggests that to anticipate better and avoid tipping points or thresholds in social-ecological systems will require adaptive governance. This is where adapting institutions, networks, and processes generate social learning about changes in social ecological systems. This chapter considers how governance in the context of tipping points differs from conventional forms of adaptation governance. While there are an increasing number of networks and partnerships underway, it appears that governance institutions are on the whole unable to integrate local-level adaptation solutions with large-scale ecological governance approaches.

In this companion piece to that by Joe Smith (7.1), I examine how adaptive institutional responses to climate shocks may act as proxies for institutional responses to tipping points. I offer a number of illustrative examples of how adapting institutions can offer positive coping mechanisms through learning feedbacks that avoid maladaptation following climate shocks. The illustrative examples presented are of systems that are in the phase of reorganization (the 'back loop' in the adaptive cycle). The idea is that a shock may result in a reorganization that maintains the system within the desired state, yet shifts thinking to new ways of governing and adapting to climate change. Examples of institutional reorganization following shocks are given from the Mumbai floods of 2005, dieback in Amazonia in 2005–10, and the Sahel drought in 2012. In the discussion, I reflect on the weak linkages that exist between local-level adaptations and large-scale environmental change problem-framing, and current barriers to adaptive governance.

The context

Environmental change is increasingly interpreted in terms of urgent, abrupt, and large-scale transformations, or tipping points. It is also conceived in the context of biophysical limits, as outlined by Tim Lenton in Chapter 2.1. Tipping points feature prominently in the literature addressing: climate change (Lenton *et al.* 2008; New *et al.* 2011); Amazonian forests (Nepstad *et al.* 2008; Nobre and De Simon Borma 2009, Mahli *et al.* 2009; Betts *et al.* 2008; and Toby Gardner (4.3)); and ecological resilience (Rockstrom *et al.* 2009). The idea of tipping points first originated with Tom Schelling (1971) who applied a dynamic model of segregation in the racial composition of neighbourhoods in the United States. Others have used the concept to model the spread of behaviour and innovation through social networks (e.g. Granovetter 1978; Gladwell, 2000; Watts 2002, 2003).

Where there is a tipping point, a threshold condition is overstepped and cascades into a runaway set of events. This could be a rapid U-turn in a policy, which is driven by protests expressing fundamental societal preferences. The Arab Spring – a wave of revolutionary protests across the Arab world which began in December 2010 – is an example of such a runaway process whereby critical masses in people lead to the rapid collapse of existing political regimes. Other chapters in this volume – Paul Ekins (6.2), Joe Smith (7.1) – and commentaries – Paul Brown (7.3) and Jonathan Sinclair-Wilson (7.5) – comment on the social interpretations of this urgency. In this chapter I examine what is new about coping with environmental tipping points by looking at the ways in which governments, businesses, and civil society are building strategies at all scales to respond, adapt, and transform as we enter the Anthropocene. It is the first time in human history that a complex array of global, national, and local institutions and networks are preparing with foresight to govern the Earth system for an uncertain future. The challenge for these institutions is that there is limited knowledge about what types of social, political, and economic enabling conditions need to be met to enable the successful handling of anticipated response strategies in a timely manner.

One challenge to governance institutions involves accounting for biophysical threshold conditions, e.g. how a flood might trigger a change in institutional learning. History shows that society is not always successful in the ways that it manages change. Trade-offs, maladaptations, and externalities are all risks that result from taking action in one arena that may have unintended negative consequences elsewhere in space and/or time. For example, managing water supply in one part of a river basin may result in people downstream losing out on the benefits of improved water availability for their upstream neighbours. Another example in the global south is where trees and forests are protected to act as carbon sinks, resulting in the social exclusion of entire communities, including women and the elderly who have limited access to natural resources under traditional land-tenure regimes. In the global north, an example would be building an eco-village on a floodplain, which is exposed to flood risk, and is insured currently but may not be in the future, as climate change alters the timing and ferocity of flooding. The introductory chapter (1.1) explains why such malfunctions in governance occur and may be becoming even more brittle.

Adaptive governance

Adaptive governance theory explains change processes as being driven by feedbacks mediated through leadership, networks, and social learning (Folke *et al.* 2005; Boyd and Folke 2012). The overarching feature of adaptive governance is the 'adaptive' dimension of governance. In order to buffer change, resilience provides insights into the importance of diversity, modularity, and feedbacks in governing complexity in social-ecological systems. It is defined by Folke *et al.* (2005) as global in scale, in terms of the converging trends of rapid, interconnected global change (Duit *et al.* 2010), and in relation to how institutional responses and constraints interact between scales and levels (Termeer *et al.* 2010), and it is inherently a response to uncertainty and vulnerability of social and biophysical systems. These features make adaptive governance an interesting framework for considering how to manage tipping points. It is inherently about the function of networks (and shadow networks) as mechanisms of learning and building adaptive capacity. Adaptive governance stipulates co-management and collective actions across scales (interdependence). It is a way of thinking about preparing societies, businesses, and governments for large-scale and fast onset change; thus it has a temporal dimension of great importance to managing tipping points.

Resilience and panarchy theory

Resilience and 'coupled social ecological systems' thinking offers ideas for understanding the adaptive nature of change in institutions, organizations, and groups in the context of tipping points. Resilience may be introduced here as the ability of a system to absorb disturbance and reorganize while undergoing change, and without losing its identity, function, structure, and feedback. It can be considered as the way that communities respond to crises and progress their pathways of development (Folke *et al.* 2010). Olsson *et al.* (2008) drew on resilience theory to explain how the management of the Great Barrier Reef in Australia reached a tipping point, fuelled by a sense of urgency about the increased pressure from terrestrial runoff, overharvesting and global warming so that the reef, as a coupled social ecological system, was transformed into a sustainable and integrated management model. The transformation process included a shift in governance from a focus on chosen individual reefs to a broader stewardship of the large-scale reef system. In theory, the closer a system is to a tipping point, the lower its resilience and the smaller the shock needed to shift the regime. Resilience can also therefore be thought of as 'the capacity of a linked social-ecological system to absorb recurrent disturbances, such as hurricanes or floods, so as to retain essential structures, processes and feedbacks' (Adger *et al.* 2005).

Panarchy theory (see Chapter 1.1) explains that the basis for change lies in the adaptive cycle (Gunderson and Holling 2002). The adaptive cycle contains four phases:

- Rapid growth (r) – typically characterized by pioneer species, innovators or entrepreneurs;
- Conservation (K) – where resources are increasingly available and locked up in existing structures;
- Release (omega) – that is often triggered by a disturbance (e.g. fire, flood, disease) which exceeds the system's resilience;
- Reorganization and renewal (alpha) – where invention, experimentation and re-assortment are common.

The adaptive cycle has two ways of responding to change. The r and K phases operate together and are called the 'front loop', and the omega and alpha phases are considered the 'back loop'. The front loop characterizes the development phase and it features things like the accumulation of capital, stability, conservation, and development. Empirical studies of complex adaptive systems often focus on the front loop, which are systems that are undergoing gradual change, such as forest conservation (but see Ashlin 2009). In contrast, this chapter considers systems that are in the phase of reorganization (the back loop) following a fast and abrupt change. The idea is that a shock may result in a reorganization that maintains the system within the desired state, yet shifts thinking to new ways of framing, adapting to, and governing, climate shocks (Ashlin 2009). Thus, given the fast and abrupt change generated in the adaptive cycle, new forms of governance are emerging, which navigate the barriers to sustainability via networks and multi-sector learning platforms (e.g. see Ashlin 2012).

Adaptive governance and institutional fit

One emerging framework developed from the observation of several hundred cases of ecosystems management over the past twenty years is 'adaptive governance', which emphasizes complexity, rather than the steady-state equilibrium, as a pre-determinant of successful governance. The concept of adaptive governance focuses on the organizational and institutional flexibility for dealing with uncertainty and change (Dietz *et al.* 2003; Folke *et al.* 2005). Fundamental to this framework is a multi-scalar approach, which acknowledges and integrates the knowledge of a diversity of stakeholders to inform resource allocation decisions (Folke *et al.* 2005). Adaptive governance requires the formation of social networks, formal or informal, which create opportunities for collective action, engagement, and learning (Olsson *et al.* 2006). Adaptive processes within networks are then fostered by learning mechanisms, which generate and disseminate information (Folke *et al.* 2005; Olsson *et al.* 2006).

Adaptive governance is an 'ideal' form of environmental governance that consists of four principles: (1) explicit understanding of the system; (2) monitoring; (3) flexibility in management and administration through networks; and (4) strategies that prepare for 'surprise'. Adaptive governance requires adapting institutions:

> The capacity of people, from local groups and private actors, to the state, to international organisations, to deal with complexity, uncertainty and the interplay between gradual and rapid change.
>
> (Boyd and Folke 2012: 3)

Adapting institutions are evident at the local level in self-organized institutions and networks, and leaders, in public institutions that are responding to uncertainty and complexity, and in multilevel, hybrid institutions that are coping with environmental crisis (Boyd and Folke 2012). The adaptation processes are normative in as far as principles of fairness and effectiveness are embedded in co-management regimes. In theory one could have an adaptive system that is not equitable but still capable of adjusting to surprise: however there is limited empirical work on this.

The challenge of institutional fit

The challenge of institutional fit is the trade-off between robustness/efficient approaches to existing problems and the flexibility and redundancy required to meet new challenges. In essence, organizations have developed responses for one problem set and are not readily adapted for other problems. This is the key to 'the challenge of the fit' (Folke *et al.* 2005). Olsson *et al.* (2006: 29) highlight the problem of fit in the example of the management of watersheds, which have specific area/system boundaries, but where the administrative boundaries and the area of the watershed do not correspond. The mismatch of boundaries could be across national borders or at the local county and municipal level. They suggest that it is often the case that the jurisdictional, administrative, and institutional responses are not well matched with the biophysical system boundaries, due to historical reasons of national security or ethnic specificity. This suggests a need for flexibility in governance structures (Dietz *et al.* 2003) to allow for ecosystem-based management and stewardship of multifunctional landscapes and seascapes (Folke *et al.* 2005), while incorporating diverse features of governance that allow for ecosystem stewardship and relationships to multiple and cross-scale complex social-ecological interactions (Duit and Galaz 2008).

From principles to practice of adaptive governance

The illustrative examples presented here are of systems that are in the phase of reorganization (the back loop). The idea is that a shock may result in a reorganization that maintains the system within the desired state, yet shifts thinking to new ways of governing and adapting to climate change.

Amazon dieback

Peter Cox and colleagues (Cox *et al*. 2000) were among the first scientists to make predictions about the collapse of Amazonian rainforest by 2050. They presented a scenario that climate change impacts on the region of Amazonia would risk climate-induced forest dieback converting large areas of tropical forests to savannah by the end of the twenty-first century. While many were sceptical at first, two consecutive droughts in 2005 and 2010 (discussed by Toby Gardner (4.3)) have caused scientists to ask questions about the potential irreversible damage of the combination of deforestation, changing precipitation patterns, fire, and rising global temperatures. Forecasting and monitoring of Amazonia has become more integral to detecting early warning signals since then. A report by the World Bank (Vergara and Scholz 2011) suggests that dieback in Amazonia – one of several major, non-linear, positive-feedback responses to global warming – has the potential to create major disruptions in global climate systems (see also Patricia Howard (4.2)). It also calls for governance of deforestation (despite a notable decrease since 2005). Deforestation is largely driven by cattle ranching, large-scale soybean cultivation, and commodity markets, opening up roads and access for small-scale farming settlements.

The experience of the 2005 Amazonian drought provides important lessons about the adaptive governance response capacity. Brazil experienced one of the worst droughts in thirty years, compounded by extensive forest fires. The cause appears to have been warmer global temperatures, which led to measurable increases in ocean surface temperatures in the Atlantic and, ultimately, lower rainfall across several regions of the country (Aragão *et al*. 2008). The drought impacted the northeast, as well as southwest and western Amazonia. A state of emergency was called, and the Brazilian government mobilized its army to provide water and medical supplies to isolated communities and contend with the intense forest fires in Brazil's western state of Acre. The resulting smoke pollution affected more than 400,000 people, and the fire damaged more than 300,000 ha of rainforest; direct costs amounted to more than US $50 million (Brown *et al*. 2006). The true monetary and health costs could be far higher as the widespread damage caused to forest cover has made the area more susceptible to repeated burning.

What was particularly important about the 2005 Amazonian drought was the speed and magnitude of the events that unfolded. An important insight is that ecological systems do not respond to stress (such as high temperatures or extreme weather events) in a linear or predictable manner. In fact, even small disturbances can bring about large and sometimes irreversible changes. In the case of forest dieback it is still debated whether a small change can bring about large-scale change. Nevertheless, the governance system that tackled the 2005 crisis was unconventional both in its rapid response and in the establishment of a situation room, extensive networks, and reliance on available information on the internet. One may wonder whether such a 'flexible' governance system can be institutionalized, strengthened, or replicated to cope with the future climate-related surprises.

Elsewhere I have explained that critical to the disaster response was the availability of the adaptive governance ingredients of early warning, effective actors, and rapid self-organizing action, with strong feedback data-gathering (Boyd 2008). This process included satellite imagery, hot-spot data and meteorological data, which first persuaded the Governor of Acre to act by prohibiting fires. Near-real-time data on hot-spot distributions, derived from MODIS (moderate resolution imaging spectro-radiometer) images and custom-designed analysis software, were voluntarily made available to state government officials by a team of NASA-supported scientists working on the large-scale biosphere–atmosphere experiment in Amazonia (http://lba.cptec.inpe.br/lba/site/). The Acre government in turn established a 'situation room' staffed by two civil defence coordinators, three state employees from INPE (the national space agency) and several researchers and students from the LBA-ECO team. Using both satellite imagery and on-the-ground information, the team provided daily briefings by email on the locations of fires to the local authorities and the Brazilian army, helping to coordinate and focus state and national efforts. Following the successful response to the crisis, access to the China Brazil Earth Resources Satellite (CBERS) second-generation satellite imagery is now granted to Brazilian institutions and more widely across South America. The CBERS has been successfully up-scaled by the provision of free-of-charge CBERS data (www.dgi.inpe.br/CDSR). CBERS has also launched a CBERS project for Africa (Epiphanio 2008). The Environmental Institute of Acre has also since established a permanent situation room that incorporates the use of multiple satellite sensors to monitor the extent of fire and drought conditions (Berkes and Seixas 2004).

The gravity of the drought in 2010 has led experts to renew their interest in Amazonia. For example, in 2011 the EU 7th Framework research programme and various national organizations funded a new €4.7 million research project called AMAZALERT to establish a multilevel early warning system for the whole region. This project includes fourteen European and Latin American institutions under the leadership of Dr Bart Kruijt, of Wageningen University, and Dr Carlos Nobre, of the Brazilian National Space Research Institute (INPE). They plan to design a data-retrieval procedure to detect the signs of widespread forest degradation, and to enable early warning if irreversible forest loss appears plausible. The project will also assess the impacts and effectiveness of public policies and mechanisms to prevent further deforestation. Over three years, scientists and decision-makers will engage in dialogue to develop the models and to contribute to a blueprint for an early warning system. The project aims to provide tools for decision-makers on future management and monitoring of Amazonia (Wageningen University and Research Centre 2011). What is unclear with the emergence of large-scale early warning systems is how local adaptation arrangements are factored into the system. If the governance of early warning is predominantly at global and national scales, is there a risk that important local sources of risk knowledge and collective memory will be overlooked? Taking a cue from Chapter 1.1, this response could lead to maladaptations by legitimizing a 'one size fits all' policy, such as Reduced Emissions from Deforestation and Forest Degradation (REDD), which does not account for complex and diverse ecosystems and may penalize activities that help to restore ecosystems (Hurteau 2008; cf. Ostrom 2010) and which could lead to potential implementation problems with negative impacts on local communities. In other words, 'solving problems through centralized controls and global blueprints tends to create its own vulnerabilities in the long term' (Boyd 2009: 3; cf. Ostrom 2010). If new mechanisms such as REDD are to work in practice they will also have to consider lessons on the barriers to local engagement (Hall 2012: 22).

The Sahel drought

The Horn of Africa is currently experiencing one of the most severe droughts in 60 years. In addition to the 30-year trend of declining precipitation, there is evidence that variability in amount and timing of rainfall from year to year is increasing, which would further compound food insecurity in the region (UNEP 2011). An accompanying trend of higher temperatures – estimated to be equivalent to an additional 10 to 20 per cent reduction in rainfall in its impact on crops – has exacerbated the reduced and increasingly variable rainfall. Air temperatures in the area have increased by over 1 ºC since the 1970s. As with rainfall, there is evidence that average annual temperatures have become more variable as well. During roughly the same time that these trends in temperature and rainfall have made rain-fed agriculture less secure, the combined population of Darfur and South Sudan has roughly tripled (UNEP 2011).

Research conducted by Sendzimir *et al.* (2011) on the 're-greening of the Sahel' illustrates an example of the solutions to the problems that are currently facing East Africa through adaptive institutions in the Niger region. They found in their study that a massive reforestation of 5 million hectares has taken place in the past 20 years in the Maradi and Zinder regions of Niger. They explain that these solutions emerged from interactions between multiple actors, institutions, and processes that were operating at different levels, times, and scales, and which contributed to this recovery in terms of biophysical, livelihoods, and governance challenges. The key finding of their study shows that 'reversing the direction of reinforcing feedbacks in existing processes' can break 'bad' patterns of interaction and poor management of natural resources. Bad practice began with the colonial structures that weakened rural governance structures and redirected the economy for export. This was followed by a period (1935 to 1970) when resources and institutions were centralized, and large-scale tree clearance for land use occurred. Conditions were exacerbated by the 1970s drought conditions, resulting in large-scale famine. A reversal of interactions started in the 1980s with a push from the international community for better management of natural resources and a political vacuum which emerged following the death of a highly respected political leader, President Kountché. A 'window of opportunity' opened up for local-level communities to take action at this time.

The adaptive response emerged through a co-evolution of local village committees with improved functional ties to regional and national organizations. Ties were built between institutions and across scales, thus breaking the 'pathological dominance from the national government' (Sendzimir *et al.* 2011: 12). The study shows that the assistance of international NGOs helped to establish direct linkages to national governments in ways that built new healthy relations, thus breaking down old power relations that had been institutionalized by corrupt forest officers. New local organizations were supported and rebuilt by international projects and programmes. Similarly to the case of Amazonia, external funding and support played a role in creating the response capacity. Currently Niger is resilient enough to sustain itself under normal conditions and withstand drought better than many other countries in the region, but it remains at risk from growing demographic pressures (doubling its population since 1920) (Sendzimir *et al.* 2011).

Urban mega-cities flood risk

A key social ecological tipping point that is currently overlooked is the risk of urban exposure to climate change. The IPCC (2001) and more recently the IPCC (2012) Special Report on Managing the Risks of Extreme Events and Disasters to Advance Climate Change Adaptation (SREX) warn of climate risks to low-lying coastal cities like Mumbai, which are likely to face the brunt of sea-level rise and salt-water intrusion into underground aquifers. Moreover, some models indicate that the intensity of heavy rainfall events may increase, whilst the number of rainy days may decrease along India's coastal zones (Challinor *et al.* 2006). Mumbai-Pune, located on the west coast of Maharashtra, has the highest number of people (50 million) exposed to coastal flooding, with unprecedented growth and development of all the Asian mega-cities (Nicholls *et al.* 2008). Mumbai is occasionally hit by cyclones and by frequent periods of heavy rainfall. The main concern for Mumbai is that much of the vulnerable poor live in the low-lying parts of the city most at risk from flooding (Huq *et al.* 2007).

In 2005 the city of Mumbai experienced severe flooding across 100 km^2, resulting in the death of over a thousand people and significant damage to property. In the space of 24 hours the city received 95 cm of rainfall – a 'once in a 100 year' event. The event caught city residents unaware. Revi (2005) recalls that the majority of the city services were shut for five days, a first in the history of the city. The unprecedented rainfall affected both wealthy and poor Mumbaikars, with people trapped away from their homes, telephone landlines and mobile phone services cut, and city transport halted for up to 24 hours. The most affected area of the city was the densely populated area of the northwest, inhabited by a mixture of social groups. The main cause was inundation, which was brought about by the accumulation of heavy local rainfall and draining congestion; the drainage process was unable to match the rate of rainfall coupled with the high tide (Kelkar 2005).

Efforts to address climate change at the city level are largely driven by NGOs, activists, and university groups, and include urban 'greening', conservation area protection, and local pollution-prevention campaigns.

Some call for engagement of politicians and elites in helping to address climate change in urban planning (Revi 2008). De Sherbinin *et al.* (2007) suggest that because Mumbai's formal institutions are too many and too weak, hope for climate change adaptive action is most likely to come from strong civil society organizations, such as the national slum-dwellers federation, with support from the overseas diaspora. Yet, the Municipal Corporation of Mumbai plays an important bridging role in the city, and points out that it lacks funds to support city-level change to prepare for long-term climate change.

In the aftermath of the floods a variety of government-supported actions sprang up, indicating that some level of institutional learning had taken place. The response to the crisis was almost immediate, with NGOs and civil society joining forces to launch the Concerned Citizens' Commission (CCC) only three weeks after the event on 4 August 2005 (CCC 2005). The CCC acted as a bridging organization between local humanitarian organizations, families, and individual slum-dwellers, which in turn acted collectively and cooperatively in response to the crisis, while the official response was less effective, despite the existence of city disaster risk management plans. Although the city's officials have come under scrutiny from the CCC for ineffective institutional responses, since 2005 officials from the Municipal Corporation of Mumbai have introduced thirty early warning rain gauges across the city that are able to monitor rainfall every 15 minutes and update every hour during heavy rainfall (Chatterjee 2010), and new satellite technology is anticipated to help monitor rainfall. A new project is underway, funded by the local authorities, which aims to tackle sewage and waterways, as well as map the city, using aerial photography. Local government funds have also been provided to support interdisciplinary scientific research at the India Institute of Technology into the impacts and solutions to flooding impacts in Mumbai.

Following the floods, a change in opinion among some of the elite, the decision-makers, and organizations that govern Mumbai has been observed, indicating a shift in perception about the risks of climate change. For example, a Climate Action Plan for Mumbai has been announced, financed by the state of Maharastra, which aims to examine projected climate change impacts on hydrology and water resources, agriculture, coastal areas, marine ecosystems, and livelihoods, including impacts on migration in Mumbai (Ghoge 2010). More recently, the city has been putting in place coastal defences to protect the city from breaches from the sea, based on a longer-term adaptation perspective. While these large-scale infrastructural and engineering solutions are important for the citizens of Mumbai, the CCC also provided the government with recommendations for a broader multi-layered approach to adaptation and mitigation. Nevertheless, the Municipal Corporation of Mumbai has opted for a narrower technical and infrastructural development approach to flood risk and adaptation predominantly, which does not consider flood risk as one of unequal distribution of resources (Chatterjee 2010). Plans and strategies for Mumbai are similar to those developed for many other cities in that they tend to focus on large-scale technological solutions. To build long-term resilience and sustainability Mumbai will also need to think about issues of risk mitigation, risk sharing and risk redistribution and about how marginalization is linked to risk governance and vulnerability (Chatterjee 2010).

Patterns and limits of adaptive governance

This chapter now draws on the resilience lens and the metaphor of the adaptive cycle of change to reflect on three examples of how institutions reorganize following rapid and sudden shocks. Sendzimir and colleagues (2011) lend three important insights to help us to think through what the examples show. First, crises can result in the formation of rapid communication and reactive policy responses that are single-issue explanations, often with narrow technical framings: these often lead to failure (as was the case in the management of the Sahel crises in the 1970s). Secondly there is no silver bullet: in the case of the Sahel, NGOs stepped in where the state was weak, and the lack of centralized control opened up an opportunity for local small-scale adaptations through agro-ecological experimentations to take shape. The platform and local networks were supported by outside (NGO) ideas, knowledge, and funds. Thirdly, what is most important is the reversibility of the reinforcing feedbacks in adjustment processes. For example, the incidence of farmer-led natural regeneration in the Sahel was a result of sufficient time passing for this type of innovation to become more familiar, backed by the appropriate knowledge and resources from international organizations.

The 2005 Mumbai floods are revealing because of the magnitude of coupled social-ecological risks facing urban areas. Mumbai shows how extreme poverty co-exists with environmental risk in a resilient city where there is a burgeoning middle class and financial centre with property prices equivalent to London, Paris, and New York. However, given that the whole cityscape of Mumbai persists on the poverty margins with little or no buffering capacity, it requires that the introduction of complex adaptation strategies be implemented through the leadership of the Municipal Corporation of Mumbai. In this regard, the public institution is providing adaptation arrangements, but there are problems over who should fund this provision, given that the benefits fall to individuals and private entities. Moreover, in India the risks of climate change are linked to its aversion to accept external interference in its adaptation strategies and policies. The events of 2005 illustrate that institutional responses in India can be reactive and self-organizing among civil society, but are limited due to the presence of too many uncoordinated government institutions. De Sherbinin *et al.* (2007) suggest that a more radical transformation is necessary which involves moving the low-lying old city of Mumbai to the suburbs. This introduces normative and ethical questions about whether this is a desirable strategy. This example shows that reorganization in the back loop of the adaptive cycle cannot be about structural and technological fixes alone, but also needs to incorporate reorganization of social and ethical considerations (Chatterjee 2010). Adaptive governance challenges in a highly human-dominated system like Mumbai encompass basic infrastructure impediments, as the city is historically located on a delta that is unable to absorb the multiple shocks induced by today's societal needs. What is certain, however, is that Mumbai's city officials and citizens will have to engage in changing urban planning practices and factor neighbourhood integration for adaptation into everyday life (Revi 2005).

In Amazonia, it is evident that the governance and management strategies have in the past fallen short of adequately protecting both people and ecosystems. To blame are both global economic demand for raw materials, minerals, and agricultural commodities and weak enforcement of policies at the national level. In Brazil, federal command and control structures have failed to deliver forest conservation (Fearnside 2005), and state-level administration has failed to enforce the law relating to forests and land-use change or to provide incentives to reduce deforestation (Chomitz *et al.* 2006). More recently, scientists have shown that establishing and implementing protected areas in zones under a high level of current or future anthropogenic threat in Amazonia offers high payoffs in reducing carbon emissions and as a result should receive special attention in planning investment priorities for regional conservation (Soares-Filho *et al.* 2010). It seems that Brazilian environmental policy has created a sustainable core of protected areas in the Amazon that buffers against potential climate-tipping points and protects the drier ecosystems of the basin (Walker *et al.* 2009).

As in the case of the Sahel, it is perhaps a window of opportunity that international scientific institutions and funding are stepping up to the plate. While the 2005 drought response illustrated a particularly important role for the state, future integration of international funds and national/regional organizations in adaptation measures is likely to occur. Any attempt to manage Amazonia will require a suite of approaches and mechanisms, such as local innovations and scientific research, coupled with national regulation and markets. National institutions will need to provide better extension support, agricultural implements and technology to farmers, regulate medium and large agribusinesses, and prioritize those areas most threatened and vulnerable in the 'crescent of deforestation' covering the regions south and east (see also Toby Gardner (4.3)).

Limits to adaptive governance

Some say that historical reflections are a limited guide to the future. Davis (2004) gives the example of urban areas, which he points out are 'evolving with "extraordinary" speed and in directions that are unpredictable'. He explains that in this rapid process the accumulation of poverty undermines security and poses vast challenges to the survival mechanisms of the poor. While it is not necessarily appropriate to rely on past understandings to predict climate futures, it is also not possible to predict the future with certainty. We can use existing metaphors to think about the possible outcomes. The adaptive cycle and tipping points as metaphors help to illustrate, in the case of climate-related shocks, how institutions and social systems respond to rapid and shock events. The limitations lie in the need to draw on historical references of 'what happened' in the period of 'creative destruction' in the adaptive cycle. Moreover, the practical application to what this means for buffering future events to save lives needs further thought. The adaptive cycle specifically is a useful metaphor as it allows us to think about ways in which societies reorganize and respond to uncertainty. As these cases show, there are old and new cross-sectoral climate partnerships and networks that mobilize across scales. Nevertheless, while examples are informative to begin our discussions, our collective understanding of how to reorganize on a global scale remains a much greater challenge.

References

Adger, W.N., Hughes, T.P., Folke, C., Carpenter, S.R., and Rockström, J. (2005), 'Social-Ecological Resilience to Coastal Disasters', *Science*, 309 (5737): 1036–39.

Aragão, L.E.O.C., Malhi, Y., Barbier, N., Lima, A., Shimabukuro, Y., Anderson, L., and Saatchi, S. (2008), 'Interactions Between Rainfall, Deforestation and Fires During Recent Years in the Brazilian Amazonia', *Philosophical Transactions of the Royal Society B, Biological Sciences*, 363 (1498): 1779–85.

Ashlin, A. (2009), 'Biodiversity and Natural Disasters: Opportunities for Change in Post-Tsunami Sri Lanka' (unpublished D.Phil. thesis, University of Oxford).

Ashlin, A. (2012), 'Adaptive Governance and Natural Hazards: The 2004 Indian Ocean Tsunami and the Governance of Coastal Ecosystems in Sri Lanka', in E. Boyd and C. Folke (eds), *Adapting Institutions: Governance, Complexity and Social-Ecological Resilience* (Cambridge: Cambridge University Press), 216–39.

Berkes, F. and Seixas, C.S. (2004), 'Lessons from Community Self-Organization and Cross-Scale Linkages in Four Equator Initiative Projects' (Winnipeg: Centre for Community-Based Resource Management Natural Resources Institute, University of Manitoba).

Betts, R.A., Malhi, Y., and Roberts, J.T. (2008), 'The Future of the Amazon: New Perspectives from Climate, Ecosystem and Social Sciences', *Philosophical Transactions of the Royal Society B, Biological Sciences*, 363 (1498): 1729–35.

Boyd, E. (2008), 'Navigating Amazonia under Uncertainty: Past, Present and Future Environmental Governance', *Philosophical Transactions of the Royal Society B, Biological Sciences*, 363 (1498): 1911–16.

Boyd, E. (2009), 'Governing the Clean Development Mechanism: Global Rhetoric Versus Local Realities in Carbon Sequestration Projects', *Environment and Planning A*, 41 (10): 2380–95.

Boyd, E. and Folke, C. (eds) (2012), *Adapting Institutions: Governance, Complexity and Social-Ecological Resilience* (Cambridge: Cambridge University Press).

Brown, I.F., Schroeder, W., Setzer, A., De Los Rios Maldonado, M., Pantoja, N., Duarte, A., and Marengo, J. (2006), 'Monitoring Fires in Southwestern Amazonia Rain Forests', *Eos, Transactions, American Geophysical Union*, 87 (26).

CCC (2005), 'Mumbai Marooned: An Enquiry into the Mumbai Floods' (Mumbai: Conservation Action Trust).

Challinor, A., Slingo, J., Turner, A., and Wheeler, T. (2006), 'Indian Monsoon: Contribution to the Stern Review', http://www.hm-treasury.gov.uk/d/Challinor_et_al.pdf (accessed 8 June 2012).

Chatterjee, M.L. (2010), 'Resilient Flood Loss Response Systems for Vulnerable Populations in Mumbai: A Neglected Alternative' (unpublished D.Phil. thesis, Rutgers University).

Chomitz, K.M., Buys, P., de Luca, G., Thomas, T.S., and Wertz-Kanounnikoff, S. (2006), 'At Loggerheads? Agricultural Expansion, Poverty Reduction, and Environment in the Tropical Forests' (Washington DC: World Bank).

Cox, P.M., Betts, R.A., Jones, C.D., Spall, S.A., and Totterdell, I.J. (2000), 'Acceleration of Global Warming Due to Carbon-Cycle Feedbacks in a Coupled Climate Model', *Nature*, 408: 184–87.

Davis, M. (2004), 'Planet of Slums: Urban Involution and the Informal Proletariat', *New Left Review*, 26: 5–30.

de Sherbinin, A., Schiller, A., and Pulsipher, A. (2007), 'The Vulnerability of Global Cities to Climate Hazards', *Environment and Urbanization*, 19 (1): 39–64.

Dietz, T., Ostrom, E., and Stern, P.C. (2003), 'The Struggle to Govern the Commons', *Science*, 302 (5652): 1907–12.

Duit, A. and Galaz, V. (2008), 'Governance and Complexity – Emerging Issues for Governance Theory', *Governance*, 21 (3): 311–35.

Duit, A., Galaz, V., Eckerberg, K., and Ebbesson, J. (2010), 'Governance, Complexity, and Resilience', *Global Environmental Change*, 20 (3): 363–68.

Epiphanio, J.C.N. (2008), 'CBERS: Remote Sensing Cooperation between Brazil and China', *Imaging Notes*, 23: 16–19.

Fearnside, P.M. (2005), 'Deforestation in Brazilian Amazonia: History, Rates, and Consequences', *Conservation Biology*, 19 (3): 680–88.

Folke, C., Hahn, T., Olsson, P., and Norberg, J. (2005), 'Adaptive Governance of Social-Ecological Systems', *Annual Review of Environment and Resources*, 30: 441–73.

Folke, C., Carpenter, S.R., Walker, B., Scheffer, M., Chapin, T., and Rockström, J. (2010), 'Resilience Thinking: Integrating Resilience, Adaptability and Transformability', *Ecology and Society*, 15 (4): 20.

Ghoge, K. (2010), 'Climate Change Action Plan for Mumbai in Two Years', *Hindustan Times*, 1 April.

Gladwell, M. (2000), *The Tipping Point: How Little Things Can Make a Big Difference* (New York: Little Brown).

Granovetter, M. (1978), 'Threshold Models of Collective Behavior', *American Journal of Sociology*, 83 (6): 1420–43.

Gunderson, L.H. and Holling, C.S. (eds) (2002), *Panarchy: Understanding Transformations in Human and Natural Systems* (New York: Island Press), 493.

Hall, A. (2012), *Forests and Climate Change: The Social Dimensions of REDD in Latin America* (Cheltenham: Edward Elgar Press).

Huq, S., Kovats, S., Reid, H., and Satterthwaite, D. (2007), 'Editorial: Reducing Risks to Cities from Disasters and Climate Change', *Environment and Urbanization*, 19 (1): 3–15.

Hurteau, M.D., Koch, G.W., and Hungate, B.A. (2008), 'Carbon Protection and Fire Risk Reduction: Toward a Full Accounting of Forest Carbon Offsets', *Frontiers in Ecology and the Environment*, 6 (9): 493–98.

IPCC (2001), *Climate Change 2001: Impacts, Adaptation and Vulnerability* (Cambridge: Cambridge University Press).

IPCC (2012), *Managing the Risks of Extreme Events and Disasters to Advance Climate Change Adaptation: A Special Report of Working Groups I and II of the Intergovernmental Panel on Climate Change*, ed. C.B. Field *et al.* (Cambridge: Cambridge University Press).

Kelkar, R.R. (2005), 'Understanding the Extreme Weather Events', *IWRS News Letter November 2005*, http://rrkelkar.files.wordpress.com/2007/08/kelkar-understanding-extreme-weather-events.pdf (accessed 21 June 2012).

Lenton, T.M., Held, H., Kriegler, E., Hall, J., Lucht, W., Rahmstorf, S., and Schellnhuber, H.J. (2008), 'Tipping Elements in the Earth's Climate System', *Proceedings of the National Academy of Sciences USA*, 105 (6): 1786–93.

Malhi, Y., Aragao, L.E.O.C., Galbraith, D., Huntingford, C., Fisher, R., Zelazowski, P., *et al.* (2009), 'Exploring the Likelihood and Mechanism of a Climate-Change-Induced Dieback of the Amazon Rainforest', *Proceedings of the National Academy of Sciences USA*, 106: 20610–15.

Nepstad, D.C., Stickler, C.M., Filho, B.S., and Merry, F. (2008), 'Interactions among Amazon Land Use, Forests and Climate: Prospects for a Near-Term Forest Tipping Point', *Philosophical Transactions of the Royal Society B, Biological Sciences*, 363 (1498): 1737–46.

New, M., Liverman, D., Schroder, H., and Anderson, K. (2011), 'Four Degrees and Beyond: The Potential for a Global Temperature Increase of Four Degrees and its Implications', *Philosophical Transactions of the Royal Society A, Mathematical, Physical and Engineering Sciences*, 369 (1934): 6–19.

Nicholls, R.J., Hanson, S., Herweijer, C., Patmore, N., Hallegatte, S., Corfee-Morlot, J., *et al.* (2008), 'Ranking Port Cities with High Exposure and Vulnerability to Climate Extremes Exposure Estimates' (OECD Environment Working Papers No. 1 ENV/WKP (2007)1).

Nobre, C.A. and Borma, L.D.S. (2009), '"Tipping Points" for the Amazon Forest', *Current Opinion in Environmental Sustainability*, 1 (1): 28–36.

Olsson, P., Gunderson, L.H., Carpenter, S.R., Ryan, P., Lebel, L., Folke, C., and Holling, C.S. (2006), 'Shooting the Rapids: Navigating Transitions to Adaptive Governance of Social-Ecological Systems', *Ecology and Society*, 11 (1): 18.

Olsson, P., Folke, C., and Hughes, T.P. (2008), 'Navigating the Transition to Ecosystem-Based Management of the Great Barrier Reef, Australia', *Proceedings of the National Academy of Sciences*, 105 (28): 9489–94.

Ostrom, E. (2010), 'A Polycentric Approach for Coping with Climate Change', *Policy Research Working Paper* (Washington DC: World Bank).

Revi, A. (2005), 'Lessons from the Deluge: Priorities for Multi-Hazard Risk Mitigation', *Economic and Political Weekly*, 40 (36): 3911–16.

Revi, A. (2008), 'Climate Change Risk: An Adaptation and Mitigation Agenda for Indian Cities', *Environment and Urbanization*, 20 (1): 207–29.

Rockström, J., Steffen, W., Noone, K., Persson, A., Chapin, F.S., Lambin, E.F., *et al.* (2009), 'A Safe Operating Space for Humanity', *Nature*, 461 (7263): 472–75.

Schelling, T. (1971), 'Dynamic Models of Segregation', *Journal of Mathematical Sociology*, 1: 141–86.

Sendzimir, J., Reij, C.P., and Magnuszewski, P. (2011), 'Rebuilding Resilience in the Sahel: Regreening in the Maradi and Zinder Regions of Niger', *Ecology and Society*, 16 (3): 1.

Soares-Filho, B., Moutinho, P., Nepstad, D., Anderson, A., Rodrigues, H., Garcia, R., *et al.* (2010), 'Role of Brazilian Amazon Protected Areas in Climate Change Mitigation', *Proceedings of the National Academy of Sciences*, 107 (24): 10821–26.

Termeer, C.J.A.M., Dewulf, A., and van Lieshout, M. (2010), 'Disentangling Scale Approaches in Governance Research: Comparing Monocentric, Multilevel, and Adaptive Governance', *Ecology and Society*, 15 (4): 29.

UNEP (2011), 'Food Security in the Horn of Africa: The Implications of a Drier, Hotter and More Crowded Future', *Global Environmental Alert Service* (Nairobi: UNEP).

Vergara, W. and Scholz, S.M. (eds) (2011), 'Assessment of the Risk of Amazon Dieback' (New York: World Bank, Latin America and Caribbean Region).

Wageningen University and Research Centre (2011), 'New EU-South America Research on Amazon Dieback, Climate and Deforestation Starts in October', *ScienceDaily*, 26 September, http://www.sciencedaily.com/releases/2011/09/110926081904.htm (accessed 25 February 2013).

Walker, R., Moore, N.J., Arima, E., Perz, S., Simmons, C., Caldas, M., Vergara, D., and Bohrer, C. (2009), 'Protecting the Amazon with Protected Areas', *Proceedings of the National Academy of Sciences*, 106 (26): 10582–86.

Watts, D. (2002), 'A Simple Model of Global Cascades on Random Networks', *Proceedings of the National Academy of Sciences*, 99 (9): 5766–71.

Watts, D. (2003), *Six Degrees: The Science of a Connected Age* (New York: Norton).

Commentary 7.3

Reflections of a journalist

PAUL BROWN

A 'tipping point' is a useful phrase for a journalist. It is one of those bits of jargon used to describe a situation where some bad events begin to happen ever more rapidly and cannot be reversed. The term is borrowed from scientists who, my colleagues say, use it to describe the same continuous or discontinuous sequence of events. But in their perspective a tipping point can sometimes be reversible, as pointed out by Tim Lenton in Chapter 2.1. This provides a recipe for considerable public and journalistic misunderstanding and confusion.

The simplest illustration of this confusion in environmental terms (to a journalist) is the melting of the Greenland ice cap. Once the temperature reaches a certain level – say, 1°C warmer than present – the Greenland ice cap will begin progressively more rapidly to melt, and not stop melting until it is gone. Whether it is a 1°C or 2°C increase in temperature that will push the ice cap into unstoppable ice melt is up for scientific debate: and how quickly the melting will take place is likewise a matter of conjecture. What is certain (and of interest to journalists) is the catastrophic consequences of reaching that point for many of the world's cities located on low-lying coastlines.

Politically there are tipping points too. In the recent Arab Spring there comes a point when the old regime cannot hang on, and the revolution, velvet or violent, is bound to succeed. The characteristic of both tipping points is that there is no going back to the status quo. Greenland will not suddenly get cold again and the same tyrants will not resume power.

Scientists studying behaviour and journalists reporting in other fields could both use the term and there would be no misunderstanding. For example, consider describing situations in which rioting occurs. The tipping point in this case for both journalist and academic reports would be the police shooting of an unarmed suspect. The shooting is the tipping point that precipitates public disorder that then escalates into riots. This is an example of a tipping point that can be reversed by political action and public order restored.

As Joe Smith tells us, global warming is a difficult subject nowadays to get news desks interested in, which is why tipping points in the context of escalating transformation become so important. Journalists struggle to sell a story to their news desks because science in this area is incremental rather than a series of easily reportable 'new' discoveries. The politics too, particularly lately, have been glacial and at best inconclusive. A tipping point is therefore an interesting idea about which an invigorated discussion can take place. A good example is the long-running debate about parts per million by volume of carbon dioxide in the global atmosphere. What is the tipping point at which global warming begins to escalate, becomes runaway, and therefore unstoppable, thus ensuring most of the human race will be consigned to oblivion? Is the tipping point 350, 400, or 450 parts per million by volume of carbon dioxide? Discuss this and you will get your story in the paper. The key point is that it is irreversible. Politicians (and scientists) are seemingly fiddling while ensuring that the Earth burns.

Let us be controversial here. The difficulty in finding a hard and fast new fact on which to base a news story has been made worse by the weaknesses and fears of the scientific community. Scientists have retired to their bunkers aware of the power of the climate deniers to make their lives miserable. There has been a staggering campaign against scientists. Journalists have failed to expose this concerted, highly sophisticated, and frequently illegal persecution of scientists, and consequently failed to assist them in standing up to this powerful political lobby. This is surprising since the effort to discredit the science is paid for largely by the fossil fuel lobby and free market fanatics who are not particularly popular with newspaper journalists and the internet community. The motives of this dangerous bunch should have been questioned at every opportunity – but have not been.

In 25 years of covering climate change, initially at least, I thought there would be a tipping point when the overwhelming scientific consensus on the need for action, backed by Nicholas Stern and other economists, would finally tip the politicians into action. Lately it has been clear that this will not happen, and partly this has been due to the rapid disappearance of the mainstream media and its replacement by internet communication in all its forms. This has undermined objective, science- and fact-based journalism, which needs time and resources to get it right. The internet is instant, and leaves no room for either. Anything goes, and when it comes to serious issues like climate change, a lot of what is reported is simply rubbish.

There are lots of other factors that make the reporting of climate issues difficult. Newspapers, radio, television, and blogs are obsessed with the size of their audience. Content is dictated by the need to survive. Thousands of newspapers and magazines have died in the last ten years, particularly in the United States, where much serious journalism has disappeared. This is why British newspapers are now among the best read in the world – online. It is impossible to buy a print version of any serious newspaper in many North American cities.

Within news organizations battles have to be fought to get climate change reported. Eyes of news editors and editors glaze over at mention of the issue. Offered the choice of the prosecution of an international footballer for a racial slur, or a piece on the displacement of a million people because of climate change, there would be no contest. You might get somewhere on the climate story if all the one million had reached a political tipping point and decided the only way to get their message across was to get in boats, arrive in the south of England, and ask for a new homeland. Then it would be an interesting immigration story.

Journalists need to be able to use simple triggers or hooks to capture the news editor's attention – 'new', 'the first time', 'never before'. A tipping point provides a trigger for environmental journalists, a bad situation getting worse with no return to the status quo. But it has to be a real tipping point. A drought with some dieback of trees is reversible, a tipping point beyond which the forest cannot recover is another much more newsworthy event altogether. When we use these words, all of us need to be clear exactly what we mean.

Commentary 7.4

Making sense of the world

CAMILLA TOULMIN

We all use mental maps and various models to make sense of the world, and understand how the different elements relate to each other. Some of these models are based on close observation of cause and effect, while others rely on a looser set of assumptions. In the first case, the biophysical world provides many settings in which we can be fairly sure that one set of actions will produce a given result. For example, planting a belt of trees will provide a sufficient windbreak for crops, animals, and pastures on the leeward side, thereby significantly increasing their productivity.

But in many other cases, particularly where people and decision-making are involved, we have to work with far looser connections, and less confidence in cause and effect. As a policy-focused research centre, the International Institute for Environment and Development (IIED) works with a 'theory of change' that is based on a set of assumptions around the importance of well-crafted information, ideas, and evidence. We seek to address what we would like to believe to be a benign, far-sighted political leadership, ready to listen and act on sound evidence, as part of a government responsive to the needs of citizens rather than narrow self-serving interests of particular lobby groups.

In practice, we recognize that many of these assumptions are only partially true and consequently we need to adapt our activities to cope with the existence of short-sighted politics, psychological denial, and the power of certain interests to both contest sound science and ensure government acts in their favour (see 6.7). We also recognize that government is not the only actor that counts, and hence the importance of working through citizen engagement, and encouraging competition amongst business leaders to show stronger sustainability credentials.

Many of us imagined that in Copenhagen in 2009, world leaders would make bold, courageous choices in favour of cutting greenhouse gas emissions, putting aside various biases for the benefit of humanity. We were wrong. We had failed to factor in the lock-in inertia in our economic patterns, the interests spearing our political systems, and the unwillingness of our politicians to take long-term decisions that might bring short-term electoral costs.

Mental models are clearly important in helping us debate the choices we face as global citizens, and the consequences of choosing a given pathway. Our readiness to accept a particular vision of the world is based on various factors, beyond rational acceptance of evidence. Kahan (2012) shows that adherence to a particular social group and its associated values may be more important than a careful weighing up of scientific arguments. He notes that people tend to filter out information and attitudes that would tend to drive a wedge between themselves and their peers (see also 3.2).

The study of global environmental change offers plenty of room for close observation of the biophysical and the human dimensions, as well as their multiple interactions. Communicating the complexity of global environmental change has been a big challenge, for which the concept of 'tipping points' has offered a valuable metaphor (see 3.1 and 7.1), although it brings its own baggage.

There have been key moments in recent and more distant history when the pattern of ideas has undergone major shift and re-adjustment. Such movement does not happen all at once. Historically, we can point to Galileo and Copernicus whose ideas and writings confirmed a radical shift in people's conception of the Earth's place in the universe; or to Hutton and Darwin, for their proof of the dizzying length of time that must have passed for particular geological features to have been produced, and for the slow painstaking process of evolution to generate such marked differences in animal and plant varieties.

More recently we have seen acceptance by governments and publics of the link between smoking and lung cancer, which has led to smoking bans in public places and controls on advertising. On the environmental front, one of the key insights of Barbara Ward, founder of IIED, has now started to take hold, 30 years after her death. This is that the cumulative actions of individual people and nations can collectively render our planet Earth unfit for human life. Having seemed limitless in scope and scale, this planet is showing its biophysical limits. In a world of scarcity and limits, Ward argued that it will be vital to address inequality, and provide means to privilege the needs of the many over the wants of the few.

Social theorists suggest that it can take 30–40 years for new ideas to become accepted and integrated as the new norm. Humankind exhibits a wide range of responses to new thinking – from denial, argument, and resistance, to broad acceptance, integration, and regulation (see also Sara Parkin in Chapter 6.3). As creatures of habit, with considerable investment in tried and tested ways of doing business, it often takes great force to achieve changes in behaviour, given the inertia, cognitive capture, and the press of interests keen to keep things as they are. The forces pushing back on achieving change can be evermore potent when there is a mismatch between the politico-administrative unit and the scale of the problem, as we see with nation states grappling with global challenges yet constrained by domestic interests, sovereignty, and competition.

Climate change and development

At IIED, we have focused on building resilience to climate change, by strengthening existing mechanisms and introducing new ways to cope with change. Such actions are premised on the costs of preparation for hazards usually being much smaller than the costs of coping with impacts after the event, and on the value of local knowledge and expertise in understanding and responding to shifting local conditions. There is a growing body of expertise around community-based adaptation (CBA), drawn in part from research in the 1970s and 1980s on coping with drought and establishing early warning systems. The six annual international workshops on CBA organized by IIED have also now built up a global constituency of people and ideas, able to share learning and offer practical insights. Key elements from the field of building resilience include:

- Recognizing local rights and agency, to manage and control access to resources;
- Supporting diverse livelihoods, putting eggs into many baskets;
- Bridging local and modern science, in ways which recognize their complementary value;
- Supporting the revolution in ICT to maximize connectivity and access to information;
- Investing in social infrastructure and social learning, through building cooperation, trust, and mutual obligations;

- Setting up safety nets, for food or income support, and establishing payments for ecosystem services;
- Building low-carbon collective infrastructure, especially for water, transport, and energy.

In Europe and North America, we have much to learn from adaptation and resilience in poorer countries. Our current economic models are pushing us in the opposite direction from resilience, leading to increased fragility in our economic and social infrastructure, through 'just in time' sourcing, long elaborate supply chains, few local connections, and eroded social capital.

Given the slow global response to cutting greenhouse gases, we now face the likelihood of a 3–4 degree rise in average temperatures by mid-century. Hence, adaptation will be critical to enable people to survive and hopefully prosper. Adaptation is not cost-free. While there may be multiple ways in which people cope with change, it tends to absorb resources that could have been used in other ways. Equally, it should be remembered that there are limits to adaptation. Language amongst donors and analysts asserts the availability of innovations which can bring 'win–win–win' solutions for climate adaptation, low-carbon mitigation, and pro-poor growth, sometimes referred to as the 'sweet spot'. Such optimistic language needs to be tempered by recognition of the fundamental unfairness of climate impacts affecting poor people and vulnerable countries most of all.

The Rio+20 summit was another opportunity to get our political leaders to focus attention on the challenges of sustainability. In contrast to COP15 (the Copenhagen climate change summit) in 2009, most observers had fewer ambitions for the outcome of such a global summit. With an outcome document with few if any commitments, even these low expectations were barely met. Our political leaders seem to be way behind many of their voters. The multilateral system is at a low ebb, but it is unclear how long the tide will be out. There is an absence of trust between nations, and the continued unhelpful dichotomy of developed versus developing countries, through the maintenance of the G77, no longer represents global reality and its greater complexity. International negotiation tactics are taken from the trade sector, with many country negotiators coming from a GATT and WTO background, where there is an emphasis on win–lose, rather than everyone contributing to a collective goal.

We hope that the next three years' work to draw up a set of sustainable development goals (SDGs), as agreed in Rio, could offer a better place to focus attention. The post-2015 agenda needs to be built up from below, and to address the multiple priorities of low- and middle-income countries as well as bringing change to the consumption patterns of rich nations.

Reference

Kahan, D. (2012), 'Why We Are Poles Apart on Climate Change', *Nature,* 488: 255.

Commentary 7.5

Endgame

JONATHAN SINCLAIR-WILSON

HAMM (anguished): What's happening, what's happening?
CLOV: Something is taking its course.

(Samuel Beckett, *Endgame*)

Metaphors are revelatory. At least successful ones are. They expand our understanding, but they hardly provide explanations. 'Juliet is the sun'? On the other hand, as Susan Sontag's caustic assault showed, they can be misleading or worse, obstructive; particularly when trying to grapple with life-threatening conditions such as cancer or HIV/AIDS, where what is required is diagnosis and treatment, and explanation that offers at least the prospect of management or even cure (Sontag 1978).

So are tipping points, or rather 'tipping points', a metaphor, and if so an illuminating or an obscuring one – faced as we are with the mounting and incontrovertible evidence of damage to the life-support systems on which we all depend, and the need above all for diagnoses and effective responses?

'The final straw' may be a metaphor for a tipping point, and one that results in abrupt, irreversible, and systemic, or at least structural, change. But we don't have to rely on analogical understanding to grasp the idea of an incremental variation that passes a critical threshold, resulting in a fundamental change of state. So while the graphic sense of 'tipping' may apply better to some such changes than others, such as the potentially reversible tipping of scales, or the potentially irreversible tipping of a glass of wine, it stretches 'metaphor' out of shape to think that 'tipping points' is one (unless we go to the vertiginous, and vacuous, lengths of saying all language is metaphor).

Behind the idea of it as a metaphor there may however be a different and also troubling thought: that what we see as critical thresholds, or tipping points, are a construct of our own forms of explanation, imposed on rather than reflective of an underlying reality which would require a different approach if we were ever properly to grasp it. Again, we don't need to go to the lengths of speculating on a metaphysical realm that puts what is really going on permanently out of our reach, but the worry is nonetheless salutary. It reminds us that, faced with the immense complexity of the natural and social worlds we are trying to encompass and – as far as possible – manage, identifying and relating all the relevant causal factors involved is anything but straightforward, and the lines we fear to cross over may simply be ones we've drawn ourselves.

Yet, even if we recognize that abruptness is relative to the frame of reference applied, that irreversibility – at least where that means more than the sense in which all change is irreversible or the continuous fulfilment of the second law of thermodynamics – may be a function of our limited knowledge, and that the system subject to change is one that exists first and foremost through our construction, it remains hard to deny that radical and sudden changes do occur. And moreover, with more than seven billion of us now on the scales, that in all probability significant geo-biophysical changes will occur and as a result of human activity.

Having acknowledged as much, what then? In controlled environments, science is able by elimination and confirmation to predict when states will alter, when water will freeze or critical mass be achieved. But confronting the biosphere, a mother of all complex systems, and the possibility of transgressing its vital boundaries, what we most evidently lack is any semblance of comparable control. Nor, without limitless spare planets, not to speak of spare centuries within which to test for the crucial variables, have we much hope of approximating to the probative value of experimental results in figuring out what the relevant causal factors are in its metabolism. We have no option but to fall back on constructed models, with all their admitted limitations. In the light of which, however exactly these models may capture experimental results and the limited historical data available to reflect current understanding, relying on them seems to be akin to looking under the streetlamp for the car keys you've lost, not because you dropped them there but because that's where the light is. Even with oscilloscopes going haywire, suggesting a major disruption is pending, the unknowns, both known and unknown, undermine confidence that our models have included and correctly weighted all the significant causal variables, so as to enable us correctly to anticipate what is coming or analyse it when it has.

Take the most publicized of the thresholds we may be approaching, a 2°C average global warming. Ignoring the element of political expediency in fastening on it, and the arbitrariness of drawing any line across a range of more or less graduated climate impacts, it is difficult to see how climate models can tell us not only the initial distribution of impacts from this level of warming but also the subsequent, cumulative cascade of further, ever-less-tested-for consequences, and to believe they can give us an accurate picture of the state in which the biosphere will eventually stabilize. If not for 2°C, there is no reason to suppose the picture is different for any other level of warming, including the 1.5°C already generated over the last 250 years (according to the recent Berkeley Earth Surface Temperature project (Muller 2012)) – or that we can say what the final reckoning of the experiment we have already begun with the Earth's systems will be. It seems perfectly conceivable that we may already have passed crucial thresholds, and that fundamental and, by the appropriate measures, abrupt changes in the conditions for life on Earth are under way. We have to hope otherwise, but without knowing exactly what counts as the relevant evidence, that may be what we have to fall back on, as the balance of probabilities appears to be imprecise and subjective. Our position is one of justifiable apprehension: a lot to suggest that we're approaching a precipice, but little assurance that we know precisely where it is or how far we may fall. In a collectively rational world, one would expect this to be a very strong incentive to arrive at a collectively rational response.

Given the state of the world as it is, however, the idea of a collectively rational response may seem absurd. If not, it does at least take us into quite a different area where tipping points may need to be found, or engineered: in our behaviour and in the social realm. It was here that Malcolm Gladwell's book, which pushed tipping points into the limelight, focused (Gladwell 2002). His account, like Sontag's, was grounded in medicine, in the spread of epidemics, using the poorly understood phenomenon of emotional contagion to extend from there to the rapid adoption of new technologies and behaviours, new social forms and norms (though his story did stretch the analogies and arguably itself tip over into metaphor).

Nevertheless, the communication of feeling, from earliest infancy on, is at the heart of our common humanity, and may indeed underpin the 'moral sentiments' that motivate and justify our concern for others, including those spatially and temporally distant from us. So our response should perhaps be, not to try and geo-engineer a way round confining planetary boundaries, but to look for ways to reinforce and employ the bonds we do share so as to inspire widespread change of social attitudes and behaviour. Replacing the self-fulfilling picture we have of ourselves, as greedy, short-sighted, and fundamentally maladapted individuals – for which the accumulating stock of atmospheric greenhouse gases could stand as an expression – may be where we need to start. Only with an expanded understanding of how we toll for one another are we likely to be able to inch our way back together from whatever precipices lie ahead.

References

Gladwell, M. (2002), *The Tipping Point: How Little Things Can Make a Big Difference* (London: Abacus).

Muller, R.A. (2012), 'The Conversion of a Climate Change Sceptic', *New York Times*, 30 July: A 19.

Sontag, S. (1978), 'Illness as Metaphor', *New York Review of Books*, 26 January.

Commentary 7.6

Beyond the linear
The role of visual thinking and visualization

JOE RAVETZ

If tipping points are more than just technical events – if they are equally significant in human hearts and minds – it follows that we need more than just technical means to understand, anticipate, or respond to them.

So here I would like to explore the role of visual thinking and visualization in the understanding and communication of tipping points. This is part of a wider programme on 'synergistic thinking for the one planet century' (Ravetz 2012), which brings in a parallel track as experience as an occasional 'graphic facilitator', with basic drawing skills from my previous life as an architect. During the Kavli Tipping Point workshop, I was keen to explore some of the more wide-ranging themes from alternative perspectives, in parallel to the more linear 'text and reasoning' mode of thinking. A sketchbook was filled in 24 hours with original raw materials, some of which have filtered through to this commentary.

My aim is both to argue the case for the visual thinking approach, and to demonstrate it. This draws on the help of some virtual friends: like Rosencrantz and Guildenstern, such characters remain quite fuzzy, but they seem to follow me around everywhere – arguing, questioning, thinking aloud, and flying off on crazy tangents.

There are four main stages to this argument: each has a section of graphic storyline. The first stage looks at the understanding of tipping points through visual thinking, in order to appreciate multiple forms of cause–effect and of human agency. The second is about the understanding of tipping points, which are complex or 'beyond complex', where visual thinking may be more effective than rational analysis. Thirdly we look at the communications side, where the flow of information and knowledge becomes part of the system. Finally, there is an overarching role for communications as catalysts for social tipping points which can respond to such interconnected problems. To set the scene, here are some background comments on visual thinking.

Background: visual thinking for research and policy

Generally, visual thinking (and/or visualization) can be a powerful enabler for new insights on complex problems (Tufte 1983; Horn 1998). There is a more technical-analytic approach which can focus on human–computer–information interfaces (Humphrey 2008; Huang *et al.* 2010). In parallel there is a more experiential and creative approach, which uses the visual medium to access the unconscious, right brain and lateral types of thinking (Nachmanovitch 2007; de Bono 1985). Such visual thinking then points the way towards more holistic ways of 'complex adaptive thinking', which might be better equipped than 'linear rational thinking', for the interconnected and multi-scale challenges all around us (Waltner-Toews *et al.* 2009). Through many diverse channels, techniques, audiences, and cultural platforms, visualization can offer the following for the research task:

- A trans-disciplinary perspective, grounded in social experience, with open and inclusive cognitive processes;
- Applications, on a spectrum from systems analysis and problem mapping to experiential envisioning and creative policy design and synthesis.

This suggests a landscape of visual thinking possibilities with two main axes (Ravetz 2011):

- One axis spans between analytic and mechanical concepts (focusing on abstractions), over to synthetic and holistic experiences (focusing on figurative substance).
- Another axis spans between discrete and disaggregated objects (specific purposes such as building designs), and fuzzy/embedded fields (general purposes such as artworks or other aesthetic communications).

This analytic approach is useful for mapping out the possibilities. But there is an alternative approach where the visualization speaks for itself, rather than as an explanation of text. In the fine arts, there are many interpretations and levels of analysis, but the primary purpose is clearly aesthetic and experiential. Likewise if we approach tipping points as 'experiences' as much as technical objects, then a fine art approach can be at least as significant as rational analysis. This can be applied to process-oriented deliberation, which again is about experience as much as technical information. For instance, 'graphic facilitation' is now established as a valuable technique in process-focused workshops, with a London institute and practitioner network (www.vizthink.co.uk). In parallel the practice of 'relational visualization' emerged from sustainability research and futures workshop processes, where visual material (from on or off site) can be a powerful catalyst to creative group thinking (Ravetz 2011). To summarize, there are two strands here:

- Visualization *as* a process – used in workshop or discussion situations – visioning, consensus building, conflict mediation, strategy forming, negotiation, and bargaining.
- Visualization *of* a process – directly capturing dialogue, debate, argument and even conflict. The classic cartoon strip is one example where a dialogue can communicate a nuance of thinking and multiple meaning which is hardly possible in any other way.

Visual thinking to understand multiple cause–effects

Our characters are trying to plan out a TV documentary on our subject – 'tipping points and the role of visual thinking'. The unplanned tipping point of a glass then sparks off various trains of thought. One is about visual technical analysis with charts, maps, or systems diagrams. Another is about experiences, sentiments, literary nuances, cultural resonances, all wrapped up with the drinking or wasting of wine. One consequence of such joined-up thinking is that the physical tipping point of another broken glass, leads to a possible social tipping point for an alcoholic on the path to reformation.

Visual thinking to understand multi-scale complexity

In search of an iconic visual theme, the image of the planet Earth turns up, but this is a very large and complex system to understand. If we zoom in, then any one tipping point – such as a forest fire – seems to be entangled with other tipping points or 'balancing points' at other scales. If we look

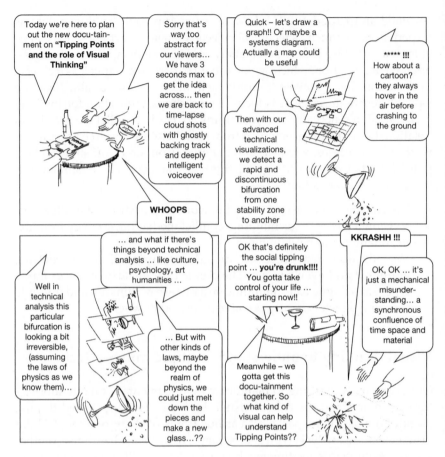

Figure 7.1 Visual thinking to understand multiple cause–effects

for the ends of the chains of cause and effect, we have to zoom back out to the global scale. Here there is a very complex technical system of feedbacks and amplifier effects, combined with human effects such as denial, displacement, conspiracy, and corruption, along with positive features such as learning, creative innovation, social responsibility, etc. The result could be summarized as 'beyond complexity' – in which case we would need all possible channels of communication to access the subconscious and supra-conscious human psyches. Then, as we are faced with multiple and existential tipping points – climate change, water and energy, food and soil, nitrogen and phosphorus, mass extinction, political terrorism, financial

Figure 7.2 Visual thinking to understand multi-scale complexity

crisis, and mental illness (to name but a few) – then we can better access other parts of the human psyche which are implicated in such problems.

Visualization in communicating tipping point situations

The focus now shifts from 'understanding' to 'communications', and the role of images is clearer. We are surrounded by images, many generated for profit, and most striving to be iconic and memorable. Perhaps the most

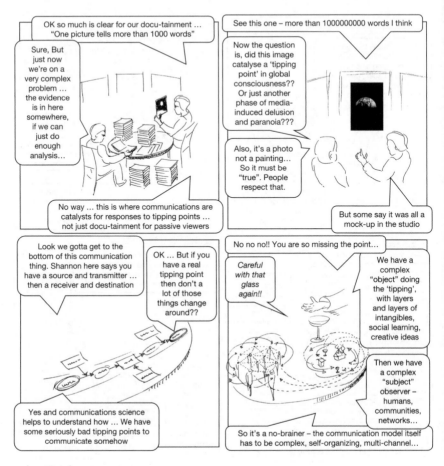

Figure 7.3 Visualization in communicating tipping point situations

famous for our generation is the 'earthrise', as seen from the moon (Poole 2010). But the implications are not so clear – did this image enable new kinds of global consciousness, or further layers of manipulation by global interests and corporate elites? To explore such questions reveals a debate on communications: starting with the communications theory which paved the way for the digital age (Shannon and Weaver 1949). But this points towards something more – the role of communications as enabler for complex feedback systems, which interpolate between complex tipping point 'objects', and observation by complex tipping point 'subjects'. We can

294

start to envisage a holistic tipping point system, in which object, subject, and media are all interconnected.

Visualization for synergistic tipping point responses

Ultimately the role of visual thinking (and other multiple channels of communication) can emerge. The example of the multi-scalar problem – including a house fire / forest fire / corrupt planning / irresponsible urbanization / climate-induced desertification – shows this graphically. The humans involved here work with multiple ways of thinking and 'intelligences' – technical intelligence, social, entrepreneurial, ethical, ecological, political intelligence, and some others. So how can decisions be made in 'wild' situations of urgency and controversy, which can respond to such a tipping point in an integrated way, using local resources and enabling global synergies? (Ravetz *et al.* 2011). Again, self-organizing and multichannel communications are not the whole of the solution, but enabling resources for solutions to emerge. This of course is not easy to 'communicate' in the two-second sound-bite culture of modern visual media. So again there is a search for iconic images which have depth and resonance – which contain or evoke conceptual mappings, so that participants can better appreciate where they are, places where they want to be, and possibly ways to move towards them.

Conclusions and ways forward

This brief think-piece or 'looking-piece' explores some territory which is maybe intuitively obvious. Faced with a crisis or catastrophe, we humans need to 'see' it. And such visual thinking is not only about technical information on risks or responses, but a multilevel multichannel experience which resonates with different parts of the human psyche.

So what to do next? There are global-level tipping points in all directions, and the technical evidence for existential crisis for our civilization seems overwhelming. Yet to generate any kind of response needs political legiti-macy, economic acceptance, behavioural change, collective responsibility, psychological resolve, and similar qualities. Few of these are technical in nature or respond to technical stimulus – rather they are socio-cultural dynamics of learning, creative action, shared intelligence, and so on. The

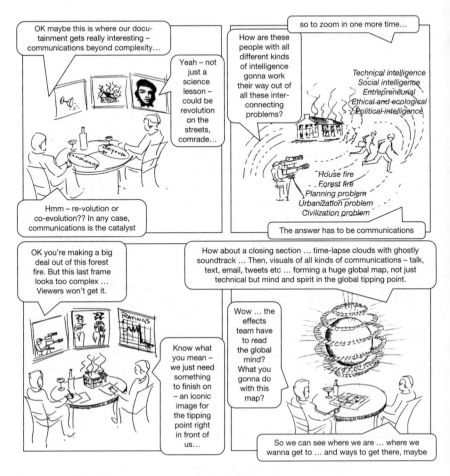

Figure 7.4 Visualization for synergistic tipping point responses

role of visual thinking, and other types of media, is crucial in appreciating the problems and designing effective responses.

References

De Bono, E. (1985), *Six Thinking Hats: An Essential Approach to Business Management* (New York: Little, Brown).

Horn, R.E. (1998), *Visual Language: Global Communication for the 21st Century* (London: Macro VU Press).

Huang, Mao Lin, Nguyen, Quang Vinh, and Zhang, Kang (eds) (2010), *Visual Information Communication* (Berlin: Springer).

Humphrey, M.C. (2008), *Creating Reusable Visualizations with the Relational Visualization Notation*, Interactive Visual Communication working paper: available on www.iviz.com (accessed April 2010).

Nachmanovitch, S. (2007), 'Bateson and the Arts', *Kybernetes* 36 (7/8).

Poole, R. (2010), *Earthrise: How Man First Saw the Earth* (London: Yale Books).

Ravetz, J. (2011), 'Exploring Creative Cities for Sustainability with Deliberative Visualization', in Girard, L.F. and Nijkamp, P. (eds) *Creativity and Sustainable Cities* (Oxford: Heinemann).

Ravetz, J. (2012), 'Urban Synergy Foresight', in Forward Planning Studies Unit (ed.), *Urban Governance in the EU: Current Challenges and Forward Prospects* (Brussels: EU Committee of the Regions), 31–44. Available on: http://urban-intergroup.eu/wp-content/files_mf/corurbangoverancefinal.pdf (accessed 31 October 2012).

Ravetz, J., Miles, I., and Popper, R. (2011), *European Research Area Toolkit: Applications of Wild Cards and Weak Signals to the Grand Challenges and Thematic Priorities of the ERA* (Manchester: Institute of Innovation Research, University of Manchester), http://community.iknowfutures.eu/news/toolkit.php (accessed 31 October 2012).

Shannon, C.E. and Weaver, W. (1949), *The Mathematical Theory of Communication* (Champaign: University of Illinois Press).

Tufte, E.R. (1983), *The Visual Display of Quantitative Information* (New York: Graphics Press).

Waltner-Toews, D. with Kay, J., and Lister, N. (2009), *The Ecosystem Approach: Complexity, Uncertainty and Managing for Sustainability* (New York: Columbia University Press).

PART 8
A PRECARIOUS FUTURE

8.1
Into a precarious future

TIM O'RIORDAN AND TIM LENTON

In the run-up to the UN Conference on Sustainable Development held in Rio de Janeiro in June 2012, the leaders of the global scientific convention *Planet under Pressure* concluded:

> Research now demonstrates that the continued functioning of the Earth's system as it has supported the well-being of human civilization in recent centuries is at risk. Without urgent action, we could face threats to water, food, biodiversity and other critical resources: these threats risk intensifying economic, ecological and social crises, creating the potential for a humanitarian emergency on a global scale.
>
> (Brito *et al.* 2012: 3)

GEO 5, the fifth Global Environmental Outlook of the UN Environment Programme, reached similar conclusions:

> As human pressures on the Earth system accelerate, severe critical global, regional and local thresholds are close or have been exceeded. Once these have been passed, abrupt and possibly irreversible changes to the life support functions of the planet are likely to occur, with significant adverse implications for human well-being.
>
> (GEO 5 2012: 5)

We are starting to stray outside the 'safe operating space for humanity' as introduced by Rockström *et al.* (2009) and extended in Rockström and Klum (2012). Rockström and his many colleagues believe that they have the scientific evidence that humanity is near or past safe boundaries in the areas of climate change, biodiversity loss, nutrient cycling, and ocean acidification. Although such boundaries are fiendishly difficult to define, the concerted scientific effort on the contingent outcomes of ubiquitous climate change shows that it is reasonable to agree on them (in this case, staying below 2°C global warming). The real difficulty lies in staying within the boundaries. Now the World Bank (2012) has begun to address a world of 4°C temperature increase by 2100, once considered at the outside range of scenarios. The Bank suggests that human institutions of adaptation and adjustment have no precedent for coping and 'the risks of crossing critical social system thresholds will grow'. The Bank concludes: 'that simply must not be allowed to occur' (2012: xviii).

Regional navigation between social foundations and planetary boundaries

We suggest that sharing a common view of what is just and safe for all is also what will make our future sustainable. Fundamental considerations of what is just, especially what is equitable, must be considered alongside planetary boundaries on what is safe.

In the planetary boundaries framework, protecting human well-being is the rationale for limiting natural resource use in order to avoid tipping points in critical Earth system processes. At the same time, human well-being clearly depends upon each person having claim upon the natural resources required to meet their dignified human rights, such as decency in life, health, water and sanitation, food, shelter, and subsistence.

Meeting these basic human rights for everyone is what Kate Raworth (2012) at Oxfam calls the 'social foundation' for human betterment. Although we need to use resources to provide this social foundation, the amount of additional resource use necessary is modest compared to current global overconsumption. Instead we have a distribution problem – resource use and availability are profoundly not equitable, and a small minority are massively overusing global resources. The UN Human Development Report (2011: 2) shows that overall poverty is increasing, that environmental stresses and associated diseases are afflicting the poor and the powerless and women in a particularly adverse manner, and that there is a 'turning point' for general human ill-being in the least developed countries well before 2050, if present trends continue.

This inefficient overuse of resources is overstepping the planetary boundaries that represent an outer limit on our collective activities. Between the social foundations and the planetary boundaries lies a 'doughnut' (or torus) that prescribes the 'just and safe operating space for humanity' – the 'Oxfam doughnut' as devised by Kate Raworth, building on the work of the Stockholm Resilience Centre (www.oxfamblogs.org/doughnut).

The challenge then is to ensure that there is sufficient resource use and distribution to achieve human rights and well-being, while simultaneously ensuring that total resource use remains within planetary boundaries. We suggest the pathway to achieving this goal is a regional approach.

The reality or otherwise of planetary boundaries has been questioned (Nordhaus *et al.* 2012) with arguments that 'boundaries' are fuzzy, that regional variations make nonsense of global guardrails, and that huge differences in cultures and economies mean that any such boundaries are highly elastic in every particular human setting. These criticisms are partly helpful, and partly spurious. We take them as an impetus not to throw out planetary boundaries, but to try to define regional and local ones.

Of the nine original 'planetary' boundaries, only four clearly involve globally well-mixed variables: climate change, ocean acidification, stratospheric ozone depletion and phosphorus cycle boundaries. Carbon dioxide is well-mixed in the atmosphere and affects the climate and ocean acidification boundaries, well-mixed chlorofluorocarbons affect the stratospheric ozone boundary, and excess phosphorus leaking into the global ocean is also well-mixed, and might ultimately trigger excess removal of oxygen from deep ocean waters – an oceanic anoxic event.

However, for the other five proposed 'planetary' boundaries there are more immediate and evident thresholds and clearer management opportunities at regional or local scales. The corresponding boundary variables – namely atmospheric aerosols, chemical pollution, freshwater availability, land system change, and biodiversity – are regionally very variable. Conditions can sometimes exceed local or regional scale thresholds, but currently there is a lack of evidence for a global-scale threshold.

Furthermore, even where a 'planetary' boundary may exist, say, for phosphorus input to the global ocean, the original boundary was set at a level far beyond the point at which multiple regional systems – including lakes, coastal seas, and their fisheries – could pass tipping points into anoxic conditions (Carpenter and Bennett 2011). It clearly makes more sense in this case to set boundaries for regional systems, and then aggregate them through their catchments to a global scale. By iterating between such efforts to define regional and global thresholds, the boundaries concept can be placed on a firmer scientific foundation.

There are other compelling human reasons for a more regional and local approach. The regionalization of boundaries fits with existing scales of communities and governance, and it reflects the scales at which democratic social foundations have relevance. Furthermore, the impacts of ecosystem degradation are experienced most strongly within national or regional economies – long before global boundaries of resource pressure may be reached. Already, natural resource management takes place predominantly at smaller scales, as part of national and regional development planning. Therefore, analytical tools that map resources and their boundaries at these scales of governance are more likely to have relevance and traction.

In the context of global population growth coupled with extreme income inequality – within and between countries – many nations and regions face significant and urgent challenges to ensure that available resources are used to meet the rights of all, whilst also seeking to guarantee that total use of regional resources stays within boundaries necessary to protect human well-being. Nations therefore need the analytical tools to define both an environmentally safe operating space and a socially just one. This theme is most eloquently addressed by the report published by the Royal Society entitled *People and the Planet* (Sulston 2012). This emphasized the necessity to address the relationships between population growth, increasing inequalities of health, wealth, and opportunity, and overconsumption as an integrated totality for discerning targeting of policy. It pushed the case for more investment in the well-being of the one billion poor and the further two billion disadvantaged, and for much more sensitive planning and socially caring development of the emerging world's cities, which will dominate human occupation within a decade.

Happily, the thickness of the 'doughnut' is not fixed for certain critical social foundations and environmental boundaries at regional scales – for example, those processes involving the use of the nutrients nitrogen and phosphorus to produce food. By shifting to much more efficient and targeted use of fertilizers and food, along with more recapture and recycling of nutrients, we can simultaneously produce human betterment whilst reducing the pressures tending to tip lakes or coastal seas into anoxic states. There is room for manoeuvre, and we need a creative interplay between regional and global scales of analysis and governance, to define and then live within the 'doughnut'.

The message of this book is that although tipping points are hard to predict and corresponding boundaries even harder to define, they are taking form on an advancing horizon. Reviewing the ecological evidence, Barnosky *et al.* (2012: 57) conclude that only with a combination of organized scientific effort, together with serious transformations in the institutions of global cooperation, plus widespread cultural recognition of the moral need to share and care, can we 'steer the biosphere towards conditions we desire, rather than those that are thrust on us unwittingly'. How might the world approach this task?

On trifurcations

Tipping points carry options. John Fowles, in his novel *The French Lieutenant's Woman*, offered two storylines for the outcome of the fateful meeting of his lovers. When contemplating tipping points we can only see stories. In astronomical time, nothing of our earthly human experience eventually will matter. As Filipe Duarte Santos (2011: 285–96) reminds us, the ultimate fate of the Earth is either spinning away into the outer realms of the solar system as a frozen lifeless rock, or being engulfed in an expanding, and subsequently contracting Sun. Before the planet is destroyed, life on Earth will be cooked to death by our steadily brightening Sun, in roughly a billion years' time. So we have time to consider our inevitable fate. The human race, even if it were to become truly sustainable, is unlikely to last for more than a few more millions of years. Given the essence of this text, such a prolonged prospect for a survivable humanity is extremely unlikely.

In this book we have so far offered two broad scenarios. One is the 'lock-in' effect of succumbing to combinations of Earth system phase changes, even in the full knowledge of possible catastrophic outcomes – especially for the most vulnerable people, the human majority. The other is the creeping mass realization that positively creative transformations are increasingly unavoidable, and that if this is so, then some form of creative adaptation towards localized resilience is necessary.

In framing our conclusions, we feel it is realistic to suggest that three distinct scenarios for the coming generation of 30 years are plausible – our 'trifurcation' of tipping points.

The first scenario

The first scenario is that the 'lock-in' effect will prevail. This will be marked both by prolonged overall economic decline and turmoil, punctuated by and coupled to real successes of emergent eco-friendly and socially beneficial technology. We envisage advances, such as: in 3D computing; in recyclable photo-voltaics which are so thin that they can coat objects; in robotics; in portable programmable computers with blossoming 'apps'; in human genetics to increase survival; and in permaculture married to targeted plant, fungal, and animal genetics to enhance food production. But these advances will not push the economic system towards sustainable paths. On the contrary, they seem more likely to reinforce efforts to keep the globalized industrial show on the road. The more there is technological hope for 'fixing' the wicked problems generated by economic growth and the explosions in production and demand, the more the lock-in effect will be relentlessly pursued. In fact it may influence the future pathways of the much touted 'resilience'. This is because such technology will be seen as the basis for successful adaptation to global and regional change. Hence 'tipping points' may lose some of their frightening qualities and 'non-adaptive' resilience will prevail.

In this scenario, tipping points of various combinations introduced in this book will become unavoidable before the century is out. Indeed, they will begin to reveal their physical dangers in the coming three decades and in some cases (summer Arctic ice removal, degradation of the Amazon) even sooner. As for social system disruption, we have repeatedly claimed that these thresholds are much more menacingly nearer.

The second scenario

The second scenario is that some form of accommodation to such approaching probable calamities will take place as an adjunct to the lock-in scenario, with a significant effort to establish 'adaptive' resilient communities across the planet. These will embrace sustainable energy, low-carbon, low-water, and low-waste technologies, behavioural change in consumption habits more generally, and the emergence of the local, more autonomous, community. Social enterprise, sensitive mentoring, and creative learning for flexible employment will flourish. Locally sourced resources will be generated by levies on non-sustainable consumption and behaviour, with the proceeds being incorporated into community-based not-for-profit cooperatives. These might be created by community charitable trusts and subject to community forums for advice, linked to media and web-based scrutiny. They could build resilience and leadership from within the vulnerable and establish the scope for sustainability enterprises. Most challenging will be the formation of such resilience in the poorer communities lying within wealthy, prosperous, and impoverished societies.

Local resilience will reflect capability and inequality of opportunity. But at least it could offer signposts.

Tipping points in this scenario will be mixed – positive and negative – but overall will contribute to human disruption and misery, despite many islands of resilience and hope.

The third scenario

The third scenario is the progressive combination of the first two, where the spectre of calamitous tipping points and the encouragement of 'islands of hope' begin the transformation of governing, of politics, of markets, and of learning into a world of sustainable living. This optimistic scenario will be seen as unrealistic by many. Positive narratives and expectations, however, can generate action, encouraging a drive for innovation and a willingness to embrace change, even when the initiating institutional conditions are very hostile. We feel it is possible for humanity to shift towards cooperative living for its own civilized survival in the light of emerging risks of serious social violence, economic disintegration, widespread destitution, and irrecoverable global damage. But as we concluded in Chapter 1.1, we may have first to be 'shocked and awed' into such dramatic transformations.

We believe that aspects of all of these scenarios are likely to develop and shape our choices and constraints by 2050. It is partly the purpose of this book to offer the reader the scope for considering the ways in which we may avoid the first scenario, embrace the emergence of the second, and realize we need to capture the third over the coming two decades. This is the message of Matthew Taylor (3.2), namely to respect, to listen, and to cooperate through mutual vision, understanding, and action.

The politics of lock-in

It is dangerous to extrapolate from immediate trends into distant prospects. As we write in late 2012, the signs for both the European and the global economies are distinctly unhappy. Official growth predictions summarized in the April 2012 World Economic Outlook (International Monetary Fund 2012) verge on recession in the European theatre where even the more powerful economies of Germany and the Scandinavian countries are weakening. In May 2012, the manufacturing sectors in Europe and the

USA fell to their lowest levels in three years, with few signs of sustained recovery. In the USA there is such turmoil in domestic politics that sustained recovery seems to be thwarted by political anger. Paul Krugman and Robin Wells summarize the dismal scene:

> Ultimately the deep problem isn't about personalities or individual leadership; it's about the nation as a whole. Something had gone very wrong with America, not just its economy, but its ability to function as a democratic nation. And it is hard to see when or how that wrongness will get fixed.
>
> (Krugman and Wells 2012: 2)

The 2012 UK Democratic Audit (Wilks-Heeg *et al.* 2012) has recorded a widespread and disturbing lack of confidence in politicians and political institutions, with deepening dismay over the failure of legislatures to be responsive to public needs, and an overwhelming perception that politicians are in the grip of big self-serving corporations. The authors conclude that long-term representative democracy is in persistent decline, though local informal activism is strengthening. The loss of faith in overall political democracy adds to the huge difficulties facing legislatures in credibly tackling tipping points.

The normally dynamic propulsions of the emerging economies are also slowing down. Given their population growth and burgeoning cities, what looks like high rates of growth may not mop up the huge numbers of people seeking employment. Furthermore the rising rates of job-seeking amongst young people in many member states of the European Union do not bode well for their well-being and self-confidence. Overall the unemployment rate for young adults in the EU is 22.6 per cent. There is a real danger that many millions of young adults could become a 'forgotten generation'. In May 2012, there were 5.52 million unemployed young people in the EU, a figure that has been steadily rising since 2007.

EU policymakers and stakeholders are aware of this potential catastrophe of creating a 'lost generation', but so far appear powerless to halt the rising unemployment among young people:

> This is a huge problem to tackle, but it is essential that young people are encouraged to develop skills that are in demand and that they are given the chance to obtain meaningful work experience that enables them to gain a foothold in the labour market.
>
> (Andrea Broughton of the Institute for Employment Studies 2012 http://www.employment-studies.co.uk/press/10_12.php)

The Prince's Trust (2012) found that two in five of youngsters not in employment, education, or training were deeply pessimistic about their ability to cope with their lives, exhibiting very little self-confidence about their abilities to enter into meaningful work. The Trust has launched a campaign over this *Undiscovered Generation* (Prince's Trust 2012).

While the Western nations are reassessing means to force-feed growth, they are also paying lip-service to 'green economies'. Even the most optimistic supporter of the green economic transition realizes that little can be achieved in a hurry, that by no means all of the currently unemployed can be mopped up by this transition, and that it will not sidestep the real risks of ecological breakdown. The Commons Environment Audit Committee (2012: 3–5) concluded that: the government in the UK do not give high priority to a green economy, favouring instead established, carbon-intensive investments in infrastructure; there were no measures of success or sense of direction in the transition to any coherent version of a green economy; there were conflicting and unhopeful prospects for many net new jobs without extensive training and work experiences; and there was no central mechanism to promote a full-scale environmentally and socially robust transition to such an economy.

From this we conclude that lock-in is rife, and that any transition towards our alternative tipping scenarios is still in its infancy and lacking in leadership. Beetham (2011) sees the weakening of democratic processes as fuelled by a combination of: market fundamentalism; corporate globalism; the hollowing out of the public service in favour of 'cherry picking' privatization; and the informal influence and ready access to politicians by those who donate to political parties. He also points to the 'revolving door' of senior civil servants moving to lucrative consultancies in the private sector they once managed; the perfidious entry of corporate advisers into the public service, often without any accountability; and the weakness of any individual politician to stand up to this onslaught. Even if he is half right, this is surely a recipe for lock-in.

The International Institute for Applied Systems Analysis (IIASA) is a highly respected modelling and policy advising interdisciplinary group of top-level researchers. In October 2012 it organized an impressive conference, *Worlds Within Reach: From Science to Policy* (IIASA 2012a). In the run-up to this event it published a number of reports seeking to show how indeed it is possible to turn around the big conundrums of the age: climate change, water and energy security, and sustainable urban living (IIASA 2012b). What is evident from these massive exercises in systems-led policy prescription is both the huge danger of lock-in (where IIASA modellers give to 2030 at most for successful transformation) and the challenging requirements they seek for ensuring that their clever and comprehensive recommendations are acted upon.

What they seek seems remote from the present economic and political realities: strong international leadership; consistent and durable regulation to provide reliable investment conditions for business to commit resources and inventiveness; significant joint public–private investment of many new billions of US dollars guaranteed every year for over 25 years; and the scope for entrepreneurial technology and enterprise across the face of the planet. This is genuinely stirring stuff. And it comes from many person-years of painstaking modelling and discussions amongst some of the brightest minds in the sustainability business. But it does appear fanciful in the harsh realities of limited available cash, deep divisions over climate change verities and solutions, touching faith in as-yet-untested technologies, and optimism over relatively rapid and enduring behaviour change coordinated across nations and time.

For us, the IIASA optimism lies at the cusp of our two scenarios: deeply dependent on the smashing of lock-in and heroically cheerful about untried ways of inventing, working, managing, and leading which should be the hallmark of a human species searching for joyous salvation.

Pavan Sukhdev (2012), the doyen of sustainable accounting, also places great faith in transformations to capitalism which, as yet, show little sign of being embraced by global financial markets and debt-plagued politicians. Perverse subsidies would be reduced (when billions are spent annually on lobbying to keep them (Heinrich Böll Foundation 2012)). Taxes would be reformed and new 'green' incentives created, with future infrastructure geared towards ecosystem sensitivity and alignment (while at present there seems only talk of more airports, roads, pipelines, and transmission lines). Public ownership of the commons and community ownership of common pool resources would be the new economic reality (while critical minerals and land are being purchased by international speculators and acquisitive governments and the global biodiverse hotspots, such as the mangrove and coral, fade). Socially responsible regulations would extend to the corporates generally, and advertising would be forced to follow strict ethical and accountable codes. Resource and pollution (including greenhouse gases) levies would steadily replace corporate taxes.

These are the recommendations we support for our second scenario. What all of these powerful and well-analysed reports reveal is the lack of alignment between the frantic regrowth-policy desperation of beleaguered politicians, their failure to connect these recommendations in an unprecedented era of recurring Euro crises and deep social malaise as austerity strips family after family of their accustomed dignities, and the emerging realities of fundamental political and social failure. Yet it is precisely this combination of excellent science, policy analysis, and unavoidable crises which we feel stimulates the conditioning for our second and third scenarios.

Beginning the journey

Throughout this book, we have sought from authors some sense of what needs to be done to break the lock-in effect. There are signs of hope. Jeffrey Sachs, the special adviser to the Director General of the UN, Ban Ki-moon, has begun the process of determining what would constitute the Sustainable Development Goals (SDGs) for all nations which formed a centre piece of the Rio+20 UN Conference on Sustainable Development:

> One of the key planks of the SDGs is that we need better measurement of well-being and one way is to ask people how well they feel they are doing, one crude measure of life satisfaction. A legion of scholars have been studying this and picking up great traditions as brought by Buddhism and Bhutan in particular. We can now identify pretty systematically places where people are deeply unhappy, highly anxious and also identify systematically the reasons why.

> Second, people are, like Aristotle said, social animals. We depend on our sense of participation in communities, and if there is a lack of trust, our lives are miserable, and if we live in unhappy places where people do not co-operate with each other and altruism is not a moral virtue that is defended, where cheating is rife and pervasive, then unhappiness soars.
> (Jeffrey Sachs, quoted in the *Guardian*, 22 June 2012)

Sachs is highly critical of the lobbying powers of big business which result in distortion of commodities prices, profound undervaluing of natural and social capital (as outlined by Sara Parkin (6.3)), and the undermining of political democracy as governments seem unable to withstand their financial and self-serving political purposes.

In order to understand how we might make the move towards alternative scenarios avoiding lock-in, we consider below some of the signals of change and instability of our time, within a conceptual framework of 'landscape, regime and niche' (Geels 2002) that can help us map the terrain and chart paths towards better futures.

Turchin (2011: 7–9) suggests that there are long waves of stability and instability in many societies lasting for about a century at a time. His neo-Malthusian approach regards the disintegrative cycles as being marked by rising populations, increasing scarcity of food, insupportable urban migration, and bulges in the young to middle age ranges, releasing great social dissatisfaction. More of a trigger is the sequestering of wealth by elites and competition amongst rising numbers of aspiring elites to get hold of diminishing amounts of remaining wealth, leading to factionalism and social turmoil. The diminishing state coffers mean that the rising costs of military and police control, and associated surveillance, exceed the capacity of the state to finance their voracious demands on the tax purse. The outcome is deep social turbulence and loss of central authority.

There are signs in the troubled Eurozone of the latter stages of this sequence beginning to occur. So we need to consider how best to avoid the worst and begin to address the better. We began this journey in Chapter 6.1. We also asked Andrew Dobson (8.2) and Ian Christie (8.3) to take us further on this path.

Well-being and betterment

The New Economics Foundation (2012: 6) regards well-being as a combination of *feelings* (contentment, joy, satisfaction) and *functions* (competence, self-esteem, worthwhileness). Placing these in the context of external *opportunities* (work, social connectedness, trust in others, democratic involvement) and *personal propensities* (health, resilience, optimism, diversity of experiences) gives a sense of flourishing (self-realization) and capabilities.

What lies behind well-being is the beginning of a whole new approach to measuring and appreciating social betterment. The scope rests on the assets of what is possible for an individual to achieve, alone or with others, in creating inner satisfactions as well as empowerment over apathy or disillusionment. It also offers, crucially, the chance to avoid seeing real loss of income and ageing as negative aspects of economic failure. Rather, well-being offers the scope for regarding household flourishing as a far more appropriate measure than income, and ageing into health a basis for extending experience for community enhancement.

One outcome of well-being is the current interest in *social investment*. This is of two kinds. One is essentially charitable giving, where investors place funds in schemes which are designed to better people and society who are otherwise disadvantaged. The other is to offer schemes and support to those who are a cost to themselves and to society more generally, so that they take on responsibility and avoid future financial burdens on the public and private purse.

It is too early in the development of a social investment bank to assess its overall value. There is a grumbling amongst market fundamentalists that this is not 'real value' but some kind of 'charity' of a kind more commonly found in Victorian times. Consequently social investment will require a concerted effort from businesses which are either strapped for cash as the banks restrict and channel lending for measurable gains, or which are really only prepared to pay lip-service to what they regard as government responsibility. This is the message of the commentaries from Amanda Long (6.4), John Elkington (6.6), and Thomas Lingard (6.8). Mike Barry (6.9) and Ian Christie (8.3) make an even more forceful point. The failure of governments to provide for publicly funded support for the planet or even for social capital may create a void which the private sector will simply have to fill. Social investment may have to be privately financed. This is the line also strongly advocated by Sukhdev (2012).

The second form of social investment is more promising. This depends on the intervention in the lives and consumption habits of people who are proving a cost to themselves (alcoholism, obesity, type 2 diabetes, self-harm, early and unwished-for pregnancy, and substance abuse). All this tends to result in expenditures to various other parties, such as insurance-premium contributors, or health authorities. For example, the cost of obesity to the UK alone is estimated to be over £5 billion annually, and the cost of treating depression over £4 billion per year (see Foresight 2008).

Mulgan (2011) offers seven criteria for success in this kind of endeavour:

- The programme is clearly preventative and sufficient funding is available.
- The programme demonstrably improves social well-being and ameliorates undesirable outcomes.
- The specific impacts and advantages of the programme can be measured.
- Sufficient participants offer robust evidence of a wider success.
- Beneficiaries can be identified.
- Their benefits are shown to be larger than the overall costs of the interventions.
- There is scope for rolling this out into a social investment bank.

In many ways key aspects of sustainability should apply here. For example, helping poor families to cut wasteful energy and water use could

313

result in incentives from utilities and reduce carbon emissions and water shortages in drought-prone areas. Such eco-orientated approaches fit in with the vision of socially responsive capitalism offered by our contributors to Part 6. Reconstituting waste, especially used consumer goods such as bicycles or electrical appliances, should provide reusable products for poor families who otherwise could not afford them. Mentoring potential depressives or would-be drug abusers provides significant benefits on the hard-pressed public purse, as well as possibly benefiting the well-being of both the helper and the assisted.

Maybe it is precisely in the realm of well-being and community support that sustainability can find a new home. This would be where it has never entered before. It is to the disadvantaged, the new household poor, the frustrated unemployed, and the incipient depressive that sustainability can now reach out. So, if the conditions of sustainable capitalism do begin to take hold nationally and internationally, this sets the scene for sustainable localism. It is here that we finally must turn.

Redesigning locality

Getting to an effective role for localism will not be easy. Central governments dislike giving too much power and discretionary money to local governments, for the obvious reason that many local governments are run by other political parties. But equally relevant is the real crisis of reduced overall cash in local government coffers due to austerity measures. Along with this financial suffocation come losses of staff and discontinuity of programmes. In many cases the projects where local government excel, namely where they create a trusting and bonded relationship with less advantaged peoples and associated charities, are those which are cut and where well-liked personnel are made redundant.

The Economist (2012) offers the emergence of a revolution in local government, especially in London where councillors are well educated and amenable to creative experimentation. They are trying out 'John Lewis' cooperative partnerships and 'easy' (low cost, no frills) partnerships with communities where all manner of people are getting involved with bettering social services and care. These well-intentioned schemes are still very embryonic, but they do show the scope for really effective adaptation and resilience if the management innovations are shared, and if 'failure' is regarded as a source for learning and recalibrating.

In essence there is little prospect of successful transfer to localism for sustainability unless several conditions are met:

- Local government needs to have powers to raise their own income from activities which are proven to be non-sustainable and carbon-generating.
- Most, if not all, of this revenue should be in the form of local not-for-profit investments which are handled by community charitable trusts for the benefit of viable local sustainability initiatives run on a partnership basis with the public and private sectors.
- Young people should be enabled to work on a host of sustainability schemes in the arenas of energy auditing, mentoring appropriate energy, water, waste, and food use by forming social enterprises which engage with communities on a neighbourhood level, and which embed real empathy with their peer groups.
- There should be a targeted programme of 'resilient streets' through which this effort can be enacted by young people who are from disadvantaged neighbourhoods so that neighbourly households can work together on common sustainability projects.
- Schools should also be involved with schemes for enabling their pupils to gain in mental toughness and confidence-building, and through such programmes to twin with schools in less advantaged areas (including in emerging and developing economies) to instigate resilient schools and streets programmes.
- The local media should support this enthusiastically, with lots of positive news coverage, information-rich websites, and schemes for community-based visits for other neighbourhoods to look and learn.
- All of this should also be promoted by social networking sites and the kinds of web-based schemes for linking people with skills to those who need support and confidence-building.
- The cascade of success should be progressively rolled out across the totality of the settlement to begin the process of creating a true sustainable city and a resilient community.

This is essentially Local Agenda 21 at work. This is the programme of conveying sustainability to the local scene and creating forms of democracy which genuinely introduce cooperative governance. Ideally there should be supportive sustainable community-based citizens' charitable or not-for-profit trusts which work alongside local politicians in a non-partisan way, so that effective collaborative democracy triumphs.

315

We are some way short of this. In particular the freedoms sought here for local government are very variably available throughout the world. For the most part central administrations prefer to tether their local brethren. But surely here is the path to our second conception of a more socially tolerant transformation, drawn from its collective self-belief rather than the fear of impending economic and social collapse. But much more needs to be done. It may be more through economic and social desperation, coupled with local business leadership, that the necessary changes will eventually occur.

Islands of hope and transformational tipping points

Following the casework of the Resilience Alliance, recognizing the heartening examples offered by Emily Boyd (7.2) and Camilla Toulmin (Commentary 7.4), and reading countless websites of sincere community action for sustainability – together these offer a sense of 'islands of hope'. These are the myriad of trials, of pilots, of courageous innovation, of community or personal leadership which add up to a transformational movement.

What seems to kill the enlarging of these islands is a combination of the themes outlined in Chapter 6.1 and in this chapter so far: inadequate international leadership; hopeless indecision and contradiction; possible deliberate hypocrisy; and failing institutions unready for change because of complexity, lobbying, and lock-in. There is also the very real difficulty of trying to alter human behaviour when cultural norms and peer pressure intervene, as we saw in the commentaries by Matthew Taylor (3.2), Charles Clarke (6.7) and Camilla Toulmin (7.4). Andrew Dobson takes this further in his companion chapter (8.2).

We add another dimension. This is a moral envelope of the kind introduced by Laurence Freeman (5.1) and by Andrew Dobson (8.2). Social nudge, regulatory shaping, economic incentives are not in themselves sufficient to produce the kinds of across-the-board transformational behavioural change in what are very habitual, peer-guided, and market-driven actions. There needs to be an inner drive: what Ernst Schumacher (1972) called 'the centre'. This is the coherent inner certainty which directs supportively and creatively the kinds of sustainability citizenship addressed by Dobson. How this can be achieved and in a timescale of decades, remains deeply problematic. We rely on a combination of 'awe and shock' as the wider and longer effects of the human footprint become more evident through scientific research, evidence collection, unavoidable warnings, and exceptionally damaging hazard. We sense that many people, especially younger people, are becoming more aware of the scale of the challenges and seek to be better informed and more in tune. We see the 'islands of hope' enlarging and gaining in publicity and attractiveness. We believe well-being and betterment will take over as the mainstay of human endeavour within a decade. We support the Sulston working group conclusions (Sulston 2012) that inequality in all of its pernicious manifestations in all nations must be reversed. For only a society of progressive, but earned, fairness can embrace sustainability. And we see business and government being goaded by customers and encouraged by reconstructed regulations and markets (in that order) to turn the corner.

So we salute these islands of hope, their visionary leaders, and their 'centred' supporters. We thoroughly support the abundance of websites which proclaim their existence and learning pathways for others to emulate. And we share the optimism of Joe Smith (7.1) that we can communicate hope much better than despair.

But we also realize we will have to travel further into the uncharted territory of advancing tipping thresholds, before we move in the directions offered in Part 6 and Part 7. It would be so very sad if the human family, with its magnificent science and information-processing skills, and new forms of communication, cannot work creatively and purposefully to prepare us all for the positive transformations we all must eventually embrace. Civilizations have failed in the past, but never comprehensively, and always with some aftermath. We believe the prospect of global dismay, and with it a sense of failing our offspring, will provide the current that potentially will turn the tide. But we are not sanguine. The lock-in effect and the sheer magnitude of social and institutional transformations which grow more irreversible by the month, particularly in times of austerity which are a function of our folly, may make tipping points the beginning of human nemesis. This is why we humbly believe this book, with its marvellous contributions, is so very timely.

References

Barnosky, A.D., Hadly, E.A., Bascompte, J., Berlow, E.L., Brown, J.H., Fortelius, M., *et al.* (2012), 'Approaching a State Shift in Earth's Biosphere', *Nature,* 486 (7401): 52–58.

Beetham, D. (2011), *Unelected Oligarchy: Corporate and Financial Dominance in Britain's Democracy* (London: Democratic Audit).

Brito, L. and Stafford-Smith, M. (eds) (2012), *State of the Planet Declaration* (London: Planet under Pressure).

Carpenter, S.R. and Bennett, E.M. (2011), 'Reconsideration of the Planetary Boundary for Phosphorus', *Environmental Research Letters,* 6 (1): 014009.

Duarte Santos, F. (2011), *Humans on Earth: From Origins to Possible Futures* (New York: Springer).

The Economist (2012), 'Political Petri Dishes', 22 September.

Environment Audit Committee (2012), *The Green Economy* (London: Stationery Office).

Foresight (2008), *Mental Capital and Well-being: Making the Most of Ourselves in the 21st Century* (London: Government Office of Science).

Geels, F.W. (2002), 'Technological Transitions as Evolutionary Reconfiguration Processes: A Multi-Level Perspective and a Case-Study', *Research Policy,* 31 (8–9): 1257–74.

GEO 5 (2012), *Environment for the Future We Want* (Nairobi: UN Environment Programme).

Heinrich Böll Foundation (2012), *Low Hanging Fruit: Fossil Fuel Subsidies, Climate Finance and Sustainable Development* (Washington DC: Heinrich Böll Stiftung).

IIASA (2012), 'Rio+20', *Options* (Summer): 12–25.

IIASA (2012a), *Global Energy Assessment: Toward a Sustainable Future* (Laxenburg, Austria: IIASA).

International Monetary Fund (2012), *World Economic Outlook* (New York: IMF).

Krugman, P. and Wells, R. (2012), 'Getting Away With It', *The New York Review of Books,* 7 July, 1–2.

Mulgan, G. (2011), *New Ways of Financing Social Outcomes* (London: The Young Foundation).

New Economics Foundation (2012), *Measuring Wellbeing: A Guide for Practitioners* (London: NEF), http://www.neweconomics.org/publications/happy-planet-index-2012-report (accessed 22 February 2013).

Nordhaus, T. Shellenberger, M., and Blomqvist, L. (2012), *The Planetary Boundaries Hypothesis: A Review of the Evidence* (Washington DC: Breakthrough Institute).

The Prince's Trust (2012), *The Undiscovered Generation* (London: The Prince's Trust).

Raworth, K. (2012), *Planetary and Social Boundaries: Defining a Safe and Just Operating Space for Humanity* (Oxford: Oxfam).

Rockström, J. and Klum, M. (2012), *The Human Quest: Prospering Within Planetary Boundaries* (Stockholm: Langenskiolds).

Rockström, J. *et al.* (2009), 'Planetary Boundaries: Exploring the Safe Operating Space for Humanity', *Nature*, 461: 472–75.

Schumacher, E. (1972), *Small is Beautiful: Economics as if People Mattered* (New York: Harper Row).

Soderholm, P. (2010), *Environmental Policy and Household Behaviour: Sustainability and Everyday Life* (London: Earthscan/Routledge).

Sukhdev, P. (2012), *Corporation 2020: Transforming Business for Tomorrow's World* (New York: Island Press).

Sulston, J. (Chair) (2012), *People and the Planet* (London: Royal Society).

Turchin, P. (2011) 'Social Tipping Points and Trend Reversals: A Historical Approach', http://cliodynamics.info/PDF/TrendReversal.pdf.

UN Human Development Report (2011), *Sustainability and Equity: A Better Future for All* (New York: UN Development Programme).

Wilks-Heeg, S., Blick, A., and Crone, S. (2012), *How Democratic Is the UK? The 2012 Audit* (London: Democratic Audit).

World Bank (2012), *Turning Down the Heat: Why a 4°C Warmer World Must Be Avoided* (Washington DC: World Bank).

8.2
Improving our chances
of transition to sustainability

The role of values and the ethics
of solidarity and sympathy

ANDREW DOBSON

Sustainability is a moral and ethical issue, so it is vital to see that we will not reach the tipping point at which it becomes the new common sense until its ethical dimensions are much more deeply rooted in the minds of citizens and policymakers alike. In this regard things do not look especially positive, especially in the realm of policymaking.

Policymakers have a range of tools at their disposal. First they can legislate. Laws may or may not be informed by moral and ethical considerations, but law-making is certainly an opportunity for governments to make ethical and moral points. In the context of climate change, for example, a government might decide on a regime of congestion charges in a country's major cities. These charges might be explained in terms of revenue-raising – a fiscal measure designed to raise money. But they might also be explained as being underpinned by the recognition that transport accounts for about a third of greenhouse gas emissions, that climate change affects the life chances of near and distant others, that it is usually the most vulnerable who are least able to cope with these challenges, and that it is therefore the duty of responsible governments to encourage their citizens to drive less.

Legislation seems an obvious vehicle through which to establish the moral and ethical 'weather' in a society – a great opportunity to engage citizens in these dimensions of the sustainability question. Up to about 40 years ago, UK governments governed through enacting legislation and expecting citizens to comply with it. The legitimacy of this approach was grounded in the democratic nature of the political system – if citizens didn't like the legislation they could vote out the government and give another one a try.

This model where the state, through its agent the democratically elected government, was the origin and author of policy, was called into question during the mid-1970s by the theoreticians of the New Right and, subsequently, the governments of Margaret Thatcher in the UK and Ronald Reagan in the USA. The postwar settlement between state, citizens, and government was undermined as the market challenged the legitimacy of elected governments to set policy, and governments in return increasingly absented themselves from the public policy space, transferring to markets ever greater scope and freedom. The effects of the success of this challenge are plain to see, from the selling off of previously state-owned assets, such as the railways and telecommunications, to the outsourcing of public services, such as waste collection and care for the elderly, to the inundating of the public sphere with market-based language (we are often referred to by local authorities as customers rather than citizens).

In liberal-capitalist countries over the past 40 years governments have been increasingly reluctant to govern, in the sense of taking responsibility for a country's political, social, and economic direction of travel, and offering arguments for preferring that direction of travel to others. Instead, the market is the constraint on, and opportunity and reference point for, policymaking. Governments hide behind the market by presenting it as a series of 'facts that speak for themselves', thereby absolving themselves of the need for ideological debate, and presenting policymaking as a matter of following common-sense. The result has been the virtual disappearance of the moral and ethical dimension of the politics of sustainability, at least in so far as the business of government is concerned.

Governments have compounded this moral and ethical 'hollowing out' by digging around in the policymaking toolbox and coming up with two further options which make it even less likely that morals and ethics will be part of the sustainability debate. The first is fiscal incentives and disincentives, and the second is rooted in behavioural economics – or what has come to be known as 'nudge'.

The logic of the fiscal approach is simple: people will want to avoid fiscal pain (fines) and embrace fiscal pleasure (rewards), so as long as the incentives and disincentives are set up in the right way, people's environmental behaviour can be altered. One important benefit of this approach is that it

321

can work very fast, often resulting in observable positive outcomes as soon as a charge is put in place (e.g. a congestion charge for vehicles). In the context of the urgency with which some environmental problems need to be dealt with – the most obvious being climate change – policy tools that secure behaviour change quickly are obviously attractive.

But from the mainstream point of view there is one huge advantage. People need have no environmental commitment whatsoever for it to work. No hard work needs to be done persuading people of the environmental and other reasons for getting out of their cars – just go with the grain of human nature, understood as the pursuit of self-interest, set up the incentive structure, then sit back and watch the environment heal.

In the longer run this advantage can turn to disadvantage. People respond to the fiscal prompt and not to the principles underlying it, so they are likely to relapse into their previous behaviour patterns once the incentive is removed. Car drivers, for example, drive less in cities with a congestion charge, but they do so because they do not want to incur the congestion charge, not in order to reduce carbon emissions. Their behaviour is changed by a superficial response to a carrot or a stick, rather than through commitment to a point of principle.

From a policy point of view this is a marked weakness of the fiscal incentive tool. But from the point of view of a politics of the environment the damage is much greater. In removing all talk of morals and ethics from the debate, the fiscal incentive approach encourages the idea that sustainability makes no moral or ethical demands on us. To grasp how bizarre this is, think of a similar claim being made in the context of votes for women or the ending of slavery. Would we be happy with a policy approach to these issues based on fiscal incentives? Can we imagine being 'incentivized' not to manacle people and put them in the hold of a ship before sending them to work for nothing in sugar plantations? No, and not just because it might not work, but because these issues demand ethical and moral reflection. Votes for women and the ending of slavery are the right thing to do, and we are selling these issues a long way short (misunderstanding them, indeed) if we rely on people's short-term financial self-interest as the sole motivation for them.

The other approach to environmental policymaking is 'nudge', drawing on the eponymous book by Richard Thaler and Cass Sunstein (2009), and deploying the insights of behavioural economics. This book has rapidly became required reading in the higher reaches of the UK government. In May 2010 the Cabinet Office and the Institute of Government published a document called *Mindspace* which aimed to bring nudge to wider attention among policymakers. Fiscal incentives bypass norms, but at least those subject to the policy are aware that there is a policy, and that they are subject to it. Nudging also eschews normative debate – but it goes even further by hiding even itself from view. Nudging works best when no one knows they are being nudged. This could well turn out to be the high (or rather, low) point of a particular approach to policymaking – including environmental policymaking – which effectively depoliticizes (and certainly de-democratizes) politics. And by 'politics', here, we mean not the institutions of government and the people who occupy them. We refer to the Aristotelian understanding of politics – debating and enacting what is right and wrong, and what is just and unjust.

'Mindspace' works as follows: 'For policymakers facing policy challenges such as crime, obesity, or environmental sustainability', writes one of the report's authors, Paul Dolan:

> advances in behavioural science offer a potentially powerful new set of tools. Applying these tools can lead to low-cost, low-pain ways of 'nudging' providers, consumers and citizens into new ways of acting by going with the grain of how we think and act. This is an important idea at any time, but is especially relevant in a period of fiscal constraint.
>
> (Dolan 2009)

Rather than operating at the level of normative reasoning as to why we think and act in the way we do and debating those reasons in terms of right and wrong, just and unjust, the Mindspace approach seeks to influence behaviour by changing the contexts which encourage people unconsciously into one course of action rather than another. Mindspace takes behavioural science to the very heart of policymaking – and simultaneously displaces politics.

One key reason given by its advocates for 'nudging' is that it 'goes with the grain of how we think and act', as Dolan (2009) puts it. This makes nudging seem hard-headed and realistic – characteristics that the electorate like to see in their politicians (or so the politicians would have us believe). Dolan goes on to say:

> In simple terms, we can seek to change behaviour in two main ways. First, we can seek to change minds. If we change the way they think about and reflect upon things, then we can change their behaviour. The success of these kinds of interventions has been somewhat mixed. Second, we can seek to change people's behaviour by changing their contextual cues. If we change the 'choice architecture', then we can change their behaviour. It turns [out

323

that] our behaviour is a lot more 'automatic' and somewhat less 'reflective' than we have previously thought.

(Dolan 2009)

This makes it clear that 'nudgers' aren't interested in normative debate – or what Dolan calls the 'changing minds' approach to politics. This, apparently, is because of 'mixed results' – i.e. policymakers don't always get what they want. Instead they propose to look at the world in the same way as consumer experts look at supermarkets. These experts know that consumer behaviour is affected by how the supermarket is designed – we are encouraged to buy this product rather than that one by the siting of shelves and signs, the smells and sounds we encounter, and the direction we walk round the shop. An environmental example of nudging – which appeared on the *Nudge* website not so long ago – is making recycling bins larger and general waste bins smaller in the expectation that people will begin to recycle more and throw away less.

In thinking of sustainability as a matter of tweaking behaviour, nudgers commit what philosophers call a 'category mistake'. Ethics, norms, and values are not an optional extra in sustainability – they are constitutive of it. From this point of view, it is as absurd to see sustainability as a matter of re-sizing waste bins as it would have been to nudge slave owners towards ending slavery by making their ships a little shorter and narrower. Unsustainability is a moral and ethical affront with severe practical consequences for all beings – human and non-human – that suffer from it.

An alternative approach is sustainability citizenship. We define sustainability citizenship as 'pro-sustainability behaviour, in public and in private, driven by a belief in fairness of the distribution of environmental goods, in participation, and in the co-creation of sustainability policy'. More particularly, the sustainability citizen:

- believes that sustainability is a common good that will not be achieved by the pursuit of individual self-interest alone;
- is moved by other-regarding motivations as well as self-interested ones;
- believes that ethical and moral knowledge is as important as techno-scientific knowledge in the context of pro-sustainability behaviour change;
- believes that other people's sustainability rights engender environmental responsibilities which the sustainability citizen should redeem;
- believes that these responsibilities are due not only to one's neighbours or fellow-nationals but also to distant strangers (distant in space and even in time);

- has an awareness that private environment-related actions can have public environment-related impacts;
- believes that market-based solutions alone will not bring about sustainability.

The sustainability citizen will therefore recommend social and public action.

As policy tools, fiscal incentives and nudge make sustainability less likely. First, this is because they deliberately avoid engaging the public in debates around ethics, norms and values – yet the deployment and internalization of this language is essential if we are to debate (a) what sustainability is, and (b) what we need to do to achieve it. Second, long-term sustainability policy success requires the sort of buy-in that can only be achieved through citizen participation and the co-creation of policy. One of the biggest obstacles to the realization of sustainability citizenship is the abdication of government from governing. It is not simply a matter of rolling back the state and expecting citizens in the guise of the Big Society to take over. Sustainability citizenship is a tender plant that needs nurturing by public agencies – the very agencies that are under attack from the market fundamentalists of the present Coalition government.

Government has a key role to play in sustainability citizenship. The trade-off between state and society is not a zero-sum game; less state will not automatically mean more society. In fact as the Young Foundation recently reported:

> When government cut back sharply in places as varied as US inner cities, and countries like Russia, the promised revival of civil society didn't happen. Often the spaces left by government were filled by organised crime or gangs. Ordinary citizens became more afraid, not more trusting, and the evidence from around the world shows that, surprisingly perhaps, the countries where civil society is often strongest are also ones with active government, even in such diverse countries as Brazil, Denmark and Canada.
>
> (Young Foundation 2010: 6)

Government can help by providing greater opportunities for citizens to participate in environmental policymaking, and for making clear the ethical and normative questions at stake. It can provide more support for grassroots initiatives and create more opportunities for civic engagement. Government can provide appropriate funding streams and build social capital. But above all, government must reconsider its overall role.

Sustainability citizenship invites government to recover its nerve, to govern once again, to engage citizens in the cut-and-thrust of ethical and

325

normative debate, and to resist the temptation to bypass politics in the name of an easy life. These ways lie the routes to infantilization, disillusion, and a vacuum where politics ought to be, filled with nudges and financial inducements. Aristotle was surely right:

> Man is a political animal . . . [since] humans alone have perception of good and evil, right and wrong, just and unjust. And it is the sharing of a common view in these matters that makes a household or a city.
>
> (Aristotle 1962: 28–29)

References

Aristotle (1962), *Politics* (Harmondsworth: Penguin).

Carolan, M. (2007), 'Introducing the Concept of Tactile Space: Creating Lasting Social and Environmental Commitments', *Geoforum* 38: 1264–75.

Carter, N. and Huby, M. (2005), 'Ecological Citizenship and Ethical Investment', *Environmental Politics*, 14 (2): 255–72.

Dolan, P. (2009), 'Mindspace: A Simple Checklist for Behaviour Change', http://www.socialsciencespace.com/2011/01/mindspace-a-simple-checklist-for-behaviour-change/ (accessed 15 February 2013).

Gilbert, L. and Phillips, C. (2003), 'Practices of Urban Environmental Citizenships: Rights to the City and Rights to Nature in Toronto', *Citizenship Studies*, 7 (3): 313–30.

Jagers, C., Sverker, C., and Matti, S. (2010), 'Ecological Citizens: Identifying Values and Beliefs that Support Individual Environmental Responsibility among Swedes', *Sustainability*, 2: 1055–79.

Thaler, R. and Sunstein, C. (2009*), Nudge: Improving Decisions about Health, Wealth and Happiness* (Harmondsworth: Penguin).

Wolf, J., Brown, K., and Conway, C. (2009), 'Ecological Citizenship and Climate Change: Perceptions and Practice', *Environmental Politics*, 18 (4): 503–21.

Young Foundation (2010), *Investing in Social Growth: Can the Big Society Be More Than a Slogan?* (London: Young Foundation), http://www.youngfoundation.org/files/images/YF_Bigsociety_Screen__2_.pdf.

Commentary 8.3

Turning the tides?
Parallel infrastructures and
the revolt of the corporate elites

IAN CHRISTIE

At the end of 2012, the signs were proliferating of the lateness of the hour for a global turn towards sustainable development. The projections for greenhouse gas emissions suggest that humanity is well on course for a 4–6°C global average temperature rise by the end of the century. The scenarios for economic, social, and ecological disruption, or even collapse, are ever more alarming. Yet in the US general election campaign of 2012, neither climate change nor wider ecological stresses and resource crises were discussed or even discussable. The presidential candidates studiously avoided all mention of climate disruption. Only when the election was won did President Obama dare to raise the issue, and then only when the devastation wrought on the north-eastern US seaboard by Hurricane Sandy had made it 'safe' to talk freely about it. Such has been the group-think of US policymakers, lobbies, and media about climate change and the broader question of ecological limits: these issues are so deeply disturbing to the settled assumptions of neoliberal economics and politics that they cannot be allowed to be made real.

Yet this is the unavoidable truth for modern states and businesses. No matter how much they hubristically feel they are entitled to define the 'facts' of the world to suit themselves, hard reality will have the final word. Already in the aftermath of the elections of 2012 and the impact of Hurricane Sandy, US politicians are beginning to break ranks and abandon the conspiracy of silence about global ecological risks and tipping points. That said, the weight of established interests lobbying for business as usual remains immense. And the persistence of the Western economic crisis that

327

broke in 2007 means politicians will continue for some time to be distracted by financial fire-fighting and the challenges of unemployment, recession, and debt.

What can potentially lead to a change in the 'lock-in' to a network of systemic dependencies and constraints that inhibit any honest and far-sighted confrontation with global ecological risks and the threat of dangerous tipping points? There is so much to overcome, as summarized in Chapters 6.1 and 8.1:

- Deep internalization of the neoliberal view of the primacy of free markets, deregulatory policy, and individualistic consumer choice;
- The consequences of this in actual market development, leading to oligopolistic business powers exercising immense influence over politics, especially in the USA;
- A demoralization of political discourse and professional ethos, as evident in the financial scandals exposed since 2007 and in the hollowing-out of the idea of citizenship (see Andrew Dobson's analysis in 8.2);
- Path-dependency on a vast scale, with lock-in to fossil fuel-powered centralized infrastructures for energy, transport, and food;
- A profound mismatch between the timetables of politicians and democratic culture and the timescales of investment and adjustment for resilience and sustainable energy use;
- Little political gain for anyone confronting the need for radical changes in production and consumption as part of a century-long strategy for sustainable development.

In the light of all this, it seems clear that we cannot expect leadership and 'tipping conversion' among those most embedded in the neoliberal system, namely policymakers at national level and producers in resource-based industries. They are likely to confront change rather too little and too late, largely in response to the experience of being 'awed and shocked' into action by environmental and social change. So we need other agents of systemic change, capable of offering leadership, exemplary influence and leverage over the political system. These need to be capable of:

- deploying sufficient power in production and consumption systems to change existing interests, or to confront them in political lobbying;
- connecting with sympathetic community interests and energizing citizens for sustainable living, in a context of deep loss of trust in politics and widespread lack of agency for change;

- holding sufficient financial power to have a major role in funding investments in sustainable technologies along entire value chains.

My contention and hope are that agents already exist who can meet these requirements. They have in common a capacity to influence behaviour, values, and investment at significant scale; dismay at the lack of urgent action on climate disruption and other global risks; a long-range perspective, transcending in some ways the electoral cycles of nation states, and less vulnerability to the lobbies so powerful at national level in politics; and potential to inspire 'followership' in national politicians, who might be encouraged to act in the wake of these agents' pioneering work. They are all capable of forming alliances and action-oriented partnerships for what Elinor Ostrom (2010) calls the 'polycentric governance' needed for resilient societies and sustainable development paths (see 5.1, 6.6, 8.1):

- Corporations and major public sector investors concerned with the risks arising from fossil-fuel dependency and climate disruption;
- Religious organizations and communities;
- Cities and local/regional governments.

Corporations such as Unilever have become increasingly outspoken about the risks being run by the global economic system and by its dominant national governments. They see their long-term competitiveness or even survival jeopardized by business as usual. Truly striking denunciations of neoliberal economic culture have come in the past year from Paul Polman, CEO of Unilever, whose global strategy for sustainable development is remarkable for its ambition and radicalism. For example:

> The very essence of capitalism is under threat as business is now seen as a personal wealth accumulator.
>
> We have to bring this world back to sanity and put the greater good ahead of self-interest.
>
> We need to fight very hard to create an environment out there that is more long term focussed and move away from short termism.
>
> (Paul Polman, quoted in Confino 2012)

Other corporations are making similar moves – for example, Wal-Mart, Marks and Spencer, Puma, Patagonia. Far more needs to be done. But the makings of a coalition of the willing are clear among major corporations whose interests are threatened by ecological disruption and whose collective financial clout could enable them to form 'parallel infrastructures' for investment, accounting, reporting, and engagement with customer-citizens.

Many of these companies are concerned with food supply and have greater sensitivity to what is happening at local and regional levels to ecosystems than any major fossil interests or national governments do. Their interests in long-term security are shared by the US Department of Defense. The Pentagon is now a major investor in renewable energy, motivated by self-interested security concerns but capable, like Unilever and other global corporations, of being a catalyst for change across many important supply chains.

My hope is that by the end of this decade these corporations will do three things. First, they will begin to construct parallel infrastructures for 'doing capitalism' to challenge the existing models of finance, accounting, reporting, and investment. Second, they will become openly and consistently hostile to fossil capitalist interests. Third, they will deliver ultimatums on climate action and low-carbon energy investment to political elites. Democratic policymakers will thereby be given an incentive to lead and to break ranks from the carbon-generating interests. This will not be a noble or inspiring spectacle, but it is the best we can hope for, and it will be effective.

These efforts will be accompanied and supported by a gradual shift towards an 'ecological awakening' among the major religions. This is already in evidence in Christian churches, some parts of the Islamic world, and in Buddhist and Daoist traditions. The global population remains overwhelmingly committed to religious identity and observance in varying degrees. We may witness a major expansion in religious belonging in China and elsewhere, galvanized by the onset of scarcities and ecological disruption. Such a development will not be automatically for the good, of course: heightened religious sentiment could well be a factor in local and regional conflict. But the potential for religious traditions, which have immense holdings of land, money, and buildings and which have potentially unrivalled resources of community trust and influence, to be positive catalysts for change and members of 'coalitions of the willing' with pro-sustainability advocates in business and civil society, is very great. The faith communities too can form 'parallel infrastructures' for finance, investment, and enterprise, and already are doing so, as evidenced by the many initiatives promoted and documented by the Alliance of Religions and Conservation (Palmer and Finlay 2003; Colwell *et al.* 2009; see also www.arcworld.org).

A third force for change is the emergent 'parallel infrastructure' of local and regional governance for sustainable development. Ever since the Rio conference of 1992 the Local Agenda 21 framework has inspired considerable local and regional action on environment and renewables worldwide. It has also generated a political narrative of increasing potency. The full force of this widely shared analysis was expressed in the wake of the Rio+20 Conference in 2012. Mayors, regional governors and local authorities released damning statements on the performance of national leaders. A quotation from the international network of local authorities for sustainability, ICLEI, exposes the frustration:

> We now see that all the good will, energy, brain capacity and money that went into the Rio+20 process have resulted in dozens of pages of paper, which contain hardly any commitment by governments. Instead, national governments reaffirm what they had already resolved long ago, list non-binding intentions, and acknowledge the activities by other actors such as local governments . . . Do cities have to step in where governments are failing to take effective action? Cities are cooperating internationally without borders, without customs, without military forces. They can address the issues of the future without the global power play that we see going on at inter-governmental level . . . We suspect that the mechanisms, rules and routines of international diplomacy are outdated and incapable of designing and bringing about a sustainable future.
>
> (ICLEI 2012)

The failure of national politics to match up to the challenges at hand has reinvigorated alliances of mayors, cities, and localities. This robust response from many local decision-making elites has been marked by the emergence of numerous coalitions for investment and sharing of experience across the world, with business, and with other sectors of civil society. As with business and religious elites alarmed by unsustainable developments, these policy elites have the capacity to make major investments in new forms of production and consumption; they have procurement power on a significant scale; they can command in many cases more trust and influence than can national politicians; and they can often plan for the long run more effectively than national policymakers can.

An objection to this analysis might be that in the absence of national action, none of these agents for bottom-up and 'together-across' change can make the difference we need to see. But the combined force, whether coordinated or not, of these interests operates at international scale, and can catalyse change in multiple value chains. Crucially, all of these forces have the capacity to develop self-reinforcing institutions for investment, engagement of citizens, and for sharing of technologies, bypassing those embedded in carbon-intensive business as usual. Should they deploy this power, they could embolden and champion national politicians who are otherwise boxed in.

This is the scenario for transformational tipping thresholds. The essential elements of this revolt – or gradual build-up of revolts – are in place now. The agents for change will extend and devise what I have called 'parallel infrastructures' for finance, energy, production, and consumption. The coalitions needed to make the revolts succeed need to be formed, active and bold in leadership well before the end of this decade. My hope and expectation are that this will be the case.

References

Colwell, M. *et al.* (eds) (2009), *Many Heavens, One Earth: Faith Commitments to Protect the Living Planet* (Bath: Alliance of Religions and Conservation/UNDP).

Confino, J. (2012), 'Rio+20: Unilever CEO on the Need to Battle on to Save the World', Guardian Sustainable Business, 21 June; http://www.guardian.co.uk/sustainable-business/rio-20-unilever-battle-save-world.

ICLEI (2012), ICLEI at Rio+20 statement: http://local2012.iclei.org/fileadmin/files/ICLEI_at_Rio_20.pdf.

Ostrom, E. (2010) 'Beyond Markets and States: Polycentric Governance of Complex Economic Systems', *American Economic Review*, 100 (3): 641–72.

Palmer, M. and Finlay, V. (2003). *Faith in Conservation: New Approaches to Religions and the Environment* (Washington DC: World Bank).

Index

ABC *see* atmospheric brown cloud
abrupt basic change 178
accommodation 15, 306
accountability 184, 226, 227
Action Aid 78
adaptation xiv, 4, 7–8, 15, 241, 244, 283;
    adaptive cycle 15, 261–2, 271, 272;
    adaptive governance 8, 258–76;
    Amazon rainforest 137;
    community-based 282; creative
    305; current thinking on 122;
    ecosystem-based 79; institutions 302;
    local initiatives 314; media coverage
    250–1, 253, 254; private sector 239;
    response to early warning 39;
    restorative redirection 5
Adger, W.N. 261
adjustment 15, 16, 302
aerosols 38, 97, 303
Africa: climate change 251;
    ecosystem-based adaptation 79;
    IAASTD report 85; Sahel 26, 29, 110,
    112, 258, 266–8, 270, 272
ageing 10, 227–8
agency 289
agriculture: Amazon region 133, 134–5,
    136, 138, 139; biodiversity 79, 117,
    121; deforestation 130; emissions
    77–8; food security 90, 94–6, 97, 99;
    mechanized 138
albedo effects 109, 110, 111
algal blooms 30
Alliance of Religions and Conservation
    (ARC) 330
AMAZALERT project 265–6
Amazon rainforest 15, 32, 79–80, 110,
    127–48, 259, 271–2; bifurcation
    approach 12; biodiversity loss 105;

challenges for governance 135–40;
    challenges for science 140–2;
    dieback 26, 28, 33, 35, 112, 128–31,
    258, 264–6; dry season 11; food
    products 118; future scenarios 306;
    impact on human well-being
    115–16; transitions 131–5
Anglian Water 216–17
Anhang, J. 92
Annan, Kofi 194
anticipation 16
Aquinas, Thomas 154
'Arab Spring' (2011) 6–7, 226, 259, 277
Arabian Peninsula 118
ARC *see* Alliance of Religions and
    Conservation
Arctic sea-ice 25–7, 31, 32, 33–4, 35
Arima, E.Y. 135
Aristotle 53, 57, 326
art 290–1
Atkinson, David 48, 150, 165–7
Atlantic thermohaline circulation
    (THC) 26, 29, 32, 33
atmospheric brown cloud (ABC) 29–30
attitudes 7, 205, 288
attractors 6, 61
Australia: food security 85, 93, 94;
    Great Barrier Reef 261; media 250;
    Queensland flood 191; subtropical
    jet 34; vulnerability 109
autonomy 184
awareness 184, 253

Bahti, T. 57
Ban Ki-moon 194, 311
Bangladesh 250
banks 7, 220, 232, 241
Barlow, J. 141

333